LATIN EPIGRAPHY

LATIN EPIGRAPHY

AN INTRODUCTION TO THE STUDY OF LATIN INSCRIPTIONS

BY

SIR JOHN EDWIN SANDYS, LITT. D. F.B.A

Second Edition, Revised by
S. G. Campbell, M.A.,
Fellow of Christ's College, Cambridge

WITH FIFTY ILLUSTRATIONS

ARES   PUBLISHERS   INC.
CHICAGO   MCMLXXIV

Unchanged Reprint of the Edition:
London, 1927
ARES PUBLISHERS INC.
150 E. Huron Street
Chicago, Illinois 60611
Printed in the United States of America
International Standard Book Number:
0-89005-062-7
Library of Congress Catalog Card Number:
74-82058

Cum maximas per urbem...reliquias undique solo disiectas aspexisset, lapides et ipsi magnarum rerum gestarum maiorem longe quam ipsi libri fidem et notitiam praebere videbantur. Quam ob rem et reliqua per orbem diffusa videre atque litteris mandare proposuit (1424).

FR. SCALAMONTI, *Vita Kiriaci Anconitani* (p. 22 *infra*), p. lxxii, ed. Colucci, *Delle Antichità Picene*, T. xv, Fermo, 1792.

Inscriptiones Latinae aetatis Romanae per totum orbem terrarum antiquum dispersarum colligi non possunt neque unius hominis opera neque omnino certorum aliquot hominum ad id delectorum. Immo, ut eiusmodi inceptum perficiatur, populi omnes litterarum Latinarum heredes concurrant consocienturque necesse est.

W. HENZEN, *Praefatio ad Inscriptiones Urbis Romae Latinae*, *C.I.L.*, vol. vi (1), Berolini, 1876.

Studia epigraphica hoc praecipuum habent et quasi divinum, ut ex sui quemque cubiculi angustiis in publicum campum eruditos viros evocent, et, dum communis humanitatis nostrae originis admonent, diversarum nationum optimos quosque consocient...

Cf. MOMMSEN, *Praefatio ad C.I.L.*, vol. iii (1), 1873.

E tenebris lux facta est, et desperationem successus excepit (1852—1883).

ID. *Praefatio ad C.I.L.*, vol. ix-x, 1883.

Fig. 1. Tomb of Scipio Barbatus, consul 298, censor 290 B.C., in the Vatican Museum, Rome; photograph by Alinari, Rome (cp. Fig. 17f). Behind the (unidentified) bust may be seen the epitaph of a son of Barbatus (cp. Fig. 19); and of two other Scipios (Dessau, *Inscr. Lat. Sel.*, 8, 9).

PREFACE

EIGHT years ago, I had the privilege of editing for the Syndics of the Cambridge University Press a work which was prepared by the loyal co-operation of seven and twenty contributors, under the title of *A Companion to Latin Studies*. On its first appearance, it was well received by classical scholars at home and abroad, and especially in the United States of America; and it was republished, in a partially revised form, only three years later. In editing that work, I had originally hoped that the Chapter on Latin Epigraphy might possibly be written by a recognised expert in the practical study of Roman Inscriptions. As my hope remained unfulfilled, I found it necessary to add this item to the list of my own undertakings as editor. Fortunately, I was already familiar with the general course of the study of the subject in the last five centuries, as unfolded in the second and third volumes of *A History of Classical Scholarship*; and I was easily able to learn more from the published works of the principal modern authorities. The result appeared in the form of a Chapter filling thirty-seven pages, and including twenty-two illustrations.

Early in 1916 I received two letters from a member of the great teaching profession in one of the lands across the seas, a stranger to myself, suggesting that this brief Chapter might serve as a basis for a short and inexpensive 'Introduction to the study of Latin Inscriptions', which might be useful to classical students who were interested in Latin literature, but were not necessarily aiming at becoming specialists in Latin epigraphy. Accordingly, after conferring with my friend the Master of Emmanuel, I submitted a proposal for the preparation of such a work, which was promptly accepted by the Syndics.

Hitherto, there has been a kind of consensus as to the topics which ought to be treated in any such Introduction: the principal

divergence has been on points of order and arrangement. Thus, in all the three well-known treatises published in Germany (1886 etc.) and France (1885 etc.), and in the United States (1896 etc.), and respectively bearing the names of the late Professor Hübner of the Berlin Academy, of M. René Cagnat of the French Institute, and of Professor James C. Egbert of Columbia University, now President of the Archaeological Institute of America, an elaborate dissertation on Roman Names fills many pages before the reader is permitted to reach the study of the actual Inscriptions, while, in the second and third of those treatises, there are also long lists of Roman Officials, with disquisitions on the intricacies of the *cursus honorum*, and a great series of Roman Emperors, with tabulated conspectuses of their complicated chronology. Similarly, even in the handy little volume produced at Milan (in 1898) by Dr Serafino Ricci, Director of the Numismatic Museum in the Brera, these three vast subjects, and others of a similar character, are the theme of no less than seventeen excursuses, which present themselves as perhaps unduly distracting episodes in the general course of the student's progress.

The present work (which is the first introductory manual of Classical Latin Epigraphy to be published in England) begins with a survey of the principal references to, or quotations from, Latin inscriptions in Classical authors. This has not hitherto been attempted in any manual. Had the survey been brought down to the Latin literature of England, it might have included some mention of William of Malmesbury's quotation of a vanished Latin inscription, MARII VICTORIAE, which he had himself seen when it was part of the Roman work in the walls of Carlisle[1]. This survey of Classical authors is succeeded by a general outline of the modern study of Latin inscriptions, first in Italy, and next in Germany, Switzerland, and France, with some account of modern 'collections of inscriptions', whether in published works or in public museums.

As soon as the various forms of the letters of the Alphabet have been sufficiently treated for ordinary practical purposes, the student is introduced to the two great classes of Inscriptions; (I) inscriptions proper, with their subdivisions of sepulchral, dedicatory,

[1] *Gesta Pontificum Anglorum*, p. 209 in Rolls Series (1870).

honorary inscriptions; inscriptions on public works, or on portable objects; and (II) documentary inscriptions, such as copies of laws, or legal agreements. Both of these classes are exemplified by means of selected inscriptions, with a few facsimiles of each. This part of the work ends with a chapter on Language and Style, and another on the Restoration and Criticism of Inscriptions.

Roman Names, Roman Officials, and Roman Emperors are reserved for the first three *Appendices*. The addition of the last of these is mainly due to the fact that a knowledge of the peculiar methods used for recording the 'regnal' years of Roman emperors is absolutely necessary to enable us to determine the date of a very large number of imperial inscriptions.

Next follows an Appendix consisting of *Six Historical Inscriptions*. This includes the whole of the available Latin text of the *Res gestae divi Augusti*, by far the most important of the historical inscriptions of the early Roman empire—an authoritative document written by Augustus himself near the close of his life, in the form of a supremely dignified retrospect of his public career. For the purpose of forming a revised recension of the text, I have naturally begun with Mommsen's monumental edition of 1883, which was mainly founded on the copy of this great inscription which is still preserved on the walls of a Roman temple at Ancyra in Galatia, now well known as *Angora*, in north-central Asia Minor; I have also examined, at first-hand, almost the whole of the widely scattered literature of this subject, which has appeared in the thirty years from 1883 to 1913; and I have ended with the latest and most welcome evidence supplied by the diminutive fragments of the Latin text discovered in June, 1914, by Sir W. M. Ramsay at Antioch in Pisidia. This Appendix also includes an extract from one of the harangues which Hadrian, the greatest traveller of all the Roman emperors, addressed to one of his armies in Northern Africa, and the preamble (and a specimen of one of the schedules) of the celebrated Edict of Diocletian, which aimed at fixing a maximum price for provisions and, indeed, for all articles of commerce, as well as a maximum rate of wages.

As the main difficulty that confronts us in the study of Latin Inscriptions lies in the numerous Abbreviations, Appendix V supplies a classified and graduated series of *Sixty Inscriptions with*

PREFACE

abbreviated phrases, and Appendix VI an alphabetical *List of Abbreviations* selected from such as appeared most likely to be of service to students.

The twenty-two 'illustrations', which appeared in the Cambridge *Companion to Latin Studies*, have been reproduced with a single alteration (4), and with certain additions bringing the total number to fifty. I may here repeat, from the preface to the *Companion*, the statement that seven of the inscriptions had been reproduced on a smaller scale from Ritschl's *Priscae Latinitatis Monumenta Epigraphica*, and eight from Hübner's *Exempla Scripturae Epigraphicae*, 'the two great repertories of facsimiles from the inscriptions of Republican and Imperial Rome'. Two more inscriptions have been borrowed from the former, and six from the latter. Hülsen's important opinions (1) as to the probable form of the *elogia* in the Forum of Augustus, and (2) as to the arrangement of the *Fasti Consulares*, and the *Acta Triumphorum*, on the outer walls of the Regia which once adorned the Roman Forum, have been made clear by means of a copy of his restoration of the *elogium* of Appius Claudius Caecus (31), and by two architectural elevations of the Regia (43*a* and *b*), which have been drawn for this work by Miss Talbot of Cambridge. Naples and its neighbourhood are represented by an electioneering placard from Pompeii (11), and by a military diploma of Vespasian (49) found at Resina in 1746. The latter was published many years ago in the *Museo Borbonico*, and again in 1795 by the able Italian epigraphist, Gaëtano Marini, in a work which has also supplied an excellent specimen of a stamped Roman tile (40), which had long formed part of his extensive collection, now incorporated in the Vatican Museum. A resident in Rome, the Rev Father Mackey, of the Collegio Angelico, a life member of the 'Society for the Promotion of Roman Studies', has kindly procured on my behalf three important photographs, those of (1) the archaic inscription in the Roman Forum (by Vasari), (2) the celebrated sarcophagus of Scipio in the Vatican (by Alinari), and (3) the famous Arch of Trajan at Beneventum (by Moscioni). Several of the other illustrations (15, 36, 38) are borrowed, by permission, from Daremberg and Saglio's great Dictionary of Antiquities, which has now happily reached its completion. The British Museum is represented by a

Roman funerary altar (23), by the tombstone of an *eques singularis Augusti* (25), and by a reproduction of the Roman Society's cast of a very fine tablet from the Antonine Wall (37), the original of which was inaccessible owing to the temporary closing of the National Museum of Antiquities in Edinburgh. The exact source of these and all the other 'illustrations' is given on the pages where they appear. For information on some points of detail I am indebted to Mrs Arthur Strong, Assistant Director of the British School of Archaeology in Rome, and Mr Arthur Hamilton Smith, Keeper of Greek and Roman Antiquities in the British Museum, and to their published works.

The *Select Bibliography* is mainly meant for purposes of reference. It includes, among many other details, a concise statement of the contents of each of the forty volumes of the *Corpus Inscriptionum Latinarum*. This great collection, published at the price of more than £110, or 550 dollars, is hardly accessible to the student except in some of the larger University or College or Departmental Libraries.

The successful study of Latin Epigraphy calls for the highest degree of industry, and affords an excellent training in accuracy. Unlike the conjectural criticism which aims at removing corruptions in the text, or at filling up *lacunae* in Latin literature, it leaves little play for what the author of *The Analogy of Religion* has described as 'that forward, delusive faculty',—the imagination. In restoring an incomplete inscription, Epigraphy almost wholly depends on the exact knowledge of a multitude of nearly invariable precedents and customary conventions. The founder of the modern science of Latin Epigraphy, Bartolommeo Borghesi (1781 —1860), living on the isolated rock of the still independent republic of San Marino, carried on a vast correspondence with archaeologists in every part of Italy; he counted among his most famous pupils Mommsen, who was destined to become the great epigraphist of Germany[1], and he was ultimately honoured by a complete edition of his collected writings, which was admirably published by France.

---

[1] *I.R.N.L.* (1852), 'Ascendi Sancti Marini montem Appenninum Tuam domum petiturus, quam artis nostrae quasi quoddam sanctuarium reddidisti' (1845).

That eminent Italian archaeologist laid down in practice some of the leading principles of epigraphical science, which have been formulated in part by one of his French admirers in two rules of permanent importance: one of these is:—*rien ne se devine, tout s'explique*; and the other:—*la même chose s'y écrit toujours de la même façon*[1].

For the beginner, probably the best course, in pursuing this study, would be to use, together with an introductory manual, some fairly comprehensive collection of select inscriptions, e.g. the two volumes of Wilmanns (1874), or the first two volumes (at least) of Dessau (1892—1916). One or both of these collections ought to be found in any large classical library. A set of facsimiles should also be studied, either the *Inscriptiones Latinae* of Diehl (1912), or the twenty-eight plates at the end of the fourth edition of M. Cagnat's *Cours d'Épigraphie Latine* (Paris, 1914). It would be a great boon to purchasers of the earlier editions, and especially to students in many lands, if these plates could be published separately.

In the preparation of this volume, my largest debt has been due to the latest edition of the luminous and masterly work last mentioned; I am fully conscious of the exact value of other manuals, all of which have their merits, but I have mainly depended throughout on a first-hand acquaintance with the general literature of the subject. All obligations are, so far as possible, definitely acknowledged in foot-notes directing the student's attention to the works in question. My revision of the text of the *Res gestae* of Augustus has been aided, in various ways, by three of my most esteemed colleagues as Fellows of the British Academy,— Sir W. M. Ramsay, now of Edinburgh, Dr J. S. Reid of Cambridge, and Professor Haverfield of Oxford, whose unrivalled knowledge of the Roman Inscriptions of England and of Wales has also enabled me to discriminate between the minor museums, and other accessible collections of inscriptions, and to select those which are mentioned in the first note on p. 33.

[1] René de la Blanchère's pamphlet (1887), *Histoire de l'épigraphie romaine*, p. 49. Cp. René Cagnat, *Cours d'épigraphie Latine*, ed. 1914, p. xvi, *L'épigraphie n'est pas affaire d'intuition, mais bien de science et de pratique; on ne la devine pas, on l'apprend*.

Even students who are unable to visit the sites of either of the Roman Walls of Britain may learn much from excellently illustrated works such as Dr George Macdonald's *Roman Wall in Scotland* (MacLehose, 1911), and from the seventh and latest edition of Dr J. Collingwood Bruce's inexpensive *Handbook to the Roman Wall* in England (Longmans, 1914). With the aid of such works, which represent a direct and first-hand knowledge of those memorable monuments, even students across the seas may realise many matters, which cannot adequately be treated within the severely limited compass of the present Introduction. That Introduction is now offered to classical scholars, and to classical students, who belong to the *nomen Anglicum*—who claim English as their mother tongue, whether at home or abroad, including those who are happily bound to the United Kingdom by many strong and (we trust) enduring ties, whether they ordinarily dwell in the United States, or in the United Empire.

J. E. SANDYS.

CAMBRIDGE, 19 *October*, 1918.

NOTE TO THE SECOND EDITION

In the revised edition the scope and plan of the late Sir John Sandys' book have not been altered. A number of passages have been re-written and many minor corrections in the text and notes have been made. References to Part II (1) of the new edition of of *C. I. L.* vol. 1, published in 1918, have been added throughout, while most of the references to Wordsworth's *Fragments and Specimens of Early Latin* have been deleted, as the out-of-date philology might lead the unwary astray. The brief bibliography has been brought up to date by the addition of some of the more important recent works, and references to the periodical literature since 1918 have been introduced, though somewhat sparingly, into the notes. A chapter on Christian Epigraphy might have been added, as more than one reviewer suggested, but this seemed unnecessary in view of the easily accessible English translation of Marucchi's manual.

S. G. C.

CAMBRIDGE, 1926.

Ès médailles et inscriptions, il y a tant de choses que nous ne sçavons ce que c'est; si nous les sçavions, les belles choses que nous découvririons!

Scaligerana, ed. 1667, p. 153.

L'épigraphie n'est pas une science à part, se suffisant à elle-même et sans point de contact avec le faisceau des connaissances qui forment le fond de nos études. Ce n'est, à vrai dire, que l'un des éléments, mais c'est un élément essentiel de la philologie, l'une des sources auxquelles doit puiser quiconque veut connaître la religion, les lois, l'histoire politique, la vie privée et le langage des anciens.

R. Cagnat, *Cours d'Épigraphie Latine, Introduction*, Douai, 1884 ; p. xiii f, ed. 4, Paris, 1914.

Aujourd'hui l'épigraphie est loin d'être connue de tous ceux qui devraient la connaître, c'est-à-dire de quiconque s'occupe quelque peu de l'antiquité ; néanmoins elle a pénétré partout où elle peut être utile. En dehors des hommes du métier, elle est étudiée par d'autres savants.

R. de la Blanchère, *Histoire de l'Épigraphie Romaine*, Paris, 1887, p. 40.

Parmi les diverses branches de la philologie ancienne, qui a pour objet de décrire toutes les faces de la vie matérielle, intellectuelle et morale des anciens, il n'en est pas une qui ne trouve dans l'épigraphie des détails nouveaux, et ces détails expliquent les monuments littéraires ou suppléent à leur silence.

J. P. Waltzing, Professeur de Liège, *L'Épigraphie Latine depuis 50 Ans*, Louvain, 1892, p. 16.

CONSPECTUS OF CONTENTS

		PAGES
	List of Illustrations	xvi—xvii
	Select Bibliography	xviii—xxiii
CHAPTER I.	The Study of Latin Inscriptions. Latin Inscriptions in Classical Authors	1—19
CHAPTER II.	Modern Collections of Latin Inscriptions	20—33
CHAPTER III.	Archaic Latin Alphabet. Earliest Latin Inscriptions. Scriptura monumentalis, actuaria, cursiva, uncialis. Shapes of the several letters. Ligatures. Punctuation. Numerals. Process of making Inscriptions. Stamps. Scriptura vulgaris	34—58
CHAPTER IV.	Classification of Inscriptions (I) (i) Epitaphs	59—82
CHAPTER V.	(ii) Dedicatory Inscriptions	83—92
CHAPTER VI.	(iii) Honorary Inscriptions (A) Elogia	93—104
	(B) Other Honorary Inscriptions	104—110
	Cursus honorum	110—117
CHAPTER VII.	(iv) Inscriptions on public works	118—142
CHAPTER VIII.	(v) Inscriptions on portable objects	143—155
CHAPTER IX.	(II) Documents	156—188
CHAPTER X.	Language and Style	189—195
CHAPTER XI.	Restoration and Criticism of Inscriptions	196—206
APPENDIX I.	Roman Names	207—221
APPENDIX II.	Roman Officials (Cursus honorum)	222—229
APPENDIX III.	Roman Emperors	230—256
APPENDIX IV.	Six historical inscriptions	
(1) Senatus consultum de Bacchanalibus, 186 B.C.		257—258
(2) Res gestae divi Augusti (Mon. Ancyranum), 14 A.D.		258—276
(3) Speech of Claudius in the Senate, 48 A.D.		276—280
(4) Lex de Imperio Vespasiani, 70 A.D.		280—282
(5) Hadriani adlocutio ad exercitum Africanum, 128 A.D.		282
(6) Diocletiani edictum de pretiis rerum venalium, 301 A.D.		283—285
APPENDIX V.	Sixty abbreviated inscriptions	286—290
APPENDIX VI.	Abbreviations. List of abbreviations	291—311
Index		312—324

LIST OF ILLUSTRATIONS

FIG.		PAGE
1	Tomb of L. Cornelius Scipio Barbatus; Vatican Museum, Rome . . . . . *Frontispiece*	
2	Greek Alphabet on the Formello Vase, formerly in the Palazzo Chigi, now in the Museo della Villa di Papa Giulio, Rome	34
3	The *Fibula Praenestina*; Museo Kircheriano, Rome .	38
4	Inscription on the archaic *cippus* in the Roman Forum .	39
5	The 'Duenos' inscription, on the 'Vasculum Dresselianum', Berlin	40
6	Dedicatory inscription on a column at Tusculum .	41
7	Epitaph of Caecilia Metella; Via Appia, near Rome .	42
8	Inscription from an obelisk formerly in the Circus Maximus; Piazza del Popolo, Rome . . .	43
9	Alphabet of *scriptura monumentalis*, Augustan age .	43
10	Alphabet of *scriptura actuaria* (*a*) Augustan age .	44
	,, ,, ,, (*b*) Claudian age .	44
11	An electioneering placard; Pompeii . . .	44
12	Inscription on a Pompeian pedestal; Naples Museum.	45
13	Graffiti, with quotations from the poets; Pompeii .	46
14	Inscription on a pedestal at Timgad; North Africa .	47
15	Ancient Latin alphabets	48
16	Inscription on the 'written rock'; on the river Gelt .	58
17	Tomb of L. Cornelius Scipio Barbatus; Vatican Museum	66
18	Epitaph of L. Cornelius Scipio Barbatus . .	66
19	Epitaph of L. Cornelius Scipio, f. Barbati; Palazzo Barberini, Rome	67
20	Epitaph of L. Cornelius Scipio, son (?) of Hispallus; Vatican Museum	68
21	Epitaph of P. Cornelius Scipio, flamen Dialis; Vatican Museum	68
22	Inscription on a sarcophagus; Lyon Museum . .	70
23	Roman funerary altar; British Museum, London .	73
24	Tablet from the columbarium of Livia, Via Appia, near Rome	74
25	Tombstone of an eques singularis Augusti; British Museum	76
26	Cenotaph of a Roman centurion; Bonn Museum .	77

LIST OF ILLUSTRATIONS xvii

FIG.		PAGE
27	Altar-tomb with *ascia*; Lyon Museum	79
28	Votive inscription of Mummius, conqueror of Corinth; Vatican Museum	84
29	Dedication to an unknown god; on the Palatine, Rome	89
30	Inscription on *Columna Rostrata*; Palazzo dei Conservatori, Rome	96
31	Restoration of *elogium* of Appius Claudius Caecus; Rome	98
32	Tomb of Bibulus; Via di Marforio, Rome	105
33	Local record of the elder Scipio's recovery of Saguntum	107
34	Arch of Trajan (114 A.D.); Beneventum	124
35	*Miliarium* of Popilius (132 B.C.); Polla in Lucania	132
36	Milestone of Claudius (41 A.D.); near Nîmes	137
37	Tablet from the *Vallum* of Antoninus Pius; National Museum of Antiquities, Edinburgh	139
38	*Tessera hospitalis*, found near *lacus Fucinus*; Museo Nazionale, Rome	145
39	Stamp of an oculist, found at Reims	151
40	Stamps on a Roman tile (203-5 A.D.); Vatican Museum	153
41	*Lex parieti faciendo* from Puteoli; Naples Museum	160
42	Decree of L. Aemilius Paullus (189 B.C.); Louvre, Paris	162
43	Conjectural arrangement of *Fasti Consulares* and *Acta Triumphorum* outside the Regia, Rome	168 f.
44	From the *Fasti Consulares*; Palazzo dei Conservatori, Rome	171
45	From the *Acta Triumphorum*; Palazzo dei Conservatori, Rome	172
46	From the *Fasti anni Iuliani*; Palazzo dei Conservatori, Rome	173
47	From the *Monumentum Ancyranum* (14 A.D.); Angora	178
48	From a speech of Claudius (48 A.D.); Lyon Museum	179
49	Military diploma of Vespasian (70 A.D.); Naples Museum	182
50	Pompeian writing-tablet (59 A.D.); Naples Museum	186

SELECT BIBLIOGRAPHY

EARLY PRINTED EDITIONS OF LOCAL INSCRIPTIONS:
(1) **Ravenna**; Desiderius Spretus, *De amplitudine urbis Ravennae*, Venetiis, 1489; (2) **Augsburg**; Conrad Peutinger, *Romanae vetustatis fragmenta*, Augustae Vindelicorum, 1505 (ed. 2, Moguntiaci, 1520); (3) **Mainz**; Johannes Huttichius, *Collectanea antiquitatum*, Moguntiaci, 1520; ed. 2, 1525; (4) **Rome**; Mazochius, *Epigrammata antiquae urbis*, Romae in aedibus Iacobi Mazochii, 1517; ed. 2, 1521.

EARLY CORPORA INSCRIPTIONUM etc.:
(1) Petrus Apianus et Bartholomaeus Amantius, *Inscriptiones sacrosanctae vetustatis, non illae quidem Romanae, sed totius fere orbis...*, Ingoldstadt, 1534; (2) Martinus Smetius († 1578), *Inscriptionum antiquarum liber* (1551), ed. Lipsius, Antwerp, 1588; (3) Janus Gruterus, *Inscriptiones antiquae totius fere orbis Romani in corpus absolutissimum redactae*, 2 vols., Heidelberg, 1603 (ed. Graevius, Amsterdam, 1707); (4) Joh. Baptistae Donii († 1647),...*Inscriptiones antiquae*, ed. Ant. Franc. Gorius, Florence, 1731; (5) Marquardus Gudius († 1689), *Antiquae inscriptiones* (1662), ed. Franc. Hesselius, Leeuwarden, 1731; (6) Thomas Reinesius († 1667), *Syntagma inscriptionum antiquarum*, Leipzig, 1682; (7) Rafaello Fabretti († 1700),... *Inscriptionum antiquarum quae in aedibus paternis asservantur explicatio et additamentum*, Rome, 1699; ed. 2, 1702; (8) A. F. Gori († 1757), *Inscriptiones antiquae in Etruriae urbibus extantes*, 3 vols., Florence, 1726–43; (9) L. A. Muratori († 1750), *Novus Thesaurus veterum inscriptionum*, 4 vols., Milan, 1739–42; (10) Scipione Maffei († 1755), (*a*) *Museum Veronense*, 1749, (*b*) *Ars Critica Lapidaria*, in vol. i (1765) of Sebastiano Donati's *Veterum inscriptionum...novissimus thesaurus*, 2 vols. (the last of the early *Corpora*), Lucca, 1775;

(11) Gaetano Marini († 1815), (*a*) *Iscrizioni delle ville e de' palazzi Albani*, Rome, 1785; (*b*) *Gli atti e monumenti de' fratelli Arvali*, 2 parts, *ib.* 1795; (*c*) *Iscrizioni antiche doliari*, De Rossi and Dressel, *ib.* 1884; (12) Bartolommeo Borghesi († 1860), *Œuvres complètes*, 10 vols. Paris, 1862–97; (13) Th. Mommsen († 1903), *Inscriptiones regni Neapolitani Latinae*, Leipzig, 1852 (superseded by *C.I.L.* vols. ix, x *infra*);

(14) Mommsen, *Inscr. confoederationis Helveticae*, 1854 (cp. *Nachstudien* in *Hermes*, xvi 445—494 (1881), and *Beiträge* in *C.I.L.* xii pp. 20—27, 806), 'Alpes Poeninae'; pp. 328—336, 830, Genava; pp. 651–5, 858; 'via per vallem Poeninam,' 1887; also in *C.I.L.* xiii.

MODERN TEXTS, (1) *Corpus Inscriptionum Latinarum (C.I.L.)*, *editum consilio et auctoritate Academiae Regiae Borussicae* (Berolini, 1863—1916...).

i. *Inscr. Latinae antiquissimae* (down to 44 B.C.), also *Elogia, Fasti*

SELECT BIBLIOGRAPHY xix

anni Iuliani, ed. Mommsen; and *Fasti Consulares*, ed. Henzen, 1863. Ed. 2, part i, *Fasti Cons.* ed. Henzen, Hülsen; *Elogia*, ed. Mommsen, Hülsen; *Fasti anni Iul.* ed. Mommsen, 1893; part ii fasc. i ed. Lommatzsch, 1918.

    ii. Spain, ed. Hübner, 1869; Suppl. 1892.

    iii. Egypt[1], Asia, Greek provinces of Europe, and Illyricum, ed. Mommsen, 1873. Part (1) including the above, with Illyricum (parts 1—5); Part (2), Illyricum (parts 6, 7). Res gestae divi Augusti (ex monumentis Ancyrano et Apolloniensi). Edictum Diocletiani de Pretiis Rerum, Privilegia militum veteranorumque (Diplomata militaria). Instrumenta Dacica (tabulae ceratae). Suppl. fasc. 1 (Greek provinces of Europe), 1889; fasc. 2, Illyricum, parts 1—3, 1891; fasc. 3, Illyricum, parts 4—7, Edictum Diocletiani, Diplomata militaria, 1893; fasc. 4—5, Suppl. to Part (1) and to Illyricum (parts 1—7), ed. Mommsen, O. Hirschfeld, Domaszewski, 1902.

    É. Desjardins, *Desiderata du Corpus Inscriptionum*, t. iii, fasc. i, *Le Musée Épigraphique de Pest*, Paris, 1873; fasc. ii—v, *Les balles de fronde de la république*, 1874-76 ('glandes plumbeae,' from Asculum, cp. *C.I.L.* ix, *infra*, under Picenum).

    iv. *Inscr. Parietariae* of Pompeii, etc., ed. Zangemeister, *Vasorum inscr.* ed. R. Schoene, 1871; Suppl. (1) *tabulae ceratae*, ed. Zangemeister, 1898; (2) *graffiti, vascula*, ed. Mau, 1909.

    v. Gallia Cisalpina, ed. Mommsen; in two parts (1) Venetia and Istria, 1872; (2) Liguria, Gallia Transpadana, Alpes Cottiae et Maritimae, 1877 (Aemilia being reserved for vol. xi). Supplementa Italica, fasc. i, ed. Et. Pais, in *Atti* of *Regia Academia dei Lincei, serie quarta*, vol. 5, Rome, 1884-8.

    vi. Rome, collected by Bormann, Henzen, Hülsen, and De Rossi, 1876—1902:—(1) ed. Bormann, Henzen, 1876; (2) and (3) ed. Bormann, Henzen, Hülsen, 1882-86; (4) fasc. 1, 2, ed. Hülsen, 1894—1902; (5) 'inscr. falsae' (cp. p. 206 *infra*), ed. Bormann, Henzen, Hülsen, 1885; (6) indices. Fasc. 1, ed. Bang, 1926.

    B. L. Ullman, *Additions and Corrections to CIL* (vi and xi), in *Classical Philology*, iv 190-8, Chicago, 1909.

    vii. Britain, ed. Hübner, 1873; Suppl. in *Ephemeris Epigraphica*, iii (1877), iv (1881), and by F. J. Haverfield, *ib.* vii (1890), ix (1913), 509—690, and in *Archaeological Journal*, xlvii 229—267 (1890), xlix 176—201, 215—233 (1892), l 279—321 (1894)[2].

    viii. Africa, in two parts, (1) proconsular Africa, Numidia, (2)

---

[1] Cp. Letronne, *Inscr. grecques et latines*, 1842-48.
[2] Cp. J. C. Bruce († 1892), *Lapidarium Septentrionale*, Newcastle-upon-Tyne, 1870—1875; *The Roman Wall*, *ib.* 1851; ed. 3, 1867, and *Handbook to the R. W.*, ed. 7, revised by R. Blair, 1914; G. Macdonald, *The Roman Wall in Scotland*, 1911; Haverfield, British Academy Papers, *Roman Britain in 1910-14*, esp. 1913-4, published in Proceedings 1912-5 (and the literature there quoted), *The Romanization of Roman Britain*, 3rd ed. 1915, *Roman London*, in *Journal of Roman Studies*, i 141—172, *Roman Britain* in *Cambridge Medieval History*, i (1911), Appendix to revised ed. of Mommsen's *Roman Provinces* (E.T. 1910), also Illustrated Catalogues of inscriptions, etc., (*a*) in Durham Cathedral Library (Durham, 1899), (*b*) in Chester Museum (Chester Society, vol. 7, 1900); and contributions to Victoria County Histories, etc.

Mauretania 'collegit G. Wilmanns, ed. Mommsen,' 1881; Suppl. in four parts, ed. Cagnat, J. Schmidt, and Dessau, 1891, 1894, 1904, 1916[1].

ix. Calabria, Apulia, Samnium, Sabini, Picenum, ed. Mommsen, 1883.

x. In two parts, (1) Bruttii, Lucania, Campania; (2) Sicilia, Sardinia, ed. Mommsen, 1883.

xi. In two parts, (1) Aemilia, Etruria, ed. Bormann, 1888; (2) fasc. 1, Umbria, viae publicae, ed. Bormann; Instrumentum, ed. Ihm, 1901.

xii. Gallia Narbonensis, ed. O. Hirschfeld, 1888[2].

xiii. Tres Galliae et duae Germaniae, in seven divisions, part 1, (1) Aquitania et Gallia Lugudunensis, 1899[3]; (2) Belgica, 1904, both by O. Hirschfeld; part 2 (fasc. 1)=(3) Germ. Superior, ed. Zangemeister, 1905; (fasc. 2)=(4) Germ. Inferior, ed. Domaszewski etc. 1907[4]; part 3 (fasc. 1)=(5) Instrumentum, ed. O. Bohn, 1901; part 3 (fasc. 2)=(6) Id. with Signacula Medicorum, ed. Espérandieu, 1906; part 4=(7). Addenda to parts 1 and 2, 1916....

xiv. Latium vetus, ed. Dessau, 1887.

xv. Urbis Romae Instrumentum domesticum, in two parts (1) and (2) fasc. 1, ed. Dressel, 1891-9.

(2) *Ephemeris Epigraphica* (1872—), *Addenda to C.I.L.* i (*Addenda to C.I.L.* i, ii, iv, vi); ii (i—iii); iii (i, ii, vi, vii); iv (i—iii, vi, vii); v (iii, viii); vi, *glandes plumbeae* cp. p. 148 *infra*; vii (vii, viii, xiv); viii (ix, x, and *Acta fratrum arvalium*, cp. p. 165 *infra*); ix (ii, vii, xiv, with Mommsen's comm. on *lex municipii Tarentini* (cp. p. 158 *infra*), reprinted in *Ges. Schr.* i (1905) 146—161.

For discussions on inscriptions published in the *C.I.L.*, see esp. the collected works of:—

(1) Ritschl, *Opuscula Philologica*, vol. iv, *ad epigraphicam... spectantia*, Lipsiae, 1878.

(2) Mommsen, Bibliography by K. Zangemeister and E. Jacobs, *Theodor Mommsen als Schriftsteller*, Berlin, 1905, followed by *Gesammelte Schriften* in nine vols., Berlin, 1905— , 1—3, *Juristische*; 4—6, *Historische*; 7, *Philologische*; 8—9, *Epigraphie und Numismatische Schriften*; see index to vols. 3, 6, 7, and esp. vol. 8 (1913); vol. 9 not yet published.

See also Cagnat and Besnier's *L'Année Épigraphique* (1) 1888–1900, (2) 1901—1910, (3) 1911-13, 1914—1923; Bursian's *Jahresbericht*, 144 (1909) pp. 157—434, 176 (1918) pp. 57—97, 184 (1920) pp. 175—187; *The Year's Work in Classical Studies*, chapters on Latin Inscriptions or cognate subjects, by Haverfield, G. L. Cheesman and others, for 1906-24.

[1] Cp. L. Renier *Inscr. romaines de l'Algérie*, Paris, 1855-8; St. Gsell, *Inscr. latines d'Algérie* 1, Paris, 1922; R. Cagnat, A. Merlin, L. Chatelain, *Inscr. latines d'Afrique*, Paris, 1923.
[2] Cp. Michel Clerc, *Aquae Sextiae*, Aix, 1916.
[3] Cp. Allmer et Dissard, *Musée de Lyon*, vols. 1—5, Lyon; A. de Boissieu, *Inscr. Antiques de Lyon*, 1846–54; C. Jullian, *Inscr. romaines de Bordeaux*, 1887–91; C. Robert et R. Cagnat, *Épigraphie Gallo-romaine de la Moselle*, 1873–88; Seymour de Ricci, *Répertoire épigraphique* (a) *de la Bretagne occidentale*, 1897, (b) *du département d'Ille-et-Vilaine*, 1898.
[4] Brambach, *Corpus Inscr. Rhenarum*, 1867.

SELECT BIBLIOGRAPHY xxi

FACSIMILES, etc.:
(1) *Priscae Latinitatis Monumenta Epigraphica* (*P.L.M.E.*), *tabulae* 98, ed. Ritschl, Berlin, 1862; Suppl. in 'Opuscula' iv, 1878, with Atlas of 23 plates, Leipzig, 1878; (2) *Exempla Scripturae Epigraphicae Latinae a Caesaris dictatoris morte ad aetatem Iustiniani* (*Ex.* or *Exempla*), Introduction and Commentary, with Facsimiles of 1216 genuine and 13 spurious inscr., ed. Hübner, Berlin, 1885; (3) *Res gestae divi Augusti*, Humann's facsimile of Latin and Greek text of *Monumentum Ancyranum, tabulae undecim*, with Mommsen's Text and Commentary (out of print, and very scarce), Berlin, 1883; (4) E. Diehl, *Inscriptiones Latinae* (50 plates), in Lietzmann's Tabulae, no. iv, Bonn, 1912 (most useful for students); (5) O. Gradenwitz, *Index* to ed. 7 (1909) of C. G. Bruns, *Fontes Iuris Romani Antiqui*, pp. 183, 8vo, with 40 first-rate *Simulacra*, pp. xxxv, folio, Tübingen, 1912; cp. references in Dessau, *Inscr. Lat. Sel.*, III ii 1916, p. clxix ff, and, under the inscr. concerned, in notes or index to the present work. See also *Facsimiles* in the various Manuals: 87 in 28 plates in Cagnat's 4th ed. (1914, the best in any Manual), *c.* 90 in Egbert's (1896, 1908), *c.* 111 in 65 tavole, in Ricci's (1898), and 50 in the present work.

SELECTIONS etc.:
(1) J. C. Orelli, *Amplissima Collectio*, Zürich, vols. i, ii, 1828; vol. iii, Supplementa et Indices, ed. Henzen, 1856; (2) C. G. Bruns, *Fontes Iuris Romani Antiqui*, 1860; ed. 2, 1870; ed. 3, 1875; ed. 4, 1879; ed. 5, Mommsen, 1886-7; ed. 6 (incl. 'scriptores'), Mommsen-Gradenwitz, 1893; ed. 7, Gradenwitz, pars prior, 'leges et negotia, pp. 435, pars posterior, 'scriptores,' pp. 91, Tübingen, 1909. For *Index* and *Simulacra*, ed. Gradenwitz, 1912, see *supra, Facsimiles* (5); (3) C. G. Wilmanns, *Exempla*, 2885 inscr. classified, with notes and full indices, 2 vols. Berlin, 1873 (as two vols. bound in one, this is still a most handy and convenient collection); (4) John Wordsworth, *Fragments and Specimens of Early Latin*, including selections from *C.I.L.* i[1] on pp. 156—250, 266—271, with notes, Oxford, 1874; (5) R. Garrucci, *Sylloge Inscr. Lat.—usque ad C. Iulium Caesarem plenissima*, Prolegomena Grammatica, (*a*) pars palaeographica; (*b*) orthographica; (*c*) numismatica; (*d*) epigraphica, pp. 655, with Indices, and two plates, Augustae Taurinorum, 1877; (6) F. D. Allen, *Remnants of Early Latin*, Boston (U.S.A.), 1880; (7) W. M. Lindsay, *Handbook of Latin Inscr., illustrating the history of the language*, Boston and Chicago, 1897; (8) A. Ernout, *Recueil de Textes Latins Archaiques*, esp. 'Textes Epigraphiques,' pp. 1—121, Paris, 1916; (9) G. McN. Rushforth, 100 *Latin Historical Inscr. illustrating the History of the Early Empire*, with introduction and bibliography, pp. xxvii + 144, Oxford, 1893 (useful for historical students); (10) Bücheler, 1858 *Carmina Epigraphica*, Teubner text, Leipzig, 1895-7 (cp. A. W. Hodgman, in *Harvard Studies*, ix (1895) 133—168; B. Lier, in *Philologus*, lxii f (1903 f), and J. A. Tolman, Chicago, 1910); (11) H. Dessau, 9522 *Inscr. Selectae*, classified and annotated, Berlin, I (nos. 1—2956) 1892; II i (nos. 2957 —7210) 1902; ii (nos. 7211—8883) 1906; (nos. 8884—9522) in III ii,

[1] A convenient selection of 27 inscr. of the Roman republic (with references to Ritschl's plates) had already been published in Roby's *Latin Grammar*, i (1871), 416—432.

xxii LATIN INSCRIPTIONS

1916; III i (Indices 1—9) 1914; III ii (Indices 10—17, 'Addenda et Corrigenda') 1916; (12) Lietzmann's *Kleine Texte*, Bonn, 1908 (most useful for students), including E. Diehl (*a*) *Res gestae divi Augusti*, 1908; ed. 2, 1910; (*b*) *Alltateinische Inschr.*, ed. 2, 1911; (*c*) *Vulgärlateinische Inschr.* 1910; (*d*) *Pompeianische Inschr.*, 1910; (*e*) F. Richter, *Sacralinschr.* 1911; (13) H. Willemsen, *257 Lateinische Inschr. für den Gebrauch im Schulunterricht*, Berlin, 1913; (14) A. H. Smith, *Guide to Inscriptions in British Museum*, Latin Inscr. on pp. 38—43, 1917 (cp. evidence from inscr. in British Museum *Guide to the Exhibition illustrating Greek and Roman Life*, ed. F. H. Marshall, 1908); (15) E. Diehl, *Inscriptiones Latinae Christianae veteres* I, II i, Berlin, 1925.

DICTIONARIES:

(1) *Antiquities* etc.: De Ruggiero, *Dizionario Epigrafico di Antichità Romane*, Rome, 1886— , fasc. 139, 1925, ends with 'Interamna'; (2) *Biography*; *Prosopographia Imperii Romani*, i ed. Klebs; ii ed. Dessau, 1897; iii ed. von Rohden and Dessau, 1898.

LANGUAGE:

(1) G. N. Olcott, (*a*) Word-formation, Leipzig, 1898; (*b*) *Thesaurus linguae Latinae epigraphicae*, Rome, 1904— published as far as *ascr*, 1912; (2) Diehl, *De m finali epigraphica*, Leipzig, 1899; (3) Spain, A. Carnoy, Louvain, ed. 2, 1906; (4) Gaul, J. Pirson, Brussels, 1901; (5) Gallia Narbonensis, pronunciation and orthography, F. Neumann, Trieste, 1897; (6) Africa, Kübler in *Archiv für Lateinische Lexicographie*, viii 161—202; Etruscan Analogies, Lattes, *ib.* 495-9 (cp. Lattes, *Iscrizioni paleolatine*, 1892); (7) Syntax, H. Martin, Baltimore, 1909 (Suppl. in *A.J.P.* xxxv, 1914, pp. 401—420).

Cp. Indices in Orelli-Henzen (1856), Diehl (*b*) and (*c*) *supra*; Wilmanns, ii pp. 605—707; also to Dessau, *Inscr. Lat. Sel.* III ii (1916), pp. 802—875, Grammatica quaedam:—Notabilia de litteris (802—839); assimilatio praepositionum neglecta vel contra usum admissa (839 f); declinatio (842—857); genera nominum permutata (857); comparatio adiectivorum, numeralia (858); pronomina (859 f); verba (861 f); adverbia (864), praepositiones (865 f), coniunctiones, interiectiones; syntaxis (869 f); vocabula rara (871 f); alliteratio (873); scripturae vitia (873 f); tituli bilingues (874); analecta nonnulla (875). Acclamationes (876 f). Nominum ratio (921-9).

HISTORY OF THE STUDY OF LATIN EPIGRAPHY:

(1) Hübner, Introduction to his *Exempla* (1885) and to his articles in (*a*) *Encyclopædia Britannica* (1881 and 1910) and (*b*) in Iwan Müller's *Handbuch*, i, 1886 and 1892; (2) R. de la Blanchère, *Histoire de l'Épigraphie Romaine* (pp. 63), Paris, 1887; (3) De Rossi, *Inscr. Christianae urbis Romae*, II (i) 1—33, 356—387, Romae, 1888; (4) J. P. Waltzing, *Le Recueil général des inscriptions Latines (C.I.L.), et l'Épigraphie Latine depuis 50 ans*, Louvain (pp. 155), 1892. Cp. Desjardins, *Nécessité des connaissances épigraphiques pour l'intelligence de certains textes classiques*, in *Rev. de Philol.* 1877, p. 7 f; and notes to (4), pp. 1—31.

MANUALS, etc.:

(1) [F. A. Zaccharia], *Istituzione antiquario-lapidaria*, Roma, 1770; 2nd ed. (with the author's name) Venezia, 1793; (2) S. A. Morcelli (*a*)

SELECT BIBLIOGRAPHY   xxiii

de stilo inscr. Lat. Libri iii, Roma, 1780; vols. i—iii (1819-22) of his
Opera Epigraphica, 5 vols. Padua, 1818-23; (*b*) *lexicon epigraphicum,*
4 vols. Bologna, 1835-43; (3) Carl Zell, *Handbuch,* in two parts (*a*)
Auswahl von (1974) *Röm. Inschr.*, Heidelberg, 1850; (*b*) *Anleitung, ib.*
1852; 2nd ed. 1874; (4) C. Bone, *Anleitung zum Lesen, Ergänzen
und Datiren römischer Inschriften,* Trier, 1881 (elementary); (5) E.
Hübner (*a*) *Roman Inscriptions,* first printed in *Encyclopædia Britannica,* ed. 9, vol. xiii (nearly 20 columns), 1881, revised and abridged by
W. M. Lindsay in ed. 11, vol. xiv (16 columns), 1910; (*b*) Introduction
to *Exempla* (166 columns, folio), Berlin, 1885; (*c*) *Römische Epigraphik,* in Iwan Müller's *Handbuch,* i, 73 pp., Munich, 1886; 2nd ed.
95 pp., 1892; (6) Chr. Hülsen, in new ed. of the same *Handbuch,*
announced in 1913.

(7) R. Cagnat (*a*) *Cours d'Épigraphie Latine,* Paris, 1885, 1889,
1898; ed. 4, revised and enlarged, pp. 27+504, 1914; (*b*) *Inscriptiones*
in Daremberg-Saglio, *Dictionnaire des Antiquités,* v 526 f; (*c*) *Sur les
manuels professionnels des graveurs d'inscriptions romaines,* in *Revue
de Philologie,* 1889, p. 447; (*d*) *Bibliographie critique de l'épigraphie
latine,* Paris, 1901; (8) J. C. Egbert, *Introduction to the Study of Latin
Inscriptions,* pp. 468, New York, 1896; revised ed. with Suppl. pp. 469—
480, 1908; (9) Serafino Ricci, *Epigrafia Latina, trattato elementare,*
447 pp., Milan, 1898; (10) O. Marucchi, *Christian Epigraphy* (with
bibliography), E.T., Cambridge, 1912.

The most recent select bibliography is that of Cagnat (*Bibliographie
de l'Épigraphie Latine*) in *Cours d'Épigraphie Latine* (ed. 4, 1914),
pp. xix—xxvii,—an abridgment of fasc. 13 contributed by himself to
the *Bibliothèque de bibliographies critiques publiée par la Société des
Études Historiques,* Picard, Paris, 1901.

De lapidariae Latinitatis usu recentiore testimonia

Si quis breve dictum, quod in gladii capulo, vel in annuli legatur emblemate: si quis versum lecto, aut cubiculo, si quis insigne aliquod non argento dixerim, sed fictilibus omnino suis desiderat, illico ad Politianum cursitat, omnesque tam parietes a me, quasi a limace videas oblitos argumentis variis et titulis.

> Angelus Politianus, *Hieronymo Donato*, Florentiae, 1490, *Epp.* ii 13, *Opera*, p. 26, Basileae, 1553.

Of the English epitaph in honour of Sir James Macdonald in the Island of Skye, Dr Johnson said, 'the inscription should have been in Latin, as everything intended to be universal and permanent should be.'

> Cp. J. Boswell, *Journal of a Tour to the Hebrides*, 5 Sept. 1773.

An inscription, to the scholars of those days [1823], *was like the sound of a bugle to a war-horse....'It is all very well to say that So-and-so is a good scholar,' said Samuel Parr to Samuel Butler of Shrewsbury, 'but can he write an inscription?'*

> Cp. Dr Samuel Butler, Head-Master of Shrewsbury School, 1798—1836, *Life and Letters*, by his grandson, Samuel Butler, author of "Erewhon," i 255, 1896.

CHAPTER I

THE STUDY OF LATIN INSCRIPTIONS

LATIN INSCRIPTIONS IN CLASSICAL AUTHORS

THE science concerned with the classification and interpretation of inscriptions is known by the name of Epigraphy, a term ultimately derived from ἐπιγραφή, the Greek word for an 'inscription.' The name, and the science denoted by it, are comparatively modern. 'The science of epigraphy,' says the *Saturday Review* for 18 July 1863, 'seems still, as far as Britain is concerned, to be quite in its infancy.' Strictly speaking, Epigraphy is a branch of Palaeography. Latin Epigraphy may be defined as the science concerned with all the remains of the Latin language inscribed on durable materials, such as stone or metal, but inscriptions on coins which, under this definition, form a part of Epigraphy, are generally reserved for the domain of Numismatics[1]. Latin Palaeography is, in practice, confined to that which is written on less durable materials, such as papyrus, parchment or paper. Writings on tablets covered with wax may be treated as belonging to the domain of Epigraphy, but they are more closely connected with that of Palaeography. The province of Epigraphy is, in one respect, wider than that of Palaeography, for, while Palaeography confines itself to the study of the forms of writing found in ancient manuscripts, Epigraphy not only deals with the lettering, but is even apt to concern itself with the subject-matter of ancient inscriptions, thus unduly encroaching on the provinces of History, and of Public and Private Antiquities.

margin note: Epigraphy defined

[1] Similarly, inscriptions on gems are usually reserved for special treatment in works on Ancient Gems.

Latin inscriptions supply us with the oldest extant evidence for the orthography and for the ancient forms of the Latin language. This evidence is far earlier than that of our oldest Latin manuscripts, and it sometimes enables us to correct the manuscript text of Latin authors[1]. All the more important documents relating to public life were inscribed on metal or on stone. Inscriptions thus provide us with valuable information on matters of Geography, History, or Chronology, and serve to supplement the records preserved in Latin literature. They also throw light on every department of Public and Private Antiquities, while they have saved from destruction many a detail of passing interest, which formed part of the daily life of the ancient world, but failed to find any notice in the pages of Latin authors. It must also be remembered that the language of many of our extant inscriptions is more closely connected with that of ordinary life than with that of literature.

Value of Latin Inscriptions

Inscriptions are the main source of our knowledge of the three following points: (1) the history and chronological development of the *Roman name*; (2) the *Cursus honorum*, or sequence of public offices held by senators or equites, the successive titles being carefully recorded either in ascending or in descending order, while both principles may be exemplified in two different inscriptions relating to the same individual; (3) *the Names and Titles of the Roman Emperors*, and of members of the imperial family. A knowledge of all these points is no necessary part of the approach to the study of inscriptions, but it often enables us to ascertain the date of an inscription, and it is an important aid towards the restoration of *lacunae*. The details in question fill a large space in some modern manuals; in the present Introduction each of these three subjects will be, either wholly or in part, reserved for comparatively brief treatment in the Appendix.

---

[1] Thus, in Cicero's *Orator* § 157, the inscription ending with **EIDEMQVE PROB[AVIT]** on the temple of Iuppiter Capitolinus (Ritschl, tab. lxix, c), suggested to Heerdegen the correction: 'et in templis: EIDEM PROBAVIT.' The *Monumentum Ancyranum* (printed in Appendix, iv 2) is our best authority for the orthography of the Augustan age.

LATIN INSCRIPTIONS IN CLASSICAL AUTHORS.

Classical inscriptions have sometimes been regarded as forming a subordinate department of classical literature; but, in practice, they are most conveniently studied as a special branch of classical archaeology. Latin inscriptions are noticed from time to time by classical authors. The treaties between the rising state of Rome and its immediate neighbours were among the earliest documents drawn up in Latin prose, and several of these treaties are definitely mentioned by Dionysius of Halicarnassus in the age of Augustus. Thus, he informs us that duplicate copies of the agreement between Tullus Hostilius and the Sabines were drawn up on tablets, and deposited in the temples[1]. He incidentally states that Ancus Martius caused the sacrificial ordinances of Numa to be inscribed on tablets of bronze, instead of panels of oak[2]. He also mentions the treaty between Servius Tullius and the Latins, adding that the terms of this treaty (inscribed with letters resembling those formerly used in Greece) were recorded on a bronze tablet which was preserved down to the writer's day in the temple of Diana on the Aventine[3]. The treaty between Tarquinius Superbus and Gabii was inscribed in archaic characters on a shield covered with ox-hide, which was kept in the temple of Iuppiter Sancus[4]. Lastly, Dionysius describes the *lex Icilia* of 456 B.C. as inscribed on a bronze tablet which was set up in the temple of Diana on the Aventine[5]. Polybius records the 'first treaty' between Rome and Carthage in 509 B.C., and quotes its terms, adding that, in certain passages, the Latin forms were hardly intelligible to the most learned antiquaries[6]. After mentioning two other treaties with Carthage, he implies that the text of all three of them was inscribed on tablets

Inscriptions in classical authors

Dionysius of Halicarnassus

Polybius

---

[1] *Antiquitates Romanae*, iii 33, τῶν ὁμολογιῶν στήλας ἀντιγράφους θέντες ἐν τοῖς ἱεροῖς.

[2] *ib.* iii 36.   [3] *ib.* iv 26.

[4] *ib.* iv 58, cp. Festus, s.v. *Clipeum*, p. 48, 19 ed. Lindsay.

[5] *ib.* x 32. In Dionysius we also find ἱεραὶ δέλτοι (i 73); τοῦ παρὰ τοῖς ἀρχιερεῦσι κειμένου πίνακος (i 74); and ἐν ταῖς ἐνιαυσίοις ἀναγραφαῖς (iv 30).

[6] Polybius, iii 22.

of bronze preserved in the archives of the aediles in the temple of Iuppiter Capitolinus[1].

Livy refers to a treaty with the Latins, in 493 B.C., as inscribed on a bronze column, and Cicero, speaking in 56 B.C., says that it had lately been inscribed on a bronze column behind the *rostra*[2]. Livy states that the 'laws of the twelve tables' (450 B.C.) were 'incised on bronze'[3]; and he implies that the treaty made with Ardea in 443 was inspected by the annalist, Licinius Macer[4], who, in connexion with the exploits of C. Cossus, duly examined the *libri lintei* containing the lists of Roman magistrates in the temple of Iuno Moneta[5]. When Augustus examined in the temple of Iuppiter Feretrius the *spolia opima* won by Cossus, and stated, on the authority of the *titulus ipse spoliis* (*in thorace linteo*) *inscriptus*, that Cossus was described as consul (when all the authorities had made him a military tribune at the time of his exploit), Livy professes to leave it as an open question[6]. Livy tells us that (in 200 B.C.) Athens decreed the removal of all statues, and forbade all inscriptions, in honour of the Macedonian king, Philippus[7]. He quotes the inscription on the tablet placed in the temple of Mater Matuta by Ti. Sempronius Gracchus in memory of his conquest of Sardinia[8], and supplies us with a perfect rendering of the Greek epitaph which the Acarnanians, in the event of their falling in battle, desired the Epirotes to place upon their tomb :—*hic siti sunt Acarnanes, qui adversus vim atque*

---

[1] Polybius, iii 26, ἐν χαλκώμασι.

[2] Livy, ii 33, 9, columna aënea insculptum. Cicero, *pro Balbo*, 53, in columna ahenea...incisum et perscriptum, probably 'not the original foedus, but a copy made in 358, when it was renewed' (Reid).

[3] iii 57, 10; cp. Diodorus, xii 26. Dion. Hal. *Ant. Rom.* x 57, 7, στήλαις χαλκαῖς. Pomponius, in the Digest, i 2, 2, 4, has *eboreas*, for which Scaliger suggested *roboreas*. The standard critical edition is that of R. Schöll (1866); see also F. D. Allen's *Remnants of Early Latin* (1880), 84—92, and A. Ernout's *Recueil de textes latins archaïques* (1916), 114—121.

[4] iv 7, 12.   [5] iv 20, 5—7.

[6] *l. c.* There may have been some confusion between cossus and cos., the abbreviation for *consul*. It has, indeed, been suggested that the inscription may have belonged to a time when A. Cornelius M. f. Cossus appeared in the form A · CORNELIO · M · F · COSO (O. Hirschfeld, *Kleine Schriften*, 398 f).

[7] xxxi 44, 4 f.

[8] xli 28, 8—10. Cp. xl 52, 5, p. 5 n. 4, and p. 6 n. 6 *infra*.

iniuriam Aetolorum pro patria pugnantes mortem occubuerunt[1]. Apart from the inscription on the above-mentioned tablet of Ti. Sempronius Gracchus, two passages of Livy have found their way into modern collections:—(1) the dedication of the temple of Iuppiter Capitolinus by M. Horatius in 509 B.C.[2], and (2) the inscription *his ferme incisa litteris* referring to the nine towns captured by T. Quinctius in 380[3]. Lastly, the historian quotes, in an imperfectly preserved form, the inscription on the temple vowed by L. Aemilius Regillus on the occasion of his naval victory over Antiochus in 190 B.C.[4]

Varro, in support of his opinion that *meridies* was derived from *medius dies*, states that the word was formerly spelt, not with an R, but with a D, as he had himself seen it inscribed on a sun-dial at Praeneste[5]. He is quoted by Macrobius as mentioning a very ancient law on the intercalary month, 'incisam in columna aerea'[6], in 472 B.C., and by Pliny[7] as stating that public documents were in early times inscribed on sheets of lead, and private ones on linen or wax. But there is no proof that lead was thus employed by the Romans. Its use was apparently confined to maledictory inscriptions such as those mentioned by Tacitus in connexion with the death of Germanicus[8]. Oak is said to have been the material used, not only for recording the ordinances of Numa[9] but also for the *sortes Praenestinae*[10].

Cicero quotes the beginning of an inscription in honour of A. Atilius Calatinus, consul in 258 and 254 B.C. :—

    Hunc unum plurimae consentiunt gentes
    populi primarium fuisse virum[11].

Varro

Cicero

---

[1] xxvi 25, 14.   [2] vii 3, 8.

[3] vi 29, 9. See *C. I. L.* vi (5) p. 1*, *a* and *d*, *Epigrammata antiqua ex libris scriptis desumpta*.

[4] xl 52, 5 f.   [5] *De lingua Latina*, vi 4.

[6] Macrobius, *Sat.* i 13, 21.   [7] xiii 69.

[8] *Ann.* ii 69, 'nomen Germanici plumbeis tabulis insculptum.'

[9] p. 3 *supra*.

[10] Cicero, *De Div.* ii 85, 'sortes in robore insculptas priscarum litterarum notis.'

[11] The name has suggested the forged inscription, *C. I. L.* vi (5) 3422*, A. ATILIVS | CALATINVS | COS, quoted by Fabretti 673, 12 from papers in the Chigi library.

He adds 'notum est totum carmen incisum in sepulcro'[1]. In quoting the same words elsewhere, he describes the tomb as placed *ad portam*[2], while, in a third passage, he states that it was outside the *porta Capena*, with the tombs of the Scipios, the Servilii, and the Metelli[3]. The epitaph is written in the same Saturnian metre, and partly in the same words, as that in honour of a consul of the year immediately preceding the first consulship of A. Atilius Calatinus, namely L. Cornelius Scipio, son of Barbatus :—

Honc oino ploirume cosentiont, etc.[4]

Saturnian verses, set up 'in the Capitol' to commemorate triumphs over Antiochus in 191 f B.C., (*a*) by M'. Acilius Glabrio, and (*b*) by L. Aemilius Regillus, are preserved in the following form by the grammarian, Atilius Fortunatianus[5] :—

(*a*) fundit fugat prosternit maximas legiones.
(*b*) duello magno dirimendo, regibus subigendis[6].

Similar verses are quoted by Atilius (*c*)[7], and in a spurious treatise ascribed to Censorinus (*d*)[8]:—

(*c*) summas opes qui regum regias refregit.
(*d*) magnum numerum triumphat hostibus devictis.

In the *De Oratore* Cicero refers as follows to the origin of the *annales maximi* :—'res omnes singulorum annorum mandabat litteris pontifex maximus, referebatque in album et proponebat tabulam domi, potestas ut esset populo cognoscendi'[9]. As quaestor in 75 B.C., he discovered the tomb of Archimedes near one of the gates of Syracuse, where it was almost hidden among briars, and even forgotten by the Syracusans themselves. Archimedes had died during the siege of the city by Marcellus in 212 B.C. His tomb was marked by a small column bearing the figure of a sphere inscribed in a cylinder, in commemoration of his discovery that

---

[1] *De Sen.* 61. [2] *De Finibus* ii 116.
[3] *Tusc. Disp.* i 13. [4] See p. 67 *infra*.
[5] Keil, *Gr. Lat.* vi 265.
[6] For (*a*) cp. the commentators on Livy, xxxvii 46, 1; and for (*b*) see further in Livy, xl 52, 5.
[7] Keil, *u. s.* 294. [8] Keil, *u. s.* 615.
[9] *De Or.* ii 53.

the volume of a sphere was equivalent to two-thirds of that of the circumscribing cylinder. There were also several lines of iambic verse, the latter halves of which (as Cicero tells us) had been worn away[1].

The beginning of the epitaph of Ennius on Scipio Africanus Maior (c. 183 B.C.) is quoted by Cicero:—HIC EST ILLE SITVS[2], and the rest by Seneca:—CVI NEMO CIVIS NEQVE HOSTIS | QVIVIT PRO FACTIS REDDERE OPIS PRETIVM.[3]. Scipio, who died in retirement at Liternum, is said to have directed that the following words should be placed on his tomb:

INGRATA PATRIA, NE OSSA QVIDEM MEA HABES[4].

The first, second, and fourth lines, and the first half of the third line, of Ennius' epitaph on himself are quoted by Cicero in the *Tusculan Disputations*[5], and the whole of the third line in the *De Senectute*[6].

The complete epitaph is as follows:—

> Aspicite, o cives, senis Enni imaginis formam.
> Hic vestrum panxit maxima facta patrum.
> Nemo me lacrumis decoret, neque funera fletu
> faxit. Cur? volito vivus per ora virum[7].

Cicero tells us that the name of Scipio Africanus Minor (who died in 129 B.C.) was inscribed in large letters on the pedestal of a statue of Diana at Segesta, which Scipio had restored to Segesta on his conquest of Carthage[8]. He further implies that a statue of the younger Scipio, inscribed with the *elogium* COS and CENS, was erroneously copied by Q. Caecilius Metellus Scipio on a statue of his great-grandfather, Scipio Nasica Sarapion, although the latter

---

[1] *Tusc. Disp.* v 64—66.

[2] *De Legibus* ii 57. He adds (§ 58) that the discovery of a bronze tablet bearing the word HONORIS led to the building of an *Aedes Honoris* outside the Colline gate.

[3] *Epp.* 108 § 33, first combined with the previous quotation by Scaliger.

[4] Valerius Max. v 3, 2. The alleged epitaph was probably suggested by Livy, xxxviii 53, 8.

[5] *Tusc. Disp.* i 34.   [6] *De Sen.* 73.

[7] Cp. *C. I. L.* vi (5) p. 3* d.

[8] *Verr.* ii 74.

had never held the office of censor[1]. It is from Cicero that we learn that, in a temple at Syracuse, certain silver tables were, according to Greek custom, inscribed BONORVM DEORVM[2]. In the prosecution of Verres he informs us that he had seen at Syracuse an inscription describing Verres as not only PATRONVS but also SOTER of Sicily[3]; and, in Rome, certain statues inscribed as presented to Verres A COMMVNI SICILIAE[4]. In the *Philippics* we find mention of three statues dedicated to Antonius as PATRONO[5], while Antonius himself placed on the statue of Caesar the inscription PARENTI OPTIME MERITO[6]. Laws, or Senatus consulta, are quoted in several of the *Philippics*, and in the *pro Cluentio*, and the *de Legibus*. Lastly, from one of the Letters we learn that Atticus informed Cicero that Clodius had placed on the door of the Senate House a *caput legis* in the form of an inscription NE REFERRI NEVE DICI LICERET[7].

Asconius, in commenting on Cicero's speech *in Pisonem* (§ 44), records the fact that Marcellus, the grandson of the conqueror of Syracuse, set up statues of himself and his father and grandfather bearing the simple and modest inscription, III MARCELLI NOVIES COSS., the fact being that he had himself been consul thrice, his father once, and his grandfather on five occasions[8].

According to Velleius Paterculus, the hot-springs of mount Tifata and the surrounding lands were a sacred precinct dedicated to Diana by Sulla in memory of the victory there won in 83 B.C.[9]

Seneca tells us that the crown of oak-leaves bore the inscription OB CIVEM SERVATVM[10]; he also quotes a line from the epitaph of a comic actor: HOSPES RESISTE ET

---

[1] *Ad Atticum* vi 1, 17, with Tyrrell and Purser's excursus in vol. iii² 344-6 of *The Correspondence of Cicero*, where there is a discussion of Mommsen's opinion in *C. I. L.* i (p. 278¹, 186²) that Metellus had placed a statue of the elder Africanus over the *elogium* of Sarapion (COS) and a statue of Sarapion over the *elogium* of the elder Africanus (COS. CENS).

[2] *De Nat. Deorum*, iii 84.
[3] *Verr.* ii 154.
[4] *Verr.* ii 114, 154, 168.
[5] *Phil.* vi 12, 13, 15.
[6] *Ad Fam.* xii 3.
[7] *Ad Atticum*, iii 15, 6.
[8] p. 12, ed. A. C. Clark.
[9] ii 25, 4. This is confirmed by local inscriptions; Dessau, *Inscriptiones*, i 251 and ii 3240.
[10] *De Clementia*, i 26, 5.

SOPHIAM DOSSENNI LEGE[1], and records the fact that Statilia (Messalina) directed that her epitaph should state that she had attained the age of ninety-nine[2].

In Petronius we have an imaginary inscription on a kind of trophy of rods and axes and rostra which was presented to Trimalchio[3], and also an imaginary epitaph purporting to be composed by Trimalchio himself. It runs as follows: *Petronius*

> Cn. Pompeius Trimalchio Maecenatianus hic requiescit. Huic seviratus absenti decretus est. Cum posset in omnibus decuriis Romae esse, tamen noluit. Pius, fortis, fidelis, ex parvo crevit, sestertium reliquit trecentiens, nec unquam philosophum audivit. Vale; et tu[4].

The elder Pliny mentions the custom of recording public ordinances on tablets of bronze:—'usus aeris ad perpetuitatem monumentorum iam pridem tralatus est tabulis aereis in quibus publicae constitutiones inciduntur'[5].   *Pliny the elder*
He describes the method of manufacturing bronze for this purpose[6]. He also states that Cn. Flavius recorded on a bronze tablet the fact that the temple of Concord, which he had vowed, was built (in 303 B.C.) 204 years after the dedication of the Capitoline temple (in 507)[7]. He tells us that the statue of 'Hercules tunicatus,' near the Rostra, bore three different inscriptions referring to its origin, its dedication, and its restoration[8]. He mentions a very old oak-tree on the Vatican hill, bearing an inscription 'aereis litteris Etruscis'[9]. He quotes the four hexameter lines inscribed on the painted walls of the ancient temple of Iuno at Ardea[10], adding that they were written *antiquis litteris Latinis*[11]. He records the inscriptions placed in the temple of Minerva in memory of the victories of Pompey[12]; and cites in full

[1] *Epp.* 89 § 7; see Wilkins on Horace, *Epp.* ii 1, 173.
[2] *Epp.* 77 § 20.   [3] c. 30.
[4] c. 71, cp. Mommsen, *Ges. Schr.* vii 200 f.
[5] xxxiv 100.   [6] xxxiv 97, *aes tabulare*.
[7] xxxiii 19.   [8] xxxiv 33.
[9] xvi 237.   [10] xxxv 115.
[11] He is even interested in inscriptions in other languages than Latin. He knows that, on certain islands of Arabia and Ethiopia, 'there are tablets inscribed with unknown letters' (vi 150, 174). See also xxxvi 71.
[12] vii 97 f.

the record on the *Tropaeum Alpium* setting forth the names of the Alpine tribes conquered by Augustus, beginning with the words :—'Imperatori Caesari divi F. Aug., pontifici maximo, imp. XIII, tribuniciae potestatis XVII, S. P. Q. R.'[1] He also quotes ten lines of elegiacs placed by Cicero's freedman Tullius Laurea beside the hot-springs of Cicero's villa at Puteoli[2], mentions monumental inscriptions as 'giving a longer life to men's name and memory'[3], and, elsewhere, incidentally refers to the satirical epitaph, 'illa infelix monumenti inscriptio, turba se medicorum perisse'[4]. He states that Appius Claudius, 'the consul of 259 A.U.C.' (495 B.C.), was the first to place the images of his ancestors on shields in the temple of Bellona, with the record of their public offices[5]; but it was Appius Claudius *Caecus*, consul in 307 and 296 B.C., who in his second consulship vowed to erect a temple to Bellona. He adds that the precedent of setting up shields was followed by M. Aemilius Lepidus, in 78 B.C., in the Basilica Aemilia, and in his private house[6]. He has only a vague reference to the *columna rostrata* set up in the Forum in honour of Duilius[7], while Quintilian definitely draws attention to the frequent appearance of the final D in that monument[8]. His report of the speech of Q. Caelius Metellus, in honour of his father, consul in 251 and 249 B.C.[9], has been made the foundation of a modern inscription[10]. Pliny observes that Varro's statement that, in 149 B.C., Scipio Africanus the younger received the *corona obsidionalis*, was also recorded beneath Scipio's statue in the *Forum* of Augustus[11]. Elsewhere he observes that the example set by Athens in erecting statues of public benefactors had been followed throughout the world. 'Statues began to adorn the *Fora* of every municipality; the memory of men was immortalised, and their honours were no longer engraven on their tombstones alone, but were handed down for posterity to read on the pedestals of their statues'[12].

[1] iii 136; cp. pp. 19, 122 *infra*.
[2] xxxi 8.
[3] ii 154.
[4] xxix 11.
[5] xxxv 12.
[6] xxxv 13.
[7] xxxiv 20.
[8] Quint. i 7, 12; cp. p. 95 f *infra*.
[9] vii 139—141.
[10] *C. I. L.* vi (5) p. 1*f.
[11] xxii 13.
[12] xxxiv 17.

The younger Pliny twice records, and severely censures, the epitaph of the upstart Pallas, the wealthy freedman of Claudius:—'huic senatus ob fidem pietatemque erga patronos ornamenta praetoria decrevit et sestertium centies quinquagies, cuius honore contentus fuit'[1]; and, in two of his Letters, he quotes with pride and pleasure the couplet inscribed on the still unfinished monument of Verginius Rufus (15—99 A.D.), the patriotic conqueror of Vindex :—

Pliny the younger

> Hic situs est Rufus, pulso qui Vindice quondam
> imperium asseruit non sibi, sed patriae[2].

He also describes Titinius Capito as composing verses in honour of famous men, and as possessing in his own house busts of the Bruti, the Cassii, the Catones, and setting up a statue of L. Silanus in the Forum[3].

Pliny himself proposes to place a statuette of Corinthian bronze in the temple of Iuppiter at Comum, and asks a friend to arrange for preparing a pedestal bearing his own name, and (perhaps) his public offices[4].

Tacitus relates that the victory of Germanicus over the tribes between the Rhine and the Elbe was celebrated by a trophy 'superbo cum titulo:—debellatis inter Rhenum Albimque nationibus exercitum Tiberii Caesaris ea monimenta Marti et Iovi et Augusto sacravisse'[5]; and that his death was commemorated by arches in Rome and on the Rhine and on mount Amanus in Syria, 'cum inscriptione rerum gestarum ac mortem ob rem publicam obisse'[6]. He also tells us that the conspirator Scaevinus inscribed the words IOVI VINDICI on the dagger, with which he had resolved on slaying Nero[7]. Before Vespasian's entry into Rome, the Senate appointed commissioners to examine and to replace the bronze tablets of the laws, which had fallen down through lapse of time, and to free the *Fasti* from the additions with which they had been disfigured by the adulation of that age[8]. Tacitus elsewhere implies that Vespasian's younger son, Domitian, in memory of his preservation amid various perils,

Tacitus

---

[1] *Epp.* vii 29, 2, and viii 6, 1. [2] *Epp.* vi 10; ix 19.
[3] *Epp.* i 17. [4] *Epp.* iii 6, 5.
[5] Tacitus, *Ann.* ii 22. [6] *Ann.* ii 83.
[7] *Ann.* xv 74. [8] *Hist.* iv 40.

dedicated a shrine IOVI CONSERVATORI, and a great temple IOVI CVSTODI¹.

Roman *senatus consulta* are repeatedly translated in the Greek text of Josephus². Frontinus, besides quoting six *senatus consulta*, and several legal documents and imperial edicts, mentions the lengthening by Trajan of the aqueduct called the *Anio novus*, 'novum auctorem IMPERATOREM CAESAREM NERVAM TRAIANVM AVGVSTVM praescribente titulo'³.

Josephus.
Frontinus

Suetonius quotes a decree of the Senate and a censorial edict on the *rhetores*⁴. In his *Life of Julius Caesar*⁵, he describes an important *lex* proposed by Marcellus as 'in aes incisa et in aerarium condita.' Shortly before the conspiracy against Caesar, the statue of Lucius Brutus, the first consul, was inscribed with the words VTINAM VIVERES, and the statue of Caesar with the lines,

Suetonius

BRVTVS QVIA REGES EIECIT CONSVL PRIMVS FACTVS EST.
HIC QVIA CONSVLES EIECIT REX POSTREMO FACTVS EST⁶.

After Caesar's death, the people set up a marble column in the Forum inscribed PARENTI PATRIAE⁷. In the *Life of Augustus*, the inhabitants of Nursia are said to have recorded on a public monument to those who had fallen in the battle of Mutina, *pro libertate eos occubuisse*⁸. The biographer of the Caesars tells us that he once possessed a bronze statuette of the young Augustus, on which his earliest *cognomen*, Thurinus, was inscribed in faintly visible letters of iron⁹; that statues of the great generals of the Roman Republic, bearing laudatory inscriptions, were set up by the emperor in the Forum of Augustus¹⁰; that, shortly before the emperor's death, the first letter of his full name (C) on the

---

¹ *Hist.* iii 74.
² Treaty with the Jews in *Antiq.* xii 6, 10; see also decrees in xiii 9, 2; xiv 8, 5, and 10, 9. Cp. Ritschl, *Opusc.* v 111 ff; and L. Mendelssohn, *Acta soc. phil. Lips.* (1875), 87 ff.
³ *De Aquae Ductibus*, 93. ⁴ *De Rhetoribus*, § 1.
⁵ *Caesar*, c. 28. ⁶ c. 80.
⁷ c. 85. ⁸ *Aug.* c. 12.
⁹ *ib.* c. 7.
¹⁰ *ib.* 31, 'opera cuiusque (ducis) manentibus titulis restituit et statuas omnium triumphali effigie in utraque fori sui porticu dedicavit.' Cp. p. 97 *infra*.

pedestal of one of his public statues was struck by lightning[1]; and that, on his death, he left behind him (in addition to his will) three 'volumes,' one of which his biographer describes as 'indicem rerum a se gestarum, quam vellet incidi in aëneis tabulis'[2]. This last is the document of which we possess the completest copy in the *Monumentum Ancyranum*[3]. He also tells us that Augustus caused an *elogium*, composed by himself, to be engraved on the tomb of Drusus[4]. He quotes the elder Pliny as supporting his own opinion that Caligula was born at a village among the Treveri by appealing to the fact that certain altars near that village bore the inscription *ob Agrippinae puerperium*[5]. He states that Caligula, on finding himself urged to give notice of a law relating to certain new taxes, caused it to be published 'et minutissimis litteris et angustissimo loco, uti ne cui describere liceret'[6]. He mentions three swords, prepared for the assassination of Caligula, which that emperor 'Marti Vltori, addito elogio, consecravit'[7]. He cites an inscription describing the father of Vitellius as 'pietatis immobilis erga principem'[8], and also mentions a 'lapidem memoriae Othonis inscriptum'[9]. Lastly, he relates that Vespasian took in hand the restoration of 3000 bronze tablets[10], which had been destroyed in the recent conflagration of the Capitol[11]. Shortly before the death of Commodus in 194 A.D. almost all the public documents in the Palace were destroyed by fire[12].

From the *Imagines* of Varro, Aulus Gellius quotes a Latin

Gellius   rendering of an imaginary epitaph on Homer, ascribed to the inhabitants of Ios.

> Capella Homeri candida haec tumulum indicat,
> Quod hac Ietae mortuo faciunt sacra[13].

Gellius also records the fact that Pompey, on dedicating the Aedes Victoriae as a memorial of his third consulship (52 B.C.)

---

[1] *ib.* 97.
[2] *ib.* 101.
[3] Appendix IV (2), *infra*.
[4] *Claud.* 1.
[5] *Cal.* c. 8.
[6] *ib.* c. 41.
[7] *ib.* c. 24 *ult.*
[8] *Vitell.* c. 3.
[9] *Vitell.* c. 10.
[10] *Vesp.* c. 8.
[11] Tacitus, *Hist.* iii 72.
[12] Dion Cassius, lxxii 24, τὰ γράμματα τὰ τῇ ἀρχῇ προσήκοντα.
[13] Gellius, iii 11, 6.

found that experts were divided between the forms *consul tertio* and *consul tertium*, whereupon he consulted Cicero, who persuaded him to adopt the form *consul tert.*, which might answer for either[1]. He also quotes the epitaphs of Naevius (d. 202), Plautus (184) and Pacuvius (130), which he supposes were written by the poets themselves. They run as follows:

(a) Mortalis immortalis flere si foret fas[2],
     Flerent divae Camenae Naevium poëtam,
     Itaque postquam est Orchi traditus thesauro,
     Obliti sunt Romae loquier lingua Latina.

(b) Postquam est mortem aptus Plautus, comoedia luget,
     Scaena est deserta, dein Risus, Ludus, Iocusque,
     Et Numeri innumeri simul omnes conlacrimarunt.

(c) Adulescens, tam[3] etsi properas, te hoc saxum rogat,
     Vt sese[4] aspicias, deinde quod scriptum est legas.
     Hic sunt poëtae Pacuvi Marci sita
     Ossa. Hoc volebam nescius ne esses. Vale[5].

Of these three epitaphs, only that in honour of Pacuvius is entirely in keeping with actual contemporary inscriptions[6], the other two having been probably composed in a later age as epigrams on the literary characteristics of the poets in question[7]. All these may have been derived by Gellius from the works of Varro[8].

A literary example of the use of inscriptions as advertisements may be found in the *Rudens* of Plautus (l. 1294), where one of the characters declares he will advertise in letters an ell long, that, if any one has lost a valuable wallet, he is to apply to

---

[1] xiii 25, 14. Pompey is described as *cos. ter* | in an inscription of Auximum (Dessau, i 877).
[2] 'Inmortales mortales si foret fas flere,' ed. Hertz.
[3] *tamen* MSS.   [4] *se* MSS.
[5] Gellius, i 24.
[6] Cp. 'adulescens, tametsi properas, hic te saxsolus
    rogat ut se aspicias, deinde ut quod scriptust legas.
    hic sunt ossa...sita....
    hoc ego voleba(m) nescius ni esses. Vale.'
Diehl, *Inscr. Lat.* 6 d; Dessau, ii (2) 7703, cp. *ib.* i. 1932,—'sunt ossa heic sita.—hoc voluit, nescius ne esses. Vale.' Cp. p. 63 *infra*.
[7] Jahn, in *Hermes*, ii 242; Bücheler, in *Rhein. Mus.* xxxvii 521.
[8] Bormann, *Arch. Epigr. Mitt.* xvii 227 f.

the speaker. Propertius has a poetical advertisement on the loss of his writing tablets, concluding with the couplet:—

> I, puer, et citus haec aliqua propone columna;
> Et dominum Esquiliis scribe habitare tuum[1].

Among imaginary literary inscriptions may be mentioned the line in which Virgil describes Aeneas as dedicating the shield of a Greek warrior on the temple-gate at Actium:—

> Aeneas haec de Danais victoribus arma[2].

An imaginary epitaph[3] is to be found in the last two lines of the *Culex*. The hundred and first poem of Catullus may be regarded as an inscription on his brother's tomb. Propertius gives us (in addition to an epitaph on himself[4]) two dedicatory inscriptions[5], and an epitaph on Cynthia:—

> Hic Tiburtina iacet aurea Cynthia terra;
> Accessit ripae laus, Aniene, tuae[6].

> Here golden Cynthia lies in Tibur's ground;
> Thy banks, O Anio, with fresh fame are crowned.

Ovid has an epitaph on Corinna's favourite parrot:—

> Colligor ex ipso dominae placuisse sepulcro;
> Ora fuere mihi plus ave docta loqui[7];

and on Hypermnestra:—

> Exsul Hypermnestra, pretium pietatis iniquum,
> Quam mortem fratri depulit, ipsa tulit[8].

Tibullus provides parallels to the customary *formulae*:—*hic situs est*, and *sit tibi terra levis*[9]. He also writes his own epitaph in an elegiac couplet[10], and is imitated in the epitaphs of the imperial age.

Horace makes Hypermnestra bid Lynceus engrave his regretful lament upon her tomb, 'nostri memorem sepulcro scalpe querelam'[11]. He recalls the primitive custom of inscribing laws

---

[1] Propertius, iv 23. [2] *Aen.* iii 288.
[3] *Elogium*. [4] Propertius iii 4 (5) 35 f.
[5] *ib.* iii 5 (6), 27 f, and v 3, 72, 'salvo grata puella viro.'
[6] *ib.* v 7, 85.
[7] *Amores*, ii 6, 61 f; cp. 13, 25 'adiciam titulum SERVATA NASO CORINNA'.
[8] *Heroides*, xiv 129. [9] iii 2, 29, and ii 4, 50.
[10] i 3, 55. [11] *Carm.* iii 11, 51 f.

on tablets of wood¹. He describes the virtues of Augustus as recorded for ever 'per titulos memoresque fastos'²; and alludes to the pedestals of the statues of great generals in the Forum of Augustus, as 'incisa notis marmora publicis'³. He has more than one mention of the 'tabula votiva'⁴, and also refers to the custom of describing the dimensions of a burial-place, with the proviso that the monument erected thereon was not to pass to the heirs of the property :—

> mille pedes in fronte, trecentum cippus in agrum
> hic dabat: heredes monumentum ne sequeretur⁵.

In allusion to a *locus sacer*, Horace's imitator, the satirist Persius, quotes parallels to the modern warning, 'commit no nuisance'⁶. Men may be ambitious of fame, in the form of an epitaph, says Juvenal, but even the tombs on which those epitaphs are carved have their destined day of doom⁷.

Lucan quotes the epitaph of Pompey:—HIC SITVS EST MAGNVS⁸, and the language that he ascribes to the wife of Cato, 'liceat tumulo scripsisse *Catonis Marcia* '⁹, has prompted the forging of the epitaph MARTIA MARCI CATONIS ¹⁰.

Martial incidentally mentions the *inscripta basis* of a statue¹¹. In allusion to a faithless wife who had buried seven husbands, and had written *Chloë fecit* on each of their tombs, the poet satirically suggests that the verb did not really refer (as usual) to the erection of the monument, but was obviously a candid confession of her guilt :—

> Inscripsit tumulis septem scelerata virorum
> se fecisse Chloë. Quid pote simplicius?¹²

---

¹ *Ars Poetica*, 399, 'leges incidere ligno.'
² *Carm.* iv 14, 4; cp. iii 17, 4, 'per memores genus omne fastos' (see also O. Hirschfeld, *Kleine Schriften*, 352 n.), and 24, 27 'si quaeret PATER VRBIVM subscribi statuis.'
³ *Carm.* iv 8, 13; cp. Suetonius, *Aug.* 31, quoted on p. 12 n. 10 *supra*.
⁴ *Carm.* i 5, 14; *Sat.* ii 1, 33; cp. i 5, 65 'ex voto,' and Ovid, *Met.* viii 744 f, 'memoresque tabellae—voti argumenta potentis.'
⁵ *Sat.* i 8, 12 f. ⁶ Persius, *Sat.* i 112—114.
⁷ Juvenal, x 143-7; cp. Mayor on viii 69.
⁸ viii 793. ⁹ ii 343.
¹⁰ *C. I. L.* vi (5) p. 2* *l*. ¹¹ ix 44. ¹² ix 15.

His epigrams include at least twenty epitaphs. The following admirable tribute to the memory of an actor, who was put to death by Domitian, was not published until three months after the emperor's decease :—

> Quisquis Flaminiam teris, viator,
> Noli nobile praeterire marmor.
> Urbis deliciae salesque Nili,
> Ars et gratia, lusus et voluptas,
> Romani decus. et decor theatri
> Atque omnes Veneres Cupidinesque
> Hoc sunt condita, quo Paris, sepulcro[1].

In the *Scriptores Historiae Augustae* we have several epitaphs on emperors and their connexions, for example that in honour of the father-in-law of Gordian III.   *Scriptores Historiae Augustae*

Timesitheo[2], eminenti viro, parenti principum, *praefecto* praetorii [totius urbis], tutori rei publicae, senatus populusque reipublicae vicem reddidit[3].

The epitaph of Gordian himself was inscribed in Greek, Persian, Hebrew, and Egyptian, as well as in Latin, as follows :

> Divo Gordiano, victori Persarum, victori Gothorum, victori Sarmatarum, depulsori Romanarum seditionum, victori Germanorum, sed non victori Philipporum[4].

Valerian the younger, who received from his father, the emperor Valerian, the title of Caesar, and from his elder half-brother, Gallienus, that of Augustus, was slain with Gallienus at Milan in 268 A.D. and was there buried in a tomb inscribed, by the orders of Claudius II, with the misleading title 'Valerianus imperator'[5]. Saloninus, son of Gallienus, was honoured with a statue in Rome, in which the words 'Gallieno iuniori' were followed by

---

[1] xi 13; for other epitaphs, see i 88, 93, 101, 116; iv 63; v 34, 74; vi 28, 29, 52, 76; vii 40, 96; x 61, 71; xi 41, 69, 91; xii 52.

[2] This is the true form of the name, which is found in an inscription (Dessau, i 1330). A name of exactly the opposite meaning is here given in the MSS, and in Gruter's inscription, 439, 4, which is probably a forgery founded on the corrupt text, which has *Misitheus*. Cp. *C. I. L.* vi (5) p. 2* r, also H. Stuart-Jones, *Companion to Roman History*, pp. 394, 398.

[3] *Gordiani tres*, c. 27, 10.

[4] c. 34, 3; cp. §§ 4—6, and Gibbon, i 191, note 67 (ed. Bury, 1896). Cp. *C. I. L.* vi (5) p. 2* s.

[5] Trebellius Pollio, *Valeriani duo*, c. 8 (*Hist. Aug.* ii 72 Peter).

S. L. I.

'Salonino'¹. Of Censorinus, the last of the 'thirty tyrants' (269 A.D.), we are told: 'extat eius sepulcrum circa Bononiam, in quo grandibus litteris incisi sunt omnes eius honores; ultimo tamen versu adseri (adscribi?) potest: *felix omnia, infelicissimus imperator*'; but no such inscription has been discovered, and the concluding words are clearly due to the biographer². The emperor Probus (276—282 A.D.), who rose to distinction by his military abilities, is said to have been commemorated in the following terms:

HIC PROBVS IMPERATOR ET VERE PROBVS SITVS EST, VICTOR OMNIVM GENTIVM BARBARARVM, VICTOR ETIAM TYRANNORVM³.

A statue of the emperor Numerianus (283), placed in the Bibliotheca Ulpia, bore the words:

NVMERIANO CAESARI ORATORI TEMPORIBVS SVIS POTENTISSIMO⁴.

A large part of an edict of Firmus (*ob.* 273), which was publicly set up in Rome, is quoted by Vopiscus, and about thirteen other edicts are cited by the *Scriptores Historiae Augustae*, but we cannot be certain that all of them were actually inscribed in marble or bronze⁵, and, in any case, literary quotations of legal documents lie beyond the limits of the present survey⁶.

After the close of the *Historia Augusta* we find Ausonius, in the course of the fourth century, moralising over a mutilated epitaph, which has ceased to record the exact name of the person whom it professes to commemorate:—

Ausonius

> Vna quidem, geminis fulget set dissita punctis
> Littera, praenomen sic <·L·> nota sola facit.
> Post ·M· incisum est, puto sic <·M·> non tota videtur:
> Dissiluit saxi fragmine laesus apex,
> Nec quisquam, MARIVS seu MARCIVS anne METELLVS
> Hic iaceat, certis noverit indiciis.

¹ *Hist. Aug.* ii 88, 23 Peter. Cp. *C. I. L.* vi (5) p. 2* *t*.
² Trebellius Pollio, *Tyranni Triginta*, c. 33, 2. (*Hist. Aug.* ii 122 Peter.)
³ Vopiscus, *Probus*, c. 21, 4 (*Hist. Aug.* ii 201). Cp. *C. I. L.* vi (5) p. 2* *u*.
⁴ Vopiscus, *Carus* etc. c. 11 (*Hist. Aug.* ii 221).
⁵ 'non credam singula haec monumenta in marmore, aut aere exarata fuisse,' Maffei, *Ars Critica Lapidaria*, col. 50.
⁶ Livy, i 26, quotes from a 'lex horrendi carminis'; and many laws are cited by Cicero, and in the *controversiae* of the Elder Seneca.

IN CLASSICAL AUTHORS

> Truncatis confusa iacent elementa figuris,
> Omnia confusis interiere notis.
> Miremur periisse homines? monumenta fatiscunt;
> Mors etiam saxis nominibusque venit[1].

In the above survey we have found that, in Latin literature, inscriptions are alluded to in about 50 passages, and are actually quoted in about 30 others. Omitting imaginary epitaphs in Virgil, Propertius, and Ovid, and the literary epitaphs on Naevius and Plautus, we have only the following inscriptions, which merit special mention in the present place by reason of their being recorded in Latin literature:—The epitaphs of Ennius and Pacuvius[2]; those on A. Atilius Calatinus, and Scipio Africanus Maior[3]; the dedications of M'. Acilius Glabrio, and L. Aemilius Regillus[4]; the inscription on the Marcelli[5]; and those on Pompey (in the temple of Minerva)[6]; the record of the victories of Augustus[7] and of Germanicus[8]; the epitaphs of Pallas, and of Verginius Rufus[9]; the inscriptions on Agrippina, Otho, and the father of Vitellius[10], and that on Trajan's restoration of the Anio novus[11]; and, lastly, six epitaphs of emperors in the *Historia Augusta*[12]. Of these inscriptions the only one even partially preserved to our own day is that on the *Tropaea Augusti*, and of this only a few letters are now discernible[13].

[1] Ausonius, *Epitaphia* xxxii = *Epigrammata*, 35.
[2] pp. 7, 14 *supra*.
[3] pp. 5, 7.
[4] p. 6.
[5] p. 8.
[6] p. 9.
[7] p. 10.
[8] p. 11.
[9] p. 11.
[10] p. 13.
[11] p. 12.
[12] p. 17 f.
[13] pp. 10, and 122 *infra*.

Maffei, in his *Ars Critica Lapidaria* (posthumously published in Donati's *Supplementum* (1765) to Muratori's *Novus Thesaurus Inscriptionum*), has a chapter 'de inscriptionibus, quae in veterum Latinorum libris referuntur' (II 2 col. 33—50). The absence of any complete collection of the inscriptions quoted in Latin literature has been noticed in Hübner's *Römische Epigraphik* in Iwan Müller's *Handbuch*, i 478 (ed. 1886), 628 (ed. 1892). The present chapter is an attempt to supply this want.

CHAPTER II

MODERN COLLECTIONS OF LATIN INSCRIPTIONS

MODERN collections of Latin inscriptions begin with the age of Charles the Great. About 800 A.D. a pilgrim from the North made a journey to Rome, where he collected seventy-five inscriptions of a public and official character, adding five more from Pavia in the course of his return. A fragment of his collection was discovered by Poggio about 1417, and a tenth-century copy of the whole was found at Einsiedeln by Mabillon, who, in 1685, published it in the fourth volume of his *Analecta*. The author is called the *Anonymus Einsiedlensis*. It is probable, however, that the unknown pilgrim, whose work was found at Einsiedeln, was really a monk of Reichenau, the island in the Untersee below the Lake of Constance[1].

Anonymus Einsiedlensis

At Bologna, in the thirteenth century, it is in a tone of regretful admiration that the Florentine grammarian Buoncompagno refers to the splendidly sculptured forms of the old Latin inscriptions :—'olim fiebant sculpturae mirabiles in marmoribus electissimis, quas hodie plenarie legere vel intelligere non valemus'[2].

Buoncompagno

There were certain minor collections, mainly concerned with Christian epitaphs. After a long interval, these were followed by collections made by humanists and others during the Revival of Learning. In the language of Gibbon, it was in that age that Rienzi, the friend of Petrarch, 'perused

Rienzi

[1] *Corpus Inscriptionum Latinarum*, vi (1), p. ix f, nos. 1—80 ; De Rossi, *Inscr. Christianae urbis Romae*, II i (1888), 9 f—33, 338—342 ; Ziebarth in *Ephemeris Epigraphica* ix (1905), 248 f; Mommsen, *Ges. Schriften*, viii 64—100.

[2] *Formula litterarum scholasticarum*, quoted by R. de la Blanchère in his pamphlet, entitled *Histoire de l'Epigraphie Romaine* (1887), p. 6.

CHAP. II]   MODERN COLLECTIONS   21

with indefatigable diligence the manuscripts and marbles of antiquity', devoting himself to deciphering the ancient inscriptions on the Roman walls, and on coins and gems, and composing, about 1344, the first 'description of the city of Rome'[1]. In the church of St John Lateran he discovered the bronze tablet recording the decree of the Senate, which granted the most ample privileges to the emperor Vespasian[2]. This long-forgotten inscription, which had been concealed in the structure of an altar by pope Boniface VIII[3], he disclosed to view, making it the text of an eloquent discourse on the rights which had been lost by the Senate and People of Rome[4]. Rienzi assumed the title of tribune in 1347, and, after his cruel death in 1354, was long remembered as 'the last of the Roman patriots'. His collection of inscriptions was overlooked for a time, but it was not wholly lost; for it was brought to light again, in the time of Martin V (1417–31), by Nicola Signorili, the Secretary of the Roman Senate[5].

The same branch of classical archaeology attracted the attention of another friend of Petrarch, Giovanni Dondi, who visited Rome in 1375, and, besides measuring the Pantheon, the Colosseum, and the Column of Trajan, copied the inscriptions on the triumphal arches and on other ancient Roman buildings[6].

Dondi

The inscriptions of Rome were also collected by Poggio of Florence (1380—1459), who made note of many of them during his earliest residence in the eternal city (1403-14). He had been partly prompted by the Florentine

Poggio

---

[1] *Decline and Fall of the Roman Empire*, c. lxx. Cp. Hülsen's *Roman Forum*, p. 34.

[2] The *lex de imperio Vespasiani*, now in the Capitoline Museum; Rushforth, *Latin Historical Inscriptions*, no. 70; Dessau, i 244, and Appendix IV (4), *infra*.

[3] Rienzi's Letter to the archbishop of Prague (1350), 'in odium imperii occultavit et de ea re quoddam altare construxit, a tergo litteris occultatis' (de la Blanchère, *l. c.*, p. 7). The tablet had been turned inwards, so as to conceal the inscription.

[4] Gibbon, *l. c.*, vii 261 Bury (ed. 1900).

[5] *C. I. L.* vi (1), p. xv; De Rossi, *Inscr. Christianae urbis Romae* II i (1888), p. 316; Voigt, *Wiederbelebung des classischen Alterthums*, i³ 53, 267.

[6] De Rossi, p. 329 f; Voigt, *l. c.* i³ 267. *C. I. L.* vi (1) p. xxvii.

chancellor, Coluccio Salutati, who enthusiastically declared that, if Poggio persevered in his quest, he would soon have transcribed all the inscriptions of Rome. In one of his excursions from Constance (*c.* 1417) Poggio discovered in the neglected library of an unnamed monastery the first four pages of a copy of the collection of inscriptions already ascribed to a pilgrim from Reichenau[1]. In these pages Poggio identified those of the inscriptions which were no longer to be found in Rome, and incorporated them with his own collection, which he completed in 1429[2]. This collection, with that of Signorili, formed the basis for the later collections of Ciriaco Pizzicolli, Giovanni Marcanova, and Fra Giocondo of Verona.

Ciriaco, the merchant, traveller, and amateur archaeologist of Ancona (*c.* 1391—*c.* 1450), began his antiquarian career by copying at his birth-place the Latin inscription that is still visible on the triumphal arch of Trajan[3]. He continued that career in Rome (1424), where he first became conscious of the historic value of the evidence from inscriptions, as compared with that derived from ordinary literature[4]. He also explored the archaeological remains of Italy, and of the distant East, and, during his later visits to Rome (1431–34), he collected inscriptions at Tivoli and Ostia. He was an indefatigable archaeologist, but he is now remembered mainly as an industrious and trustworthy recorder of ancient inscriptions, which were originally comprised in three vast volumes, only fragmentary remains of which have survived. The doubts once thrown on the accuracy of his transcripts have been triumphantly dispelled[5].

Ciriaco

One of the pleasantest pages in the early history of the study of Latin inscriptions in Italy is to be found in the jubilant memorial

---

[1] p. 20 *supra*.

[2] E. Walser, *Poggius Florentinus* (1914), pp. 28, 60, 144–6, 488; *C. I. L.* vi (1) p. xxviii—xl (nos. 1—86); and Ziebarth in *Ephemeris Epigraphica*, ix (1905) 248 f. [3] Dessau, i 298; p. 125 f *infra*.

[4] 'maiorem longe quam ipsi libri fidem et notitiam praestare videbantur'; cp. Voigt, *l. c.* i³ 272 n. 1.

[5] Cp. *History of Classical Scholarship*, ii 39 f; Voigt, i³ 269—286; *C.I.L.* iii p. xxii, 129 f; v p. xvi; vi p. xl; ix—x p. xxxvi ff; De Rossi, *Inscr. Christianae urbis Romae*, II i (1888) 356—387; and Ziebarth, *De antiquissimis inscriptionum syllogis*, in *Ephemeris Epigraphica*, ix (1905) 188—213.

of an antiquarian excursion on the Lago di Garda in the autumn of 1464. The writer, Felix Felicianus of Verona, tells us that, at that time, a merry company from Verona, Padua and Mantua met on the western shore of the lake. They crowned themselves with ivy and myrtle, and, after visiting the ruins of the temple of Diana, made copies of all the inscriptions they could discover. When they left the shore for the islands, their barque was dressed with laurel, and the notes of the lyre floated over the waters as they sailed southward for Sirmione, where they finally entered the little church of San Pietro to give thanks for a happy and successful day. Two and twenty inscriptions had been copied by this joyous and grateful company, all of whom were members of an antiquarian confraternity[1]. One of these, Giovanni Marcanova of Venice, a physician and philosopher of Padua and Bologna (d. 1467), was the first to follow the example of Ciriaco as a collector of inscriptions[2]. More was accomplished by Felix Felicianus, the poet, printer, publisher, and antiquarian, whose collection of inscriptions[3] was dedicated to Mantegna. Mantegna himself (1431—1506), the most antiquarian of artists, introduced into his pictures careful copies of inscriptions, and the two that he has placed on the arches among the frescoes of the life of St James in the Eremitani Chapel at Padua, have, mainly on the authority of Mantegna, been included in the *Corpus Inscriptionum Latinarum*[4]. Inscriptions are also to be found in the sketch-book of Mantegna's father-in-law, Jacopo Bellini[5], and in the manuscript collection formed by the accomplished architect, Fra Giovanni del Giocondo (d. after 1520)[6].

Felicianus

Marcanova

Mantegna

Bellini. Giocondo

[1] Felix Felicianus, *Jubilatio*; complete text first published in Kristeller's *Andrea Mantegna*, Engl. ed. (1901), p. 472.
[2] *C. I. L.* ii p. v; iii p. xxix; v (2) p. xx; vi (1) p. xlii; ix–x, p. li.
[3] *C. I. L.* iii p. xxiv; v (2) p. xvii; vi (1) p. xlii; ix–x p. xxxix. His collection accidentally included some forgeries.
[4] *C. I. L.* v (1) nos. 2528, 2989, (2) pp. 1072 f.
[5] v (1) nos. 2428, 2542, 2553, 2623, 2669, 3464, and 4653.
[6] *C. I. L.* ii p. vi; iii p. xxviii; v (2) p. xviii; vi (1) p. xliv; ix–x p. xlvi; xiv p. xvi. On Fra Giocondo, cp. De Rossi, *Inscr. Christ.* II i 395 ff, and Ziebarth, in *Neue Jahrbücher* (1903) 480—493, and in *Eph. Epigr.* ix (1905) 221—245.

There are many other names of minor interest among the early collectors of inscriptions in Italy[1]. Among those of wider fame, Pomponius Laetus, the founder of the Roman Academy (1425—1498), formed a collection of inscriptions within the walls of his own house, and the autograph of a small part of his transcripts has been discovered in the Vatican[2]. It includes the earliest modern copy of the monument set up by the *magistri vicorum urbis* in honour of Hadrian[3]. As early as 1488, Pomponius Laetus was familiar with a large and important fragment of the *Fasti Consulares*[4].

About 1513, Battista Brunelleschi of Florence made some fine drawings of the ruins of Rome, including careful copies of certain inscriptions, the originals of some of which are now lost[5]. Later in the same century, Onophrius Panvinius (1529—1568) and Fulvius Ursinus (1529—1600) were among the Roman correspondents of Antonius Augustinus of Saragossa, ultimately archbishop of Tarragona (1517—1586)[6], who, in his work *De legibus et senatus consultis* (Rome, 1583), applied his knowledge of inscriptions to the study of law, and whose important dialogues on coins, inscriptions, and other antiquities were posthumously published in 1587.

Pomponius Laetus

Brunelleschi

Antonius Augustinus

The earliest printed collections were those embracing the inscriptions of Ravenna (1489), Augsburg (1505), and Mainz (1520, '25). These were followed by the inscriptions of Rome, as printed by Mazochi (1517–21)[7], and by a more comprehensive collection (*inscriptiones...totius fere orbis*) published in geo-

Printed inscriptions of Ravenna, Augsburg, Mainz, and Rome

[1] Cp. in general, Hübner, in Iwan Müller's *Handbuch*, I (ed. 1892), p. 632 f.
[2] *C. I. L.* vi (1) p. xliii; ix-x p. xlvii; xiv p. xvi; De Rossi, *Inscr. Christ.* II i 401 f. [3] Dessau, ii 6073.
[4] *C. I. L.* i, ed. 2 (1893), p. 1.   [5] *C.I.L.* vi (1) p. xlv.
[6] *C. I. L.* ii p. xv; vi (1) p. xlix; ix-x p. xxviii.
[7] This work was originally prepared by Francesco Albertini in 1517, and was revised for the edition of 1521 by Marcangelo Accorso. There are copies of this second edition recording further corrections by A. Laelius Podager, identified as Antonio Lelli by De la Blanchère, *l.c.*, p. 20. Cp. *C. I. L.* vi (1) p. xlvi.

graphical order by Petrus Apianus of Ingoldstadt (1534). The collector and editor of the Augsburg inscriptions above-mentioned was the celebrated German humanist, Conrad Peutinger, a pupil of Pomponius Laetus. In the second edition of his work (Mainz, 1520) the number of the inscriptions rose from twenty-three to thirty-five, all of them admirably reproduced in the Roman style of the age of the Antonines. *Petrus Apianus*

In and after 1488, only a few fragments of the *Fasti Consulares* were known to Pomponius Laetus, and to Giocondo, and Mazochi[1]. *Fasti Consulares*

In 1546 a number of large marble blocks, including thirty fragments of those *Fasti*, down to 766 A.V.C., and twenty-six of the *Acta Triumphorum*, down to 735, were discovered on the East side of the Forum, between the Temples of Faustina and of Castor. It is now generally agreed that they formed part of the walls of the marble *Regia* rebuilt in 718 (= 36 B.C.)[2].

At first, they were deposited in the Farnese Palace; soon afterwards, under the directions of Michael Angelo, they were transferred to the walls of the newly formed *Sala dei Fasti* in the Palace of the Conservatori on the Capitol. They are accordingly often described as the *Fasti Capitolini*. They were first edited by Marliani (Rome, 1549), and afterwards by Sigonius (Modena, 1550; and, with commentary, Venice, 1556, etc.), Robortelli (Venice, 1555), and Panvinius (Venice, 1557 and 1558). Smaller portions of the same *Fasti* were discovered in 1816–18, and in 1870.

An ancient Calendar of Roman festivals of B.C. 8—A.D. 3 was discovered in 1547, and was for a time in the possession of Bishop Hieronymus Maffaeus, secretary to the Cardinal Farnese, in whose Palace it was preserved for more than 150 years. There are manuscript copies of early date in the Florentine Museum, and in the Bodleian, the latter by Ligorio. It was first printed by Paulus Manutius as an appendix to the *text* of the *Fasti Consulares* and the treatise on Roman names, published by Sigonius at Venice in 1555; and it was reprinted by the younger Aldus in *Fasti anni Iuliani (Maffeiani)*

[1] *C. I. L.* i, ed. 2 (1893), p. 1. [2] Cp. Fig. 43, p. 168 f, *infra*.

26   LATIN INSCRIPTIONS   [CHAP.

1566, in the second edition of his early work on Latin Orthography, which is founded on the study of Inscriptions, and includes copies of more than 1500. These *Fasti Anni Iuliani* are generally known as the *Fasti Maffeiani*[1].

The earliest discoveries of the *Acta fratrum Arvalium* were made in 1570 in the *Vigna Caccarelli* outside the *Porta Portuensis*, less than five miles S.W. of Rome; and, on the same site, further discoveries of these documents followed in 1699, 1792, and 1868.

Acta fratrum Arvalium

Outside the *Porta Capena*, at the beginning of the *Via Appia*, the epitaph of Scipio, the son of Barbatus, was found in 1614, and the famous sarcophagus of Scipio Barbatus himself, and the epitaph of Scipio, the Flamen Dialis, in the same burying-place of the Scipios in 1780[2].

Epitaphs of the Scipios

Panvinius (1529—1568) collected no less than 3000 inscriptions, and formed a grand scheme for publishing all the inscriptions of the Roman world. In the second book of his *Fasti* he writes :—*Magnum inscriptionum totius orbis opus adorno, quod quamprimum Deo auspice evulgabitur; in quo omnia singillatim inscriptionum loca accuratissime descripta sunt.* This collection has never been found, but it has been surmised that it may have been merged in some manner with that of one of his companions in Rome, Martin Smetius, of Bruges[3], who made his first manuscript collection of the inscriptions of Europe in 1545, and, when a large part of this had been destroyed by fire, made another in 1551. He died in 1578. Ten years later his work was published at Antwerp by the great Latin scholar, Lipsius (1588), who added more than 500 to the 3500 inscriptions collected by Smetius. The arrangement according to *subjects*, public inscriptions, sacred inscriptions, etc. adopted in this work, was continued in later *thesauri*.

Panvinius

Smetius

Lipsius

The encyclopaedic genius of Joseph Justus Scaliger (1540—1609) formed a comprehensive plan for publishing a complete *Corpus inscriptionum*. The task was

Scaliger.
Gruter

---

[1] *C.I.L.* i, ed. 2, pp. 222—228 ; p. 172 *infra*.
[2] See *Frontispiece*, and Figs. 17—21, pp. 66—68, *infra*.
[3] *C.I.L.* vi (1) p. liii. Cp. Maffei in Tiraboschi, vii (Modena, 1792) 829.

entrusted to Janus Gruter (1560—1627), who included the collections made by Smetius in a work published by himself at Heidelberg in 1603 (and inadequately republished by Graevius and others at Amsterdam in 1707). Scaliger had not only supplied a large part of the materials, but had also devoted the strenuous toil of ten months to the construction of twenty-four admirably methodical indexes. In the body of the work, the arrangement was in order of *subjects*, instead of the geographical order of *provenance*.

About the same time, a work of the same general character was prepared by the Italian antiquary Giovanni Battista Doni (1594—1647); it was ultimately published, in an incomplete and inaccurate form, by Antonio Francesco Gori at Florence in 1731. Meanwhile, under the title of *Syntagma Inscriptionum*, a supplement to the work of Gruter by Thomas Reinesius (1587—1667), had been produced at Leipzig in 1682. Inscriptions were also largely represented in the works of Jacques Spon of Lyons, in his *Antiquités...de Lyon* of 1673, and his *Miscellanea* of 1685.   *Doni. Reinesius. Spon*

At Padua, Count Sertorio Orsato (1617—1678) studied inscriptions in connexion with Latin scholarship in a work entitled *I marmi eruditi* (1669), and collected all the abbreviations then known in a treatise *De notis Romanorum* (1672). He also protested against the local belief (once accepted by Petrarch[1]) that the epitaph preserved in the *curia* of Padua was that of the historian Livy.   *Orsato*

In Rome, Rafaello Fabretti (1619—1700) gave proof of an extraordinary accuracy in all matters relating to inscriptions by his works on the Roman aqueducts (1680), and on the Column of Trajan (1683, 1690), as well as by his edition of the inscriptions in his father's collection (1699), in which the 430 inscriptions he had inherited are followed by nearly 4600 derived from other sources. He was the first to draw attention to the date-stamps on Roman bricks.   *Fabretti*

In 1726–43, the inscriptions of the ancient cities of Etruria were carelessly collected in three volumes by Gori, already men-

---

[1] *Epp. Fam.* xxiv 8.

tioned as the editor of Doni. A far higher degree of merit was displayed by the genuine archaeologist, A. S. Mazzochi of Naples (1684—1771), in his memoirs on Campanian inscriptions (1727), and on the *lex Iulia municipalis* (1754 f)[1]. In 1739-42, the new edition of Gruter's *Corpus* was followed by the *Novus thesaurus veterum inscriptionum* prepared by the learned Italian historian, Muratori (1672—1750)[2]. This proved to be an inadequate and unsatisfactory compilation. The arrangement being according to subjects, some of the inscriptions were repeated as many as six times. The large number of carelessly copied or actually forged examples, which had been allowed to appear in it, compelled Scipione Maffei of Verona (1675—1755) to examine the originals, and to reject all that were found to be spurious. In the *Museum Veronense* (1749) Maffei published the inscriptions and reliefs of his native city, with an appendix of inscriptions from Rome and the rest of Italy, and from France, Spain, Britain, and the Netherlands, and Africa. He also formed a plan for a *generalis collectio inscriptionum*, and invited the co-operation of his learned correspondent, the French jurist, Jean François Séguier of Aix[3]. His treatise *De arte critica lapidaria* (1765), published ten years after his death in pp. 1—432 of the first volume of Sebastiano Donati's supplement to Muratori's *Thesaurus*, gives proof of the keen and unsparing criticism which he applied to the inadequate work of other archaeologists.

Such criticism was all the more necessary owing to the fact that the forging of Latin inscriptions was not unknown in and after the second half of the sixteenth century. Among those responsible for these forgeries were Pirro Ligorio of Naples, a painter and architect in Rome and Ferrara (1530—1586)[4]; J. J.

Margin notes: Mazzochi; Muratori; Maffei; Forgers: Ligorio, Boissard, Resende, Higuerra, Gutenstein

[1] *In...tabulas Heracleenses*, 1754-5.
[2] Cp. *C. I. L.* vi (1) p. lxiii. [3] *C. I. L.* xii p. 387.
[4] *C. I. L.* ii p. xii; v (2) p. xix; vi (1) pp. li—liii; vi (5) p. 19*—213*; and ix-x p. xlviii f; De la Blanchère, pp. 23, 31; cp. P. de Nolhac, *Notes sur Pirro Ligorio*, in *Mélanges Renier*, 1887, pp. 319—328; and F. F. Abbott, in *Classical Philology*, 1908, pp. 22—30, *Some Spurious Inscriptions and their Authors*.

Boissard of Besançon (1528—1602)[1]; the Portuguese, Luis Andrea de Resende (1498—1573), canon of Evora[2]; the Spanish Jesuit, Hieronymus Roman de la Higuera (1551—1624)[3]; and the German, Leonhard Gutenstein, who, in making extracts for Gruter from the collections of Ursinus and Smetius, interpolated forgeries of his own, as well as those by Ligorio[4]. One of the keenest critics of Ligorio's forgeries was Annibale Camillo degli Abbati Olivieri of Pesaro (1708—1789)[5].

An interesting introduction to the study, and to the writing, of Latin inscriptions was supplied by Stefano Antonio Morcelli (1737—1821), librarian of Cardinal Albani, in his works On the style of Latin inscriptions (1780)[6], and in his Select inscriptions, with comments (1783).

Morcelli

His contemporary, the eminent archaeologist, Gaetano Marini (1742—1815), published the inscriptions of the Albani Villa and Palace in 1785, and the high expectations thereby aroused were completely fulfilled in the two quarto volumes of the inscriptions of the *Fratres Arvales* (1795), in which the *Acta* of that ancient religious body were explained and emended, and no less than 1000 other inscriptions published for the first time.

Marini

Marini found an eminent successor in the person of Count Bartolommeo Borghesi (1781—1860), who began his archaeological career by the study of numismatics, and became the founder of the modern science of Latin epigraphy. As citizen and *podestà* of the still-independent Republic of San Marino, he spent the last thirty-nine years of his life in the smallest of the Italian states, but his archaeological correspondence extended over the whole of the Italian peninsula. He devoted a large part of his labours to the study of the *Fasti Consulares*, producing in 1818-23 his papers on the newly-discovered fragments. These were reprinted in 1885 in the ninth volume of his collected

Borghesi

[1] *C. I. L.* iii p. xx; vi (1) p. lv, (5) pp. 216*—221*; ix–x p. xxx; Mommsen, *Ges. Schriften*, viii 205-15.
[2] *C. I. L.* ii p. xi 17.
[3] *C. I. L.* ii p. xvii.
[4] *C. I. L.* iii p. xxxii; vi (5) p. 222*—227*; and ix–x p. xliv.
[5] Cp. Orelli's *Sylloge*, i p. 43 ff.
[6] 2nd ed. in three vols. quarto (Padua, 1819 f), with portrait.

works, published in Paris in ten volumes in 1862–97, a series in which volumes 3—5 are entirely devoted to Latin inscriptions[1].

Maffei's Swiss correspondent, Hagenbuch, had often insisted on the importance of a critical basis for the further publication of the vast mass of extant Latin inscriptions. His annotations formed a part of J. C. Orelli's excellently planned *Amplissima Collectio*, produced in two volumes at Zürich in 1828[2]. The usefulness of these volumes was greatly enhanced by the supplements and corrections, and, above all, by the *indices rerum ac notarum*, published in a third volume by W. Henzen in 1856.

Hagenbuch and Orelli

The scheme for a complete *Corpus Inscriptionum Latinarum*, formed, with the support of Borghesi, by Olaf Kellermann of Copenhagen (1805—1837), who spent the last nine years of his life in Italy[3], and by Emiliano Sarti, and further promoted by Letronne and others as members of the French Academy during the ministry of Villemain, was ultimately taken up by the Berlin Academy. The early preparations for carrying out the scheme are associated with the names of the Latin grammarian, K. G. Zumpt (1792—1849), and his nephew, A. W. Zumpt (1815—1877). The younger Zumpt aimed at little more than extracting and re-arranging all the inscriptions that had been already published. His papers on inscriptions[4] brought him into frequent conflict with Theodor Mommsen (1817—1903), who laid his own scheme before the Academy in 1847[5]. During the last two years Mommsen had been studying inscriptions in Italy with the aid of Borghesi and Henzen. In his 'Inscriptions of the Kingdom of Naples' (1852), he showed a consummate skill in applying the results of epigraphical research to the elucidation of the constitutional history and the law of the Italian communities. Mommsen's scheme was ultimately approved by the Academy, and finally carried forward with complete success[6].

Proposed Corpus Inscriptionum Latinarum

Mommsen

[1] Cp. De la Blanchère, *l. c.* pp. 45—58.
[2] i 29—66; 525 ff (*Epp.*), and ii 361—378.
[3] O. Jahn, *Specimen epigraphicum*, 1841; cp. *C. I. L.* vi (1) p. lxvi.
[4] Collected in *Comm. Epigraphicae*, 1850-4.
[5] Reprinted in Harnack's History of the Berlin Academy, ii (1900) 522 f.
[6] Obituary notice of Mommsen, reprinted in O. Hirschfeld's *Kleine Schriften*, esp. pp. 932—944.

The way for the publication of the proposed *Corpus Inscriptionum* had been partly prepared by the preliminary labours of Henzen and of G. B. de Rossi in Rome, and by the study of inscriptions in relation to early Latin by Friedrich Ritschl (1806— 1876) at Bonn. In 1862 Ritschl published the *Priscae Latinitatis Monumenta Epigraphica* in a vast folio volume containing 98 lithographed plates and including a very large number of facsimiles of early Latin inscriptions, some of the most important being exact reproductions of the large bronze plates inscribed with ancient Roman laws. The plates were preceded by 127 pages of descriptive text, with elaborate indexes classifying and summing up all the results relating to the early history of the Latin language.

Ritschl

In the first volume of the *Corpus Inscriptionum*, published in 1863, the *Fasti consulares* were edited by Henzen; and the rest of the inscriptions of the Roman Republic, including the *Elogia clarorum virorum*, and the *Fasti anni Iuliani*, down to the death of Julius Caesar, by Mommsen, who also prepared for subsequent volumes the Oriental inscriptions (III), and those of *Gallia Cisalpina* (V), and Central and Southern Italy, and Sicily and Sardinia (IX, X). The inscriptions of Pompeii etc. (IV) were edited by Zangemeister and others; those of Northern Italy (XI) by Bormann; those of Rome (VI) by Bormann, Henzen, Hülsen, aided by De Rossi; those of ancient Latium (XIV) by Dessau; and those of the *instrumentum domesticum* of Rome, including inscriptions on pottery (XV), by Dressel. *Gallia Narbonensis*, or Southern Gaul, was undertaken by Hirschfeld (XII); the 'three provinces of Gaul and the two of Germany' (XIII) by Hirschfeld and Zangemeister, with the *Instrumentum* by Bohn, and the *Signacula Medicorum* by Espérandieu; Africa by Wilmanns and by Cagnat, J. Schmidt, and Dessau (VIII). Meanwhile, Spain (II) and Britain (VII) had been dealt with by Hübner. The number of volumes published between 1863 and 1906, including supplements, was about forty, while the total number of the inscriptions came to about 100,000. Among collections of select inscriptions for the use of students, that of Wilmanns (1873) includes 2885, and that of Dessau (begun in 1892 and completed in 1916) as many as 9522. It will be observed that the latter figure

Corpus Inscriptionum Latinarum, 1863—1906

is more than 400 times greater than that of all the inscriptions, about 22 in number, which we find definitely quoted by classical authors[1].

Ritschl's vast volume of 1862, the *Priscae Latinitatis Monu-*

Facsimiles: *menta*, had supplied lithographed facsimiles of most
Ritschl,
Hübner, of the important inscriptions of the Roman Republic.
Diehl The corresponding volume on the Roman Empire was published in 1885 by Hübner (1834—1901), under the title of *Exempla Scripturae Epigraphicae Latinae*, including outline specimens of no less than 1216 inscriptions from the death of Caesar to the age of Justinian, with 68 ample pages of palaeographical Introduction. The *Inscriptiones Latinae* prepared by Diehl (1912) contains 50 comprehensive plates of photographic facsimiles, 19 of which are concerned with Christian inscriptions;

Cagnat, and reproductions of inscriptions form an important
Egbert, feature of the handbooks prepared by Cagnat
Ricci (fourth edition, Paris, 1914), Egbert (New York, 1896, 1908), and Ricci (Milan, 1898).

Among the epigraphical discoveries made in Rome towards
Modern the close of the nineteenth century, few have rivalled
discoveries in interest the archaic inscription found in the Forum in 1899, and the *Acta ludorum saecularium* of 17 B.C., which were discovered in 1890, and are now preserved in the new Museum formed out of the ancient Baths of Diocletian. The successive excavations of the Forum, and the chronological order of its inscribed monuments, have been clearly set forth by Jordan (1877)[2], while the archaeological exploration of the site, from the Revival of Learning to the early years of the twentieth century, has been briefly reviewed by Hülsen in his *Roman Forum* (1906)[3].

Of the many thousands of inscriptions included in the *Corpus*,
Inscriptions very few (such as those carved upon rocks) are still
in public in the positions which they originally occupied.
Museums Many have either been lost since the time when they were copied, or are only to be found in private collections. But

[1] p. 19 *supra*.
[2] *Ephemeris Epigraphica* iii (4), 1877, pp. 237—310, *Sylloge Inscriptionum Fori Romani*, including *Annales* (238—248) and chronological list of inscribed monuments (248—250). [3] pp. 33—55.

MODERN COLLECTIONS

by far the greatest number are still preserved in public museums. In Rome, the most important collection is in the *Galleria lapidaria* of the Vatican Museum, where whole walls are covered with inscriptions. There are also the collections in the Capitoline Museum, the *Palazzo dei Conservatori*, and the Lateran Museum, the inscriptions now (or formerly) in the *Museo Kircheriano*, and those in the *Museo Nazionale* (*delle Terme*), with those in the Villas Albani, Borghese, and Boncompagni (late Ludovisi). Among the rest of the museums of Italy, the most important are those of Naples, Florence, Milan, Turin, Verona, Brescia, Venice, Padua, Mantua, Parma, Modena, Bologna, Perugia, Arezzo, and Cortona. In Paris the galleries of the Louvre include inscriptions found in France, and not a few from Italy and North Africa (many of these last being also preserved in the various local museums of Algeria, and of Tunis). Besides these, there are collections in the *Bibliothèque Nationale*, and at St Germain-en-Laye, near Paris; and also in Boulogne, Lyon, Vienne, Nîmes, and Arles. In Switzerland, there are museums at Geneva, Lausanne, and Avenches, as well as Basel, Bern, and Zürich. In Spain, at Seville, Tarragona, Madrid, and Barcelona. In Germany, in Berlin, Cologne, Bonn, Mainz, Mannheim, Augsburg, Stuttgart, Trier; in Bavaria, in Munich: and, in Austria, in Vienna, Salzburg, and Graz. In Hungary, there is a museum at Buda-Pest; in Holland, at Leyden; while, in Great Britain, we have the British Museum in London, and the local museums at Colchester, Chester and Cirencester, at Bath, York, Carlisle, Newcastle, Durham, and in Edinburgh and Glasgow[1]. In the United States of America, there is a collection at the Johns Hopkins University, Baltimore[2], and another at the University of Michigan[3].

[1] There are also museums at Caerleon, Shrewsbury, and South Shields, and accessible private collections at Chesters on the Wall, Lanercost abbey, Castlesteads, and Netherhall park, Maryport (Bruce's *Handbook to the Roman Wall*, pp. 214, 222, 252, ed. 7, 1914).

[2] 111 of these Latin Inscriptions are described in the *American Journal of Philology* for 1907, 1909–12, by H. L. Wilson, who died in 1913.

[3] 'Some New Inscriptions from Puteoli, Baiae, Misenum and Cumae' in this collection were published in the *American Journal of Archaeology* for 1898, pp. 373—398, by Walter Dennison, who died in 1917. See *University of Michigan Studies, Humanistic Series*, xii (1918) 167 f.

CHAPTER III

THE LATIN ALPHABET

The alphabet

ALL the Italian alphabets, whether Etruscan, Umbrian, Oscan, Faliscan, or Latin, were derived from the alphabet of the Dorian Greeks of Italy and Sicily. This Greek alphabet belonged to the western colonies of the Euboean city of Chalcis, viz. Cumae, Neapolis and Rhegium in Italy, and Zankle, Naxos and Himĕra in Sicily. The forms of the Greek letters are preserved on coins and in inscriptions and syllabaries. The ordinary types of these letters are given in the following line :—

A B C D E F I H ⊖ I K L ʍ N O Γ Q P ⟩ T V X ⊕ V
α β γ δ ε ϝ ζ η θ ι κ λ μ ν ο π ϙ ρ σ τ υ ξ φ χ

The variants found in Chalcidic texts may here be added :—

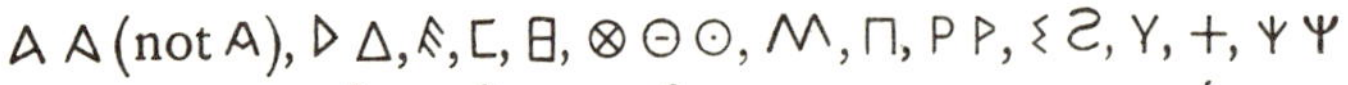

Λ Λ (not A), Ͻ Δ, ⟨, Ϲ, ⊟, ⊗ ⊙ ⊙, ᗰ, Π, P Ρ, ⟩ Ƨ, Y, +, Ψ Ψ
α   δ ε ζ η   θ   μ π ρ   σ υ ξ χ

The following is the Greek Alphabet on the Formello vase found near Veii. It may be regarded as a link between the Chalcidian and the Italic alphabets. The letters corresponding to ε and F are accidentally transposed in the original, but the order is corrected in the almost identical second alphabet on the same vase [1].

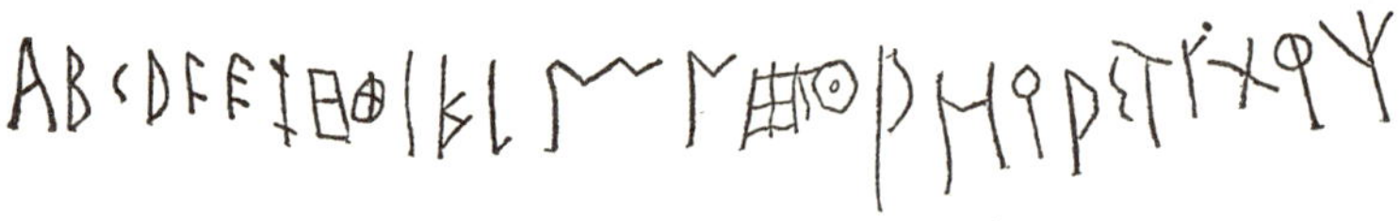

α β γ δ ϝ ε ζ h θ ι κ λ   μ   ν ⊞[2] ο π M[3] ϙ ρ σ τ υ ξ φ χ

Fig. 2. Greek Alphabet on the Formello vase.

[1] Cp. E. S. Roberts, *Greek Epigraphy*, i p. 17.
[2] Phoen. *samekh*.
[3] Phoen. *shin*.

CHAP. III]   THE ALPHABET.   35

It will be observed that this alphabet closely coincides with that used on the archaic *cippus* in the Roman Forum (Fig. 4, p. 39).

In early Latin the symbol for Ƨ soon fell out of use. The Romans also rejected the three Greek aspirates ⊕ ⊙ Ѵ as letters of the alphabet, but adopted them as numerals[1]. C, the curved form of the old Greek *gamma*, had, at first, the same value as *gamma*, but it was also used to express the sound of *kappa*. Thus the symbol C did double duty for the sounds of K and G. To prevent confusion, the symbol C, when used to represent the sound of *gamma*, was slightly changed into G. G is first found on an *as libralis* of Luceria, before 269 B.C.[2], and a distinction between C and G (⟨ and ⟨,) may be noticed about 250 B.C. on the earliest coins of Aesernia, and in the Oscan bronze of Rapino[3]. About 234 the grammarian Spurius Carvilius appears to have been the first to give the letter G its present position in the place formerly held by Z in the Greek alphabet[4]. In the *elogium* on Scipio Barbatus, probably later than 234, we find the letter G in *Gnaivod*, *prognatus* and *subigit*[5]. During the time when C was still used for G, the abbreviations C. and CN. stood for the *praenomina* pronounced as Gaius and Gnaeus, and the old spelling of these abbreviations was retained after the introduction of the new letter, G.

After the rejection of the three aspirates and Ƨ and the introduction of G, the Latin alphabet consisted of the following 21 letters. That number is mentioned by Cicero (*N. D.* ii 93), and X is called the last letter by Quintilian (i 4, 9).

A B C D E F G H I K L M N O Π Q R S T V X

Late in the seventh century of Rome, Y and Z were introduced in the spelling of words borrowed from the Greek, such as ZEPHTRVS. The Greek Y had previously been represented by V or I. Thus Ennius wrote BVRRVS for Πύρρος and BRVGES

[1] p. 54 f *infra*.
[2] Mommsen, *Die unteritalischen Dialekte*, 32.
[3] Conway, *Italic Dialects*, i 254.
[4] Cp. Plutarch, *Quaestiones Romanae*, 54. Cp. Ritschl, *Opusc.* iv 226, 228.
[5] See Frontispiece, and Figs. 17, 18 (p. 66).

for Φρύγες. Only a single example of Y has been found in Latin before the seventh century, DIONTSI on an inscription from Puteoli¹. Z, which had been found in the *Carmen Saliorum* (Varro, *L. L.* vii 26), and on a coin of Cosa² later than 273 B.C., was revived in the age of Sulla³. The Greek Z had been previously expressed in Latin by S at the beginning and SS in the middle of a word, e.g. *sona* (ζώνη) and *tarpessita* (τραπεζίτης).

Three new letters were invented by the emperor Claudius (Tacitus, *Ann.* xi 14), who used an inverted *digamma* ⅎ for the consonant or semivowel V, an *antisigma* Ↄ for the combination *bs* or *ps*, and Ⱶ (the first half of the aspirate H) for a sound between *i* and *u* in words like *optumus* and *maxumus*. The first and the third of these symbols are actually found in inscriptions of the time of Claudius to express the Latin V (as in Fig. 12, p. 45), and the Greek Y, as in AEGⰙPTI and BⰙBLIOTHECA.

Double vowels were introduced by the tragic poet, L. Accius (*fl.* 139 B.C.), to represent a long vowel. In *Latin* this doubling is confined to the vowels A, E, U, e.g. *Vaarus* and *seedes* in the Aletrium inscription⁴, and *Iuulius*. The earliest example is *paastores* in 132 B.C. (Fig. 35, p. 132). The double vowels, as well as the form *qura* and the shape of the letters, have led to the following epitaph from the *Via Appia* being assigned to the age of Accius (who died *c.* 90 B.C.) :—

> Hoc est factum monumentum | Maarco Caicilio.
> Hospes, gratum est quom apud | meas restitistei seedes;
> bene rem geras et valeas, | dormias sine qura.
>   Dessau, ii (2) 8121 (cp. iii p. 804); Ritschl, *P. L. M. E.*
>   tab. lxix D, *Opusc.* iv 142—163.

This usage is found in inscriptions from the time of the Gracchi (133 B.C.) to the Mithradatic war (75 B.C.). From that date to the second half of the third century the long vowel was distinguished by an *apex*, placed above the vowel in the form of a comma (ʼ), or (later) of an accent (´); cp. Fig. 8, p. 43.

Double consonants are said to have been introduced by Ennius (*d.* 169 B.C.). The earliest known examples are in a decree of 189 B.C., where *possidere* occurs by the side of *posedisent*⁵

¹ Ritschl, *Priscae Latinitatis Monumenta Epigraphica*, tab. lxxvi A; *C. I. L.* x 3975. ² Ritschl, tab. vii 40 *a* and *b*. ³ See Index s.v. *Zephyrus*.
⁴ p. 119 *infra*. ⁵ Cp. also *turri, essent, oppidum, vellet*.

(Fig. 42, p. 162). They are also found c. 150 and become common before 100 B.C.

In the earliest inscriptions *ei* was represented frequently by E[1]. Long *ī* was often spelt EI from about 150 B.C.[2]; occasionally from the time of Sulla and frequently from the age of Augustus to the second half of the second century it was represented by a taller form, I. The diphthong *ai* (or *aei*) survived until the age of Sulla, and was temporarily revived by Claudius. *ae* and *ai* were represented by E in a few of the oldest inscriptions and in vulgar usage, and more frequently after the end of the first century of our era. The diphthongs *oi* and *oe* for *ū* and *ou* for *ū* belong, in general, to republican times[3].

An Archaic Alphabet was used in ancient treaties, such as that with Gabii, and with the Latins and the Carthaginians[4].

On the Latin Alphabet, cp. *Index Palaeographicus* to Ritschl's *P. L. M. E.* (1862), and article of 1869, reprinted in his *Opusc.* iv 691—726; Kirchhoff's *Studien* (1863; ed. 4, 1887); Isaac Taylor, *The Alphabet*, 1883, ii 124—144; Hübner's *Exempla* (1885) liii—lvii; Cagnat's *Cours d'Épigraphie Latine*, ed. 4, 1914, pp. 1—23; Lindsay's *Latin Language*, 1—12; Giles' *Manual of Comparative Philology*, §§ 605-9; and Sir Edward Maunde Thompson's *Introduction to Greek and Latin Palaeography*, 1912, pp. 5—7.

The **earliest Latin inscription in metal** is that on the gold fibula of Praeneste, where all the letters are Greek in form. The retrograde order, the use of FH for F, FHEFHAKED for *fecit* and NVMASIOI for *Numerio*, all point to a very early date[5]. The 'Duenos' inscription (Fig. 5) also runs from right to left. The inscription on the fibula of Praeneste (Fig. 3) is assigned to about 600 B.C.

<small>Earliest Latin inscriptions. Fibula Praenestina</small>

The **earliest Latin inscription carved in stone** is that on the four sides of a rectangular pillar, or *cippus*, of tufa lying five feet below the pavement of black marble found in 1899 between the Forum

<small>The Forum inscription</small>

---

[1] Cp. *maurte* (Fig. 6, p. 41), *ploirume* (Fig. 19, p. 67).
[2] Cp. Fig. 35, p. 132.
[3] Cp. Hübner in Iwan Müller, I (1892), p. 650.   [4] p. 3 f *supra*.
[5] Cp. Bücheler in *Rhein. Mus.* xlii 317; Darbishire, *Relliquiae Philologicae*, 6—14; Lindsay, *Handbook of Latin Inscriptions*, 18 f; Ernout, *Textes Latins Archaïques* (1916), pp. 3 f.

38   LATIN INSCRIPTIONS   [CHAP.

and the Comitium (Fig. 4). (This rectangular pillar, or *cippus*, is sometimes, erroneously, called the *lapis niger*, a term which ought to be confined to the pavement of black marble five feet above it; it comes from Festus: *niger lapis in Comitio locum funestum significat—Romuli morti destinatum*... p. 184, 19 ed. Lindsay.) The letters run in lines vertical to the base; line 1 is written from below upward (right to left), line 2 from above downward (left to right), and so on, alternately. Such alternation of direction is not found in purely Latin inscriptions. The inscription is not later than the fifth century B.C., and the letters show a very close resemblance to those of the Greek alphabet, and especially

lolSA WWW:⊲⋺⋎A′⋳⋺:⋺⋳⋺:⊲⋺W:SolWAW
manios · med · fhe · fháked · numasioi
(*Manius me fecit Numerio*)

Fig. 3. Fibula Praenestina (*C. I. L.* i² p. 370, xiv 4123; slightly reduced from *Röm. Mitth.* 1887, p. 37). The points (: and ⁚) are more correctly copied in the transcript immediately below the cut.

to those on the Formello vase (Fig. 2). We here have C for G, ⋳ for H, P for R, Ϙ for Q, Ϛ for S, Y for V; the words are separated by three vertical points, as in the above *fibula*. Mention is made of the *kalator*, and the *rex* (possibly the *rex sacrorum*) in the form *recei* (for *regi*), and of *iouxmenta* (for *iumenta*).

Cp. Comparetti, *Iscrizione archaica del Foro Romano*, Firenze, 1900; Hülsen, *The Roman Forum*, E. T. 1906, pp. 103—108; E. C. Clark, *Proc. of Soc. Antiq.*, 20 June, 1901; Minton Warren, in *A. J. P.* xxviii (1907), 249 f, 373 f; further literature in Dessau, ii p. 248 no. 4913, and in *C. I. L.* i² p. 367; Giles' *Manual*, ed. 1901, § 666, with facsimile from the official *Notizie*; Bursian's *Jahresbericht*, cxxvii (1905) 257—280, cxliv (1909) 162 f; also Ernout, *Textes Latins Archaïques*, pp. 4—7. Cast in Ashmolean Museum, Oxford, and Cambridge Museum of Classical Archaeology, and in the British Museum; also in the Museums of Harvard and Johns Hopkins Universities.

THE ALPHABET

16. .. LOIVQVIOD
1. QVOI HOI......
2. SAKPOS ES-
3. ED SOR....
4. .....IA..IAS
5. RECEI.IC....
6. .....EVAM
7. QVOS.R....
8. ...M.KALATO-
9. REM.HAP....
10. ...IOD IOVXMEN-
11. TA.KAPIA.DOTAV..
12. M ITE.RI....
13. ....M.QVOI HA
14. VELOD.NEQV....
15. ....OD.IOVESTOD

Lines 1, 3, 5, 7, 9, 11, 12, 14, 16 run from right to left; 2, 4, 6, 8, 10, 13, 15, from left to right; 8, 9, 16 are upside down. (1) HOI may be HON*ce*; (2—3) SAKPOS ESED = *sacer esset*. (5) RECEI = *regi*. (6) EVAM = ?(*d*)*evam* for *deivam*. (10—11) IOVXMENTA = *iumenta*. IOVESTOD = ?*iusto*. Thurneysen inverts the order of the last four lines; the inscr ends with (16) added in smaller letters along the edge of the stone, between the fourth face and the first.

Fig. 4. Inscription on the archaic cippus in the Forum ($\frac{1}{10}$); from a photograph by Vasari, Rome.

40 LATIN INSCRIPTIONS [CHAP.

Greek influence is clearly visible in the 'Duenos' inscription, which runs, from right to left, round the outer edge of three small vases, joined together in an equilateral triangle, found near the Quirinal in 1880. The inscription is assigned to the early part of the fourth century.

The 'Duenos' inscription

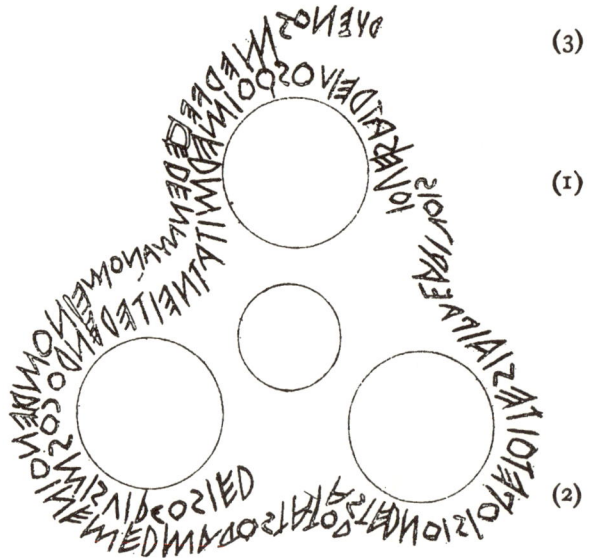

Fig. 5. The 'Duenos' Inscription (slightly reduced from Dressel, *Annali*, pl. l, 1880; *C. I. L.* i ed. 2, p. 371; Dessau, ii (2) p. 986).

(1) *Iove sat deivos qoi med mitat nei ted endo cosmis virco sied*
(2) *asted noisi ope toitesiai pakari vois*
(3) *Duenos med feced en manom einom dzenoine med mano statod*

Jordan was the first to notice that *ted endo* = *in te* (*Hermes*, 1881, 225).

Bücheler's rendering is as follows:—Iovi Saturno deis qui me mittat, ne te intus comes virgo sit | adstet, nisi Opi Tutesiae pacari vis; | Duenos me fecit propter mortuum ut die noni me mano sistito (*Rhein. Mus.* xxxvi 355).

Prof. Conway, reading *Io. Vei. Sat., Duenoi ne med*, and *malo* (for *mano*) formerly translated:—'May the Gods Jove, Vejove, Saturn, (grant) that Proserpine, to whom they suffer this vase to be despatched, show thee no favour. Unless thou, indeed, art willing to make thy peace with Ops Toitesia. Duenos made me (as a curse) against Manos, and let no evil fall to Duenos from me' (*A. J. P.* x (1889) 445—459). But *Iovestod* for *iusto* in the Forum inscription (Fig. 4, line 15) suggests that in line 1 *iove sat* should be read as one word *iovesat*, early Latin for *iurat*, an interpretation which Prof. Conway now prefers, making the sense: 'he who sends me adjures the gods not to let Proserpine be kind to thee.' It is now generally admitted that the inscription should be interpreted as a curse; it is included in Audollent's *Defixionum Tabellae* (1904).

F. D. Allen regarded the inscription as having been 'interpreted, with a fair amount of probability', either as a direction for a *novendiale sacrificium*, or as an *execration* (see *Harvard Studies* for 1898, 53 f). Thurneysen, however, regards it as a gift from a lover to his mistress (*Kühn's Zeitschrift*, 1897, 193—226). Cp. also Egbert's *Introduction to...Latin Inscriptions*, p. 346 f, Lindsay's *Handbook*, pp. 19—23; Ernout, 7—9; and the literature at the end of E. W. Fay's article in *A. J. P.* 1909, 121—138, in Bursian's *Jahresbericht*, cvi (1901) 40—46 and in *C. I. L.* i² p. 371.

Here we have A A A for A; ↄ for C and G; ᗡ and ᗡ for D; ᗯ for M; O and ᗣ for O; ⌐ for P; Ϙ for Q; ꟼ for R; Ƨ and Z for S. As in the other early inscriptions, the letters closely resemble those of the Greek alphabet (p. 34), and are, at the same time, marked by a general absence of uniformity.

The **monumental alphabet** of the last three centuries of the Republic exhibits a marked improvement. A certain inelegance and unevenness may, indeed, be noticed in the dedications from the sacred grove of Pisaurum[1], and in the ancient epitaphs from Praeneste[2]. The letters are, however, more even and more elegant in the following dedication from Tusculum assigned to the sixth century of Rome.

Scriptura monumentalis

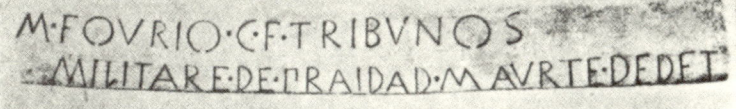

Fig. 6. Dedicatory inscription from Tusculum
(*P. L. M. E.* tab. 49 B), ⅔ of facsimile.

M. Fourio(s) C. f(ilios) tribunos militare(s) de praidad Maurte dedet
(*C. I. L.* i² 2, 49; cp. Lindsay's *Handbook*, p. 34).

[1] *P. L. M. E.* tab. xliii f; Diehl, *Inscr. Latinae*, pl. 2; Ricci, tav. v; Dessau, ii p. 2; *C. I. L.* i² 2, 368—371.

[2] *P. L. M. E.* tab. xxxvi, n. 53—61; Ricci, tav. vi, D—O; Cagnat, pl. i 3; Dessau, ii (2) p. 834; Egbert, p. 34; *C. I. L.* i² 2, 64—367.

The same general characteristics may be noticed in the epitaphs of the Scipios. See *Frontispiece*, and figs. 17—21, pp. 66–68. The fully developed alphabet of the *Scriptura monumentalis* belongs to the age of Augustus and the early Empire. The work is executed by a professional stone-cutter; the letters are exact, and, in general, square. They are the *litterae quadratae* or *lapidariae* of Petronius, who (in c. 29) has the phrase ' quadrata littera scriptum CAVE CANEM', and (in c. 58) ' lapidarias litteras scio'. But all the letters are not (strictly speaking) 'square', for that epithet cannot be applied to circular letters such as O Q C D, or to others such as I and M. The epithet seems, in fact, to be derived, not from the shape of the letters, but from the use of square-cut stones for the carving of inscriptions. Such stones are described as *lapides quadrati*, or *saxa quadrata*; the artificers are therefore called *quadratores*[1], or *artifices quadratarii*, and their work *opus quadratarium*. Sidonius Apollinaris, on composing a poetical epitaph, asks his correspondent to have it promptly inscribed on a marble tablet (*tabula*), and to take care that the stone-cutter (*lapicida*), makes no mistake, for the reader is sure to attribute any such mistake to the composer, and not to the stone-mason (*quadratarius*)[2].

The subjoined inscription from the tablet on the massive tomb of Caecilia, daughter of Q. Caecilius Metellus Creticus (consul of 69 B.C.), and wife of the elder son of the triumvir, M. Crassus, is a good example of the *scriptura monumentalis* of the early part of the Augustan age.

Fig. 7. Epitaph of Caecilia Metella on the Via Appia, Rome (Hübner's *Exempla*, no. 61), $\frac{1}{12}$.

Caeciliae | Q. Cretici f(iliae) | Metellae Crassi (*C. I. L.* vi 1274).

[1] Cassiodorus, *Variae*, ii, 7.
[2] *Epp*. iii 12, 5. See in general, Hübner's *Exempla*, p. xxvi, col. 2.

THE ALPHABET 43

The following inscription of a still more public character is an excellent example of the best monumental style of the age of Augustus.

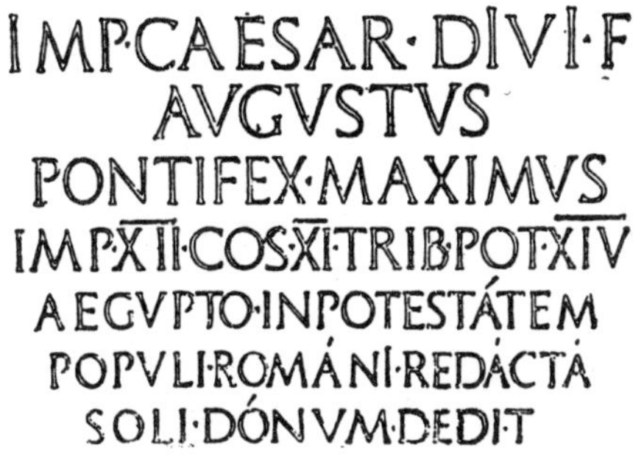

IMP·CAESAR·DIVI·F
AVGVSTVS
PONTIFEX·MAXIMVS
IMP·XII·COS·XI·TRIB·POT·XIV
AEGVPTO·INPOTESTÁTEM
POPVLI·ROMÁNI·REDÁCTA
SOLI·DÓNVM·DEDIT

Fig. 8. From an obelisk in the Circus Maximus, now in the Piazza del Popolo, Rome, 10 B.C. (reduced by ½ from Hübner's *Exempla*, no. 52). Cp. Pliny, xxxvi 71.

In both of the above inscriptions the lettering of the upper part is on a larger scale than the rest. In the four rows of a Pompeian inscription figured in Hübner's *Exempla* (no. 138), three different sizes of letters may be observed. Two varieties may be seen in Fig. 12.

The following is a typical alphabet of the *scriptura monumentalis* of the Augustan age. It is mainly founded on the immediately preceding inscription.

ABCDEFGHIL
MNOPQRSTVX

Fig. 9. Alphabet of *scriptura monumentalis*, Augustan age, founded mainly on Fig. 8 *supra* (from Hübner's *Exempla*, p. lxxx, no. ii).

The following are typical alphabets of the *scriptura actuaria*, founded on public documents of (*a*) the Augustan, and (*b*) the Claudian age.

LATIN INSCRIPTIONS [CHAP.

ABCDEFGHILMNOPQRSTVX

Fig. 10 (*a*). Alphabet of *scriptura actuaria*, Augustan age, founded mainly on the *Acta triumphorum*, Fig. 45 *infra* (from Hübner's *Exempla*, p. lxxxii, no. 13).

ABCDEFGHILMNOPQRSTVX

Fig. 10 (*b*). Alphabet of *scriptura actuaria*, Claudian age, founded on the Speech of Claudius, Fig. 48 *infra* (from Hübner's *Exempla*, p. lxxxii, no. 14).

In contrast to the large, carefully outlined, and deeply cut lettering of important public monuments, we have the smaller and simpler type used for inscriptions of a more ordinary kind. This assumed three forms:—

Scriptura actuaria

(1) The lettering used in public documents, **scriptura actuaria** (Fig. 10). In early times public announcements or advertisements were painted in black or red letters on the walls of buildings. Such also are the later placards and advertisements, and in particular, the election-notices, on the walls of Pompeii. These notices are of two classes, according as they are the work of an unpractised hand, or that of a professional calligrapher. The following is an example in which 'all the fruiterers' publicly urge the election of a *duumvir*.

M HOLCONIVM
PRISCVM·II VIR·I·D· POMARI·VNIVERSI CVM·HELVIOVESTALE·ROG

Fig. 11. A Pompeian placard (Niccolini, *Pompeii*, Seconda Fontana, tav. 1).

M. Holconium Priscum II vir(*um*) *i*(*uri*) *d*(*icundo*) *pomari universi cum Helvio Vestale rog*(*ant*). *C. I. L.* iv 202 ; Dessau, ii 6411 *a*.

The original use of the brush led to the letters assuming a free and flowing form, and this form was partially reproduced even when the document was cut in bronze or stone. As an early

III] THE ALPHABET 45

example of the documental style in bronze we have the decree of
L. Aemilius Paullus, belonging to 189 B.C. (p. 162). The *scriptura actuaria* of the Augustan age is exemplified in the marble
tablets of the *Acta Triumphorum* (p. 172)[1]. A later example may
be seen in the bronze tablet at Lyons, recording an Oration of
Claudius (p. 179)[2]. The influence of the 'painted' style is exemplified by the letters incised on the black marble of the
following Pompeian inscription. This also belongs to the age of
Claudius, as is inferred from its containing two examples of one
of the three letters which he added to the Latin alphabet (p. 36
supra).

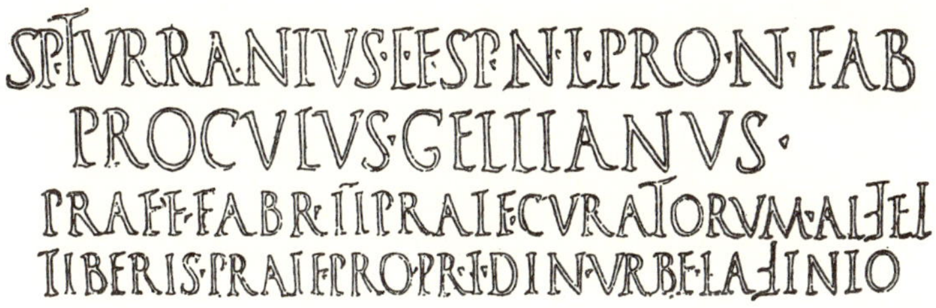

SP·IVRRANIVS·ƎESP·N·LPRO·N·FAB
PROCVLVS·GELLIANVS·
PRAEF·FABR·IIPRAIECVRAT̄ORVM·ALƎEI
TIBERISPRAIFPROPR·IDIN·VRBELAƎINIO

Fig. 12. From a Pompeian pedestal of black marble, now in the
Museum of Naples (Hübner's *Exempla*, no. 135), *c.* ⅓.

Sp. Turranius L. f(ilius) Sp. n(epos) L. pron(epos) Fab(ia tribu) | *Proculus
Gellianus* | *praef(ectus) fabr(um) II, praif(ectus) curatorum alʃei* | *Tiberis,
praif(ectus) pro pr(aetore) i(ure) d(icundo) in urbe Laʃinio.* (*C. I. L.* x 797.)
On ꟻ for V cp. p. 36 *supra*.

The other two forms are developments of the *written*, rather
than the *epigraphic* style :—

(2) The **cursive characters**, generally confined to waxed tablets, and to the *graffiti* of Pompeii (p. 46).

Scriptura cursiva

Cursive characters are used in an epitaph in the Vatican
Museum[3]. Certain isolated characters are occasionally used in

[1] Cp. Fig. 10 (*a*).
[2] Cp. Fig. 10 (*b*).
[3] *C. I. L.* vi 27556 add. p. 3534 (facsimile in Diehl's *Inscr. Lat.* 29 c).

46 LATIN INSCRIPTIONS [CHAP.

other inscriptions on stone, such as Λ for A, || for E, |¹ for F,
Ϲ for C, and |||| for M.

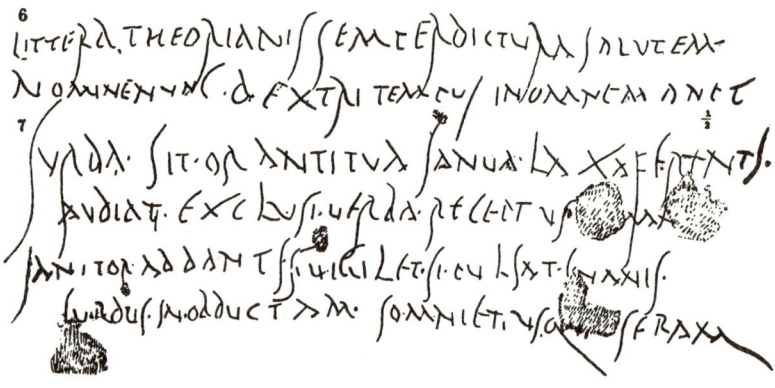

Fig. 13. Pompeian graffiti, including two quotations from the
poets (*C. I. L.* iv 1891-93-94), more than ⅓.

(6) Littera Theorianis semper dictura salutem
     Nomine nunc Dextri tempus in omne manet.   Anon.

(7) Surda sit oranti tua ianua laxa ferenti
     Audiat exclusi verba receptus [am]a[ns].
                                         Ovid, *Am.* i 8, 77.

     Ianitor ad dantis vigilet, si pulsat inanis
     Surdus in obductam somniet usque seram.
                                         Propertius, iv (v) 5, 47 [1].

(3) The **uncial letters** of rounded form and with a marked
curve above the vertical strokes. These were bor-   Scriptura
rowed from the written style of papyri and parch-   uncialis
ments, and adopted in African inscriptions from the end of the
third century, and in dedicatory inscriptions elsewhere, from the
end of the fourth[2]. In the following example the use of a form
of U for V will be noticed in lines 2, 3, 4.

  [1] See further, p. 188 *infra*, and cp. Hübner's *Ex.* pp. xliii—xlv, and Van
Hoesen's *Roman Cursive Writing*, Princeton, 1915.
  [2] Cp. Hübner's *Exempla*, p. xxxviii. On the term 'uncial' in Jerome's
Preface to Job, and in Servatus Lupus, Ep. 5, see *Hist. of Cl. Scholarship*, i
488², and E. T. Merrill, in *Cl. Philology*, xi (1916) 452-7.

III]　　　　　THE ALPHABET　　　　　47

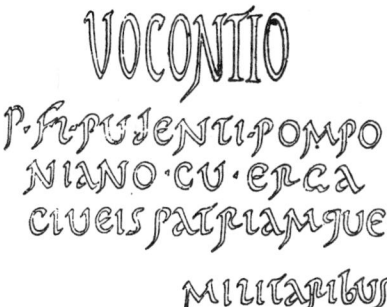

Fig. 14.　On a pedestal at Thamugadi (Timgad), N. Africa
(Hübner's *Exempla*, no. 1147), ⅓.

Vocontio | P. Fl(avio) Pudenti Pompo|niano c(larissimo) v(iro), erga | civeis patriamque | etc. militaribus (C. I. L. viii 2391). Photograph of the whole in Cagnat, ed. 1914, pl. xv, 4.

The **shapes of the letters** vary according as they are used in the monumental, the documentary, or the cursive style. Thus the horizontal stroke of A is retained **A.** in the monumental style (though it varies in height), while it is often omitted in the documentary (∧), or deflected from the right or the left (⋀ or ⋀) or made vertical (⋀) in the cursive, which sometimes omits it and prolongs the right arm upwards (⋏).

The angular type, B, is found in some early inscriptions, and in letters cut in lead under the Empire, the form depending on the material used. The rounded type **B.** is in ordinary use during all periods, with variations in the relative sizes of the two lobes. The lower lobe is rather large in copies of the *Fasti*[1]. Sometimes, in the painted style, the upper lobe entirely vanishes, and the upper part of the stem, or of the lower lobe, is curved upwards.

The archaic forms of C are ᔑ [C. The narrower forms are found in early inscriptions, while the fully rounded form belongs to the best period. In and after that **C.** period it is sometimes made larger than the next letter, especially at the beginning of the line, where it may even include the next

[1] Cp. Fig. 46, p. 173.

48 LATIN INSCRIPTIONS [CHAP.

(a)	(b)	(c)
A ᐱ ᐱ	A ᐱ	A
B B	B	B
⟨ C	C	C
D	D	D
E E ‖	E ‖	E
F F I'	F I'	F
	G	G
H	H	H
I	I	I
K ⊢	K	K
L	L L	L
M M	M M M	M
N N	N N	N
◊ O O	O	O
Γ P	P P	P
? Q	Q	Q
R R	R	R
⌇ S	S	S
T	T	T
V	V	V
X	X	X

Fig. 15. Ancient Latin alphabets (founded on Ritschl's *Priscae Latinitatis Monumenta Epigraphica*, and reproduced, by permission, from Daremberg and Saglio, i 215, Fig. 238).

(a) 475—500 A.V.C. = 279—254 B.C.
(b) 501—600 A.V.C. = 253—154 B.C.
(c) From 600 A.V.C. = 154 B.C.

THE ALPHABET

letter within its curve. Similarly, at the end, we may have a large C embracing a small o. See p. 51 *ult.*

The archaic forms of D are ▷ ▷ ▷. The fully rounded type is found on monumental inscriptions of the best age. In laws of the republican period, inscribed on metal plates, the lobe is often left partly open, either above or below. In the painted, the documental, and the cursive styles, a tail often extends to the left from the upper part of the lobe.

D.

The archaic forms of E are E ⩘ ⩘ ⩘ ‖. Under the Republic the three parallel lines are sometimes deflected downwards, but in the Augustan age these lines are horizontal, and are of very nearly (if not exactly) equal length. After the Augustan age the central horizontal line becomes shorter. In the painted style, the parallel lines are curved upwards and are sometimes very short, so that the letter E resembles the letters F, L, I, T. The form ‖ probably arose out of the use of |' for F. It is found under the Republic, and in ancient inscriptions of lower Italy, and is not infrequently used under the Empire, especially in the 'vulgar' style.

E.

F went through the same changes as E. The archaic forms are ⨍ F ⨍ |'. In the monumental style of the best age the two transverse lines are horizontal and equal. They are deflected *upwards* in ancient times, and in the second and third centuries of the Empire; and also in the painted and the 'vulgar' styles. Deflection *downwards*, which is also ancient, is not found under the Empire. |' is to be seen in the Pompeian *graffiti.* F (like P and T) is often taller than the other letters, especially at the beginning of the line. This fashion dates from the second century in Italy and the provinces, and from after the third in Rome.

F.

In the monumental style of the early Empire the very short stroke distinguishing G from C rises straight upwards and is deflected horizontally towards the left. The form in which the stroke immediately curves inwards is rare in the first century, but is common in the next two centuries, especially when the letters are small and are in the painted style. Ϛ and other cursive forms are also found in the uncial style; late in the

G.

S. L. I.

50   LATIN INSCRIPTIONS   [CHAP.

second century they even appear in some of the smaller examples of the monumental style.

H.   ⊟, the earliest form of H, may be seen in the ancient *cippus* of the Forum (Fig. 4), and on the *fibula Praenestina* (Fig. 3). H varies little. Rather broad in the early monumental style, it gradually becomes narrower. Sometimes the transverse stroke either extends beyond the two vertical lines, or joins the lower part of the first to the upper part of the second. The partial or complete omission of the upper part of the second.vertical line begins in some Roman inscriptions of the second century[1]. This is an early form of the modern h.

I.   In some of the inscriptions of the Republic and early Empire, I is perfectly plain, with no further strokes, either above or below. These are added, in a straight or curved form, in inscriptions of the painted style, in which (as in the 'vulgar' style) it often resembles T or L. I is used for the semivowel, as well as for the vowel. In Cicero's time the semivowel was sometimes expressed by a double I, as in CVIIVS, EIIVS, for *cuius, eius*. Cicero himself wrote *aiio* and *Maiia* for *aio* and *Maia* (Quint. i 4, 11), and there is also evidence for *Aiiax* and *Troiiam*; but this innovation did not become common. About the time of Sulla a tall I was used for *ei*, and this was partly continued in the Augustan age, especially in the dative and ablative plural. The tall I was also used to denote the long vowel in DIVOS and DIVI, in IVLII and CAESARI, and in PRIDIE and APRILIS; as the first letter of IMPERATOR (especially at the beginning of the line); and even in IN and ITEM, and IVSSV, and ISDEM CONSVLIBVS (87—155 A.D.)[2]. Under the Empire, I was used between two vowels, as in CVIVS and EIVS (*C. I. L.* i 1964, v 18). For the latter we even find EIIVS and EIIVS (Hübner's *Ex.* 808; *C. I. L.* ii 1687, 1953). The form J, which originated in the written style, came into occasional use in the second century. In modern alphabets this form was adopted as an initial letter in the fifteenth century. The dotted I appears about 500 A.D.

[1] Hübner's *Exempla*, 1129: cp. 1148.
[2] For DIVI cp. Fig. 8, l. 1, and 47, l. 1, pp. 43, 178

The letter K was seldom used and underwent little change. Under the early Empire the two transverse strokes were very small (Fig. 45, p. 172). In the painted style they become larger about 300 A.D.

K.

The archaic form of L was ↳ (see Fig. 19, p. 67, *infra*). The most ancient angular type gradually gave way to the various rectangular forms, and completely disappeared about 200 B.C. In the best age the horizontal line measures a little more than half the vertical. In later times it varies and becomes much shorter, sometimes differing but little from I. A tall L is often found as an initial letter. In the documental and the cursive style, the lower stroke is sometimes curved downwards. ⌊ is peculiar to the 'vulgar' style.

L.

The oldest form of M, which has five straight lines, /\/\/, is found on the *fibula Praenestina*, the Forum *cippus*, and in the 'Duenos inscription' (Figs. 3, 4, 5). This form was used as the abbreviation for Manius under the Republic and (occasionally) under the Empire; M.' (for Manius) is purely modern. The straddling form in four lines (/\/\) is the prevailing type (Figs. 7, 8, 17—21). /\ and /\\ are very rare under the Republic, the former being found on coins and small articles, and the latter only on coins, to save space. The former is not used in monumental inscriptions till after 200 A.D.; it is about 50 A.D. that the form M comes first into use in Germany. /\\, a cursive form of the best age, appears later on monuments of the lower class, while another cursive form |||| is found in the Pompeian *graffiti*.

M.

The earliest form N, in which all the strokes were oblique, was retained under the Republic, but the upright form is sometimes found in the same inscriptions as the other. N is the usual type of the best age. Extra touches were gradually added to the top and bottom of the vertical lines.

N.

The archaic forms of O were ᴖ O () ⟨⟩. In the earliest times, O was often much smaller than the other letters; this was partly continued under the Empire, especially after C, which often embraces a small O in its curve, as in the abbreviation ⓒS for *consul*.

O.

4—2

The archaic forms of P are Γ Ρ. The latter remains the
standard type. The closed form, P, is sometimes
found on the *glandes plumbeae* and the *tesserae* of
the Republic, but it is rare under the early Empire. It appears
about 100 A.D. in Germany, and about 200 A.D. in the other provinces, and in Rome. As an initial letter it is taller than the rest.

P.

The earliest form of Q is ϙ. Among other archaic forms are
Q and Q. Under the late Republic, the tail is
short and nearly straight, in the early Empire it is
longer and more curved (Figs. 47, 48, p. 178 f).

Q.

The oldest form of R is found in the retroverted Greek type
of the earliest inscriptions (Fig. 5). Among other
archaic forms are Ρ and R. In the standard monumental type of this letter, the circumference of the fully rounded
upper loop ends at the middle of the shaft, and it is at this point
that the tail begins. Cp. p. 201 *infra*.

R.

The archaic forms of S are ϟ S ϟ. The angular types belong
to the age of the Republic alone. The curved
form of perfect symmetry is characteristic of the
best period.

S.

The archaic types of T are Υ and Τ as well as T. Under
the early Empire this last was the standard form,
and it was often made taller to save space on either
side (Fig. 12, p. 45). In the documental and cursive styles, the
transverse line was slightly curved.

T.

V is fairly constant, but it sometimes slopes to the left, with
the right stroke perpendicular and the left stroke
slightly lengthened. The same letter was used for
the vowel and for the semivowel. The curved form U is used for
both in the uncial style at Rome about 200 A.D., and later elsewhere (cp. Fig. 14, p. 47).

V.

In comparatively modern alphabets, V was used in the tenth
century as the initial, and U as the medial letter, and V came
to be regarded as the semivowel, U as the vowel.

The archaic + is found on the Forum *cippus* (Fig. 4) and in
an ancient inscription from the *lacus Benacus*
(*C. I. L.* i² 2, 2166). The normal character X
underwent little change under the Empire.

X.

III] LIGATURES 53

Y and Z were borrowed, towards the close of the Republic, for the transliteration of Greek words. Y was often made taller than the other letters, and sometimes assumed a slanting form. In other respects Y (like Z) was constant in shape.

Y.
Z.

LIGATURES, ETC.

With a view to saving space, especially at the end of the line, two or three or even more letters are sometimes joined together: e.g. A preceding E, M, N, R, TR, V, VR; I preceding B, N, R, T; or following C, F, H, L, M, N, P, T, V. This practice first appears on coins about 200 B.C. and in inscriptions about 150. To save space in an inscription of c. 41 A.D., ET is represented by $\frac{E}{T}$ in the second line, and by a monogram in the third (Hübner, *Ex.* 193). O·V·F, for *orat vos faciatis*, and O·H·S, for *ossa hic sita*, are sometimes contracted into a monogram (Hübner's *Exempla*, p. lxix). Ligatures were not in general use in Italy, but became common in Gaul, Germany, and Africa. (Lists in Hübner's *Exempla*, p. lxviii; Cagnat[4], p. 24; and Egbert, p. 67.)

Ligatures

It is stated by grammarians that a *sicilicus* or laterally inverted C, Ɔ, was placed above a consonant which was to be regarded as a doubled letter. Some examples of this (e.g. SABELIO and OSA) belong to the early part of the Augustan age (*C. I. L.* v 1361, x 3743, xii 414). Cp. Isidore, *Etym.* i 27, 29, 'veteres non duplicabant litteras, sed supra sicilicos adponebant; qua nota admonebatur lector geminandam esse litteram'.

Sicilicus

The *apex* was used to distinguish vowels which were naturally long (Figs. 8, 47, pp. 43, 178). It was in use from after the age of Sulla to about 250 A.D. Its earlier forms were ⟩ ⊃ ⟩ ⟨, and, under the Empire, ʹ. It is rarely found over I. Long I was written as EI after 134 B.C., or expressed by a taller letter, c. 80 B.C. to 150 A.D.

Apex

PUNCTUATION

Punctuation

The several words were separated by means of a mark placed, not at the foot of the line of letters, but midway between the top and the bottom. These marks are nearly always absent at the ends of the lines, and they are not used to denote the termination of a clause or a sentence. When the letters are in relief this mark is round. When they are incised in stone or metal, it may be either square or oblong or triangular (Fig. 47, p. 178). This last finally assumed the ornamental form of an ivy-leaf. An inscription at Cirta expressly mentions *hederae distinguentes* (*C. I. L.* viii 6982). Towards the end of the first century the more important divisions are sometimes distinguished by branches of palm. In the more ancient inscriptions (especially in the early *leges* of the Republic) words are seldom divided at the end of the line; but this becomes common in the *acta* of the Empire[1].

In later inscriptions points are sometimes inserted between single letters or syllables. In lengthy documents these are often omitted, except after abbreviations, and similarly in the bronze lettering of important buildings, and in epitaphs written in 'vulgar' characters.

NUMERALS

Numerals

The original numerals were I (a single digit) for 'one,' V (a rudimentary representation of the five fingers) for 'five'; X (or the two hands joined) for 'ten'[2]. X, however, is sometimes regarded as an Etruscan symbol for 'ten', the upper half of which was adopted for 'five'[3]. To these ancient symbols two were added from the Chalcidic alphabets, *ch*, ↓ (altered into ↓, ⊥, L) for 50, and *ph*, Φ (Ⓓ, later CIƆ) for 1000. The sign for 100 (C) probably originated in the Chalcidic Θ, but no certain example of the use of Θ or O for 100 has yet been found[4]. The opinion that it was the three

---

[1] For pp. 47—54 the primary authority is Hübner's *Exempla*, pp. lii— lxxxiii.   [2] Mommsen, *H. R.* i 264, E. T. ed. 1894.

[3] Ritschl, *Opusc.* iv 704.

[4] Ⓓ (=φ) is the form used in the ancient inscription of Cora, *C. I. L.* i² 2, 1510. Cp. Bücheler, *Rhein. Mus.* 46 (1891), 239; p. 77 *infra*. Oxe, *Rhein. Mus.* 59 (1904), 115.

Chalcidic aspirates that were borrowed to denote 50 and 1000 and 100 is confirmed by the Etruscan alphabet, in which these aspirates, retained as letters, were slightly changed when used as numerals.

While ⏀ denotes 1000, the addition of a second circle outside the first made it mean 10,000, and that of a third, 100,000. Half of these figures was denoted by the second half of the symbol, e.g. D for 500 (cp. Cicero, *pro Q. Roscio*, 4, 11 f, 22 f, 28 f, 32 f, 40 f, 43, 48 f, 55). In early inscriptions, multiples of 100,000 were expressed by repeating the symbol as often as necessary (cp. Fig. 30, p. 96).

Towards the end of the Republic the thousands were denoted by drawing a horizontal line above the numeral, e.g. $\bar{V} = 5,000$, $\bar{D} = 500,000$. Lateral lines were further added to denote 100,000, e.g. $\overline{|X|} = 1,000,000$. These lines are first found in the *lex Rubria* of 49 B.C. (*C. I. L.* i² 2, 592). Cp. Pliny, *N. H.* xxiii 133.

The original numerals I, V, X being identical with certain letters of the alphabet, other numerals were assimilated to letters. Thus the second half of ⏀ became D, ⊖ became C, and ⊥ became L. The second of these changes was favoured by the fact that C was the first letter of *centum*. At an early date *milia passuum* was represented by ⋀·P, but the separate use of ⋀ for the word *mille* or *milia* is not found before the second century A.D., and ⋀ was never used as a mere numeral. The old form ⏀ was sometimes changed into ∞ (Cicero, *pro Q. Roscio*, 28 f; Appendix, v 14) or ⋂.

To prevent confusion in the use of the same signs as numerals and as letters, the numerals were distinguished by drawing a horizontal line either across the letter or (in the Augustan age) above. A familiar example of the early use of II as a numeral is to be seen in HS ($= duo + semis$) for *semis-tertius*, the *sestertius* of $2\frac{1}{2}$ *asses*. II, after the title of an office, denotes that it has been twice held. IIVIR is the common abbreviation for *duumvir*.

Numerals other than those above mentioned were expressed either by the method of addition, in which the higher figure comes first, or by that of subtraction, in which it comes last. Of these methods the former is the earlier, and the more usual,

Thus, IIII is earlier and more frequent than IV, while the latter belongs to writing of the lower class and is first found in the seventh century of Rome. VIII is commoner than IIX, and XXVIII than XXIIX. Besides I and X, C is used in subtraction, as CDⱢ = 450 and C∞LX = 960, but V, L, and D are not so used[1].

The single *as* was denoted by I, the *semis* by its first letter S and the *uncia* by — or o. Thus the *quadrans* of 3 *unciae* was expressed by $=-$ and the *deunx* of 11 *unciae* by S $==-$ [2].

Fractions

Process of Making Inscriptions

Some of the epitaphs of the Scipios (e.g. Fig. 17 f) include letters painted in vermilion (*minium*). The custom of painting letters in black on a white ground is mentioned in the *lex Acilia repetundarum* of 123 B.C. (*C. I. L.* i² 2, 583, 14, *in tabula, in albo, atramento scriptos*). *Fasti* painted in red or black have been found on the walls of Rome, and in black on the buildings of Pompeii, and other painted inscriptions have been preserved in large num¹ers. The lines of the lettering were either marked out previously by means of a cord covered with vermilion, or faintly cut with a rule (as in the epitaph of Scipio, the *flamen Dialis*, Fig. 21, and as in the unfinished inscription reproduced in Daremberg and Saglio, s.v. *Inscriptiones*, fig. 4068). The accuracy characteristic of the lettering of inscriptions cut in bronze or stone proves that the separate letters must have been first painted, or at least outlined, before they were incised, and there is reason for believing that patterns of the different letters were used for this purpose. The next step was for the stone-cutter (*marmorarius* or *lapidarius*) to cut the letters out of the stone (*scalpere, sculpere* or *insculpere*) with a chisel (*scalprum*) and hammer. On certain inscriptions we have actual representations of the tools used (cp. Daremberg and Saglio, s.v. *Inscriptiones*, fig. 4067, and references there given; and Hübner's *Exempla*, p. xxx ff.). The shape of the incision is neither curved

Process of making inscriptions

---

[1] See, in general, Mommsen in *Hermes*, xxii (1887) 596 ff, and xxiii (1888) 152 ff (*Ges. Schr.* vii 765—787). VL is quoted for 45 by Egbert and ∞ Ↄ (4000) occurs on *C. I. L.* x 1273.

[2] Cp. conspectus in Cagnat, 30—34, or Egbert, 72—81; also Dessau, iii pp. 797 f.

nor oblong, but an acute angle resembling the letter V. The letters, when completed, were often picked out with vermilion, a practice mentioned by Pliny (xxxiii 122, *minium...clariores litteras vel in auro* (corr. *muro* or *aere*), *vel in marmore, etiam in sepulcris facit*)[1]. The letters on bronze plates were sometimes made more distinct by being filled with white lead[2]. For large public monuments the letters were sometimes separately made of bronze or lead, and affixed to the stone with rivets. On the architrave of the triumphal Arch at Orange, it is only the holes left by these rivets that enable us to restore part of the lost inscription:— TI·CAESARI·DIVI·AVGVSTI·F·DIVI·IVLI·NEPOTI·AVGVSTO (Daremberg and Saglio, fig. 4070); and similarly with the inscriptions on the frieze of the temple at Assisi[3].

For inscriptions on bronze, the person employed was an *aerarius* or *caelator*, and the corresponding verb was *incidere*, which is also applied to inscriptions on stone. Sometimes the letters are only indicated by a series of points impressed on the surface of the plate[4]. A large *stilus* called a *graphium* was used to scratch inscriptions on the walls of buildings (generally before the cement had hardened). Many such *graffiti* have been found at Pompeii (Fig. 13). Lettering of different kinds, varying with the material, is also found on pottery, on bricks and tiles, and on plates of gold, silver, bronze or lead.

In the Museum at Palermo we have an inscription in which a professional stone-mason advertises his establishment in two parallel columns, in Greek and in Latin:—στῆλαι | ἐνθάδε | τυποῦνται καὶ | χαράσσονται | ναοῖς ἱεροῖς | σὺν ἐνεργείαις | δημοσίαις |, *tituli* | *heic* | *ordinantur et* | *sculpuntur* | *aidibus sacreis* | *cum operum publicorum* (*sic*). Similarly, in a Roman inscription :—*D*(*is*) *M*(*anibus*) | *Titulos scri*|*bendos vel* | *si quid ope*|*ris marmor*|*ari*(*i*) *opus fu*|*erit hic ha*|*bes*[5]. In the Lateran Museum we find an elaborately sculptured funerary urn, which had been prepared on specu-

---

[1] Traces of colour can be seen in the *elogium* on Scipio Barbatus in the front of the sarcophagus figured in the *Frontispiece*.
[2] Mommsen, *Eph. Epigr.* ix 1, *lex municipii Tarentini* (*Ges. Schr.* i 148).
[3] *C. I. L.* xi 5378; cp. p. 125 *infra*.
[4] Hübner's *Exempla*, p. xxxvii, and nos. 896, 926—945; Diehl, *Inscr. Lat.* tab. 3 d, *C. I. L.* i² 2, 359.
[5] Hübner's *Exempla*, p. xxx; *C. I. L.* x 7296 and vi 9556 (copied on title-page of Cagnat, ed 2—4)

lation, inscribed only with the letters D·M·, leaving the rest of the inscription to be completed to order[1].

Stamps Stamps of hard material are often used to impress letters in relief on the surface of articles made of clay or terracotta. Letters in relief are also stamped on arms and on household utensils, on pigs of metal, and on water-pipes, missiles, tablets and tokens of lead[2].

Scriptura vulgaris A rude type of lettering called *scriptura vulgaris* is characteristic of inscriptions made by an inexpert or unprofessional hand. The letters are cut without the aid of outlines. Sometimes holes are first punched out, to mark the shape of the letters. These holes are then rudely joined together, as in the inscriptions in quarries near Hadrian's Wall in the north of England, (1) by the side of Banksburn, near Lanercost (*C. I. L.* vii 872 ; Hübner's *Exempla*, no. 1185); and (2) on the 'written rock' of Helbeck, about two miles south of Brampton, *Vex(illatio) leg(ionis) II Au(gustae), of(ficina) Apr(ilis), sub Agricola optione*, a lieutenant of 207 A.D. (*C. I. L.* vii 912). The following is Bruce's copy of the first two words, where Hübner suspects that for IE we should read II, the 'vulgar' form of E, but Bruce's copy has been confirmed by Haverfield[3]. It is to the large characters of this

Fig. 16. From the 'written rock' on the river Gelt (*Lapidarium Septentrionale*, iii 469, p. 234, *c.* 1/15. Letters about 4 inches high).

'written rock' that Tennyson compares the inscription seen on certain slabs of rock in *Gareth and Lynette*:—

> In letters like to those the vexillary
> Hath left crag-carven o'er the streaming Gelt.

Similar unprofessional work is often found in the remains of fortified camps, in ordinary epitaphs, and in cases where additions are made to the normal columns of *Fasti*, or new names added to those of the emperors first mentioned on Roman milestones.

[1] Benndorf-Schöne, *Lat. Mus.* no. 189; Helbig's *Führer*, no. 638; figured in *Arch. Zeitung*, 1866, pp. 137 f, Taf. ccvii.   [2] Cp. pp. 148—152 *infra*.
[3] *Eph. Epigr.* ix p. 683; Bruce, *Roman Wall*, p. 32[7].

CHAPTER IV

CLASSIFICATION OF INSCRIPTIONS

(I) Inscriptions proper

INSCRIPTIONS (ἐπιγραφαί) are primarily divided into two classes : — *Classification*

(I) inscriptions proper (ἐπιγράμματα, *tituli*), consisting of characters inscribed on monuments or other objects to denote their purpose, the essential point in each case being the name of an individual and a statement of his relation to the monument or other object. *(I) inscriptions proper. tituli*

(II) documents, public or private (γράμματα, *acta, instrumenta, tabulae*), inscribed on durable material, such as metal or stone, with a view to their publication and more or less permanent preservation. *(II) documents. acta*

The *tituli* of class (I) are subdivided into (1) epitaphs (*tituli sepulcrales*); (2) dedicatory inscriptions (*t. sacri*); (3) honorary inscriptions (*t. honorarii*); (4) inscriptions on public works (*t. operum publicorum*); (5) inscriptions on portable objects (*instrumentum domesticum*, etc.). *Subdivisions*

The *acta* of class (II) are subdivided into (1) treaties (*foedera*); (2) laws (*leges* and *plebiscita*); (3) decrees of the Roman Senate (*senatus consulta*) and of the *coloniae* and *municipia*, the *collegia* and *sodalicia*; (4) decrees of magistrates and emperors (*decreta*, etc.); (5) consular diptychs (*diptycha consularia*); (6) sacred and public documents (*acta sacra et publica*); (7) private documents (*acta privata*); (8) *graffiti* on walls (*inscriptiones parietariae*).

The most elaborate classification of Latin inscriptions is that of Zell, who divides them into (I) sacred, and (II) profane; and subdivides sacred inscrip-

60   LATIN INSCRIPTIONS   [CHAP.

tions into those on (1) temples, and (2) tombs etc.; profane into (1) public, and (2) private; and public into (*a*) civil, and (*b*) military[1].

Among simpler classifications of *inscriptions proper* (our class I) are those of Zaccaria, and Cagnat, (1) dedicatory, (2) honorary, (3) sepulchral; Egbert and Ricci's order is (1) dedicatory, (2) sepulchral, (3) honorary; and Hübner's, (1) sepulchral, (2) dedicatory, (3) honorary. This last is the order I have retained; it has the advantage of beginning with the largest class of inscriptions, and of placing inscriptions on tombs immediately before those on temples, both of these being of the nature of 'sacred inscriptions'. But a single inscription may sometimes belong to more than one class. An honorary inscription may be combined with an epitaph (as in the monument of Bibulus, p. 105), or with a dedicatory inscription, as where Titinius Capito recites all his own honours in a dedication to a divinity (p. 87 *infra*).

(i) Epitaphs

Epitaphs

I (1). The earliest **epitaphs**, such as those of Praeneste (250—150 B.C.), simply give the name of the deceased, in the nominative case, e.g. *M'·Fabrici*(*s*)[2]·*K*(*aesonis*)·*f*(*ilios*)[3]. The nominative is also found in the epitaphs of the Turpleii and Fourii at Tusculum[4], and in the earlier inscriptions on the Scipios (first part of Figs. 17—20). The genitive and dative (Fig. 7) are later in date. The following are in constant use as the abbreviations for the most frequent *praenomina*:—

A Aulus.   D Decimus. ⋏⋁ (not ⋏⋏') Manius. Q Quintus. S(SP) Spurius.
C Gaius.   K Kaeso.   ⋏⋏ Marcus. SER Servius. TI(B) Tiberius.
CN Gnaeus.   L Lucius.   P Publius. SEX Sextus. T Titus.

Ↄ stands for Gaia, and may be used for any woman, e.g. M·ARRIVS·Ↄ·L· DIOMEDES means 'M. Arrius, freedman of Arria'[5]. On the cinerary urns, found in the vineyard of San Cesario on the *Via Appia* (150—50 B.C.), the date of the death is also given, e.g. *L. Anauis*[6] *L. f. eidibus Sex*(*tilibus*). In course of time the profession of the deceased, the age, with formulae such as *hic cubat* (H·C), *hic situs est* (H·S·E), were added, as well as laudatory epithets.

[1] *Handbuch*, ii (1852) 139 f.
[2] Old form of *Fabricius*.
[3] Cp. Ritschl *P. L. M. E.* tab. 36 inf., 45—47, and Dessau, ii (2) p. 834.
[4] Cp. Dessau, *l. c.*, and dedicatory inscription, Fig. 6.
[5] M. Arrius Gaiae (=Arriae) libertus Diomedes. Wilmanns, no. 1933; Dessau, ii 6378.
[6] *Anauis* (*Annauius*), old form of *Annaeus*. Cp. Diehl, *Altlateinische Inschriften* (ed. 1911), nos. 478—491.

In the case of distinguished persons, it had become customary, about 250 B.C., to supplement the ordinary *tituli* with poetic *elogia*. The original epitaph of Scipio Barbatus was simply his name written in vermilion (upper part of Fig. 18); at a later date an *elogium* was added below in Saturnian verse, the metre used in the case of three other Scipios[1], while Scipio Hispanus, praetor peregrinus in 139 B.C., was honoured in two elegiac couplets:—

> Virtutes generis mieis moribus accumulavi,
>   progeniem genui, facta patris petiei.
> Maiorum optenui laudem, ut sibei me esse creatum
>   laetentur; stirpem nobilitavit honor[2].

In contrast to the *elogia* we have the following simple epitaph found in Padua, which is possibly that of the historian Livy:— T. Livius C. f. sibi et | suis, | T. Livio T. f. Prisco f., | T. Livio T. f. Longo f., | Cassiae Sex. f. Primae | uxori (Dessau, i 2919).

On important tombs of the earlier time, the inscription is generally brief and simple, as on the great tomb of Caecilia Metella (p. 42). On the other hand, the tomb of a consul of 74 A.D., Tiberius Plautius, near Tivoli, included a full and elaborate enumeration of all his distinctions[3].

Epitaphs on tombs prepared by persons who are still living usually begin with the letters V·F·, *vivus fecit*, for example :—

V·F· | C(aius) Atilius | Castalii lib(ertus) | Florentinus sibi et | dis manibus Iuliae | Fortunatae uxoris | optime meritae (Dessau, ii (2) 8072).

In lists of persons commemorated by a single epitaph, the names are regularly given in the nominative. Those who are still living are distinguished by the letter V (*vivus*) prefixed to the name: those who are dead by a symbol like Θ. The latter was also used in lists of soldiers to distinguish those who were no longer living, cp. Isidore, *Etym.* i 24, 1, 'Θ Theta vero ad uniuscuiusque defuncti nomen apponebatur. Vnde habet per medium telum, id est mortis signum. De qua (*sc.* nota) Persius ait (iv 13): et potis est nigrum vitio praefigere theta.' This usage

---

[1] Bücheler, *Carmina Epigraphica*, nos. 6, 8, 9; Figs. 19, 20, 21 *infra*.
[2] *ib.* no. 958, *C. I. L.* i² 2, 15.
[3] Dessau, i 986.

(which is rare in the provinces) is mainly found in Roman and Italian inscriptions of the first century, e.g.

Θ P·AQVILLIVS·P·P·L·HILARVS
ⱯAQVILLIA·P·ET·Ɔ·L·NICE

Θ(ανὼν?) *P. Aquillius P(ubliorum duorum) l(ibertus), Hilarus.
V(iva) Aquillia P(ublii) et Ɔ (mulieris) l(iberta) Nice*[1].

Θ(?) is hardly found after the age of Augustus. It has been distinguished from various forms of Ο, such as Θ, Ө, Ꙩ, used as an abbreviation for *obiit* or *obitus*, and specially frequent in the inscriptions of Noricum[2]. Similarly, in Pannonia, we find *Memoriae ∅ M. Aureli Melliti Librari leg(ionis)* etc. (Wilmanns, 1549). O is also used for *ossa* (*ib.* 1633, 1644). Q·D, or Ꝙ, stands for *quondam*.

Many epitaphs (especially in and after the Augustan age) begin with *Dis Manibus* or *Dis Manibus Sacrum*, at first written in full, but afterwards abbreviated as D·M, or D·M·S. The tomb is sometimes called a (*locus*) *deum Maanium*, as at Hispellum[3], or is expressly dedicated to the *Di Manes*, e.g. at Padua, *hunc locum monumentumque dis Manibus do legoque*[4]. At Corduba we have the phrase *dei Manes receperunt eum*[5]. In Gallic inscriptions D·M is often followed by *et memoriae aeternae*, or (more rarely) by *quieti aeternae* or *perpetuae*. Frequently we find only *memoriae*, and, sometimes, *in memoriam*[6]. M(*emoriae*) C(*ausa*), found in Greece and Asia Minor, corresponds to the Greek formula, μνήμης χάριν[7]. D·M is normally followed by the genitive of the person commemorated; but it may also be followed by the name and description of the deceased in the nominative

---

[1] Hübner's *Exempla*, 4. Cp. Dessau, ii 6963, (2) 8150.
[2] This distinction is maintained by Hübner, followed by Egbert; but it is hardly defensible. Θ is not used in Greek for θανών or θάνατος; much less is it likely to have been so used in Latin. Both symbols are best regarded by Mommsen, Mowat (*Bulletin Épigraphique*, iv 133 f), and Cagnat[4], 292, as abbreviations for *obiit*, and by Dessau, iii p. 795, as standing for *obitus*.
[3] *C. I. L.* i² 2, 2117.
[4] Wilmanns, 217. [5] Dessau, ii (2) 8007.
[6] Wilmanns, 590; cp. Pliny, *Epp.* iii 3, 1, with Mayor's note.
[7] S. Reinach, *Épigraphie grecque*, p. 427.

EPITAPHS

with *hic situs est*, or with the dative in apposition to *Dis Manibus*. The dative singular is often followed by B · M (*bene merenti*), or, less often, A · B · M (*amico bene merenti*).

The age is most simply expressed in the genitive case, either by *annorum* (*tot*) alone, or by *natus annorum* (*tot*)[1]. When it is introduced by the phrase *qui vixit* (Q · V ·), the number of years is far more frequently expressed by the ablative *annis* (*tot*) than by the accusative *annos* (*tot*). In either case the number of years may be followed by that of the months, days, and even hours. Occasionally the ablative, *annis*, is ungrammatically followed by the accusative, *menses*, or *dies*[2]. The accusative and the ablative may be seen in two different epitaphs on the same funerary altar (p. 73). Q · V · A is used as an abbreviation for *qui* (or *quae*) *vixit annis* (or *annos*), and an approximate number of years is expressed by prefixing P · M (*plus minus*). An early example of this last formula is VIX · ANN · P · M · XXIIII[3].

Salutations addressed to the dead by the passers by are placed either at the beginning or at the end of an epitaph, e.g. AVE or HAVE, or S · T · T · L, either abbreviated, or in full as *sit tibi terra levis*.

We often find salutations purporting to be addressed by the dead to the living, e.g. *ave, salve*, or *vale, viator*; or *tu qui legis vale et cum voles venito*; or *bene valeat is qui hunc titulum perlegit meum*. In fuller form, we have the following metrical lines:—

adulescens, tametsi properas, | hic te saxsolus
rogat ut se | aspicias, deinde ut quod scriptust | legas.
    hic sunt ossa Maeci Luci sita |
    Philotimi vasculari.
hoc ego voleba(m) | nescius ni esses. vale.
    (Dessau ii (2) 7703, Diehl, *Inscr. Lat.* tab. 6 d)[4]

The deceased is also represented as saying of his present abode, *iuvenis feci, ut senex habitem* (*C. I. L.* viii 2177). The living and

---

[1] Wilmanns, 542, 1436, *annorum gnatus* or *natus*; also *annos gnatus* or *natus* (*ib.* 541, 1493).
[2] Wilmanns, 1558, 1647; and Dessau, ii (2) 8100.
[3] Wilmanns, 235; Dessau, i 1523.
[4] Cp. the epitaph of Pacuvius quoted on p. 14 *supra*.

the dead are sometimes represented as conversing, as in the following epitaph :—

D·M· | Primitiva have. Et tu quis’quis es, vale.
Non | fueram, non sum, | nescio, non ad me | pertin(et).
Alexand(er) actor coniugi kar(issimae).
(Dessau, ii (2) 8165, cp. 8125, 8162 ; iii p. 947.)

We may here quote the epitaph of an actor, *aliquoties mortuus sum, sed sic nunquam* (*C. I. L.* iii 3980), or that of the modest matron, *hic sita est Amymone Marci optima et pulcherrima,* | *lanifica pia pudica frugi casta domiseda*, and the longer epitaph ending with the line *domum servavit, lanam fecit; dixi, abei*[1]. Among simpler forms of reference to the deceased are C(*arus*) S(*uis*), or P(*ius*) I(*n*) S(*uos*), both found in Spain; B(*ene*) Q(*uiescat*) and (with reference to the survivor) P(*ro*) P(*ietate*), both in Africa.

Facts relating to the site are often added, such as *loco dato decreto decurionum* (L · D · D · D ·). It is a characteristic of the Augustan age to give the dimensions of the place of burial:— *locus patet in fronte pedes* (tot), *in agro* (or *in via*, or *retro*) *pedes* (tot)[2]. Cp. Horace, *Sat.* i 8, 12 f :—

> Mille pedes in fronte, trecentos cippus in agrum
> hic dabat, heredes monumentum ne sequeretur.

In this quotation, the last four words refer to a customary legal formula, the object of which was to reserve the property in the tomb and in its immediate surroundings, and to prevent its passing to the heirs of the adjacent land. In inscriptions, this was usually expressed by H(*oc*) M(*onumentum*) H(*eredem*) N(*on*) S(*equitur*), or S(*equetur*), and especially by—*heredem exterum non sequetur*, with variations, such as H(*ic*) L(*ocus*), or H(*aec*) A(*ra*), or H(*ic*) L(*ocus*) S(*epulturae*), H(*ic*) L(*ocus*) *et* M(*onumentum*), ending sometimes A(*d*) H(*eredem*) N(*on*) P(*ertinet*)[3]. The site is sometimes called L(*ocus*) M(*onumenti*), or *loc*(*us*) *sep*(*ulturae*)[4].

We also find phrases forbidding desecration, such as, *nolei violare* or *monumento huic nil male feceris*[5]; H(*uic*) L(*oco*), or H(*uic*)

---

[1] Dessau, ii (2) 8402 f; Bücheler, *Carm. Epigr.* i 52, p. 25.
[2] Wilmanns, *index*, p. 692 *b*, Dessau, iii p. 943.
[3] Cp. Wilmanns, 280 n. (and *index*, p. 693 f).
[4] *Ib.* 330 and *index*, p. 691.
[5] Dessau, ii (2) 8174 and 7602; cp. Wilmanns, *index*, p. 693.

M(*onumento*), D(*olus*) M(*alus*) A(*besto*)¹; and even protests against painting election placards upon the tomb:—

> ita candidatus fiat honoratus tuus
> et ita gratum edat | munus tuus munerarius
> et tu ⟨sis⟩ felix, scriptor, si hic non scripseris².

The epitaph often included the name or description of the person dedicating the monument, while the monument dedicated might be followed by a verbal phrase, such as *ponendum curavit* (P·C·), with mention of the circumstance or motive, e.g., *ob memoriam custodiendam adque propagandam*, and a description of the persons to whom it was dedicated, in the dative:—*sibi et suis* (S·ET·S), *libertis libertabus posterisque eorum* (L·L·P·Q·E).

Sometimes the sepulchral inscription is an actual document, a *laudatio funebris* of an exemplary wife or mother. From the eulogy of a wife, which, even in its fragmentary remains, fills four pages of print, we may here extract a single sentence:

> Domestica bona pudicitiae, opsequi, comitatis, facilitatis, lanificiis tuis [adsiduitatis, religionis] sine superstitione, ornatus non conspiciendi, cultus modici cur [memorem?]³.

The extant page in praise of a mother ends as follows:

> Eo maiorem laudem omnium carissima mihi mater meruit, quod modestia probitate pudicitia opsequio lanificio diligentia fide par similisque cetereis probeis feminis fuit, etc.⁴

Lanificiis and *lanificio* in the above laudations remind us of *lanifica* and *lanam fecit* in the already quoted epitaphs, which include the making of wool among the praises of women⁵.

Sometimes the inscription includes the complete quotation of the terms of a will⁶, or legal provisions relating to the place of sepulture⁷.

The most important group of extant epitaphs of the Republican age is associated with the tombs of the Scipios.

The custom of burying, instead of burning the dead, was long continued by the *gens Cornelia*, to which the Scipios belonged. Their place of burial

---

¹ Wilmanns, 252, and *index*, p. 693. ² Dessau, ii (2) 8206; cp. 8205, 8207.

³ Dessau, ii (2) 8393, lines 30 ff (the so-called *laudatio Turiae*); cp. Mommsen (1863), *Ges. Schr.* i 395—421; W. Warde Fowler, in *Cl. Rev.* xix (1905), 261—267.

⁴ *Ib.* 8394 (the *laudatio Murdiae*). ⁵ p. 64 *supra*. ⁶ *Ib.* 8379 f.

⁷ *Ib.* 8380—8392. For many examples of *tituli sepulcrales*, see *ib.* 7818—8566.

was outside the *porta Capena*, S.E. of Rome. The epitaph of L. Cornelius Scipio (consul of 259 B.C.), son of Scipio Barbatus (Fig. 19), was there found in 1614, while the tombs of Scipio Barbatus (Fig. 17, consul of 298) and of seven other Scipios were discovered in 1780.

Fig. 17. Tomb of Scipio Barbatus, consul 298, censor 290 B.C. (reduced to ⅔ of Piranesi's engraving in Ritschl, *P. L. M. E.* tab. xxxvii). See also the *Frontispiece*.

(a) The original epitaph written in red; (b) the elogium, in Saturnian metre, incised on the stone; (c) the epitaph of Cornelia, wife of Hispallus, consul of 176 B.C.

Fig. 18. Epitaph of Scipio Barbatus (reduced to more than ¼ of Ritschl, tab. xxxvii). Dessau, i 1, *C. I. L.* i² 2, 6 and 7. Cp. Lindsay, 41 f; Ernout, 12 f.

EPITAPHS

(*a*) The epitaph in its present state, after the loss of *L. Cornelio;* (*b*) the elogium ; (*c*) the epitaph of the wife of Hispallus. The elogium (*b*) is later than (*a*), and even later than the epitaph of the son of Barbatus, Fig. 19 (Ritschl, *Opusc.* iv 222 f). Wölfflin, *S. Ber. Münch. Akad.* 1892, 188—219, assigns the *elogia* in Figs. 18 ('after 200'), 19 ('*c.* 200'), 21 (*c.* 170), to Ennius (*ob.* 169), and that in Fig. 20 (*c.* 160) to Pacuvius, on grounds regarded as weak by Schanz, *Röm. Lit.* i 50³. On all the *Scipionum Elogia*, cp. *C. I. L.* i² pp. 373—382.

(*a*)   *L. Cornelio*] Cn. f. Scipio

(*b*)   Cornelius Lucius Scipio Barbatus,
    Gnaivod patre | prognatus, fortis vir sapiensque,
    quoius forma virtutei parisuma | fuit ;
    consol, censor, aidilis quei fuit apud vos ;
    Taurasia Cisauna | Samnio cepit,
    subigit omne Loucanam opsidesque abdoucit.

(*c*)   [P]aulla Cornelia Cn. f. Hispalli.

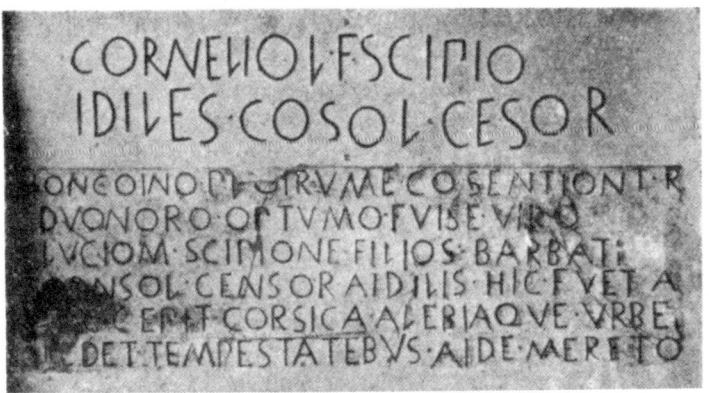

Fig. 19. Epitaph of L. Cornelius Scipio (consul 259 B.C.), son of Barbatus (reduced to ¼ of Ritschl, tab. xxxviii). Dessau, i 3, *C. I. L.* i² 2, 9. Cp. Lindsay, 39 f; Ernout, 14 f.

[L.] Cornelio L. f. Scipio | [a]idiles, cosol, cesor.
Honc oino ploirume cosentiont R[*omai*]
duonoro optumo fuise viro,
Luciom Scipione. Filios Barbati,
consol, censor, aidilis hic fuet a[*pud vos*].
Hec cepit Corsica Aleriaque urbe,
dedet Tempestatebus aide mereto . . . . .

5—2

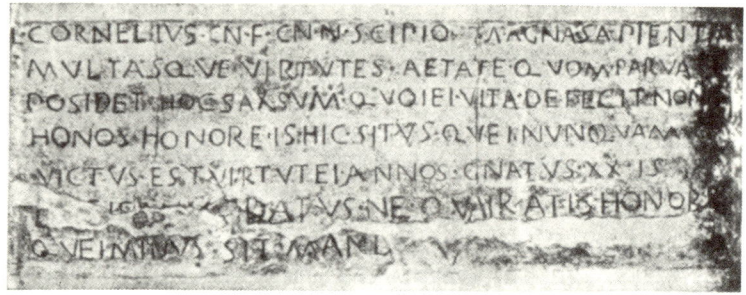

Fig. 20. Epitaph of L. Cornelius Scipio, younger brother, or son, of Hispallus (reduced to more than ¼ of Ritschl, tab. xli). Dessau, i 7, C. I. L. i² 2, 11. Cp. Lindsay, 76 f; Ernout, 19 f.

L. Cornelius Cn. f. Cn. n. Scipio.

Magna sapientia | multasque virtutes
aetate quom parva | posidet hoc saxsum.
Quoiei vita defecit, non | honos, honore.
Is hic situs, quei nunquam | victus est virtutei.
Annos gnatus XX is | 1 . . eis[1] mandatus:
ne quairatis honore | quei minus sit mandatus.

Fig. 21. Epitaph of P. Cornelius P. f. Scipio, *flamen Dialis*, who died young (*c.* 204—164 B.C.), possibly a son of Africanus maior (*c.* ¼ of Ritschl, tab. xxxix f). Dessau, i 4, C. I. L. i² 2, 10. Cp. Lindsay, 43; Ernout, 18 f.

Quei apice insigne Dial[*is fl*]aminis gesistei, |
mors perfe[*cit*] tua ut essent omnia | brevia,
honos fama virtusque, | gloria atque ingenium,

[1] *loceis* Mommsen; *diveis* Bücheler.

quibus sei | in longa licu[i]set tibe utier vita |,
facile facteis superases gloriam | maiorum.
quare lubens te in gremiu, | Scipio, recip[i]t
terra, Publi, | prognatum Publio, Corneli.

Among the largest Roman tombs, bearing extant Latin inscriptions, are the massive rotunda of Caecilia Metella (p. 42), and the vast pyramid of C. Cestius. An inscription on the latter shows that, in accordance with the will of the deceased, it was completed within 330 days:—

C. Cestius L. f(ilius) Pob(lilia) Epulo, pr(aetor), tr(ibunus) pl(ebis)|, VIIvir epulonum|.
Opus apsolutum ex testamento diebus CCCXXX | arbitratu | [L.] Ponti P. f(ili) Cla(udia) Melae heredis et Pothi l(iberti)[1]. One of the heirs was M. Agrippa[2].

Of the numerous inscriptions placed on the vast Mausoleum of Hadrian, not one has survived, save in the copies made mainly in the *codex Einsiedlensis*[3], or (in the case of the principal inscription) by humanists of the 14th and 15th centuries[4]. A finely situated monument on the promontory of Gaëta, resembling the above mentioned rotunda of Caecilia Metella, is inscribed solely with a brief record of the distinctions of L. Munatius Plancus, the founder of Lyons in the year of his consulship (42 B.C.). The inscription on this tomb is of the same general type as those of the *elogia* in the Forum of Augustus[5].

L. Munatius L. f(ilius), L. n(epos), L. pron(epos) | Plancus cos (=consul), cens(or), imp(erator) iter(um), VIIvir | epulon(um), triump(havit) ex Raetis, aedem Saturni | fecit de manibis (=manubiis), agros divisit in Italia | Beneventi, in Gallia colonias deduxit | Lugudunum et Rauricam[6].

The only important sarcophagus of the Roman Republic, now extant, that of Scipio Barbatus, bears his name on its lid and a fuller inscription on its base (Frontispiece and Fig. 17). Occasionally, a Roman sarcophagus (like those of Etruria) was surmounted by reclining figures representing a husband and wife.

[1] Dessau, i 917. [2] *Ib.* 917 a.
[3] *Ib.* i 329, 346, 349—352, 383—385, 401; p. 20 *supra*.
[4] *Ib.* 322. [5] Cp. p. 97 f *infra*.
[6] Dessau, i 886; Wilmanns, 1112; view of the monument in P. S. Bartoli, *Gli antichi sepolcri* (1704), tav. 88.

The front of such a sarcophagus was generally adorned with sculptures in relief, leaving little, if any, room for an inscription. But, on a sarcophagus from the Appian way, we find the central three of the winged Cupids (here represented as forging armour) engaged in holding up a circular shield, bearing a brief epitaph:—

>   BLAERA
>   VITALIS
>   >LEG·III·AVG
>   B·M·M·D

The person commemorated is a centurion of the *legio III Augusta*, and the letters in the last line possibly stand for *bene merenti mater dedit*[1].

When the front of a sarcophagus was filled by an inscription, triangular spaces were often added at each end, bearing the letter D in the space to the left, and M in that to the right, the two letters standing for *Dis Manibus*, the normal beginning of the epitaph.

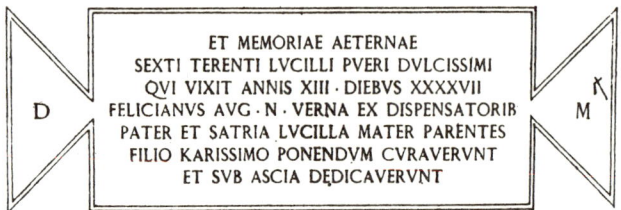

Fig. 22. Inscription on a sarcophagus (printed in A. de Boissieu's *Inscriptions Antiques de Lyon*, p. 459; *C. I. L.* xii 1824; with *ascia*, cp. p. 78 f).

Sometimes we find a portrait of the person commemorated. A sepulchral slab in the British Museum bears in deep relief the portrait busts of (*a*) a priest of the Alban Salii, and (*b*) his wife, with the following inscriptions beneath them :—

(*a*) 'L(ucius) Antistius Cn(aei) filius Hor(atia) Sarculo, Salius Albanus, idem mag(ister) Saliorum.'

(*b*) 'Antistia L(ucii) l(iberta) Plutia.'

[1] *C. I. L.* vi 3645; Duruy, *Histoire des Romains*, vi 329; Daremberg et Saglio, s.v. *Sarcophagus*, fig. 6112.

Below both we read:—

(c) 'Rufus l(ibertus), Anthus l(ibertus), imagines de suo fecerunt patrono et patronae pro meritis eorum'. Besides this record of the dedication of the two busts, there was a fuller inscription including the names of four other members of the family[1].

A monument in the museum at Trier shows us a statue of a man and his wife, standing in two niches, with the inscription showing that it was set up by the husband in his life-time:—

C · ALBINIVS · ASPER | SECVNDIAE · RESTITVTAE |
CONIVGI —— | VIVOS (*i.e. vivus*) [POSVIT?][2].

Sometimes a pair of busts is carved in relief beneath a curved niche, as in the pair inscribed with the words:—

TVRPILIANAE M · F   CACVTIO
TERTIAE   C · F ·
MATRI   PATRI[3]

These marble busts were a kind of survival of the *imagines maiorum* which adorned the halls of important families in ancient Rome.

In an oblong slab in the British Museum Aurelius Hermia stands facing his wife and clasping her hands. The husband praises his wife, and the wife her husband, in the verses which form the greater part of the inscription: the style is that of the school of Accius, about 78 B.C.

(a) To the left of the relief:

(L. Au)relius L(ucii) L(ibertus) Hermia (la)nius de colle Viminale

(H)aec quae me faato praecessit corpore casto,
(c)oniunxs, una meo praedita amans animo,
(f)ido fida viro veixsit studio parili, qum
nulla in avaritie cessit ab officio.
Aurelia L(ucii) l(iberta)

[1] *C. I. L.* vi 2170 f; A. H. Smith, *Brit. Mus. Cat. of Sculpture*, no. 2275; fig. in Hans Lamer, *Römische Kultur im Bilde* (1910), no. 128; and in article by Mrs S. A. Strong, in *Journal of Roman Studies*, iv (1914), 147—156.
[2] Hans Lamer, Fig. 127.
[3] W. Altmann, *Die römischen Grabaltäre der Kaiserzeit* (with 210 illustrations), 1905, p. 206, copied in Daremberg et Saglio, s.v. *Sepulcrum*, fig. 6344.

72 LATIN INSCRIPTIONS [CHAP.

(*b*) to the right of the relief:

Aurelia L(ucii) l(iberta) Philematio

Viva Philematium sum Aurelia nominitata,
casta, pudens, volgei nescia, feida viro.
Vir conleibertus fuit eidem, quo careo eheu!
ree fuit ee vero plus superaque parens.
Septem me naatam annorum gremio ipse recepit;
xxxx annos natā necis potior.
Ille meo officio adsiduo florebat ad omnis
* * * * * *1

The ashes of the deceased were often deposited in an urn, or other receptacle, which was placed in a funerary altar. The marble *olla*, which once contained the ashes of a son of Cicero's enemy Clodius (now in the Louvre), bears the following inscription:—
P·CLAVDIVS·P·F· | AP·N·AP·PRON· | PVLCHER Q· QVAESITOR | PR·AVGVR². The large marble urn of Agrippina the elder is still preserved in the Capitol. It is inscribed OSSA | AGRIPPINAE M·AGRIPPAE (F) DIVI AVG·NEPTIS·VXORIS | GERMANICI CAESARIS | MATRIS C· CAESARIS AVG· | GERMANICI PRINCIPIS.

A favourite form of monument was an altar of an architectural type with its two upper angles adorned by heads of oxen or of rams, or by bearded human heads with Ammon horns, or, again, by capitals with rams' heads between them³. The inscription was usually in the upper part of the front of the altar. Most of these grave-altars appear to belong to slaves or freedmen or freedwomen. It is exceptional to find such an altar (inscribed with the words *d. m. Miniciae Marcellae Fundani f(iliae), v(ixit) a(nnis)* XII, *m(ensibus)* XI, *d(iebus)* VII) commemorating a proconsul's daughter. Her death is lamented by the younger Pliny⁴.

---

[1] *C. I. L.* i² 2, 1221. Figured in A. H. Smith, *Brit. Mus. Cat. of Sculpture*, III pl. xxvii; also in *Greek and Roman Life*, p. 233; text in Bücheler, *Carm. Epigr.* no. 959, Dessau, ii (2) 7472, and Lindsay, p. 91.

[2] Dessau, 882; Fig. in Ritschl, tab. LXXXV f, and in Daremberg et Saglio, s.v. *Olla*. Q. stands for *Q(uirina tribu)*.

[3] W. Altmann, *Die römischen Grabaltäre, passim*; cp. Daremberg et Saglio, s.v. *Sepulcrum*, figs. 6342 f.

[4] *Epp.* v 16.

EPITAPHS

There are two inscriptions on the altar in the British Museum figured below.

Fig. 23. Roman Funerary Altar, in the British Museum.

The first inscription runs:—L. Cocceius M(arci) f(ilius) Dexius Clymenus vixit annum $\bar{\text{I}}$, menses $\overline{\text{VII}}$, diem unum.

The second :—C. Sergius C. fil(ius) Alcimus vixit ann(is) III, mensib(us) III, diebus tribus. Frumentum accepit die X, ostio XXXIX. Sergius Alcimus f(ilio) suo. (Dessau, ii 6069; both inscriptions in *C. I. L.* vi 10224.)

In (2) the child is stated to have received his dole of corn on the tenth day, at the office numbered 39. In other inscriptions children of four are described as having received the dole[1]. A ticket inscribed FRV for *Fru(mentatio)* was presented by persons entitled to this privilege[2]. It will be observed that a bird is figured among the fruit and foliage to the left of the epitaphs; and that, at each angle, there is a *candelabrum* exemplifying the use of 'funeral lights in Roman sepulchral monuments'[3].

In many cases a person founded a tomb *sibi et suis*, or *sibi et liberis suis posterisque suis*, or *libertis libertabus posterisque eorum*. This led to the formation of associations for sharing the different parts of a common tomb[4], and also of arrangements whereby a large rectangular chamber called a *columbarium* was built, partly above and partly below ground, with its inner walls filled with horizontal rows of niches, like pigeon-holes, for cinerary urns. There was space for as many as 3000 in the *columbarium* of the freedmen and slaves of Livia, wife of Augustus, which was in excellent preservation when it was discovered on the Via Appia in 1726[5]. In this *columbarium* each of the niches was under a small semicircular arch, and contained two urns (*ollae*) let into circular openings in the slab below the arch. There was a tablet above, recording the names of those to whom the niche was allotted, e.g.

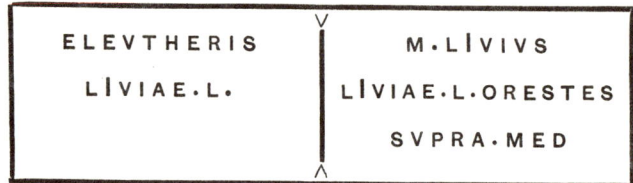

Fig. 24. Tablet in the columbarium of Livia. (Gori, p. 122, tab. LXXV.)

(*a*) *Liviae liberta*; (*b*) *Liviae libertus—supra medicos*.

[1] Dessau, ii 6067, 6070; cp. 6065f, and Hirschfeld, in *Philologus*, 1870, p. 64.
[2] *Tessaria frumentaria* in *British Museum Guide—Roman Life*, p. 10.
[3] See G. McN. Rushforth's article under the above title in *Journal of Roman Studies*, v (1915), 150—164.
[4] Cp. Wilmanns, 211.
[5] Described, with illustrations, by A. F. Gori, Florence, 1727.

IV] EPITAPHS 75

In the case of *columbaria* which belonged to an association, the total number of niches was sometimes equally divided by lot among all the partners, so that each was the proprietor of one niche in each division. Thus we have five inscriptions, relating to a freedman named P. Sontius Philostorgus, showing that, in a *columbarium* with five horizontal rows of thirty-six niches, he was the owner of niche no. 3 in row I; no. 14 in II; no. 13 in III; no. 36 in IV; and no. 23 in V. The niches, that he did not require for his own use, he could assign to his friends[1].

Among military epitaphs, special mention may here be made of those in honour of the *equites singulares Augusti*, who were instituted under Trajan, or, more probably, under Hadrian, as a troop connected with the auxiliary cavalry, but standing in a higher grade. They nearly always have the regular Italian three names. They appear to have been originally taken from the provinces on the Rhine or the Danube, and formed an imperial body-guard supplementary to the Praetorians who were mainly raised from Italy, Gaul, and Spain. They wore a helmet without any plume, and carried a sword and lance, and an oval shield[2]. The reliefs relating to them seem to show that they had slaves, and were therefore free themselves. They had a special cemetery near the third milestone on the Via Labicana. The following represents the tombstone of a Pannonian *eques singularis Augusti*, which was formerly in Rome, and is now in the British Museum. The reliefs are characteristic of the tombstones of *equites singulares Augusti*[3].

[1] Dessau, ii (2) 7892.
[2] Cp. *C. I. L.* vi 3214, 3290.
[3] Cp. A. H. Smith, *Catalogue of Sculptures in the British Museum*, III no. 2392; Daremberg-Saglio, s.v., fig. 2746–7; and Dessau, i 2199, *vir equum tenens*, and (for both reliefs) 2523 (figured in F. Hettner's *Röm. Steindenkmäler*, Trier, 1893, p. 133), also A. Müller, in *Philologus*, 40, p. 263.

Fig. 25. Tombstone of an eques singularis Augusti (in the British Museum, from a photograph by Messrs W. A. Mansell).

D M

T. Aurelio Saturnino, eq(uiti) sing(ulari) Aug(usti), tur(mae) Aeli Crispi, nat(ione) Pann(onio), vix(it) an(nis) XXX, mil(itavit) an(nis) XI, T. Flavius Marcellinus, signif(er), her(es), et T. Aur(elius) Secundinus, sec(undus) her(es) amic(o) optim(o) faciend(um) curaver(unt)[1].

The following is a military cenotaph of special interest:—

Fig. 26. Cenotaph of a Roman centurion in the Bonn Museum (reduced copy of L. Lindenschmit, *Alterthümer* (1858 f), pl. i 6, 5; cp. Baumeister's *Denkmäler*, fig. 2263).

On each side is a bust of one of his *liberti*, both named M. Caelius; and, below, is the inscription:—M. Caelio T. f(ilio), (tribu) Lem(onia), (domo) Bon(onia), o(ptioni)[2] leg(ionis) XIIX, ann(orum) LIII s(emissis); (ce)cidit bello Variano. Ossa (i)nferre licebit. P. Caelius T. f(ilius), (tribu) Lem(onia), frater fecit. *C. I. L.* xiii 8648; Dessau, i 2244.

[1] *C. I. L.* vi 3222; cp. A. H. Smith, *l.c.* III no. 2354; and, in general, *C. I. L.* vi 3173—3323, 31138 ff, 32783—32813: Dessau, i 2180—2212; and Pauly-Wissowa, vi (1) 312—322.

[2] Or *centurioni*, O or Θ standing for *centum* (Bücheler, *Rhein. Mus.* 1891, p. 239); p. 54 *supra*.

78 LATIN INSCRIPTIONS [CHAP.

Tombs of centurions were sometimes provided with portraits of the soldier commemorated, wearing his military decorations. Thus, the monument of M. Caelius, centurion (or deputy-centurion) of the 18th legion, who fell in the Varian war (9 A.D.)[1], shows him wearing a *corona civica* of oak-leaves, and a tunic and cuirass; on his shoulders are two medallions with lions' heads; on his breast, two *torques* and five *phălĕrae;* and, in his right hand, the *vitis* or vine staff, which is the emblem of his office.

Tombs were occasionally decorated with representations of the tools or instruments ordinarily used by the deceased in his daily duties. We have examples of these in the case of an architect, a bee-keeper, a butcher, a cutler[2], a shoemaker[3], a carpenter, an upholsterer, and a stone-mason[4]; and we have already noticed that carvers of inscriptions sometimes had the implements of their craft represented on their own monuments[5]. Such tools or instruments were generally carved on one of the ends of the tomb, leaving the large space in front free for the inscription. The tomb of a poetess is adorned with a lyre and a *cithara*, that of an officer of the corn-supply with a figure of the goddess Annona[6]; a representation of flowing water appears on the tomb of an engineer of the *Aqua Claudia*[7]; the prow of a ship of war recalls the *rostra* of an orator; and a *bisellium* (or 'seat of double width') the dignity of a *decurio* or of a *sevir Augustalis*. On Pompeian tombs, such a double seat, with one footstool, is accompanied by the inscription:—*Decurionum decreto et populi consensu biselli honor datus est*[8].

The above-mentioned representations of tools denoting the
sub ascia   former business of the deceased must not be con-
dedicavit   founded with the *ascia* or adze, frequently carved

[1] Fig. 26. Tacitus, *Ann.* i 60.
[2] Altmann, *l. c.* p. 173.
[3] C. Julius Helius; *ib.* p. 248; Mrs Strong's *Roman Sculpture*, opp. p. 362.
[4] Cp., in general, Daremberg et Saglio, s.v. *Sepulcrum*, p. 1237; also s.v. *Tignarius*, fig. 6989.
[5] p. 56, *supra*.
[6] Altmann, p. 243.
[7] *C. I. L.* vi 8495.
[8] Dessau, ii 6372 f; Mau's *Pompeii*, ed. Kelsey, fig. 232.

on tombstones in or near Lyons[1] from the middle of the first to a little later than the end of the third century. On these tombs the *ascia* may be seen, either incised or carved in relief. It is often placed between the two letters **D** and **M** (the ordinary abbreviation for *Dis Manibus*, Fig. 27), or above the beginning of the

Fig. 27. Altar-tomb in the Lyon Museum (from De Boissieu, *Inscriptions Antiques de Lyon*, p. 303).

D(is) *ascia* M(anibus) et memoriae aeternae L(ucii) Sabini Amandi veter(ani) leg(ionis) I Minervae (*sc*. Minervinae) Ianuarinia Verina coniunx et Sabin(us) Victor (fi)lius heredes p(onendum) c(uraverunt) et s(ub) a(scia) d(e)d(icaverunt). *C. I. L.* xiii 1885.

[1] A. de Boissieu, *Inscriptions Antiques de Lyon* (1846–54), *passim*, with discussion on pp. 103—113; cp. Allmer et Dissard, *Musée de Lyon* (*Inscriptions Antiques*, iii (1890) 148; Dessau, ii (2) 8141 n. 3. At Trier, the *ascia* is found on two tombs, (1) by itself, and (2) with a last, a hammer, and a file; Hettner's *Röm. Steindenkmäler*, pp. 88 f. See also Fig. 22, p. 70, *supra*.

80   LATIN INSCRIPTIONS   [CHAP.

inscription, and sometimes in a duplicated form; while, occasionally, it appears at the side or the end of the epitaph. The *ascia* may either appear alone, or it may be accompanied, in the latter part of the inscription, by a *formula*, such as *sub ascia dedicavit*, either in full or in some abbreviated form, such as S · A · D. Rarer varieties of this *formula* are *ab ascia fecit*[1], or *a solo et ab ascia fecit*[2], or *ad asciam* (or *ab ascia*) *dedicatum posuerunt*[3], or *consummatum hoc opus sub ascia est*[4], or *inscribendum et consummandum curaverunt et sub ascia dedicaverunt*[5]. Among the inscriptions of Lyons, so far as they are included in De Boissieu's important volume, about 150, or half of all the sepulchral monuments, have either the *formula*, or the *ascia*, or both, while there are 167 exhibiting the *ascia* in the thirteenth volume of the *Corpus Inscriptionum Latinarum* (nos. 1815—2332).

At Narbo, where most of the inscriptions belong to the early imperial age, the *ascia* and its *formula* are very rarely found; they have not been found in Aquitania, where the Celtic population appears to have been small; while, outside of Gaul, they have only been found in regions formerly inhabited by Celts, or in inscriptions in memory of persons who had possibly left Gaul and had died elsewhere[6].

The meaning of the symbol and the *formula* has been long debated. (1) In 1715 it was suggested that the symbol was a kind of talisman to preserve the tombs from violation[7]. This opinion is supported by Otto Hirschfeld, the

[1] *C. I. L.* vi (2) 8931.
[2] *C. I. L.* vi (2) 10921; Dessau, ii (2) 8090ᵇ; found on Via Labicana, two miles from Rome. See p. 81, n. 4.
[3] A · A · D · P · in *C. I. L.* xiii 5391 (near Besançon).
[4] *C. I. L.* xiii 2494; Dessau, ii (3) 9439.
[5] *C. I. L.* xii 2041 (Vienne).
[6] The *ascia* has been found in Spain, *C. I. L.* ii 1383, 4147, *Eph. Epigr.* ix 364; and the *formula* in Portugal, *C. I. L.* ii Suppl. 5144 (Dessau, ii (2) 8100), 'hoc misolio (=mausoleum) sub ascia est'; and near Rome, *C. I. L.* vi (2) 10921 (quoted on p. 81, n. 4); and both in Dalmatia, *C. I. L.* iii 1712, Caesonia Nardis—con(iugi) viva fecit ann(orum) XLV, et suis omnibus sub ascia dedicavit. There is an *ascia* between D and M in an epitaph from Colchester, now in the Fitzwilliam Museum (*C. I. L.* vii 92). It is figured in four Roman epitaphs, now in Baltimore (nos. 24, 72, 77, 84, in *A. J. P.* xxxi—xxxiii).
[7] Laisné, *Mém. de Trevoux*, Mai 1715, p. 772, and similarly Mabillon.

editor of the two volumes of the *Corpus Inscriptionum* in which by far the largest number of such inscriptions is recorded (XII and XIII). He holds that, in accordance with some very ancient Gallic custom, this symbol showed that the tombs were placed under divine protection, and that any who violated their sanctity would be visited by divine punishment[1].

(2) The prevalent opinion, however, is that the *ascia* and its *formula* implied the preparation of a perfectly new tomb, the solemn dedication of which was completed while the work was still in the hands of the stone-mason who first shaped out the block with his adze[2]. This opinion rests partly on the variety of the formula found in late examples near Rome:—*ab ascia fecit*[3], and *a solo et ab ascia fecit*[4]. It has also been surmised that the *ascia* and the *formula* may have been due to some local legal requirement involving the formal claim of a prescriptive or permanent right to a new tomb, and barring any counter-claim. It is, in any case, noteworthy that, of the 167 epitaphs of Lugudunum marked with the symbol of the *ascia*, *Dis Manibus* is followed in no less than 96 by the phrase *et memoriae aeternae*, in 17 by *et quieti aeternae*, and in 10 by *memoriae*, while there are isolated examples of *spei* (or *securitati*) *aeternae*, or *memoriae perenni*, or *securitati* (or *quieti*) *perpetuae*. Taking the first two groups alone, we have 123 epitaphs which include, with the symbol of the *ascia*, a phrase implying a desire to ensure a perpetually undisturbed possession of the tomb[5].

(3) It may here be suggested that the *ascia* and the corresponding *formula* characteristic of Celtic Gaul may be regarded as the local equivalent of the Roman *formula* :—*hoc monumentum heredem exterum non sequetur*. The object of the Roman *formula* (in all its varieties) was to prevent the tomb and its immediate site from passing (with the surrounding property) to any heir who was not a member of the family, and to ensure its being reserved in perpetuity for the deceased and his or her direct descendants. The same object was attained

[1] *C. I. L.* xiii p. 256. Cp. A. B. Cook, *Cretan Axe-cult outside Crete*, Congress of Religions, Oxford, 1908, ii 185 ff, discussed by the present writer in *Camb. Philol. Soc. Proc.* 22 Feb. 1917.

[2] Léon Renier (in Allmer et Dessard, *Musée de Lyon*, *Inscr. Ant.* iii (1890), 148; and Mau in Pauly-Wissowa, s.v.).

[3] *C. I. L.* vi (2) 8931 'D M | M. Aurelius Afrodisius Aug(usti) Lib(ertus) nomenclator se vivo ab ascia fecit monimentum muro cintum sibi et suis' etc. ending 'in agro p(edes)..., in f(ronte) p(edes)...'

[4] Ungrammatical inscr. from the Via Labicana, *C. I. L.* vi (2) 10921; Dessau ii (2) 8090ᵃ; hunc munimentum in fr(onte) p. xiii, in agro p. xvi a solo et ab ascia Aelia Isigenia Ti. Cl. Zenati memoriam marito suo dulcissimo et sibi libertis libertabusque suis posterisque eorum fecit.

[5] *C. I. L.* xiii nos. 1815– 2332. The above statistics do not include epitaphs containing the *formula sub ascia dedicavit*. Of the 150 epitaphs in De Boissieu's *Inscriptions* in which the *ascia* or the *formula* is found, 84 have *memoriae* (or *quieti*) *aeternae*. See also Allmer et Dissard, *l.c.*, iii 146 f, where *memoriae aeternae* is described as almost a 'local formula.'

S. L. I.

in Celtic Gaul by placing on the tombstone the *ascia* and the corresponding *formula*, which may have denoted that, from the time of the first hewing out of the stone, the monument was reserved for a definite person or persons. We sometimes find special mention of posterity [1]. The Celtic and the Roman *formulae* were thus two different ways of reserving a perpetual property in a sepulchral monument. The two *formulae*, here regarded as having the same purpose, are very seldom found on the same tombstone; but, in two late inscriptions near Rome, the *formula* of the *ascia* is found in combination with a statement of the dimensions of the ground reserved [2], and once, among the Ambarri, north of Lyons, in combination with the 'Roman formula' [3].

[1] *Sibi posterisque C. I. L.* xiii 1937, 2070; and note 4, p. 81, *supra*.
[2] *C. I. L.* vi (2) 8931, 10921, quoted p. 81, n. 3—4, *supra*.
[3] *C. I. L.* xiii 2494 (Dessau, ii (3) 9439), Epitaph of M. Rufius Catullus,... consummatum (?) hoc opus sub ascia est, haec o(pera?) sive l(ocus) h(eredem) n(on sequetur).

Cp. in general Saglio in Daremberg-Saglio; H. Leclercq in *Dictionnaire d'archéolcgie chrétienne*, s.v. *Ascia* (with four columns of bibliography); and Pigorini in Ruggiero, *Dizionario Epigrafico*, s.v.; also *Thesaurus linguae Latinae*, Olcott, *Thes. ling. Lat. epigraphicae*, and Mau, in Pauly-Wissowa, s.v. See also G. Boni in *Nuova Antologia*, 16 Apr. 1911, p. 21, quoted in G. Pascoli's *Inno a Roma*, p. 106, with cut on p. 15, Bologna, 1911.

CHAPTER V

(ii) DEDICATORY INSCRIPTIONS

DEDICATORY inscriptions (*tituli sacri*) are found on vases, altars, or temples, and on votive tablets or statues, belonging to or consecrated to the gods. The name of the god may be in the genitive, as in the black *paterae*, found in Etruria, inscribed in white letters with AECETIAI POCOLOM or VOLCANI POCOLOM or VESTAI POCOLO[1]. But it is more frequently in the dative, as in *Iovi optimo maximo* (I·O·M), *Genio populi Romani* (G·P·R), followed by verbal phrases such as *dono dedit* (D·D), or *votum solvit laetus libens merito* (V·S·L·L·M). Cp. Catullus, xxxvi 3 f, *sanctae Veneri Cupidinique vovit*, and Virgil, *Georg.* i 436, *votaque servati solvent in litore nautae*.

Among the earliest of such inscriptions are those from the sacred grove of Pisaurum, e.g. IVNONE·RE | MATRONA | PISAVRESE | DONO·DEDROT, i.e. Iunoni Reginae matronae Pisaurenses dono dederunt[2]. The dative after *vovit* may be either with or without the word *sacrum*, e.g. HERCOLEI | SACROM | M·MINVCI·C·F | DICTATOR | VOVIT, an inscription set up by the dictator of 537 A.V.C. (Dessau, i 11)[3]. *Sacrum* is usually combined with the dative, but we also find examples of the genitive, e.g. PIETATIS·SACRVM (*ib.* ii 3791). *Sacrum* is often abbreviated as S, SA, or SAC. The genitive with *ara* is a frequent formula, e.g. in the three altars from Antium, inscribed ARA NEPTVNI, ARA TRANQVILLITATIS, and ARA VENTORVM (*ib.* ii 3277 f).

[1] *C. I. L.* i² 2, 439—53; Ritschl, *Opusc.* iv Taf. ix; Dessau, ii 2957, 2969; C. Picard, *Mélanges de l'École Française de Rome*, 1910, 99—116; British Museum Guide (1912), p. 251.

[2] *C. I. L.* i² 2, 378; Facsimile in Ritschl, tab. xliii c, and Diehl, *Inscr. Lat.* 2 e; cp. *ib.* 2 a; Cagnat, ed. 4, pl. i 3; texts in Dessau, ii 2970—2983.

[3] *C. I. L.* i² 2, 607; Ritschl, *Opusc.* iv, taf. xv.

84   LATIN INSCRIPTIONS   [CHAP.

As an example of a dedicatory inscription in archaic Latin, we have the votive tablet of bronze recording the dedication of the twentieth part of certain spoils to Apollo:—

M. Mindios L. fi(lius) | P. Condetios Va(lesi)[1] fi(lius) | aidiles vicesma parti[2] | Apolones[3] dederi (=*dederunt*). *C. I. L.* i² 2, 37, Ritschl, *P. L. M. E.* tab. ii b; Ricci, tav. xiii; Dessau, ii 3216; Lindsay, p. 33.

The following is a facsimile of the votive inscription, in Saturnian lines, set up by L. Mummius, the conqueror of Corinth.

Fig. 28. Votive inscription of Mummius, conqueror of Corinth. 146 B.C. (reduced from lithograph in Ritschl's *Opuscula*, vol. iv, taf. iii).

L. Mummi L. f. cos.
Duct(u) | auspicio imperioque | eius Achaia capt(a),
Corinto | deleto Romam redieit | triumphans.
Ob hasce | res bene gestas quod | in bello voverat, |
hanc aedem et signu(m) | Herculis victoris |·
imperator dedicat

(*C. I. L.* i² 2, 626; Facsimile in Ritschl, tab. li A, and in Cagnat, pl. iii 4. Dessau, i 20; cp. Lindsay, p. 71 f; Ernout, p. 72 f.)

[1] = *Valeri.*   [2] = *vicesimam partem.*   [3] = *Apollinis*, cp. *decuma Herculis.*

As another example of a votive inscription in Saturnian lines, we have that set up at Sora by *M. et P. Vertuleii, Gaii filii*:—

M. P. Vertuleieis[1] C. f. |
Quod re sua di(f)eidens asper (*sic*) | afleicta
parens timens | heic vovit, voto hoc | solut(o,
de)cuma facta—poloucta[2] leibereis[1] lube|tes (*sic*)
donu danunt[3] | Hercolei maxsume | mereto.
Semol[4] te | orant se voti crebro | condemnes.

(*C. I. L.* i² 2, 1531 ; Ritschl, *P. L. M. E.* tab. lii *a*; *Opusc.* iv 130 f, Taf. v; Dessau, ii 3411; cp. Ernout, p. 70 f; Lindsay, p. 69 f.)

Many other votive inscriptions in iambic, dactylic, or elegiac verse, may be found in Bücheler's *Carmina Epigraphica*.

The next is a dedication in prose, (possibly) on the part of Juvenal, which was found near his birthplace, Aquinum :—

C(ere)ri sacrum | (D. Iu)nius Iuvenalis | (trib.) coh. (I) Delmatarum, | II(vir) quinq., flamen | divi Vespasiani, | vovit dedicav(itq)ue | sua pec(unia). (Dessau, i 2926; many other examples, *ib.* ii pp. 1—288.)

A further example may be taken from a bronze tablet, found on the Great St Bernard and now in the British Museum, in which the dedication to the Pennine Jupiter is represented by a series of dots punched into the plate, and forming the words *Poenino sacrum*, etc. (Hübner, *Ex.* 929).

Vows made by a person are often fulfilled by himself after his promotion, or, by his executors, after his death. Thus a vow made by an aedile is fulfilled by a duovir[5]. A freeman fulfils a vow which he had made as a slave, *ser(vus vovit), leiber sol(vit)*[6]. The *propylum* at Eleusis, vowed by Ap. Claudius Pulcher, as consul in 54 B.C., was begun by himself when he had been hailed as imperator in Cilicia, and was completed by his sister's husband and son. The proposed *propylum* is mentioned by Cicero, in his letters to Atticus (vi 1, 26 and 6, 2). The inscription runs as follows :—

(Ap. Claudi)us Ap. f(ilius) Pulche(r) propylum Cere(ri et Proserpi)nae cos (=consul) vovit, (im)perato(r coepit. Pulcher Clau)dius et Rex Mar(cius fec)erun(t ex testamento). (*C. I. L.* i² 2, 775, and iii 547, p. 100, with facsimile on both pages; Dessau, ii 4041.)

[1] An old nominative plural. [2] =*pollucta*. [3] =*dant*.
[4] =*simul*. [5] Dessau, ii 3312.
[6] *ib.* 3491.

The verbs used of the various acts of dedication and consecration are *dicare, dedicare,* and *consecrare,* e.g.

AARA | LEEGE·ALBANA·DICATA[1]

(where the double vowels suggest the seventh century of Rome). The other two verbs, common in inscriptions, are combined in the second fragment of Catullus, *hunc lucum tibi dedico consecroque, Priape.* The verbs, or verbal phrases, in ordinary use are *dedit* (D), *donum* or *dono dedit* (D·D), *dono dedit dedicavit* (D·D·D), *fecit* (F), *faciendum curavit* (F·C), *posuit* (P), *ex voto posuit* (EX·V·P).

On an altar discovered in 1566 at Narbonne in Provence we have a celebrated inscription of considerable length setting forth, in the age of the Antonines, a dedication to the *numen* of Augustus, the original date of which was the year 11 A.D. It describes the sacrifices annually offered to Augustus on the anniversary of his birthday, *qua die eum saeculi felicitas orbi terrarum rectorem edidit,* in accordance with the vow made by the people of Narbo:— *numini Augusti votum susceptum a plebe Narbonensium inperpetuom*[2].

In many cases the verb of dedication is not expressed, but is easily understood. Thus we have in Rome the following brief dedication to Neptune, incised on a small tablet of bronze, only two inches broad and one and a half high, which might easily have been suspended on the *paries sacer* of his temple, like the *votiva tabula,* which Horace declares he had dedicated to 'the god of the sea'[3].

Neptuno | ex voto | Cn. Domitius | Gelasus

(Hübner, *Ex.* 893; Dessau, i 893.)

The following is nominally a 'dedicatory' inscription, for it ends with a dedication to Vulcan; but it is also an 'honorary' inscription, in so far as the larger part of it consists of the recital of the public offices held by the dedicator. The person in question is a man of letters, who was a friend of the younger Pliny[4]. He was a secretary to Domitian (as well as to Nerva and Trajan),

---

[1] *C. I. L.* i[2], 2, 1439, Wilmanns, 101. Cp. p. 36 *supra.*
[2] Hübner's *Exempla,* 1099; Dessau, i 112.
[3] Horace, *Carm.* i 5, 13—16.
[4] *Epp.* i 17; v 8; viii 12.

but the name of the first emperor is here omitted; it was usually erased from public inscriptions after his death. The date is after 97 A.D., when the title of Germanicus (here mentioned) was conferred on Trajan.

> Cn. Octavius Titinius Capito, praef(ectus) cohortis, trib(unus) milit(um), donat(us) hasta pura, corona vallari, proc(urator) ab epistulis et a patrimonio, iterum ab epistulis divi Nervae, eodem auctore ex s(enatus) c(onsulto) praetoriis ornamentis, ab epistul(is) tertio imp(eratoris) Nervae Caesar(is) Traiani Aug(usti) Ger(manici), praef(ectus) vigilum, Volcano d(ono) d(edit). Dessau, i 1448.

Some twenty years later, in 118 A.D., under Hadrian, we have the following dedication to no less than nine divinities, inscribed by the *equites singulares Augusti*[1] on a marble altar found, with several others of the same type, on the site of their camp near the church of St John Lateran:—

> Iovi optimo maximo, Iunoni, Minervae, Herculi, Fortunae, Felicitati, Saluti, Fatis, Genio sing(ularium) Aug(usti), emeriti ex numero eod(em) missi honesta missione ab imp(eratore) Traiano Hadriano Aug(usto), ipso II co(n)s(ule), l(aeti) l(ibentes) m(eritis) v(ota) s(olverunt). Dessau, i 2180.

In many cases an inscription is placed on a dedicated object, stating the source from which it was derived, with the name of the dedicator, but without the name of any divinity to whom it is dedicated. Thus, on a bronze tablet found at Firmum, certain quaestors (who are named) make a gift from the proceeds of a fine, *aire moltaticod dederont* (*C. I. L.* i² 2, 383). M. Fulvius Nobilior, consul in 189 B.C., is described in two inscriptions, as having captured spoils (1) from Aetolia and (2) from Ambracia. Inscription (1) was probably set up in his native town, and (2) in a temple of the Muses in Rome: but in neither case is any divinity named[2]. Of two inscriptions relating to spoils brought back from Sicily by Marcellus in the Second Punic War, the first simply states that he captured the spoil in question at Henna, the other adds that he gave the spoil to the god of war (MARTEI— DEDIT)[3]. The source of the gift, as well as the name of the god, is mentioned by M. Furius, who, as a military tribune, makes a gift to Mars, or to Fortune, DE PRAIDAD = *de praeda*[4].

---

[1] p. 75 f *supra*.   [2] Wilmanns, 26, *C. I. L.* i² 2, 616 and 615.
[3] *C. I. L.* i² 2, 608—9; (*b*) in Ritschl, tab. 1A.
[4] *C. I. L.* i² 2, 49 and 48; Ritschl, tab. xlix B, C.

88   LATIN INSCRIPTIONS   [CHAP.

Similarly we have phrases denoting the cost, such as *de pecunia sua* (D·P·S), *ex reditu pecuniae, ex patrimonio suo*. The occasion is sometimes mentioned, e.g. *ex iussu* (EX·IV), or *iussu deorum, ex oraculo, ex visu, somnio admonitus, ex testamento* (EX·T); or the person, on whose behalf the dedication is made, as *pro filio, pro populo*; or the motive, as *pro salute* (PRO·S) *filiae suae, pro salute sua* (P·S·S) or *in honorem domus divinae* (IN·H·D·D). The site of a dedicated monument is often denoted by *loco dato decreto decurionum* (L·D·D·D), *loco* or *solo publico, loco dato publice, loco* or *solo privato* (with their respective abbreviations [1]).

The dedicatory inscription was, originally, placed on part of a temple, or on the base of a statue, and, so long as the inscription was in its original position, it was not necessary to specify the building or the statue. Nor was it necessary to name the altar on which the dedication was inscribed, but the altar is sometimes specified, e.g.

Iovi Optumo Maximo ex viso aram aedificavit P. Cornelius P(ublii) l(ibertus) Trupo[2]...

Similarly the dedication may specify the statue, or its base, or both, *basim donum dant*[3], or *signum basim*[4].

While the object dedicated may sometimes be specified, it is very rarely combined with a demonstrative pronoun, as *hoce seignum* on a bronze tablet from *Nemi*[5], and, in a dedication by Mummius, *hanc aedem et signu(m) Herculis Victoris imperator dedicat*[6]. This use of a demonstrative pronoun is sometimes regarded as an indication of a spurious inscription[7].

[1] Wilmanns, i p. 11 no. 50 n., and *Index*, ii 675–8.
[2] Dessau, ii 3005; cp. Wilmanns, 52, *aram d(e) s(uo) f(aciundam) c(uravit)*; also, of *sepulchral* altars, Orelli, 4521 f, 7357 f.
[3] *C. I. L.* ix 3910.
[4] *C. I. L.* i² 2, 1508.
[5] *C. I. L.* i² 2, 42; Dessau, ii 3234.
[6] Cp. Fig. 28 *supra*. Also, of an altar, Dessau, ii 4909, *hanc aram locumque*; and of a *sepulchral altar*, *H(aec) A(ra)? H(eredem) N(on) S(equitur)*, *ib.* ii 5208, cp. 1955.
[7] p. 204 *infra*.

For examples of dedicatory inscriptions, see Wilmanns, i 1—48, *tituli sacri*; Dessau, ii (1) pp. 1—288, *tituli sacri et sacerdotum*; and Richter, *Lateinische Sacralinschriften*, Bonn, 1906.

DEDICATORY

Dedications to Diana sometimes assume an almost poetical form :—

(1) Dianae deae nemorum comiti, victrici ferarum, annua vota dedi Fannius Iulianus praefectus cohortis II Sardorum. (In Mauretania, Dessau, ii 3257.)

(2) Umbrarum ac nemorum incolam, ferarum domitricem, Dianam deam virginem, Auxentius v(ir) c(larissimus), ubique pius, suo numini sedique restituit. (In Rome, *ib.* 3258.)

In Britain Silvanus, the god of the woodland, is gratefully thanked for the capture of a fine boar, which had long baffled pursuit:—

Silvano invicto sac(rum). C. Tetius Vetorius Micianus praef(ectus) alae Sebosianae ob aprum eximiae formae captum, quem multi antecessores eius praedari non potuerunt, v(oto) s(oluto) l(ibens) p(osuit). At Stanhope, near Lanchester, *ib.* 3562.

In making (or in restoring) a dedication to some divinity whose name was unknown, a vague formula was used, as in the celebrated 'altar to an unknown god' on the western slope of the Palatine.

Fig. 29. Dedication of an Altar to an unknown god, on the Palatine (from Ritschl, *P. L. M. E.*, tab. lvi E; cp. Dessau, ii 4015).

SEI · DEO · SEI · DEIVAE · SAC(RVM)
G · SEXTIVS · G · F · CALVINVS · PR(AETOR)
DE · SENATI · SENTENTIA
RESTITVIT [1]

Sei deus sei dea has been found at Tibur[2]; *si deo si deai*, at Lanuvium[3]; and *sive deo sive deae* in Rome[4]; while we read (of

[1] *C. I. L.* i² 2, 801. The use of G. twice (instead of C.) for *Gaius* is noteworthy. For a description of the altar cp. Middleton's *Ancient Rome*, i 173-5.
[2] Dessau, ii 4017.
[3] *Ib.* 4016.
[4] *Ib.* 4018.

the grove of dea Dia, in the *Acta fratrum Arvalium*), *sive deo sive deae in cuius tutela hic lucus locusque est*[1]. *De senati sententia* and *decurionum decreto* were among the common *formulae* for official sanction in Rome and in the Italian *municipia* respectively. The dedicator of this altar is probably the person mentioned by Cicero[2] as candidate for the praetorship in 100 B.C. He was apparently a son of the consul of 124.

Not a few names of foreign divinities, unknown in Latin literature, are solely preserved in inscriptions. Such was Iuppiter Dolichenus, a deity of Cappadocian origin, whose worship passed from port to port in the Mediterranean under the pervading influence of the soldiers of the Roman army. The name was originally connected, in some mysterious manner, with the discovery of iron mines, as implied in the following dedicatory inscription :—

Iovi optimo maximo Dolicheno ubi ferrum nascitur C. Sempronius Rectus centurio frumentarius d(ono) d(edit)[3].

Similarly, it is only through inscriptions that we know of the Celtic divinity, Camulus, who is identified with Mars, as is proved by inscriptions such as *Marti Camulo sacrum* at Cleves on the Rhine[4], and *Marti Camulo* in Glasgow[5]. The name survives in *Camulodunum*, the Latin equivalent for Colchester. Apollo Maponus, mentioned in an inscription at Hexham[6], made it possible to restore another inscription by reading *Deo san*(*cto*) (*A*)*pollini Mapon*(*o*), where the three letters *Map* are represented by a monogram alone[7]. Among other examples of the combination of Roman and Gallic names of divinities are dedications *Apollini Beleno*, *Marti Belatucardo*, and *Minervae Belisanae*. A Roman

[1] Dessau, ii 5047.
[2] *De Or.* ii 249; *Brutus*, 130.
[3] Dessau, ii 4302 ; cp. 4301, 4303—4324 ; also facsimile of inscribed relief in Marini, *Atti Arvali*, p. 539, and in Daremberg-Saglio, s.v. *Dolichenus deus Iupiter*, fig. 2489. The name is often abbreviated as I · O · M · D.
[4] Hübner's *Exempla*, 198.
[5] *C. I. L.* vii 1103.
[6] *Ib.* 1345 (Dessau, ii 4639, and *deo Mapono, ib.* 4640).
[7] *C. I. L.* vii 1345 n, where Hübner had previously read, *ib.* 218,...*Apollini et Matronis*. (The inscr. is in the third court of St John's College, Cambridge.)

V] DEDICATORY 91

soldier, who is a citizen of Reims (*civis Remus*), sets up a series of reliefs in honour of Arduinna and Camulus (who appear with the attributes of Diana and Mars respectively), and also in honour of Iuppiter, Mercurius, and Hercules[1]. There are many similar examples of the combination of Roman and of foreign names of divinities in the inscriptions of Africa, Germania, Gallia, Britannia, etc.[2] More than four hundred inscriptions attest the existence of certain 'mother-goddesses' of Celtic origin known as *Matres* or *Matronae*[3]. Similarly, it is to inscriptions that we owe practically all our knowledge of the widely extended worship of Mithras (especially as the *sol invictus Mithras*), which was introduced from the East by Roman merchants and Roman soldiers in the age of the Flavian emperors, and claimed a very large number of worshippers in the third century. In 307 A.D., at Carnuntum on the Danube, Roman emperors calling themselves *Iovii* (i.e. the 'Augusti' Diocletian, Galerius, and Licinius, and the absent 'Caesar', Maximin), or *Herculii* (i.e. the 'Augustus' Maximian, and the absent 'Caesar', the future emperor, Constantine) make a dedication to Mithras, as the protector of the empire:—

D(eo) S(oli) i(nvicto) M(ithrae), fautori imperii sui, Iovii et Herculii religiosissimi Augusti et Caesares sacrarium restituerunt[4].

On 27 October, 312 A.D., Constantine defeated Maxentius in the battle of the Pons Mulvius, to the north of Rome. Late in the same year, his restoration of the aqueduct of the *Aqua Virgo* is superintended by a *curator aquarum*, who describes himself as devoted to his numen[5]; and, at the close of the year, Constantine allows the Senate to dedicate to himself the small round temple which Maxentius had built on the Appian way in honour of his

[1] Dessau, ii (1) 4633.
[2] *Ib*. pp. 186—245.
[3] Cp. Ihm in *Bonner Jahrb.* 1887, 1—200; Haverfield in *Arch. Aeliana* 1892, 314 ff, *Romanization of...Britain*, ed. 1915, 71; and Daremberg-Saglio, s.v.
[4] *C. I. L.* iii 4413 (with Mommsen's note), and Dessau, i 659; cp. ii 4190—4250, also Cumont in Daremberg-Saglio, s.v. *Mithra*, with restoration of a *Mithraeum* at Carnuntum on p. 1950. The latest genuine Mithraic inscription belongs to 387 A.D.
[5] *D(evotus) N(umini) M(aiestati)Q(ue) eius* (Dessau, i 702). Cp. Victor, *Caesares*, 41.

son Romulus¹. In 315 he returns to Rome to celebrate the completion of the first ten years of his reign, and the 'Senate and People of Rome' hastily erect the 'Arch of Constantine', in the dedicatory inscription of which his victory over Maxentius is vaguely described as due to a 'divine inspiration', a phrase which may be interpreted either in a pagan or in a Christian sense². Meanwhile, on the coins of Constantine, his change of belief has left its trace in the fact that their dedication to Mars, or to the 'Genius of the Roman people', has already disappeared in 313, to be followed in 317 by the further disappearance of dedications to the Sun-god, such as *Soli invicto comiti*, or *Soli comiti Augustorum*³. Lastly, in 327, in the Edict of Hispellum, the emperor approves of the local *Aedes* or *Templum* of his own Flavian *gens*, with the proviso that that temple is not to be ' polluted by the frauds of any contagious superstition '⁴.

¹ Victor, *l. c.*, 40.
² *Instinctu divinitatis* (Dessau, i 694). Cp. De Rossi, *Bull. di Arch. Crist.* 1863, p. 58; and Boissier, *La Fin du Paganisme*, i 35 ff; also Lanciani, *Pagan and Christian Rome*, 20 f; p. 127 *infra*.
³ Schiller, *Gesch. der Kaiserzeit*, ii 207; Duruy, *Hist. des Romains*, vii 51.
⁴ Dessau, i 705; Mommsen, *Ges. Schriften*, viii 24 f.

CHAPTER VI

(iii) HONORARY INSCRIPTIONS

(A) ELOGIA

INTERMEDIATE between epitaphs on the one hand, and honorary inscriptions on the other, is a special variety of honorary inscription called an *elogium*. The etymology of the term has been much disputed. It has been proposed (1) to derive it from *eligere*, and to regard it as meaning a 'selection' or 'excerpt' from the family archives[1], or (2) to make it a parallel form to *eloquium*[2], or (3) to explain it (with its French derivative, *éloge*) as a Latin equivalent to the Greek εὐλογία[3], or (4) to the Greek ἐλεγεῖον[4], assuming that, originally, it was applied to an elegiac couplet. Cato the elder uses it of Greek epigrams in honour of Leonidas[5], and Suetonius of a dedicatory inscription[6]. It is mainly applied to a limited group of inscriptions, which originated in the epitaphs of the oldest family-sepulchres, and in the *tituli* attached to the *imagines maiorum* in the Roman *atrium*. The meaning 'epitaph' is found in Cicero, who uses it of the Saturnian line on A. Atilius Calatinus[7], of the Greek elegiac couplet on Solon[8], and of a sentence *in sepulcro rei publicae incisum*[9]; also in Suetonius, who

[1] Mommsen, *C. I. L.* i¹ p. 277. This is the derivation implied in *Corpus Gloss. Lat.* v p. 19, 11 (=p. 64, 11), *Elogia:* laudes electae summatimque collectae, ut puta si quis in basi statuae alicuius laudes scribat aut in titulo imaginis, elogia dicuntur.
[2] Düntzer, and Fick.   [3] Stowasser.
[4] G. Curtius, and Mommsen and Hülsen, *C. I. L.* i² p. 186.
[5] Apud Gellium iii 7, 19, 'propter eius virtutes omnis Graecia...decoravere monumentis, signis, statuis; elogiis, historiis aliisque rebus gratissimum id ejus factum habuere'.   [6] *Caligula*, 24.
[7] *De Sen.* 61; *De Fin.* ii 116; p. 5 f.   [8] *De Sen.* 73.   [9] *in Pisonem*, 72.

applies it to the verses carved by Augustus on the tomb of Drusus¹.

The earliest form of the Roman *elogium* was the *titulus* appended to the *imagines maiorum*. Suetonius mentions the family *imagines et elogia*². The *elogium* included the name, doubtless in the nominative, followed by the offices held and the triumphs won by the person commemorated. It thus corresponded to the form used in the earliest epitaphs, e.g. that on L. Scipio, consul in 259 B.C., *L. Cornelio L. f. Scipio aidiles cosol cesor* (Fig. 19, p. 67), and in some honorary inscriptions on statues, e.g. *L. Manlius L. f(ilius) Acidinus, triumvir Aquileiae coloniae deducendae* (consul 179 B.C.), and *M. Claudius M. f(ilius) Marcellus, consul iterum* (155 B.C.)³. From the end of the fifth century of Rome (or 254 B.C.) we have the addition of a poetical epigram celebrating the merits and the victories of the deceased, first in Saturnian lines (Figs. 18—21, pp. 66—69), and, later, in hexameters or elegiacs (p. 61).

The custom of setting up statues in honour of men of mark was of Greek origin, and, in some early Latin inscriptions on the pedestals of statues, the Greek custom of placing the name in the accusative and omitting the verb is retained, e.g. *Italicei L. Cornelium Sc(ip)i(one)m* (sc. *Asiagenum*) *honoris causa* (193 B.C.; in Sicily, *C. I. L.* i² 2, 612, Dessau, i 864).

Pliny, in his account of ancient statues in the Roman forum, states that the honour of a statue was usually paid to those who had been killed in violation of the law of nations (as in 230 B.C.) and that, according to the annals, such statues were three feet high⁴. He also states that all the statues of magistrates standing round the forum, except those which had been set up by decree of the people or of the Senate, were removed by the censors Publius Cornelius Scipio and Marcus Popilius⁵ (158 B.C.). Public places must have become overcrowded with statues. This overcrowding was due to the fact that, at an early date, the *imagines maiorum*, with their *tituli* or *elogia*, had found their way from

---
¹ *Claud.* 1, p. 13 *supra*.
² *Galba* 3, 'imagines et elogia universi generis exequi longum est'.
³ Wilmanns, 649—651.
⁴ xxxiv 24.   ⁵ *ib.* 30.

the *atrium* of the private house to the open spaces, and the public buildings, of the outer world. The first to adorn a public building with *clipei*, literally 'round shields' or portrait-medallions (including *tituli honorum*) of his ancestors, was Appius Claudius Caecus on the dedication of the temple of Bellona, which he had vowed during his second consulship in 296 B.C.[1]

The term *elogium* may fairly be applied to the earliest extant public inscription of an honorary type, written in prose, namely that on the *columna rostrata* in honour of C. Duilius, consul of 260 B.C., the victor of Mylae[2]. *Columna rostrata* This is only preserved in a copy discovered in the Forum in 1565, and ascribed, in its present state, to the early imperial age, and, in particular, to the time of Augustus or Claudius, in which archaic forms are inaccurately imitated[3]. See Fig. 30 (p. 96). The column, with its honorary inscription, was surmounted by a portrait-statue of the victor. This is implied by the use of *columnarum* of 'statues placed on lofty pedestals' in the context of Pliny's reference to this monument[4], and is actually mentioned in the fragments (discovered in 1890) of a briefer *elogium* in his honour[5].

The example set by Appius Claudius Caecus in 296 B.C. was followed by Marcus Aemilius Lepidus, consul in 78 B.C., who set up 'shields', or portrait-medallions, in the Basilica Aemilia[6] built by his ancestors. The *Arcus Fabianus*, built to celebrate the victory of Q. Fabius Maximus, consul of 121, over the Allobroges, was restored by his namesake, the curule aedile of 56 B.C.[7] It included statues, as well as 'shields' and emblems

[1] Pliny, xxxv 12, quoted on p. 10 *supra*.
[2] *Ib.* xxxiv 20; Quintilian, i 7, 12.
[3] 'Not before Claudius' is Ritschl's date, *Opusc.* iv 204—212. The inscription is also attacked by Mommsen, *C. I. L.* i¹ 37—40, and defended by Wölfflin, *S.-Ber. Akad.* Munich, 1890, 293—321. Cp. Allen, p. 67 f; and *C. I. L.* i² pp. 384—6; Lindsay, p. 45 f; Ernout, p. 109 f, and Tenny Frank, *Class. Phil.* 1919, pp. 74 ff; also Traexler's progr. Budweiss, 1899. Restoration of the *columna* (with its *rostra*, or metal prows of captured ships) in the Palazzo dei Conservatori, copied in Hülsen's *Forum*, p. 10, reproduced in Daremberg-Saglio, s.v. *Tropaeum*, fig. 7133.
[4] xxxiv 20 and 27. [5] Dessau, i 55, ...(*s*)*tatua q*(*uoque*).
[6] Pliny, xxxv 13. The medallions are visible on coins of 61 B.C., struck by his son, the triumvir. Cp. Daremberg-Saglio, s.v. *Clipei*, Fig. 1666.
[7] Cp. Cicero *in Vat.* 28; p. 122 *infra*; Mommsen, *Ges. Schr.* v 47—53.

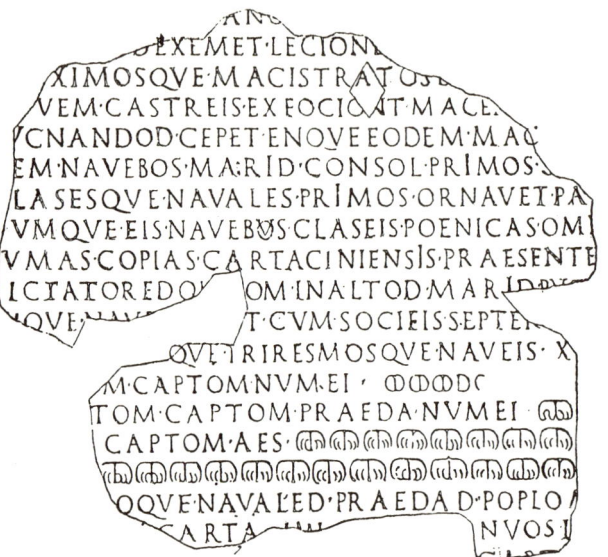

Fig. 30. From the Columna Rostrata (now in the Palazzo dei Conservatori on the Capitol) (Hübner's *Exempla*, no. 91), *c.* 1/11.

. . . . . [Secest]ano[sque . . . . op-]
[sidione]d exemet lecione[sque Cartaciniensis omnis]
[ma]ximosque macistr[a]tos l[uci palam post dies]
[no]vem castreis exfociont[1], Macel[amque opidom vi]
[p]ucnandod cepet. enque[2] eodem mac[istratud bene]
[r]em navebos marid consol primos c[eset copiasque]
[c]lasesque navales primos ornavet pa[ravetque],
[c]umque eis navebos claseis Poenicas omn[is, item ma-]
[x]umas copias Cartaciniensis praesente[d Hanibaled]
[d]ictatored ol[or]om[3] in altod marid pucn[andod vicet] |
[v]ique nave[is cepe]t cum socieis septer[esmom unam quin-]
[queresmos]que triresmosque naveis X[XX, merset XIII].
[auro]m captom : numei ↀↀↀDC[C]
[arcen]tom captom praeda numei ↈC[4]. . . . .
[omne] captom aes ↈↈↈↈↈↈↈↈ . . . .
. . . . ↈↈↈↈↈↈↈↈↈↈↈↈↈ . . . . . . [pri-]
[mos qu]oque navaled praedad poplom [donavet pri-]
[mosque] Cartacini[ens]is [ince]nuos d[uxit in]
[triumpod] . . . . . . eis . . . . . . capt . . . . . . (*C. I. L.* i^2 2, 25; Dessau, i 65).

[1] *effugiunt.* [2] *inque.* [3] *illorum.*

[4] ↈ = CCCIↃↃↃ = *centum milia*, p. 55 *supra*.

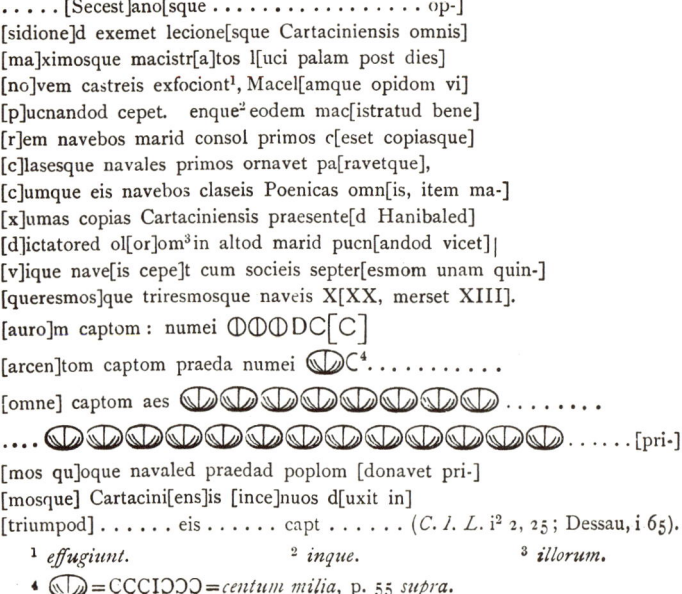

of victory¹. Among the inscriptions were two in honour of L. Aemilius Paullus, the conqueror of Macedonia, and his son, the younger Scipio. The inscriptions on these two were as follows:—

(*a*) L. Aem(il)ius L. f. Paullus | co(s. II) cens. augur, | tr(i)umphavit ter.
(*b*) P. Cornelius Paulli f. Scipio | Africanus, cos. II cens. | augur, triumphavit II (*C. I. L.* i² 2, 763, Dessau, i 43).

Paullus, consul in 182 and 168, and censor in 164, was thrice *imperator*, and is therefore wrongly credited with three triumphs instead of two, namely in Spain and over king Perses. He was also the father of Q. Fabius Maximus Aemilianus, consul of 145 B.C., and great-grandfather of the restorer of the Arcus Fabianus. The younger Scipio, a son of Paullus, was a brother of Q. Fabius Maximus Aemilianus, and is therefore counted among the ancestors of the restorer of the Arch.

The inscription on the vast rotunda at Gaeta which was once the tomb of L. Munatius Plancus (consul in 42 B.C.) is in the form of an *elogium*, beginning with the name in the nominative, and not including a single word directly suggestive of an epitaph².

The *imagines maiorum*, with their *tituli* and *elogia*, were the origin of two literary works, (1) the *Imagines* of Varro (39 B.C.), including portraits of 700 celebrities, with an epigram or *elogium* under each³; and (2) the *Imagines* of Cicero's correspondent, Pomponius Atticus. In the latter the portraits of the most distinguished statesmen and generals of Rome were placed above four or five lines of verse summing up their exploits and their public offices:—*facta magistratusque*⁴.

The term *elogium* is specially applied by scholars to certain laudatory inscriptions which are neither 'sepulchral' nor 'honorary', but are of a literary and historical type. The most important of these *elogia* were those on the famous generals, set up in the temple of Mars in the Forum of Augustus, to which reference is made by Suetonius⁵ and by Horace⁶. There was probably room

---

¹ Fabricius (*Roma*, 1500), 'scuta et signa victoriae'. Jordan in *Eph. Epigr.* iii 265, 290.   ² p. 69 *supra*.
³ It has been suggested that the epitaphs on Naevius, Plautus, and Pacuvius (quoted by Gellius, p. 14 *supra*) came from Varro's *Imagines*.
⁴ Nepos, *Atticus*, 18, 5 f.   ⁵ *Aug.* 31, quoted on p. 12, n. 10, *supra*.
⁶ *Carm.* iv 8, 13 f, p. 16 *supra*.

for statues of as many as thirty-six personages; but the names of only twenty have been in any way recorded:—

Aeneas, Lavinia, Silvius Aeneas, Romulus, M'. Valerius Maximus (dictator, 494 B.C.), M. Furius Camillus (military tribune, 401), L. Albinius (?), M. Valerius Corvus (consul, 348), L. Papirius Cursor (dictator, 325), Ap. Claudius Caecus (consul, 307), C. Duilius (260), Q. Fabius Maximus (233), L. Cornelius Scipio Asiaticus (190), L. Aemilius Paullus (182), Ti. Sempronius Gracchus (177), P. Scipio Aemilianus (147), Q. Caecilius Metellus Numidicus (109), C. Marius (107), L. Cornelius Sulla Felix (88), and L. Licinius Lucullus (74).

Of the bronze statues in each of the two porticoes not a single fragment has survived, but small portions of the *elogia* on Appius Claudius, Q. Fabius, and C. Marius have been discovered, from which it has been inferred that the name and official titles of each person were placed on the plinth of the statue, so far as there was room, while his exploits were reserved for a framed tablet on the broad pedestal below. Thus the few surviving fragments of the *elogium* of Appius Claudius, the full text of which has been preserved in a copy made at Arretium, show that the arrangement of the two parts of the inscription was as follows:

```
AP·CLAVDIVS·C·F·CAECVS
CENS·COS·BIS·DICTATOR
INTERREX·TER·PR·BIS
```

```
AED·CVR·II·Q·TR·MIL·III·COMPLVRA·OPPIDA
DE·SAMNITIBVS·CEPIT·SABINORVM·ET·TVSCORVM
EXERCITVM·FVDIT·PACEM·FIERI·CVM
PYRRHO·REGE·PROHIBVIT· IN· CENSVRA
VIAM·APPIAM·STRAVIT·ET·AQVAM·IN·VRBEM
ADDVXIT·AEDEM·BELLONAE·FECIT
```

Fig. 31. **Elogium of Appius Claudius Caecus**, censor 312 B.C., as arranged by Hülsen in *Mitt. Röm. Inst.* 1890, p. 312, and *C. I. L.* i² p. 188; cp. also Lanciani in *Bull. Comun.* 1889, pp. 73—79, and Bormann quoted *ib.* p. 481. The sixteen letters marked off in lines 1, 2, 3, 5, 6 of the lower inscription are all that survive of the Roman original.

The following is the arrangement of the above *elogium* in the copy formerly at Arretium, and now in the Florentine Museum.

(1) APPIVS·CLAVDIVS
C·F·CAECVS

CENSOR · COS · BIS · DICT · INTERREX · III   cens. 312, cos. 307, 296 B.C.
PR · II · AED · CVR · II · Q · TR · MIL · III · COM
PLVRA · OPPIDA · DE · SAMNITIBVS · CEPIT
SABINORVM · ET · TVSCORVM · EXERCI
TVM · FVDIT · PACEM · FIERI · CVM · TYRRHO   *sic pro Pyrrho*
REGE · PROHIBVIT · INCENSVRA · VIAM
APPIAM · STRAV·IT · EI AQVAM · IN   *sic pro et*
VRBEM · ADDVXIT · AEDEM · BELLONAE
FECIT

In lines 6—7, there are *apices* on *Sabínorum et Tuscórum*, and on *pácem*.

C. I. L. i² p. 192 (Dessau, i 54).

Of the *elogia* in the Forum of Augustus copies were made, on a smaller scale, in Rome itself. Such were the local reproductions of the *elogia* on M. Furius Camillus and L. Papirius Cursor[1]. Copies were also made for some of the Italian *municipia*. Among these the foremost place must be assigned to the seven from Arretium, namely those on M'. Valerius Maximus, Ap. Claudius Caecus, Q. Fabius Maximus, L. Aemilius Paullus, Ti. Sempronius Gracchus, C. Marius, and L. Licinius Lucullus[2]. In these copies ancient forms, such as *quei armatei*, and *apsens*, are modernised, and verbal statements, as to the number of times in which a particular office was held, are changed into numerical abbreviations (not to mention a few errors of transcription).

The *elogium* of Ap. Claudius Caecus has already been quoted from the Arretine copy. The literary and historic interest of these *elogia* is so great that five others are here added from the same source.

[1] C. I. L. i² p. 191 f, nos. vii, viii ; Dessau, i 52 f.
[2] Dessau, i 50, 54, 56—60.

(2) M¹·VALERIVS
VOLVSI·F
MAXIMVS
DICTATOR² · AVGVR PRIMVS³ · QVAM
VLLVM · MAGISTRATVM · GERERET
DICTATOR · DICTVS · EST · TRIVMPHAVIT
DE SABINIS · ET · MEDVLLINIS · PLEBEM
DE SACRO · MONTE · DEDVXIT · GRATIAM
CVM PATRIBVS · RECONCILIAVIT · FAE
NORE · GRAVI POPVLVM · SENATVS · HOC
EIVS · REI · AVCTORE · LIBERAVIT · SELLAE
CVRVLIS · LOCVS · IPSI · POSTERISQVE
ADMVRCIAE · SPECTANDI · CAVSSA · DATVS
EST · PRINCEPS · IN SENATVM · SEMEL
LECTVS · EST⁴

There are *apices* on *quám* (l. 4), *magistrátum* (5), *Medullinis* (7), *deduxit* (8), *senátus* (10), *liberávit* (11), and *léctus* (15).

C. I. L. i² p. 189 (v); Dessau, i 50.

The above is still at Arezzo; the following is now in the Florentine Museum.

(3)   q · f a b i u s
Q · F · MAXIMVS
DICTATOR · BIS · COS · V⁵ · CEN
SOR · INTERREX · II · AED · CVR
Q · II · TR · MIL · II · PONTIFEX · AVGVR
PRIMO · CONSVLATV · LIGVRES · SVBE
GIT · EX · IIS · TRIVMPHAVIT · TERTIO · ET
QVARTO · HANNIBALEM · COMPLVRI
BVS · VICTORIS · FEROCEM · SVBSEQVEN
DO · COERCVIT · DICTATOR · MAGISTRO
EQVITVM · MINVCIO · QVOIVS · POPV
LVS · IMPERIVM · CVM · DICTATORIS
IMPERIO · AEQVAVERAT · ET · EXERCITVI
PROFLIGATO · SVBVENIT · ET · EO · NOMI
NE · AB · EXERCITV · MINVCIANO · PA
TER · APPELLATVS · EST · CONSVL · QVIN
TVM · TARENTVM · CEPIT · TRIVMPHA
VIT · DVX · AETATIS · SVAE · CAVTISSI
MVS · ET · RE · MILITARIS · PERITISSIMVS   *sic pro rei*
HABITVS · EST · PRINCEPS · IN · SENATVM
DVOBVS · LVSTRIS⁶ · LECTVS · EST

Apices on *subsequendó* (l. 10), *profligáto*, *subvénit*, and *nómine* (14), *exercitú* (15), and *cépit* (17).   C. I. L. i² p. 193 (xiii); Dessau, i 56.

¹ *Manius.* M (Marcus) in MSS of Cicero, Livy, etc. Manius, the dictator of 494 B.C., who died in 463, had a brother, Marcus, consul in 505, who died at Lake Regillus in 496.   ² 494 B.C., cp. Livy ii 30, 4 f.   ³ sc. PRIVS.
⁴ Dessau, i 50; cp. esp. O. Hirschfeld, *Kleine Schriften*, 816—823, where Valerius Antias is conjectured to be the source of this *elogium*.
⁵ 233, 228, 215 f, 209 B.C.   ⁶ 209, 204 B.C.; Livy, xxvii 11, 12; xxix 37, 1.

VI] (A) ELOGIA 101

The antiquity of this *elogium* was doubted by Muratori and Maffei, but has been confirmed by a few fragments found in Rome. It will be observed that it does not (as implied by its impugners) profess to belong to the age immediately succeeding the death of Fabius in 204 B.C. It is at a later time (that of Augustus) that Fabius is here described as having been the most cautious commander of *his own* age. Sir John Hawkwood, the English *condottiere* (d. 1394), whose portrait was painted for the Cathedral of Florence by Paolo Uccelli in 1436, was described in the accompanying title in terms exactly identical with those of the above *elogium*, and it may well be doubted whether there was any one in the fifteenth century who was capable of forging the original[1].

IOANNES ACVTVS EQVES BRITANNICVS
DVX AETATIS SVAE CAVTISSIMVS
ET REI MILITARIS PERITISSIMVS
HABITVS EST

The three following are at Arezzo.

(4) L·AEMILIVS
L·F·PAVLLVS

COS·II[2]·CENS[3]·INTERREX·PR·AED
CVR·Q·TR·MIL·TERTIO·AVG
LIGVRIBVS·DOMITIS·PRIORE
CONSVLATV·TRIVMPHAVIT
ITERVM·COS·VT·CVM·REGE
*per*SE BELLVM·GERERET·AP
*sens f*ACTVS·EST·COPIAS REGIS
*decem dieb*VS·QVIBVS MAC*e*
*doniam atti*GIT DELEV*it*
*regemque cum liberi*S CEP*it*

8—9 *ap|sens* Bormann; *a p|opulo* Mommsen.

C. I. L. i² p. 194 (xv); Dessau, i 57.

---

[1] Zaccaria, *Istituzione antiquario-lapidaria* (1770), pp. 228—232. This *elogium* was also imitated by Francesco Barbaro (d. 1454) in the inscription on Donatello's equestrian statue of Gattamelata (d. 1443) at Padua (finished in 1453). Morcelli, i 265.
[2] 182, 168 B.C.
[3] 164 B.C.

(5)   C·MARIVS·C·F

CO͞S·VII·PR·TR·PL·¹Q·AVG·TR·MILITVM
EXTRA·SORTEM·BELLVM·CVM·IVGVRTA
REGE·NVMIDIAE·COS·GESSIT·EVM·CEPIT
ET·TRIVMPHANS·IN·SECVNDO·CONSVLATV
ANTE·CVRRV·A·SVVM·DVCI·IVSSIT
TERTIVM·COS·ABSENS·CREATVS·EST
IIII·COS·TEVTONORVM·EXERCITVM
DELEVIT·V̄·COS·CIMBROS·FVDIT·EX
IIS·ET·TEVTONIS·ITERVM·TRIVMPH*auit*
REM·PVB·TVRBATAM·SEDITIONIBVS·TR·PL
ET·PRAETOR·QVI·ARMATI·CAPITOLIVM
OCCVPAVERVNT·V̄Ī·COS·VINDICAVIT
POST·LXX·ANNVM·PATRIA·PER·ARMA
CIVILIA·EXPVLSVS·ARMIS·RESTITVTVS
V̄ĪĪ·COS·FACTVS·EST·DE·MANVBIIS
CIMBRIC·ET·TEVTON·AEDEM·HONORI
ET·VIRTVTI·VICTOR·FECIT·VESTE
TRIVMPHALI·CALCEIS·PATRICIIS
(IN SENATVM VENIT)

The Roman original had *apsens* (l. 7), *fugavit* (9), *ieis* (10), and *quei* (12).

C. I. L. i² p. 195 ; Dessau, i 59.

(6)   L·LICINIVS·L·F·
LVCVLLVS·
COS·PR·AED·CVR·Q·²
TR·MILITVM·AVG·

TRIVMPHAVIT·³ DE·REGE·PONTI·MITHRIDATE
ET·DE·REGE·ARMENIAE [E] TIGRANE MAGNIS·
VTRIVSQVE REGIS COPIIS·CONPLVRIBVS PRO
ELIS·TERRA·MARIQVE·SVPERATIS·CONLE
GAM·SVVM·PVLSVM·A·REGE·MITHRIDAT*e*
CVM·SE·IS·CALCHADONA·CONTVLISSET
OPSIDIONE·LIBERAVIT

C. I. L. i² p. 196 ; Dessau, i 60.

¹ consul 107, 104—100, 86 B.C.; praetor, 115 B.C.; tribunus plebis, 119 B.C.
² consul, 74 B.C., praetor, 77 B.C.; curule aedile, 79 B.C.; quaestor, 88 B.C.
³ 62 B.C.

VI]   (A) ELOGIA   103

Owing to the many points of similarity between the *elogia* of the Forum of Augustus, and the anonymous *liber de viris illustribus urbis Romae* (usually printed with the *Caesares* of Aurelius Victor), it was suggested by Borghesi in 1819[1] that the biographies in the *liber de viris illustribus* were ultimately derived from the *elogia*. But it has since been suggested that both had a common origin, and that the *elogia* were derived from the *Imagines* of Pomponius Atticus, which was also the ultimate source of forty-seven chapters of the *liber de viris illustribus*, while the other chapters may have been derived from the *Imagines* of Varro[2]. This view is open to the obvious objection that the work on the *viri illustres* is written in prose, whereas the literary portion of the *Imagines* of Varro and of Atticus was clearly written in verse.

The following three *elogia* form a separate group:—(1) refers to a politician and man of letters frequently mentioned by Cicero[3]. He was born about 120 B.C., was eminent as an orator and as a tragic poet, and was slain by the partisans of Marius in 90.

C. IVLIVS L. f. CAESAR STRABO,

aed. cur., q(uaestor), tr(ibunus) mil(itum) bis, xvir agr(is) dand(is) adtr(ibuendis) iud(icandis), pontif(ex)[4].

(2) The father of Augustus was commemorated as follows:

C · OCTAVIVS · C · F · C · N · C · PR(*onepos*),

Pater Augusti, tr(ibunus) mil(itum) bis, q(uaestor), aed(ilis) pl(ebis) cum C. Toranio, iudex quaestionum, pr(aetor)[5] pro cos., imperator appellatus ex provincia Macedonica[6].

(3) The *elogium* on Drusus, the celebrated tribune of 91 B.C., runs thus:

M · LIVIVS · M · F · C · N · DRVSVS PONTIFEX,

tr(ibunus) mil(itum), xvir stlit(ibus) iudic(andis), tr(ibunus) pl(ebis), xvir a(gris) d(andis) a(dtribuendis) lege sua, et eodem anno vvir a(gris) d(andis) a(dtribuendis) lege Saufe(i)a, in magistratu occisus est[7].

[1] *Œuvres*, iii 10.
[2] G. Schoene, *Die Elogien des Augustus-forum und der liber de viris illustribus urbis Romae*, Cilli, 1895. Cp. Schanz, *Röm. Litt.* IV i 64 f.
[3] *Brutus*, 177; *De Or.* iii 30.
[4] *C. I. L.* i² p. 198; Dessau, i 48.   [5] 61 B.C.
[6] *C. I. L.* i² p. 199; Dessau, i 47.
[7] *C. I. L.* i² p. 199; Dessau, i 49.

It has been suggested by Mommsen that the three *elogia* above mentioned came from a *sacrarium* of the Augustan house containing *imagines* of the emperor's ancestors and connexions.

Libraries were also adorned with portrait-busts, or other representations, of orators or men of letters. A small column found on the Palatine is inscribed with the following *elogium* on one who is described in the *liber de viris illustribus* (c. 5) as a *iuris fetialis inventor* :—'Fert(or) Erresius | rex Aequeicolus |. Is preimus | ius fetiale paravit; | inde p(opulus) R(omanus) discipleinam excepit'[1]. This *elogium* is in the archaistic style affected in early imperial times, and it may have belonged to the gallery of legislators and lawyers in the Palatine Library. The *elogium* on a portrait-bust was often simply the name of the person honoured, in the nominative case, with or without the age. Thus we have a bust of the first century, in Rome, inscribed QVINTVS HORTENSIVS; and another in Madrid bearing the inscription M·CICERO·AN·LXIIII; and a third in London, at Apsley House (ascribed to the third century), bearing the name of CICERO[2].

(B) OTHER HONORARY INSCRIPTIONS

Thus far, in our survey of 'honorary inscriptions', we have noticed that, on the pedestals of statues, the name of the person honoured may, in accordance with a Greek idiom, be put in the accusative case[3]. We have also noticed that, in a very few ancient Italian inscriptions[4], and in *elogia*, the name is in the nominative[5]. We now turn to the other 'honorary inscriptions', in which we shall find that the characteristic case is the dative of gift or of dedication, with or without the verb.

In Rome, to the north of the Capitoline hill, at the point where the Via Marforio meets the Via de' Corvi, we have a building resembling a temple, which is known as the Tomb of Bibulus. On its base is an honorary

The tomb of Bibulus

[1] Dessau, i 61.
[2] *C. I. L.* i² p. 202; Dessau, i 2915-8; Q·ENNIVS, iii (2) 9228.
See in general *C. I. L.* i² pp. 183—202, *Clarorum liberae reipublicae virorum elogia, edita a Th. Mommseno* (1863), *iterum recognovit Ch. Hülsen* (1893); also Pauly-Wissowa, s.v. *Elogium.*
[3] p. 94 *supra.*   [4] p. 94.   [5] p. 94.

VI] (B) OTHER HONORARY INSCRIPTIONS 105

inscription showing that it was granted to Bibulus by the senate and people, as a place of burial for himself and his posterity. Since the burying or burning of any corpse within the city walls was forbidden by the Twelve Tables, this tomb was doubtless just outside the Servian wall. Bibulus is here described as an *aedilis plebis*, and he may possibly be identical with a *tribunus plebis* of 209 B.C.[1]; but the lettering of the inscription suggests a century later.

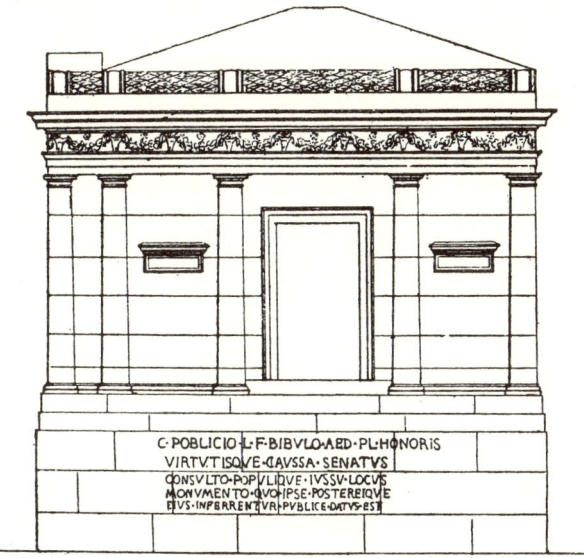

Fig. 32. The tomb of Bibulus, in Rome (after Canina, *Architettura Romana*, 1830–40, no. 212).

C. Poblicio L. f(ilio) Bibulo, aed(ili) pl(ebis), honoris | virtutisque caussa senatus | consulto populique iussu locus | monumento, quo ipse postereique | eius inferrentur, publice datus est (*C.I.L.* i² 2, 834; Wilmanns, 294; Dessau, i 862)[2].

The dative is also used in one of the earliest Italian inscriptions recording the setting up of a statue :—L · POPLILIO · C · F · |

[1] Livy, xxvii 20.
[2] See facsimile of inscription in Ritschl's *P. L. M. E.*, tab. lxxxiii A (with letterpress); and in Diehl's *Inscr. Lat.* 7a. In the original, the third letter of POBLICIO is more probably P (as read by Ritschl), than B, and the last letter of VIRTVTIS is very indistinct.

FLACCO | POPLICE · STATVTA¹. The form *poplice* probably did not last later than 104 B.C. This inscription was not found in Rome, but at Ferentinum. We have already seen that, in 158 B.C., all the statues round the Forum were removed by the censors, with the exception of those set up by decree of the people or of the Senate². At present hardly a single pedestal bearing an honorary inscription of the age of the Roman Republic has been found in Rome itself. We have a rare exception in the case of C. Vibius Pansa, the colleague of A. Hirtius as consul in 43 B.C. The honour paid to the former is inscribed in fine characters on a great block of travertine discovered in 1899 :—
*Ex s(enatus) c(onsulto) C. Vibio C. f(ilio) Pasae Caetronian(o) co(n)sul(i)*³.

From the age of Sulla onwards (80 B.C.), we frequently find the dative of dedication introduced into inscriptions of the honorary type, e.g. in four inscriptions in honour of Sulla himself, all beginning with the words L · CORNELIO · L · F · SVLLAE FELICI, with the title DICTATORI⁴, an office which he held in 79 B.C.; in one set up at Auximum in honour of Pompey in 52 B.C.,— (*Cn. P)ompeio, Cn. (filio, Ma)gno, imperatori, consuli ter(t.)*⁵, (*pa)trono, publice*⁶; in one in honour of Caesar at Bovianum during his life-time, 48 B.C. (*C. Iul)io Caesari, im(peratori), dictat(ori) iteru(m, pont)ufici max(umo, auguri, c)o(n)s(uli), patrono mu(nicipi), d(ecurionum) c(onsulto)*⁷; and in another in Rome dated after his death, *Divo Iulio iussu populi Romani statutum est lege Rufrena*⁸.

In the imperial age emperors and members of the imperial house often received the honour of a statue in Rome. The same honour was conferred on private persons with the emperor's consent. *Auctore M. Aurelio Antonino* is the phrase in several honorary inscriptions referring to statues set up in the Forum

---

¹ Ritschl, tab. lxxv *c*; Wilmanns, 655; *C. I. L.* i² 2, 1526.
² Pliny, xxxiv 30, p. 94 *supra*.
³ Livy, epit. Lib. 119; Bursian, *Jahresb.* vol. 144, p. 184; Dessau, iii (2) 8890.
⁴ *C. I. L.* i² 2, 721-4.   ⁵ Cp. p. 13 f *supra*.
⁶ Dessau, i 877; *C. I. L.* i² 2, 769.
⁷ Dessau, i 70; *C. I. L.* i² 2, 787.
⁸ Cp. Cicero, *ad Fam.* x 21, 4; Dessau, i 73; *C. I. L.* i² 2, 797; facsimile in Hübner's *Exempla*, 1.

of Trajan[1]. Honorary statues were also set up in private houses in Rome and in the provinces, and also publicly in the provinces[2].

In Spain the following inscription in honour of Scipio Africanus maior records the recovery and the restoration of Saguntum in 207 B.C.[3]; but it describes Scipio as consul, an office which he held for the first time two years later. It was once assigned to the end of the second century of our era, but it is probably not later than the time of Trajan. It seems to be a restoration in the imperial age of an honorary record of far earlier date.

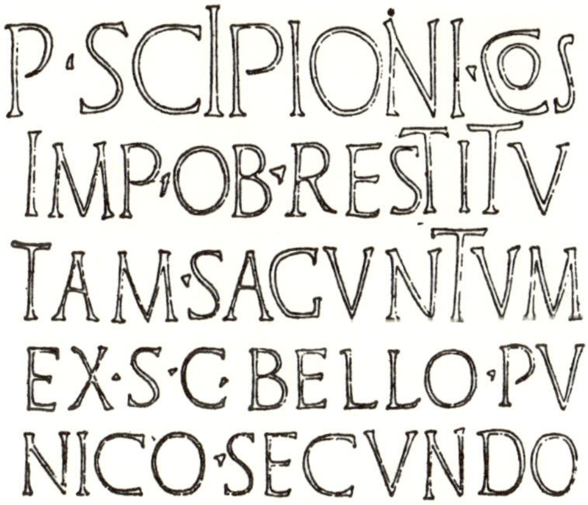

P·SCIPIONI·⊙S
IMP·OB·RESTITV
TAM·SAGVNTVM
EX·S·C·BELLO·PV
NICO·SECVNDO

Fig. 33. Honorary inscription recording the recovery of Saguntum by Scipio in 207 B.C. (Hübner's *Exempla*, no. 434), ⅛.

P. Scipioni consuli, imperatori, ob restitutam Saguntum ex senatus consulto bello Punico secundo. (Dessau, i 66.)

To the imperial age may also be assigned an inscription in memory of Marius, found near his birth-place:—*C. Mario C. f(ilio)* | *consuli* VII, *pr(aetori), trib(uno) pl(ebis)* | *q(uaestori), aug(uri), tr(ibuno) militum*[4], corresponding exactly with the name and titles

[1] Wilmanns, 636, 638—640.
[2] Pliny, xxxiv 17 (p. 10 *supra*); cp. Wilmanns, i p. 195.
[3] Livy, xxiv 42, 10; xxviii 39.
[4] *C. I. L.* x 5782.

in the *elogium* of the Forum of Augustus, except that the dative is here used instead of the nominative[1].

The first of the two inscriptions in honour of the great general Stilicho begins with the words, *Fl. Stilichoni inlustrissimo viro*, and the second ends as follows :—*populus Romanus pro singulari eius circa se amore adque providentia statuam ex aere argentoque in rostris ad memoriam gloriae sempiternae conlocandam decrevit, exequente Fl. Pisidio Romulo v. c. praef. urb.*[2] The fame of Stilicho was celebrated by the poet Claudian, and the following is the inscription placed on the pedestal of the statue of the poet in the Forum of Trajan. The genitive of the person whose statue was there placed fills the first line[3], and is followed by the usual dative of honorary dedication :—

[CL.] CLAUDIANI, V(IRI) C(LARISSIMI).

[Cla]udio Claudiano v. c., tri[bu]no et notario, inter ceteras [de]centes artes praegloriosissimo [po]etarum, licet ad memoriam sempiternam carmina ab eodem scripta sufficiant, adtamen testimonii gratia ob iudicii sui fidem, dd. nn[4]., Arcadius et Honorius, felicissimi ac doctissimi imperatores senatu petente statuam in foro divi Traiani erigi collocarique iusserunt.

EIN ENI BIPΓIΛIOIO NOON | KAI MOYCAN OMHPOY | KΛAYΔIANON PΩMH KAI | BACIΛHC EΘECAN[5]

Pedestals of a series of statues set up by Fabius Titianus, praefect of Rome, A.D. 350 f, and by other praefects, have been found in the Forum[6]. The most ancient of the formulae stating the authority for the erection of an honorary statue was *publice*, or *publice statuta*. At a later date we find formulae specifying the public body conferring the honour, the *civitas, respublica, colonia, municipium, pagus*, or the *cives, municipes, coloni, pagani*, or the *senatus populusque*[7], either in full or in the abbreviated form, S·P·Q. The following are also found, with their corre-

[1] p. 102 (5) *supra*.   [2] Wilmanns, 648 f; Dessau, i 1277 f.
[3] Cp. *Tatiani* and *Eusebii* in a separate line at the beginning of inscriptions on statues in Dessau, i 2942, 2946. It is generally a *cognomen* that is so placed (Wilmanns, 670 n).
[4] *domini nostri*.
[5] *C. I. L.* vi 1710; Wilmanns, 642; Dessau, i 2949; now in Naples; facsimile of part in Hübner's *Exempla*, 746.
[6] Bursian, *Jahresb.* vol. 144, p. 187.
[7] References in Wilmanns, *Indices*, pp. 700 f.

sponding abbreviations :—*ex senatus consulto* (E(X)·S·C), *publice decreto decurionum* (P·D·D), and, especially at the end, *decreto decurionum*, D·D, alone. Verbs such as *fecit, fecerunt* (F), *faciundum curaverunt* or *censuerunt* (F·C), *posuit, posuerunt* (P), *ponendum curavit* (P·C), or *dedit, dedicavit* are often included, but are still more frequently omitted[1]. The motive of an honorary inscription is often expressed by *honoris causa* (H·C). In Gallia Cisalpina we find *Genio*—H·C, and *Gen(io) et Hon(ori)*[2]. In and after the third century HONORI is sometimes placed in a separate line at the head of the inscription, followed, in the next line, by the ordinary dative of the person honoured[3]. We also find *virtutis ergo*[4], or *optime de republica merito*[5]; or *ob merita eius*[6], and, at the end, *statuam censuit ponendam*.

When the inscription is placed on the pedestal of a statue, the statue itself is seldom expressly mentioned[7], but, in later ages, this becomes more common, and the particular variety of statue is also specified, whether it is of marble, or of bronze, or gilded, or a *statua togata* or *loricata*, or *pedestris* or *equestris*[8]. Bassaeus, the *praefectus praetorio* under M. Aurelius, was honoured with three different kinds of statue, *aurata, civili amictu,* and *loricata*[9]. It is very rarely that the mention of the statue is accompanied by the demonstrative pronoun[10]. This is not the only example of undue emphasis that may be noticed in the inscription of 608 A.D. on the pedestal of the statue in the Forum, once the theme of Byron's apostrophe, 'thou nameless column with the buried base!', but now well known as the statue of Phocas dedicated by Smaragdus in the following terms:

hanc sta(tuam maiesta)tis eius auri splend(ore fulgen)tem huic sublimi colu(m)na(e ad) perennem ipsius gloriam imposuit ac dedicavit[11].

The compliment of a statue was often declined by the proposed recipient of the distinction. Such cases were so common

[1] Wilmanns, i p. 195 f.   [2] *Ib.* 239, 2181 f.
[3] Wilmanns, 669 n; Dessau, i 1214, 1220, 1243, ii 6696.
[4] *C. I. L.* xiv 2218.
[5] Dessau, i 1071.   [6] Wilmanns, *Indices*, p. 698.
[7] Wilmanns, 671 n.
[8] *ib.* i 299 n, and *Indices*, ii p. 668 *b*.   [9] *ib.* 638.
[10] p. 88 *supra*.
[11] *Childe Harold*, iv 110, 2; Wilmanns, 1100; Dessau, i 837.

that the refusal is not unfrequently expressed in various abbreviated forms, e.g. *honore accepto impensam remisit*[1], H·A·I·R[2], *honore contentus sua pecunia posuit*, H·C·S·P·P.

The *honores*, or 'public offices', held by a Roman are mentioned in sepulchral and dedicatory, as well as in honorary inscriptions. They might be added to his name in his epitaph[3], and also in his dedication of any object to a divinity[4]; but they are far more frequently found in those inscriptions which are distinctively known as 'honorary' (*tituli honorarii*).

Cursus honorum

The order in which public offices were held, the normal age for succeeding to them, and the intervals of time between them, were mainly determined by the *Lex Villia Annalis* of 180 B.C.[5] After ten years military service[6], from 17 to 27, the Roman might successively hold the quaestorship, curule aedileship, praetorship, and consulship; but, as the number of the praetorships was equal to that of the aedileships, he was allowed to pass straight from the quaestorship to one of the praetorships. There was also an interval of two years between the tenure of one office and the next. Before Sulla (80 B.C.), the earliest age for holding the consulship was, normally, about the fortieth year; but, after Sulla had raised the age for the quaestorship to the completion of the thirtieth year, the earliest age for the consulship was about the forty-third.

There was a group of twenty-six minor functionaries called the *vigintisex viri*. Under Augustus these were reduced to twenty, the *viginti viri*, including the *decemviri stlitibus iudicandis*, the *quattuorviri viarum curandarum*, the *triumviri capitales*, and the *triumviri monetales*, and one of these twenty minor offices had to be held before passing to any of the twenty quaestorships.

In the normal *cursus honorum* for the senatorial order a Roman might successively bear the following titles, (1) *viginti-*

---

[1] Wilmanns, 301, 2317.
[2] *ib.* 683, 1786, 2638. Cp. *Indices*, ii 674 *b*.
[3] p. 61 *supra*. [4] p. 86 f *supra*.
[5] Livy, xl 44, 1, 'quot annos nati quemque magistratum peterent caperentque.'
[6] Polybius, vi 19.

VI] (B) OTHER HONORARY INSCRIPTIONS 111

*vir*¹, (2) *quaestor*, (3) *tribunus plebis*², or *aedilis curulis*, or *aedilis plebis*², (4) *praetor*, (5) *consul*, (6) *censor*, (7) *dictator*. As the holder of a military or civil office, he might be (1) a military tribune, (2) the legate of a legion, (3) the legate of a proconsul, or of a propraetor, (4) the *curator alvei Tiberis et riparum et cloacarum urbis*, or *curator aquarum*, or *viarum* (*Aemiliae*, etc.), or *operum publicorum*, or *rei publicae*; (5) the *praefectus* (*a*) *aerarii militaris*, (*b*) *aerarii Saturni*; the *praefectus praetorio*, or *praefectus urbis Romae*; a *praeses provinciae*, or a *proconsul*. Among the religious offices held by the senatorial order, were those of *augur, flamen, frater arvalis, lupercus, pontifex, quindecimvir sacris faciundis, salius, septemvir epulonum*, and *sodalis Augustalis*, etc. The *virgines Vestales* were limited to senatorial families.

In the *cursus honorum* of the equestrian order, down to the time of Diocletian (284—305), the *eques* might successively bear the following titles:—(1) in the preliminary grades of office, he might be a *praefectus fabrum*; a *tribunus*, or a *praefectus, cohortis*; a *tribunus militum*, or *legionis*; a *praefectus equitum*. He might become (2) a *procurator provinciae*, or one of some 37 other *procuratores*³; (3) a *praefectus provinciae*, a *praefectus consularis*, a *praefectus classis, praefectus praetorio*, or *praefectus Aegypti*. As holder of a religious office, he might be a *tubicen* or a *sacerdos*. As holder of an office of special character, he might be a *procurator portorii*, or a *curator viarum*.

Under the Republic, honorary inscriptions in the dative case were only accompanied by the mention of the public offices held at the time when the honour was conferred⁴. Fuller and more elaborate forms came into use in the Augustan age. One of the earliest extant inscriptions, in which all the offices held are mentioned in the chronological order of their tenure, is an Augustan inscription in honour of L. Aquillius Florus⁵. His offices are

---

¹ Usually expressed by the specific title of the office held, *decemvir...*, *quattuorvir...*, or *triumvir....*
² Open to plebeians only. For patricians the normal order was *quaestor, praetor, consul*.
³ Ricci, p. 138 f; or, more fully, Cagnat, pp. 123–5.
⁴ Cp. pp. 104–6 *supra*.
⁵ *C. I. L.* iii 551; Wilmanns, 1122; Dessau, i 928.

named in the following order:—(1) *decemvir stlitibus iudicandis*; (2) *tribunus militum legionis nonae*...; (3) *quaestor imperatoris Caesaris Augusti*; (4) *proquaestor provinciae Cypri*; (5) *tribunus plebis*; (6) *praetor*; (7) *proconsul Achaiae*.

The *honores* may either be stated (as above) in the *direct* order, or in the *reverse* order. The *direct* order implies that the successive offices are named in the order of appointment; the *reverse* implies beginning with the highest, and ending with the lowest. The different methods of statement attracted the notice of scholars at an early date[1]; but they were first discussed fully by Borghesi in his memoir on the following inscription in the Naples Museum relating to the consul L. Burbuleius[2].

L·BVRBVLEIO·L·F·QVIR
OPTATO · LIGARIANO
COS·SODAL·AVG·LEG·IMPERAT
ANTONINI·AVG·PII·PRO·PR·PROV
SYRIAE IN QVO HONOR·DECESSIT·LEG·
EIVSDEM·ET·DIVI·HADRIANI·PRO·PR·PROV
CAPPAD·CVR·OPER·LOCOR·Q·PVBL·PRAEF·
AERAR·SATVRN·PRO·COS·SICIL·LOGISTE·
SYRIAE·LEGAT·LEG·XVI·FL·FIRM·CVR·REI·P·
NARBON·ITEM·ANCONITANOR·ITEM·
TARRICIN·CVRAT·VIAR·CLODIAE·CASSIAE
CIMINAE·PR·AED·PL·Q·PONTI·ET·BITHYN·
TRIB·LATICL·LEG·IX·HISPAN·III·VIR·KAPIT
PATR·COL
RASINIA·PIETAS·NVTR·FILIAR·EIVS
S·P·P·L·D·D·D[3]

C. I. L. x 6006; Dessau, i 1066.

Here the order in which the offices were severally held was (1) *triumvir capitalis*; (2) *tribunus legionis IX*; (3) *quaestor Ponti et Bithyniae* (after 117 A.D.); (4) *aedilis plebis*; (5) *praetor*;

[1] Morcelli (1781), *De Stylo Inscr. Lat.* ii 51, 2nd ed. (1820); Marini (1795) *Atti Arvali,* p. 754.
[2] 1838; *Œuvres,* iv 103—178.
[3] *sua pecunia posuit loco dato decreto decurionum.*

(6) *curator viarum*......; (7) *curator rei publicae Narbonensis*, etc.; (8) *legatus legionis XVI*; (9) *logistes Syriae*; (10) *proconsul Siciliae*; (11) *praefectus aerarii Saturni*; (12) *CONSUL c.* 131; (13) *curator operum locorumque publicorum*; (14) *legatus propraetore Cappadociae, c.* 138 A.D.; (15) *legatus propraetore Syriae, in quo honore decessit.*

(10) the office of *proconsul Siciliae* is here exceptionally held before the consulship, but the holder was eligible to a proconsulship as an *ex-praetor* (5).

(11) the office of *praefectus aerarii Saturni* was also given to *ex-praetors*; never to *ex-consuls*; it was often held immediately before the consulship.

(12) it will be observed that the title of *consul* is not mentioned in the body of the inscription, but is placed at the head, and that it is there immediately followed by a priestly office, that of *sodalis Augusti*. Owing to the position in which the consulship is placed, the inscription does not help us to determine the date of that office in relation to the rest.

(13) the office of *curator operum publicorum* was given to *ex-praetors* of long standing, or to recent *ex-consuls*; there is no indication whether Burbuleius held it before or after his consulship.

If the person honoured has held or is holding the office of *consul*, this office is almost always mentioned first, and is followed by the other offices, either in the *direct* or the *reverse* order. The various *sacerdotia* are generally kept in a separate group, either before or after the other offices [1]. If all the offices are mentioned in a double series of (1) *honores ordinarii*, (2) *honores extraordinarii*, or (1) *magistratus publici*, (2) *magistratus municipales*, the *sacerdotia publica* are placed, in either case, in a separate group, between (1) and (2)[2].

Among exceptions to the rule of naming the office of *consul* at the head of the list, the following inscriptions may be mentioned, beginning (1) with the nominative: M. Licinius Crassus Frugi, described first as *pontifex* and *praetor urbanus* (24 A.D.), and next as *consul* (27 A.D.)[3]; (2) with the dative, Ti. Plautio Silvano, named first as holding two priestly offices, and five other offices, and next as *consul* (*suffectus* of 45 A.D.)[4]; (3) also with

[1] Cp. Cagnat[4], 89, 97.
[2] Wilmanns, i p. 360.
[3] Dessau, i 954, probably an *elogium* on his tomb, on the Via Salaria.
[4] *Ib.* 986, honorary inscr. near Tibur.

dative, C. Calpetano Rantio, named first as holding nine offices (one of which is priestly), and next as *consul* (*suffectus* of 71 A.D.)[1]. The two orders of stating the sequence of the *cursus honorum* are well illustrated by two inscriptions on the same person, found (*a*) at Cirta (or *Constantine*), (*b*) at Thamugadi (or *Timgad*) in the Roman province of Africa. In (*a*) we have the *direct* order, and in (*b*) the *reverse*; in both, the consulship is mentioned first. This consulship belongs to the reign of Alexander Severus.

(*a*) P(ublio) Iulio Iuniano Martialiano, c(larissimo) v(iro),
consuli, quaest(ori) provinciae Asiae, trib(uno) plebei, praetori, [2]curatori civitatis Calenorum[2], curatori [3]viarum Clodiae Cassiae et Ciminiae[3], praefecto aerari militaris, proconsuli provinciae Macedoniae, legato [4]leg(ionis) I I I Aug(ustae) Severianae Alexandrianae[4],
praesidi et patrono, res publica Cirtensium decreto ordinis dedit dedicavitque.

(*b*) P(ublio) Iulio Iuniano Martialiano, c(larissimo) v(iro),
consuli, leg(ato) Aug(usti)[5] [6]pr(o) pr(aetore) provinciae Numidiae[6], proconsuli provinciae Macedoniae, praef(ecto) aerari militaris, curatori viae Clodiae, praetori, tribuno plebei, quaestori provinciae Asiae,
patrono coloniae et municipi, respublica coloniae Thamugadensium decreto decurionum[7].

The following inscription of 105 A.D. found at Aquileia is an example of the military and civil career of an *eques Romanus*. It is here printed without abbreviations, it is also broken into paragraphs, to show the various groups of the offices held in *ascending order* :—

C. MINICIO C. FILIO VELINA ITALO,

quattuorviro iure dicundo ;
praefecto cohortis V Gallorum equitatae, praefecto cohortis I Breucorum equitatae civium Romanorum, praefecto cohortis II Varcianorum equitatae, tribuno militum legionis VI Victricis, praefecto equitum alae I singularium civium Romanorum, donis donato a divo Vespasiano corona aurea, hasta pura ;

---

[1] Dessau, i 989, honorary inscr. by the *plebs urbana* of Tergeste (*Triest*).
[2] Omitted in (*b*).
[3] *Viae Clodiae* in (*b*).   [4] Partly erased.
[5] Partly erased.
[6-6] Omitted in (*a*). Martialianus is called in (*a*) *legatus legionis tertiae Augustae*, and in (*b*) *legatus—Numidiae*.
[7] Wilmanns, 1214 f; Dessau, i 1177 f.

VI] CURSUS HONORUM 115

procuratori provinciae Hellesponti, procuratori provinciae Asiae quam mandatu principis[1] vice defuncti proconsulis[2] rexit, procuratori provinciarum Luguduniensis et Aquitanicae, item Lactorae[3];
praefecto annonae, praefecto Aegypti; flamini divi Claudii;
DECRETO DECVRIONVM[4].

In the mutilated portions of another side of the pedestal the person honoured is described as serving his country (*per summos honor*)*es equestris dignitatis*. From the minor municipal office of *quattuorvir iure dicundo* he rose to various positions as a military *praefectus* and a civil *procurator*, and was ultimately *praefectus annonae* and *praefectus Aegypti*, these last being among the highest offices open to the equestrian order. He is also named at the end of the inscription as the holder of a priestly office, that of *Flamen divi Claudii*.

The highest office that could be held by an *eques* was that of *praefectus praetorio*. Among those who attained that distinction was M. Bassaeus Rufus, whose honours are enumerated as follows in *descending* order, beginning with the highest and ending with the lowest:—

praefecto praetorio M. Aureli Antonini—, consularibus ornamentis honorato et—corona murali, vallari aurea, hastis puris—donato; praefecto Aegypti, praefecto (annonae?);
procuratori a rationibus, procuratori Belgicae et duarum Germaniarum, procuratori regni Norici, procuratori Asturiae et Calleciae;
tribuno cohortis—praetoriae, tribuno cohortis X urbanae, tribuno cohortis V vigulum, primipilo bis.

About 180 A.D., with the sanction of the emperors M. Aurelius and Commodus, three statues were set up by the Senate in his honour, a *statua aurata* in the Forum of Trajan, and two others in appropriate temples, one of them *civili amictu*, and the other *loricata*[5]. An inscription of 377 A.D. in honour of a *praefectus urbi*, Symmachus, father of the famous orator, mentions an *auro*

[1] Trajan.
[2] Civica Cerealis, slain by Domitian, 88 A.D.
[3] *Lectoure*, N.E. of Aquitania.
[4] Wilmanns, 691; Dessau, i 1374.
[5] Dessau, i 1326. Cp. 1327, where the honours of L. Iulius Iulianus, *praefectus praetorio* under Commodus (and slain by that emperor), are similarly described in descending order.

8—2

inlustrem statuam, which was to be set up in Rome, as well as in Constantinople, *adposita oratione, quae meritorum eius ordinem ac seriem contineret*[1].

The terms of the *titulus honorarius* were sometimes left to be settled by the recipient of the honour. Thus, on the left side of a pedestal found at Fossombrone (*Forum Sempronii*), an *eques*, C. Hedius Verus, is described as having declined the honour of a statue; nevertheless, the municipal *duumviri* and *decuriones* once more decreed the statue, ordered it to be executed, and brought it to Verus with the appeal:—*quod superest, voluntati nostrae consule, et qualem inscriptionem dandam putas facito notum.* The inscription suggested by the recipient appears in front of the pedestal, describing his military career as *praefectus equitum* and *tribunus militum*, and his municipal career as *duumvir* in two towns, as *quaestor* and *flamen* in one, and as *aedilis* and *pontifex* in the other, and as *patronus* of both[2]. In another case, the recipient of a compliment at Cales, in Campania, is permitted to 'amplify' the inscription in his honour, *inscriptionem basis suae— ampliare*[3].

After the time of Caracalla, the office of *tribunus militum* was no longer a necessary preliminary to that of *quaestor*. Under Alexander Severus, the *vigintiviri* dropped out of the list of *honores*, and the offices of tribune and aedile were seldom filled. Under Gallienus, senators were excluded from the army; the equestrian order acquired a new importance by succeeding to all the military functions of the *legati legionum* and the *legati pro praetore*, while the senatorial order became a class of honorary officials. The praetorship became the first effective office. The quaestorship had already fallen into abeyance, and access to the senatorial order had been already obtained by becoming *adlectus inter quaestorios*. From the middle of the third century the same access was obtained by becoming *adlectus inter consulares*, a privilege which was now constantly granted to persons who had never held the consulship. Under Constantine, the senatorial order flourished anew, and members of that order were promoted to three successive classes distinguished by the following titles:

[1] Wilmanns, 641; Dessau, i 1257.
[2] Wilmanns, 694.   [3] *ib.* 695.

VI] CURSUS HONORUM 117

(1) *clarissimi* (C): (2) *clarissimi et spectabiles* (C·ET·S, or SP); and (3) *clarissimi et inlustres* (C·ET·I, or IN, or INL). Stilicho, the general of Honorius, in the honorary inscription already quoted[1], is described as *inlustrissimo viro*. His distinctions are mainly military, and are recited in rhetorical language characteristic of the age, without any distinct enumeration of the historical sequence of his *honores*.

The careers of persons below the senatorial and equestrian orders are set forth according to the same general rules. Such persons filled the subordinate places in the public administration, and served as soldiers or subalterns in the army. They also held office in the various *municipia* and *collegia*. The list of their *honores* is often reserved for their epitaphs. Thus, at Genava (*Geneva*), a centurion named M. Carantius Macrinus gives directions by his will for an epitaph, in which (as in the case of consuls) his highest office, that of *centurio*, is mentioned first, followed by his other military distinctions in the ascending order of definite dates in the imperial reigns, corresponding to the years 73 to 90 A.D.[2] Honour is elsewhere paid to a member of a *collegium* of 'fishermen and divers', named Fl. Annius Annaeus Fortunatus, as *quinquennali perpetuo—honoribus omnibus per gradus functo*[3]. Thus, even in the *municipia* and the *collegia*, the order of the enumeration of *honores* is modelled on that prescribed for the highest officials of the Roman state[4].

For Honorary Inscriptions see Wilmanns, nos. 609—696, and Dessau, i pp. 1—324, *passim*, esp. among the *tituli* (1) *imperatorum*, (2) *ordinis senatorii*, and (3) *virorum dignitatis equestris*; also iii (2) pp. xiv—xlvii.

[1] p. 108, *supra*.
[2] Dessau, i 2118; Cagnat, p. 138[4].
[3] *C. I. L.* vi 29700; Wilmanns, 1737; Cagnat, p. 154[4], n. 2.
[4] On the *cursus honorum*, see also *Appendix II*, pp. 222 ff *infra*.

CHAPTER VII

(iv) INSCRIPTIONS ON PUBLIC WORKS

Inscriptions on public works

INSCRIPTIONS on public buildings, including temples, theatres, gates and towers and walls, bridges, arches, columns, and aqueducts (*tituli operum publicorum*), are of the same general type as the most ancient honorary inscriptions. In the case of temples, the earliest dated Roman example commemorates a stage in the restoration of the temple of Iuppiter Capitolinus (in 78–60 B.C.):—*Q. Lutatius Q. f(ilius), Q. (nepos) Catulus cos.* (78) | *substructionem et tabularium* | *de s(enatus) s(ententia) faciundum coeravit* | *(ei)demque pro(bavit)*[1]. The municipal inscriptions earlier than the age of Sulla (80 B.C.) are of the same general type, e.g. on the temple of Castor and Pollux at Cora,...*Aedem Castoris Pollucis de s(enatus) s(ententia) faciendam pequn(ia) sac(ra) coeravere...*, ending *d(e) s(enatus) s(ententia) prob(arunt) (d)edicar(unt)q(ue)*[2]; on that of Hercules, at the same place,...*de senatus sententia aedem faciendam coeraverunt eisdemque probavere*[3]; on a temple of Bona Dea near Corfinium :—*pagi decreto faciendu(m) curarunt probaruntq(ue)*[4]; and, lastly, on the substructure of an ancient fort at Ferentinum,...*fundamenta murosque af solo faciunda coeravere eidemque probavere*[5]. Similarly, an inscription from the western gate of Aeclanum records the names of the persons, who built the gates and towers and walls : *d(e) s(enatus) s(ententia) portas turreis moiros turreisque aequas qum moiro faciundum coiraverunt*[6].

Temples

---

[1] Wilmanns, 700; Dessau, i 35 (now lost); cp. 35 a, and Ritschl, *P.L.M.E.* lxix C; *C. I. L.* i² 2, 737.
[2] Ritschl, lxviii A; Wilmanns, 722 ; *C. I. L.* i² 2, 1506.
[3] Ritschl, lxviii C; Wilmanns, 723; *C. I. L.* i² 2, 1511.
[4] Ritschl, lxiv J; Wilmanns, 703; *C. I. L.* i² 2, 1793.
[5] Ritschl, lxvii C, lxviii D ; Wilmanns, 708; Dessau, ii 5342 ff; *C. I. L.* i² 2, 1522–3.
[6] Ritschl, lxx C; Wilmanns, 699; Dessau, ii 5318; *C. I. L.* i² 2, 1722.

CHAP. VII] ON PUBLIC WORKS. BRIDGES 119

Agrippa dedicated his Pantheon in 27 B.C. in the following
terms :—*M. Agrippa L. f(ilius) cos. tertium fecit*[1]. *Fecit*, a characteristic verb relating to the building of a tomb, was also commonly
applied to public buildings erected by private persons, such as
Pompey's theatre. In the *monumentum Ancyranum*
Augustus applies the term *feci* to his dedication   Theatres
of the theatre of Marcellus, and *refeci* to his restoration of the
theatre of Pompey[2]. Of the 'smaller theatre' at Pompeii it
is stated that the *duumviri* '*theatrum tectum fac(iendum) locar(unt)
eidemq(ue) prob(arunt)*'[3]; and, of certain baths and other buildings,
that the same officials *faciun(da) coerarunt eidemque probaru(nt)*[4].
Phrases such as *faciendum curavit idemque probavit* are often
abbreviated (F·C·I·Q·P). The architect's name is seldom
added. An inscription in front of the temple at Aletrium, among
the Hernici, describes the local censor as having superintended
the laying out of all the streets, with the play-ground and the
meat-market, and the construction of a colonnade, a clock, a
law-court, a swimming-bath and an aqueduct[5]. The date is after
the time of the Gracchi (133—122), but before the passing of the
lex Iulia de civitate (90 B.C.)[6].

L. Betilienus L. f. Vaarus haec quae infera scripta sont de senatu sententia
facienda coiravit : semitas in oppido omnis, porticum qua in arcem eitur,
campum ubei ludunt, horologium, macelum, basilicam calecandam, seedes,
lacum balinearium, lacum ad portam, aquam in opidum adque[7] arduom[8] pedes
cccx↓, fornicesque fecit, fistulas soledas fecit. Ob hasce res censorem
fecere bis, senatus filio stipendia mereta ese iousit, populusque statuam donavit
Censorino[9].

A very ancient inscription on the *pons Fabricius* in Rome records the name of its original builder, L. Fabricius,
who was elected *curator viarum* out of the *tribuni*   Bridges
plebis of 62 B.C., and also the names of the consuls of 21 B.C.,

[1] Dessau, i 129.   [2] *Mon. Anc.* §§ 20, 21.
[3] Wilmanns, 1900; Dessau, ii 5636; *C. I. L.* i² 2, 1633.
[4] Ritschl, lxxxi E; Wilmanns, 730; Dessau, ii 5706; *C. I. L.* i² 2, 1635.
[5] Ritschl, lii B; Wilmanns, 706; Dessau, ii 5348; Allen, p. 58; Lindsay,
p. 83; *C. I. L.* i² 2, 1529.
[6] Ritschl, *Opusc.* iv. 164—182.   [7] ADOV for ADQV(E).
[8] sc. 'et in arcem.'
[9] So called owing to his having twice filled the municipal office of *censor*.

under whom the bridge was completed. There are two large arches, and, at a loftier level between them, a small arch for carrying off the water when the river was in full flood. Looking up the stream, we see, over the large arch to the left hand, the inscription

L·FABRICIVS C·F·CVR·VIAR
FACIVNDVM·COERAVIT

This is continued in the words $\frac{\text{EIDEMQVE}}{\text{PROBAVEIT}}$ on the small arch. On the back, the first of these inscriptions is repeated over the large arch, but is continued on the small arch in the slightly different spelling of the same date $\frac{\text{IDEMQVE}}{\text{PROBAVIT}}$.
On the large arch to the right of the first arch, we see the same inscription as on the arch to the left, and this is repeated on the back, with an addition, in both cases, of an inscription in smaller letters recording the completion of the bridge by the consuls of 21 B.C., the only difference being that, as we look up the stream, we see the words M·LOLLIVS·M·F·Q·LEPI(DVS) (M·F·) COS and EX·S·C·PROBAVERVNT, whereas, on the back of the same arch, the order of the two names is reversed, and the smaller inscription runs Q·LEPIDVS·M·F·M·LOLLIVS·M·F· COS and EX·S·C·PROBAVERVN(T)[1].

On the Roman bridge at Alcántara, a place on the Tagus, near the borders of Spain and Portugal, deriving its modern name from the Arabic words meaning 'the bridge', we have in large letters an inscription of 104 A.D. in honour of the emperor Trajan. Another inscription on the same bridge records the names of eleven *municipia* of Lusitania, which contributed to the cost of building the bridge. Their names are introduced by the words: *municipia provinciae Lusitaniae stipe conlata quae opus pontis perfecerunt*[2]. In Dalmatia in 184 A.D. the emperor Commodus is described as having restored the bridge over the river Hippus with the aid of contributions from some of the neighbouring

[1] Ritschl, lxxxvii; Ricci, tav. xxii; Wilmanns, 788; Dessau, ii 5892; C. I. L. i² 2, 751. Middleton's *Rome*, ii 367. See also Mommsen, *Ges. Schr.* viii 100—107. [2] Dessau, i 287ᵃ.

ON PUBLIC WORKS. BRIDGES

municipalities :—*pontem Hippi fluminis vetustate corruptum restituit, sumptum et operas subministrantibus Novensibus Delminensibus Riditis, curante et dedicante L. Iunio Rufino Proculiano, leg(ato) pr(o) pr(aetore)*[1].
Certain officials at Patavium are described as accepting a contract for building a bridge, and approving its completion :— *(p)ontem faciendum d(e) d(ecurionum) s(ententia) locarunt, eidemque probarunt*[2]. A block of stone recovered from the foundations of the 'pons Cestius' records repairs ordered and approved, in 2 A.D., by the curators of the Tiber :—*curatores riparum et alvei Tiberis ex s(enatus) c(onsulto) reficiundam (sc. ripam?) curaver(unt) idemque probaverunt*[3]. One of the finest Roman bridges now extant is that of Augustus at Ariminum (the *Ponte d'Augusto* over the Marecchia at Rimini), which was begun under Augustus, and finished in 21 A.D. under Tiberius. The two inscriptions on each side of the road run as follows :—

> imp. Caesar divi f(ilius) Augustus, pontifex maxim(us), cos. XIII, imp. XX, tribunic(iae) potest(atis) XXXVII, p(ater) p(atriae).
> Ti. Caesar divi Augusti f(ilius), divi Iuli n(epos), Augus(tus), pontif(ex) maxim(us), cos. IIII, imp. VIII, trib(uniciae) potest(atis) XXII, dedere[4].

On the S.E. side of Ariminum, at the opposite end of the Bridge of Augustus, and at the end of the Via Flaminia brought to that point from Rome in 220 B.C., rises the Arch of Augustus belonging to the year 27 B.C. It celebrates the completion of the repair of the *via Flaminia* and other important Roman roads[5]. The inscription runs as follows.

Arches

> SENATVS · POPVLVSQ(ue Romanus)
> (imp. Caesari divi f. Augusto imp. sept.)
> COS · SEPT · DESIGNAT · OCTAVOM · V(ia Flamin)IA (et reliquei)S
> CELEBERRIMEIS · ITALIAE · VIEIS · CONSILIO (et sumptib)VS (eius mu)NITEIS[6]

---

[1] Dessau, i 393.
[2] *Ib.* ii 5897.
[3] *Ib.* ii 5893.
[4] *Ib.* i 113.
[5] Suet. *Aug.* 30; *Mon. Anc.* § 20 ult.
[6] *C. I. L.* xi 365 ; Dessau, i 84 (with Bormann's restorations, in small type). For a photograph of this Arch, see Sir T. G. Jackson's *Holiday in Umbria*, 1917, facing p. 6.

Another famous 'Arch of Augustus' is that at Segusio, the modern *Susa*, erected in 9 B.C. by the ex-king Cottius, then prefect of the province of the 'Cottian Alps'. The inscription records no less than fourteen tribes as under the sway of Cottius, who sets up the arch in honour of Augustus. Many of the bronze letters of the inscription have perished.

imp(eratori) Caesari Augusto divi f(ilio), pontifici maxumo, tribunic(ia) potestate XV, imp(eratori) XIII, M(arcus) Iulius, regis Donni f(ilius), Cottius, praefectus ceivitatium quae subscriptae sunt: Segoviorum, Segusinorum, Belacorum, *Caturigum*, *Medullorum*, Tebaviorum, *Adanatium*, Savincatium, *Egdiniorum*, *Veaminiorum*, Venisamorum, Iemeriorum, *Vesubianiorum*, Quariatium, et ceivitates quae sub eo praefecto fuerunt[1].

Of these fourteen tribes the six printed in italics are also named in the list of those subdued by Augustus as recorded in the *Tropaeum Alpium* of 7 B.C. transcribed by Pliny (iii 136[2]), but, on the *Tropaeum*, the name of the third of these tribes is given as *Edenates* and that of the sixth as *Esubiani*. Only a few letters from the *Tropaeum* are now preserved in the Museum at Saint-Germain-en-Laye[3], near Paris.

Of the arches erected in Rome, the earliest were those set up in 196 B.C. by L. Stertinius from the spoils of his Spanish campaign[4]; the next was that erected in honour of P. Cornelius Scipio Africanus in 190 B.C.[5] The victory of Q. Fabius Maximus over the Allobroges in 121 B.C. was celebrated by the erection of the *Arcus Fabianus* at the east end of the Forum. This arch was restored by his grandson, Q. Fabius Q. f. Maxsumus aedilis curulis, of about 56 B.C., who adorned it with statues of his ancestors L. Aemilius Paullus, the conqueror of Perses, and of P. Cornelius Scipio Africanus, the destroyer of Carthage, and added his own statue. It is to this fact that Cicero alludes in his speech *In Vatinium* § 28, 'nihil Maximus fecit alienum aut sua virtute aut illis clarissimis Paullis, Maximis, Africanis, quorum

---

[1] Dessau, i 94; cp. Ricci, pp. 146–9, and Bursian, *Jahresb.* vol. 144, p. 330.

[2] c. 1, p. 10 *supra*, and Rushforth's *Lat. Hist. Inscr.* p. 36 f.

[3] *C. I. L.* v 7817; for an architectural restoration of the trophy, see Daremberg-Saglio, s.v. *Tropaeum*, fig. 7122.

[4] Livy, xxxiii 27, 3—5.

[5] *Id.* xxxvii 3, 7.

gloriam huius virtute renovatam non modo speramus, verum etiam iam videmus'[1].

The *Arch of Augustus*, near the temple of Castor, was set up in honour of his victory at Actium in 31 B.C. The arch itself has vanished, but, during the excavations of 1540–50, a marble block from its attic was found with the following inscription, which has since been lost.

Senatus populusque Romanus Imp(eratori) Caesari divi Iuli f(ilio) cos. quinct. | cos. design(ato) sext., imp(eratori) sept., re publica conservata[2].

The *Arch of Tiberius* was erected in 17 A.D. in honour of Tiberius, on account of the recovery by Germanicus of the standards lost by Varus in Germany. Tacitus, *Ann.* ii 41, describes it as *arcus propter aedem Saturni, ob recepta signa cum Varo omissa, ductu Germanici, auspiciis Tiberii.*

The *Arch of Claudius*, erected in 51—52 A.D., stood across the *Via Lata*, corresponding to the modern Corso. Poggio saw the arch still standing in the fifteenth century; it was destroyed two centuries later. It was erected to commemorate Claudius' 'victory over eleven British kings', probably Caractacus and his brothers in 50 A.D. (Tacitus, *Ann.* xii 35). The block containing half of the inscription is now in the Barberini Palace. The whole has been restored as follows:

Ti(berio) Clau(dio Drusi filio Cai)sari Augu(sto Germani)co, pontific(i maximo, trib. potes)tat(is) XI, cos. V, im(peratori XX (?), patri pa)triai, senatus po(pulusque) Ro(manus, q)uod reges Brit(anniai) XI (devictos sine) ulla iactur(a in deditionem acceperit), gentesque b(arbaras trans Oceanum) primus in dici(o- nem populi Romani redegerit)[3].

The capture of Jerusalem in 70 A.D. was commemorated by an arch in honour of Titus in the Circus Maximus, which bore the following inscription belonging to the year 80 A.D.

Senatus populusque Romanus imp(eratori) Tito Caesari divi Vespasiani f(ilio) Vespasian(o) Augusto pontif(ici) max(imo), trib(unicia) pot(estate) X, imp(eratori) XVII, (c)os. VIII, p(atri) p(atriae), principi suo, quod praeceptis patr(is) consiliisque et auspiciis gentem Iudaeorum domuit et urbem Hierusolymam, omnibus ante se ducibus regibus gentibus aut frustra petitam aut omnino intem(p)tatam, delevit[4].

The four arches above mentioned are no longer in existence.

[1] *C. I. L.* i² 2, 763; Wilmanns, 610; Dessau, i. 43; cp. p. 95 *supra*.
[2] Dessau, i 81.   [3] Hübner, *Ex.* 86; Dessau, i 216.   [4] Dessau, i 264.

Fig. 34. The Arch of Trajan at Beneventum (reproduced, by permission, from a photograph by Moscioni, Rome).

The emperor Titus died in 81 A.D. and the *Arch of Titus*, erected 'in summa sacra via' after his death, still bears the following inscription:

SENATVS

POPVLVSQVE ROMANVS

DIVO TITO DIVI VESPASIANI F

VESPASIANO AVGVSTO[1]

The *Arch of Trajan at Beneventum* was erected in the year 114 A.D. to commemorate the beneficent rule of the emperor, on whom the Senate had in that year bestowed the title of *Optimus*. It bears numerous reliefs on both sides, those on the side facing Beneventum and Rome referring to his home-policy, and those on the side facing the country, to his provincial policy. The former is the side here reproduced (Fig. 34). Both sides bear the same inscription.

Imp(eratori) Caesari divi Nervae filio, Nervae Traiano Optimo Aug(usto) Germanico Dacico, pontif(ici) max(imo), trib(uniciae) potest(atis) XVIII[2], imp(eratori) VII, cos. VI, p(atri) p(atriae), fortissimo principi, Senatus p(opulus) q(ue) R(omanus)[3].

The arch was never seen by the emperor himself, who had left for the East in 114 and died on his homeward journey in 117[4]. The same is true of the next arch.

The *Arch of Trajan at Ancona* belongs to the following year, namely 115 A.D. It commemorates the completion of the harbour at Ancona, and, besides the inscription in honour of the emperor, bears the names of his wife and his sister. The letters of the inscription were made of bronze; the letters have been lost; it is only by means of the holes left by the rivets, that the words have been read[5].

[1] Dessau, i 265; Diehl, 26 a.   [2] Dec. 113—114 A.D.
[3] Dessau, i 296.
[4] For a convenient conspectus of the reliefs on the arch, see A. L. Frothingham, jun., *The Triumphal Arch at Beneventum*, 1893; and Mrs Arthur Strong's *Roman Sculpture*, 1907, pp. 214—225, with the literature there quoted. See also Rossini, *Archi trionfali*, 1836, tav. 38—43.
[5] Cp. p. 57 *supra*.

	Imp. Caesari divi Nervae f(ilio) Nervae Traiano	
	Optimo Aug(usto) Germanic(o) Dacico, pont(ifici)	divae
Plotinae	max(imo), tr(ibuniciae) pot(estatis) XVIIII, imp(era-	Marcianae
Aug(ustae)	tori) IX, cos. VI, p(atri) p(atriae), providentissimo	Aug(ustae)
coniugi	principi, senatus p(opulus)q(ue) R(omanus), quod	sorori
Aug(usti)	accessum Italiae, hoc etiam addito ex pecunia sua	Aug(usti)
	portu, tutiorem navigantibus reddiderit[1].	

Returning to Rome, we notice, on the Esquiline, an unimportant archway called the *Arch of Gallienus*. This was erected by a *vir egregius*, Aurelius Victor, about 260 A.D., in honour of an accomplished, but incapable, emperor, and his wife. It is inscribed in large letters on both sides:

Gallieno, clementissimo principi, cuius invicta virtus sola pietate superata est, et Saloninae sanctissimae Aug(ustae), Aurelius Victor v(ir) e(gregius), dicatissimus numini maiestatique eorum[2].

The *Arch of Septimius Severus*, N.W. of the Forum, was erected in 203 A.D. in honour of the emperor and his sons Caracalla and Geta, after victories in Parthia and other eastern countries. It is inscribed, on both sides, as follows:

Imp(eratori) Caes(ari) Lucio[3] Septimio M(arci)[4] fil(io) Severo, Pio Pertinaci Aug(usto), patri patriae, Parthico Arabico et | Parthico Adiabenico, pontific(i) maximo, tribunic(iae) potest(atis) XI, imp(eratori) XI, cos. III, procos., et | imp(eratori) Caes(ari) M. Aurelio L(ucii) fil(io) Antonino Aug(usto), Pio Felici, tribunic(iae) potest(atis) VI, cos., procos., ⟨p(atri) p(atriae)⟩ | optimis fortissimisque principibus)[5] | ob rem publicam restitutam imperiumque populi Romani propagatum | insignibus virtutibus eorum domi forisque, S(enatus) P(opulus)q(ue) R(omanus).

From the *Arch of Trajan in Rome* (no longer in existence) were taken the fine sculptured panels with scenes from Trajan's life, as well as the main entablature and eight Corinthian columns,

---

[1] Dessau, i 298. For a fine picture of this Arch, see frontispiece to Sir T. G. Jackson's *Holiday in Umbria*, 1917.

[2] *Ib.* i 548.

[3] Exceptionally given in full, instead of L.

[4] His adoptive father, M. Aurelius, who ought to have been called *divus*.

[5] After the death of Septimius Severus, when Caracalla had murdered his brother Geta, he ordered his victim's name to be erased from all inscriptions. Additional titles after the name of Caracalla, here called M. Aurelius Antoninus Pius, fill the place of the erased name, which is conjectured to have been originally introduced as follows, *et P. Septimio L. fil. Getae nobiliss. Caesari*, Dessau, i 425 (where various irregularities in the inscription are noticed).

which now adorn the *Arch of Constantine*, erected to commemorate Constantine's victory over Maxentius in 312 A.D.

The following is the inscription above both sides of the lofty central arch, which stands between two lower arches:

imp(eratori) Caes(ari) Fl(avio) Constantino, maximo p(io) f(elici) Augusto, S(enatus) P(opulus)q(ue) R(omanus), quod instinctu divinitatis, mentis magnitudine, cum exercitu suo tam de tyranno quam de omni eius factione uno tempore iustis rempublicam ultus est armis, arcum triumphis insignem dicavit.

Within the central arch, we have on the one side 'liberatori urbis', and, on the other, 'fundatori quietis', while, above the double medallions of the two smaller arches, we have in front, on the arch to the left, VOTIS X, and on that to the right, VOTIS XX, implying 'votis decennalibus'—'votis vicennalibus'; and, on the back, in the corresponding positions, SIC X and SIC XX, i.e. 'sicut decennalia, sic vicennalia (fiant)', 'as he has reigned ten years, so may he reign twenty', the arch having been erected after the tenth year of his reign, i.e. 315 A.D. [1]

(1) The pedestal of *Trajan's column*, dedicated in 113 A.D., still bears the following inscription in letters of perfect form, each of them about four inches high [2].

Columns

SENATVS · POPVLVSQVE · ROMANVS
IMP · CAESARI · DIVI · NERVAE · F · NERVAE
TRAIANO · AVG · GERM(ANICO) · DACICO · PONTIF
MAXIMO · TRIB · POT · XVII · IMP · VI · COS · VI · P · P
AD · DECLARANDVM · QVANTAE · ALTITVDINIS
MONS · ET · LOCVS · TAN[TIS · OPE]RIBVS · SIT · EGESTVS [3]

In the last line TIS · OPE have been preserved in the *Sylloge Einsiedlensis* [4].

---

[1] Dessau, i 694; *Facs.* in Hübner's *Exempla*, 702, copied in Egbert, p. 250, and Ricci, tav. xliv; *Phot.* in Cagnat⁴pl. xx, 1, and Diehl 26 *d*; p. 92 *supra*.

On all the above Arches, and on others in many parts of the ancient Roman world, see esp. Paul Graef, in Baumeister's *Denkmäler*, vol. iii pp. 1865—1899. For inscriptions on less important arches, cp. Dessau, ii 5566—77 (the more important are printed elsewhere, under the names of the several Emperors).

[2] Facsimile in Hübner's *Exempla*, 265, and Cagnat⁴, pl. x (1).

[3] *C. I. L.* vi 960; Wilmanns, 935; Dessau, i 294. In this inscr. the side strokes of M are nearly perpendicular, and the ordinary modern form of the letter has been retained in this and the subsequent inscriptions of the present chapter.   [4] p. 20 *supra*.

The sense of the last two lines has been much discussed. Dion Cassius says that 'Trajan placed a colossal column in his Forum to be his own tomb, and also to show the amount of labour expended upon the Forum, the slope of the hill which previously occupied the site having been dug away so as to afford a level space for the Forum'[1].

(2) The *column of Antoninus Pius* was set up in 161 A.D. by his adopted sons, M. Aurelius Antoninus and Lucius Verus. The pedestal, with sculptures in high relief (including the *apotheosis* of Antoninus Pius and Faustina the elder) is now in the Garden of the Vatican. It bears the following inscription:—

DIVO · ANTONINO · AVGVSTO · PIO
ANTONINVS · AVGVSTVS · ET
VERVS · AVGVSTVS · FILII

The letters, which were originally of bronze, have been lost. The inscription only survives in the cuttings made in the marble to receive the separate letters, and consequently has a somewhat uncouth appearance[2].

(3) The *column of M. Aurelius*, 180 A.D., almost a copy of Trajan's, is exactly the same height, 100 Roman feet; hence these columns were known as *columnae centenariae*. The inscription is doubtless on that part of the original pedestal which is still buried beneath the surface of the modern Piazza. A separate tablet was, however, found in the ruins of an adjacent house, showing that this column had a custodian, *procurator columnae centenariae divi Marci*, who, in 193 A.D. under Septimius Severus, received permission to

---

[1] Dion Cassius, lxviii 16, ἔστησεν ἐν τῇ ἀγορᾷ καὶ κίονα μέγιστον—εἰς ἐπίδειξιν τοῦ κατὰ τὴν ἀγορὰν ἔργου· παντὸς γὰρ τοῦ χωρίου ἐκείνου ὀρεινοῦ ὄντος κατέσκαψε τοσοῦτον ὅσον ὁ κίων ἀνίσχει, καὶ τὴν ἀγορὰν ἐκ τούτου πεδινὴν κατεσκεύασε. Cp. Burn's *Rome*, p. 148, also Bursian's *Jahresb.* 144, 335; J. O. F. Murray and Verrall, in *Cambridge Philol. Soc. Proc.* 4 March and 13 May, 1897; Comparetti, in *Rendiconti—Acc. dei Lincei*, 1906, 577—588; Boni, *N. Antologia* 1 November 1906, 1 March 1907; Mau, *Röm. Mitt.* xxii 187—197. I understand the words, 'to show how great a height of hill', 'and space (i.e. 'as a space') for such vast buildings, has been cleared'. Cp. Livy, xxi 37, 1, 'tantum nivis fodiendum atque egerendum fuit'. The sense would have been clearer, if *quantus* had been inserted before *locus*.

[2] Hübner's *Exempla*, 294; Wilmanns, 945; Dessau, i 347. Cp. pp. 57, 125 *supra*.

build, at his own expense, a house instead of a hut, on condition of paying the usual ground-rent (cp. p. 160 (*e*) *infra*)[1].

Of the dedicatory inscriptions on the Roman aqueducts none are earlier than the Augustan age. There are three such inscriptions over the arch of the *Aqua Marcia*. On the building of the Aurelian walls this arch was used for the *Porta Tiburtina*. Three aqueducts pass over the gateway, the lowest (and earliest) of these is the aqueduct of the *Aqua Marcia*, built by the praetor Q. Marcius Rex in 144 B.C.; the next is that of the *Aqua Tepula*, constructed by the censors, Cn. Servilius Caepio and L. Cassius Longinus, in 127 B.C.; and the highest (and latest) is that of the *Aqua Iulia*, originally constructed by M. Agrippa, as aedile in 33 B.C. The rebuilding of the aqueduct of the *Aqua Iulia* by Augustus in 5 B.C. is recorded in the highest of the three inscriptions:—

Aqueducts

IMP · CAESAR · DIVI · IVLI · F · AVGVSTVS
PONTIFEX · MAXIMVS · COS · XII
TRIBVNIC · POTESTAT · XIX · IMP · XIIII
RIVOS · AQVARVM · OMNIVM · REFECIT

The lowest of the inscriptions is the record of the restoration of the *Aqua Marcia* by Titus in 79 A.D.

IMP · TITVS · CAESAR · DIVI · F · VESPASIANVS · AVG · PONTIF · MAX
TRIBVNICIAE · POTEST · IX · IMP · XV · CENS · COS · VII · DESIG · IIX
RIVOM · AQVAE · MARCIAE · VETVSTATE · DILAPSVM · REFECIT
ET · AQVAM · QVAE · IN · VSV · ESSE · DESIERAT · REDVXIT

In the space between the highest and the lowest of the three inscriptions is the record of the restoration of the *Aqua Marcia* by Caracalla, between the death of his brother Geta in 212 and his acquisition of the title 'Germanicus' in 213 A.D.

[1] Wilmanns, 2840; Dessau, ii 5920,...'praestaturo secundum exemplum ceterorum solarium'. In Middleton's *Rome*, ii 312, *sŏlarium* (which is here meant) is confounded with *sōlarium*, a sunny upper room, here apparently 'used for a whole house'! Facsimile of inscr. in Diehl, *Inscr. Lat.* 28 *b*.

IMP · CAES · M · AVRELLIVS · ANTONINVS · PIVS · FELIX · AVG ·
PARTH · MAX · | BRIT · MAXIMVS · PONTIFEX · MAXIMVS |
AQVAM · MARCIAM · VARIIS · KASIBVS · IMPEDITAM · PVRGATO ·
FONTE · EXCISIS · ET · PERFORATIS | MONTIBVS · RESTITVTA ·
FORMA · ADQVISITO · ETIAM · FONTE · NOVO · ANTONINIANO |
IN · SACRAM[1] · VRBEM · SVAM · PERDVCENDAM · CVRAVIT[2].

Above the *Porta Praenestina* there is another group of three inscriptions relating to the *Aqua Claudia* and *Anio nova*, recording (1) their completion by Claudius in 52—53 A.D., (2) their restoration by Vespasian in 71, and (3) their further restoration by Titus in 81.

(1) TI · CLAVDIVS · DRVSI · F · CAISAR · AVGVSTVS · GERMANI-
CVS · PONTIF · MAXIM | TRIBVNICIA · POTESTATE · $\overline{\text{XII}}$ · COS ·
$\overline{\text{V}}$ · IMPERATOR · $\overline{\text{XXVII}}$ · PATER · PATRIAE |
AQVAS · CLAVDIAM · EX FONTIBVS · QVI · VOCABANTVR · CAERV-
LEVS · ET · CVRTIVS · A MILLIARIO · XXXXV | ITEM · ANIENEM ·
NOVAM · A MILLIARIO · LXII · SVA · IMPENSA · IN VRBEM · PER-
DVCENDAS · CVRAVIT |

(2) IMP · CAESAR · VESPASIANVS · AVGVST · PONTIF · MAX ·
TRIB · POT · II · IMP · $\overline{\text{VI}}$ · COS · $\overline{\text{III}}$ · DESIG · $\overline{\text{IIII}}$ · P · P
AQVAS · CVRTIAM · ET · CAERVLEAM · PERDVCTAS · A DIVO ·
CLAVDIO · ET · POSTEA · INTERMISSAS · DILAPSASQVE | PER
ANNOS · NOVEM · SVA · IMPENSA · VRBI · RESTITVIT

(3) IMP · T · CAESAR · DIVI · F · VESPASIANVS · AVGVSTVS ·
PONTIFEX · MAXIMVS · TRIBVNIC | POTESTATE · $\overline{\text{X}}$ · IMPERA-
TOR · $\overline{\text{XVII}}$ · PATER · PATRIAE · CENSOR · COS · $\overline{\text{VIII}}$
AQVAS · CVRTIAM · ET · CAERVLEAM · PERDVCTAS · A DIVO ·
CLAVDIO · ET · POSTEA |
A DIVO · VESPASIANO · PATRE · SVO · VRBI · RESTITVTAS · CVM ·
A CAPITE · AQVARVM · A SOLO · VETVSTATE · DILAPSAE ·
ESSENT · NOVA · FORMA · REDVCENDAS · SVA · IMPENSA ·
CVRAVIT[3]

[1] i.e. 'imperial'.
[2] Wilmanns, 765 f; Dessau, i 98; Burn's *Rome*, pp. 63, 71; and Middleton's *Rome*, ii 340.
[3] Wilmanns, 764; Dessau, i 218; cp. Schreiber's *Atlas*, lvii 1; Burn's *Rome*, p. 65; Middleton's *Rome*, ii 344 f; and Lanciani, on *Frontinus and the Aqueducts of Ancient Rome*, in *Memorie dei Lincei*, vol. iv 215—616 (Rome, 1880), and text and translation by C. Herschel (Boston, Mass. 1899); also O. Hirschfeld, *Verwaltungsbeamten* (1905), 273—284. For inscriptions relating to aqueducts, cp. Dessau, ii 5743—5796, and *C. I. L.* xv 906 ff.

VII]   ON PUBLIC WORKS. AQUEDUCTS   131

In the original, the last paragraph above quoted forms a single line, in characters far smaller than the rest; and, throughout these inscriptions from aqueducts, M appears in a shape resembling Ⅿ.

The above records of the completion or restoration of aqueducts are drawn up in the same general style as the 'honorary inscriptions' already noticed. The distinctive and characteristic point about them is that they are inscribed on the aqueducts themselves .

The legal conditions relating to the aqueduct at Venafrum are laid down in an edict of Augustus[2]. In the *Monumentum Ancyranum* he records the fact that he doubled the supply of the *Aqua Marcia* by adding a second source (called the *Aqua Augusta*):—AQVAM · QVAE · MARCIA · APPELLATVR · DVPLICAVI | FONTE · NOVO · IN · RIVVM · EIVS · INMISSO[3]. The space of ground belonging to an aqueduct, usually 30 feet wide, was marked by *cippi*, or upright slabs of stone, of the same general type as Roman milestones. Several of those set up by Augustus have been found, e.g. IVL · TEP · MAR | IMP · CAESAR | DIVI · F | AVGVSTVS | EX S · C | LXXV | P · CCXL. This refers to the three aqueducts of the *aqua Iulia*, *Tepula* and *Marcia*, and denotes that the number of the *cippus* was 75, and the distance from the junction, 240 feet, which is equivalent to the longer side of a *iugerum* (240 × 120 feet)[4]. The number of hours, during which private houses could be supplied with water, was indicated by an inscription at the point where the small pipe left the large, e.g. 'aquae (= fistulae aquariae) duae ab hora secunda ad horam sextam'[5]. Even the names of the makers of the leaden pipes were inscribed, with the names of the emperor and the procurator, e.g. 'Imp(eratoris) Caesar(is) Domitiani Aug(usti), sub cura | Alypii proc(uratoris); fec(erunt) Esychus et Hermias[6].

We have a large number of inscriptions recording the construction or repair of roads. A slab of stone by the roadside recorded the name of the emperor, and the nature or extent of the repairs, in phrases such as *refecit*

Roads

---

[1] Cp. Wilmanns, *indices*, ii p. 658 f.   [2] Dessau, ii 5743.
[3] c. 20.   [4] Wilmanns, 776; cf. Dessau, ii 5744—5748.
[5] Wilmanns, 780; cp. *ib*. 2038; Frontinus, ii 94.   [6] Wilmanns, 2808 a.

et restituit[1]; *silice sua pecunia stravit*[2]; *viam antehac lapide albo inutiliter stratam et corruptam silice novo...fecit*[3].

One of the earliest of such documents is that found on the site of Forum Popilii at Polla in Lucania, in which one who

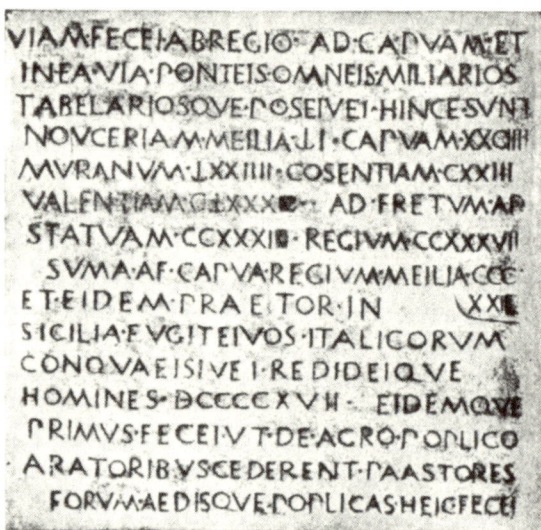

Fig. 35. Miliarium Popilianum (*P. L. M. E.* li *b*, and *Opusc.* iv, Taf. iv pp. 115—130), ⅔.

Viam fecei ab Regio ad Capuam, et in ea via ponteis omneis, miliarios tabelariosque poseivei.

Hince sunt Nouceriam meilia	⊔I
Capuam	XXCIIII
Muranum	⊔XXIIII
Cosentiam	CXXIII
Valentiam	C⊔XXXI (obliterated)
ad fretum ad statuam	CCXXXII
Regium	CCXXXVII
suma af Capua Regium meilia	CCCXXII

Et eidem praetor in Sicilia fugiteivos Italicorum conquaeisivei, redideique homines DCCCCXVII. Eidemque primus fecei, ut de agro poplico aratoribus cederent paastores. Forum aedisque poplicas heic fecei (*C. I. L.* i² 2, 638; Dessau, i 23; cp. Lindsay, 74—76).

[1] Dessau, ii 5818. [2] *ib.* 5821. [3] *ib.* 5822.

is certainly identified as P. Popillius Laenas, consul of 132 B.C., describes his building of a road from Regium to Capua, and his other services.

Near the beginning of the above inscription, we should probably understand *lapides* with *tabelarios*, as well as with *miliarios*, taking *miliarios* to mean stones bearing only the number of the miles, while *tabelarios* might imply stones bearing a *tabella* or brief inscription of quadrangular form[1].

Augustus in 2 B.C. inscribed on every milestone of his road from the Baetis to Gades :—*a Baete et Iano Augusto ad Oceanum*[2], and Claudius in 46 A.D. on those of the road founded by his father Drusus :—*viam Claudiam Augustam, quam Drusus pater Alpibus bello patefactis derexerat, munit ab Altino* (or *a flumine Pado) ad flumen Danuvium*[3].

Trajan, in 100 A.D., caused a road to be cut in the living rock close to the water's edge on the right bank of the Danube, near the 'Iron Gate',—*montibus excisi(s) anco(ni)bus*[4] *sublatis*[5], 'by hewing out the mountains, and removing the jutting crags'; and, in 111, built another road in the newly founded province of Arabia, *a finibus Syriae usque ad mare Rubrum*[6]. The *Via Traiana*, which passed from Beneventum through Barium to Brundisium, is personified on a coin of Trajan, and, on the Arch of Constantine, the *Via Flaminia* is represented reclining at the feet of Marcus Aurelius[7].

Inscriptions on milestones (*miliaria*) and boundary-stones (*cippi terminales*) include names of places and records of distances, which throw light on the topo-

Milestones

[1] Cp. O. Hirschfeld, *Kleine Schriften*, 708. A. M. Ramsay in *J. R. S.* x (1920) takes *tabelarios* = 'couriers'.

[2] Dessau, i 102. Similarly, Gaius Caesar in 39 A.D., Hübner, *Exempla*, 283.   [3] *C. I. L.* v 8002 f; cp. Dessau, i 208.

[4] 'Trabes intelligit Mommsenus, ego angulos montis', Vollmer in *Lat. Thesaurus*, s.v. *ancon*.

[5] Dessau, ii 5863, view by Bartlett in Dr W. Beattie's *Danube* (1844), p. 214.

[6] Dessau, 5834, 5845; inscriptions on milestones on the Arnon, and in other parts of Arabia Petraea.

[7] Daremberg et Saglio, s.v. *Via*, figs. 7428, 7429. On the *Via Traiana* see Ashby and R. Gardner in *Papers of British School of Rome*, viii (1916) 104—171. For inscriptions relating to roads, cp. Dessau, ii 5799—5891, iii (2) 9371—4.

graphy of Rome, and the geography of the Provinces. In all, there are nearly 4000 milestones. Of these, about one-third have been found in Africa; only about 600 in the whole of Italy; and, of these, two-thirds in the South; about 100 in Sardinia; none in Corsica and Sicily. Spain has more than 400; Gallia Narbonensis about 250; the 'three Gauls' about 200; Germania and Helvetia about 250; Britannia about 70; and the Danubian Provinces less than 400[1].

The earliest at present known was set up by the curule aediles on the *Via Appia* at a place *ad Medias*, in the Pomptine marshes, in the first half of the first Punic War :—

P. Claudio Ap. f., | C. Fourio aidiles. (*In fronte*) √||| (*a tergo*) X[2].

Not much later in date we have two milestones set up by plebeian aediles : (1) XI miles from Rome on the *Via Ostiensis*[3]; and (2) XXX miles from Rome on the left bank of the Tiber :—

P. Menates P. f. | aid. pl. | XXX[4].

In 187 B.C. we have three set up by M. Aemilius Lepidus, the builder of the *Via Aemilia* between Ariminum and Placentia, one of them marking XV miles from Bononia, and another XXI from Mutina[5]. In 148 we have a milestone of Sp. Postumius Albinus, the builder of the *Via Postumia* from Cremona to Genua, with a record of the total length of CXXII miles, and the distance of XXVII miles from Cremona, and VIIII from a station unnamed[6]. Shortly after 146 B.C. the *Via Egnatia* was constructed, and the fact that it was provided with milestones is attested by Polybius[7]. The age of the Gracchi is represented by a milestone of P. Popillius, consul of 132, builder of the *Via Popillia* between Ariminum and Atria. This was found at Atria, and it marks the distance of 81 miles between that place and Ariminum :—

---

[1] Cp., in general, O. Hirschfeld, *Die römischen Meilensteine* (1907), in *Kleine Schriften* (1913), pp. 703—743; and Daremberg et Saglio, s.v. *Via*.

[2] i.e. 53 miles from Rome, and 10 from the beginning of the 19 miles of the *decennovium* (*C. I. L.* i² 2, 21; Dessau, ii 5801); cp. *Eph. Epigr.* ix (1913), p. 494, n. 971.

[3] *Röm. Mitt.* 10 (1895), 298 ff, with facsimile; *C. I. L.* i² 2, 22.

[4] *C. I. L.* i² 2, 829; Dessau, ii 5802.

[5] *C. I. L.* i² 2, 617-18; Dessau, ii 5803-4.

[6] *C. I. L.* i² 2, 624; Dessau, ii 5806. [7] Ap. Strabo, p. 322.

P · POPILLIVS · C · F | COS | ↧XXXI[1]. We have already noticed his own record of his construction of the road between Capua and Regium[2].

The age of the Gracchi also saw the beginning of the erection of milestones in the Provinces. Several of those set up by M'. Aquillius in Asia Minor have been discovered on roads from Ephesus to Pergamon, or to Tralles and Sardis. He was consul in 129 B.C., and, as proconsul, two years later, he superintended the settlement of the boundaries on the taking over of the Pergamene kingdom. The same age is represented by a milestone of C. Cornelius Cinna, consul in 127[3], and another of T. Quinctius Flamininus, consul in 123[4]. Gaius Gracchus set up milestones on the roads which he constructed[5]; and the *Via Domitia* in Gallia Narbonensis was marked out with milestones shortly after his death in 121[6]. It was probably in the age of Sulla (80 B.C.) that the several sections of an unidentified *Via Caecilia* were contracted for, and the beginning and end of each section denoted by the number of the miles on the milestones[7]. The age of Caesar is represented by a milestone of P. Servilius Isauricus, proconsul of Asia in 46 B.C.[8]

A new epoch begins with the Empire. Augustus, in the early years of his rule, repaired the *Via Flaminia*[9], and the road between Tusculum and Alba was restored by Valerius Messalla[10]. The old tradition, that the charges for the repair of roads were sanctioned by the Senate, was maintained, as a matter of policy, by Augustus, whose milestones on the *Via Appia*, *Latina*, and *Salaria* (of 17—12 B.C.) bear the inscription S·C or EX S·C[11]. While the emperors did much for the maintenance of the *Via Appia*, they are seldom mentioned as contributing to the cost of the roads in the Provinces, the expenses of which generally fell on the owners or the communities in the vicinity of the road. The emperor's

---

[1] *C. I. L.* i² 2, 637; Dessau, ii 5807; facsimile in Ritschl, Tab. liv A*a*, and Opusc. iv, *Tafeln* xiii A (copied in Daremberg et Saglio, fig. 5029, and Egbert, p. 251). [2] p. 132 *supra*.
[3] *C. I. L.* i² 2, 654; Dessau, ii 5809.
[4] *C. I. L.* i² 2, 657; Dessau, ii 5808. [5] Plutarch, *Gaius Gracchus*, c. 7.
[6] Polybius, iii 39, 8. [7] Des au. ii 5799.
[8] *C. I. L.* i² 2, 786; Dessau, i 40. [9] Dessau. ii 84 (quoted p. 121).
[10] Tibullus, i 7, 57 ff. [11] *ex senatus consulto*.

name is often recorded either in the dative of dedication, or in the ablative of date. Even when the name is in the nominative, it does not follow that the emperor bore the expense, except in the case of the early Caesars. Thus, on a stone of 14 B.C. found between Monaco and Mentone, we read:—'imp(erator) Caesar | Augustus, imperator x, | tribunicia potestate xi | · ƎCI ' (i.e. 601 miles from Rome)[1]. Elsewhere we find the number of miles from the principal town of the region, such as Lyons, Ephesus, or Carthage[2]. Of milestones found in England, the best, one of 120 A.D., of the time of Hadrian, is now in the municipal Museum, Leicester:—'Imp(erator) Caes(ar) | Div(i) Traiani Parth(ici) f(ilius), Div(i) Ner(vae) nep(os), | Traian(us) Hadrian(us) Aug(ustus) p(ater) p(atriae), trib(unicia) | pot(estate) IV COS · III a Ratis (i.e. 'from Leicester') II[3]. In the Provinces in general the name of the Roman governor is often added. Thus a milestone at Ancyra after giving the titles of Domitian in 82 A.D., continues 'per | A. Caesennium Gallum leg(atum) | pr(o) pr(aetore) vias provinciarum | Galatiae Cappadociae | Ponti Pisidiae Paphlagoniae | Lycaoniae Armeniae minoris | stravit', and ends with the number of miles, above in Latin, VIII, and below in Greek, H[4]. But the name *Domitianus* is omitted, or mutilated, in this inscription, and in another at Ancyra, two years earlier in date[5]. The names of emperors whose memory was execrated were apt to be mutilated[6], and the maltreated and rejected milestones were sometimes collected in a *dépôt* at the chief town of the Roman road, as at Rennes and Bayeux, and also at Heidelberg[7]. In Upper Germany and in Gaul, from the time of Septimius Severus, the distances were regularly reckoned in leagues (of 1500 *passus*), e.g. in Baden, 'C(olonia) A(urelia) Aq(uensium). Ab Aq(uis) leug(ae) IIII '[8].

Milestones often indicate, not only the number of miles from the beginning of the road, but also the number from the end;

---

[1] Dessau, ii 5816.
[2] G. J. Laing, *Roman milestones and the capita viarum*, in *Trans....of the Amer. Philol. Assoc.* 1908, p. 15—34.
[3] *C. I. L.* vii 1169.
[4] Dessau, i 268.
[5] *ib.* 263.
[6] List in Appendix III, p. 232.
[7] Hirschfeld, *l.c.*, p. 734, n. 3.
[8] Wilmanns, 842 (220 A.D.).

VII] ON PUBLIC WORKS. MILESTONES 137

and Quintilian dwells on the encouragement which the traveller thus derives from the record of the diminishing distance :—*facientibus iter multum detrahunt fatigationis notata inscriptis lapidibus spatia*[1].

The forms of milestones vary. That of Popillius (132 B.C.)[2] is four feet high and two broad, and tapers towards the part inserted in the ground. Cato implies that a *miliarium* was a *columella*[3]. Between Nîmes and Arles, on the *Via Domitia* of 120 B.C., which was restored by the early emperors, the milestones of Augustus are cylindrical in shape, and only record the emperor's titles in 3 B.C.; those of Tiberius are quadrangular pillars, which add to the imperial titles of 31—32 A.D. the distance in miles; while, in those of Claudius, the inscription on

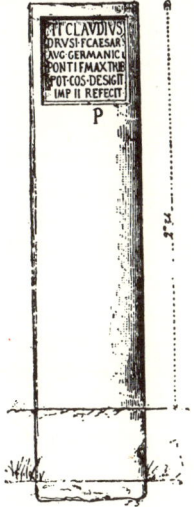

Fig. 36. Milestone of Claudius, between Nîmes and Arles (height above ground, 7 feet, 7 inches); reproduced, by permission, from Daremberg et Saglio, s.v. *Milliarium*, p. 178.

Ti(berius) Claudius Drusi f(ilius) Caesar Aug(ustus) Germanic(us) Pontif(ex) Max(imus) trib(unicia) pot(estate) cos. desig(natus) IĪ IMP II REFECIT (Dessau, i 200), A.D. 41. The meaning of the letter P, below the inscription, is unknown.

[1] Quintilian, iv 5, 22. [2] p. 134 *supra*.
[3] *De Agri Cultura*, 20, 22.

the cylindrical stone is enclosed in a quadrangular frame, making no mention of miles, but confining itself to the imperial titles of 41 A.D.[1] An example of this last is given on p. 137.

On the *Vallum* of Antoninus Pius, constructed about 142 A.D. along the 36 miles between the Firth of Forth and the Firth of Clyde, a series of inscribed tablets has been found recording the exact distance covered by the work accomplished by each legion, or detachment of the same (a *vexillatio*, probably composed of two centuries). The work was apparently begun at the eastern end, and finished on the western. Out of seventeen tablets, the eight found in the eastern portion of the *vallum* record the distance in paces (*millia passuum* usually expressed PER · M · P), varying from 4652 paces to 3000[2], while the remaining nine, found in the western portion, probably record it in feet (*pedes*, expressed P · or P · P), varying from 4411 to 3000[3]. On two of these nine, the work is described as OPVS VALLI[4]. The Second Legion, and a detachment of the Sixth, are each represented by five of the tablets; and the Twentieth, or a detachment of the same, by seven. The largest and finest of them all is that found in 1868 near the eastern end of the *Vallum*, at Bridgeness in Linlithgowshire. It includes two interesting pieces of sculpture; that on the right is a sacrificial scene, in which five men are standing, one of whom is pouring a libation on an altar, while another bears a standard inscribed LEG II AVG; below, there is a *tibicen*, and an attendant with the three characteristic animals of the *suovetaurilia*, a sacrifice known as a *piaculum Martis*, and connected with the 'lustration' of an army on taking the field[5]. On the left we have an armed horseman, of the Dexileos type, brandishing a spear, with four foemen prostrate beneath him[6]. See Fig. 37.

Distance-slabs

[1] Cp. Desjardins, *Géogr. de la Gaule romaine*, iv pp. 175, 177, 178, reproduced on a smaller scale in Daremberg et Saglio, s.v. *Milliarium*.
[2] *C. I. L.* vii 1088, 1121, 1122, 1126, 1130, 1131, 1132, 1143.
[3] 1133, 1133a, 1135, 1136, 1137, 1138, 1140, 1141, and probably 1142. P may, however, be used for *passus* as well as for *pedes*. In *C. I. L.* vi 29774 (Dessau, ii 6032), P · ∞ is used for *passus mille*, as well as for *pedes mille*.
[4] 1135, 1140.   [5] Livy, i 44, 2; viii 10, 14; Tacitus, *Ann.* vi 37.
[6] Cp. G. F. Hill, *Illustrations of School Classics*, figs. 452, 467, and Dessau, i 2512 f, 2516, 2520; also Bruce's *Handbook to Roman Wall*, p. 82[7].

VII] ON PUBLIC WORKS. DISTANCE-SLABS 139

Fig. 37. Distance-slab from the Vallum of Antoninus Pius, Scotland.
Original, 9 feet long, by 3 feet, 11 inches high, in the National Museum of Antiquities, Edinburgh; from a cast, made for the Roman Society, in the British Museum.

IMP(ERATORI) CAES(ARI)[1] TITO AELIO HADRI(ANO) ANTONINO AVG(VSTO) PIO, P(ATRI) P(ATRIAE), LEG(IO) II AVG(VSTA) PER M(ILLIA) P(ASSVVM) IIIDCL · II FEC(IT). (Cp. *C. I. L.* vii 1088.)

[1] It has here been assumed that the name of the emperor is in the dative, as is usual in honorary inscriptions. CAESARI is found in full in the distance-tablets numbered *C. I. L.* vii 1121 and 1143.

140   LATIN INSCRIPTIONS   [CHAP.

Of these seventeen tablets, fifteen are in the Hunterian Museum, Glasgow[1], while one of the others (1133 a) was purchased by the Chicago Museum, and perished in the great fire of 1871. The only similar record found on the *Vallum* of Hadrian (belonging to 122 A.D.) is a mere fragment at Chesters, restored as ⟨LEG·II⟩ AVG⟨VSTA⟩ ⟨FECIT PEDES⟩ CCCXLIII[2], while the work of a single *centuria* is recorded in about 12 other unimportant inscriptions as amounting to distances varying from 22 to 200 P(EDES)[3], and one space of 200 and two of 800 feet are described as having been finished in the fortification of Salōnae in Dalmatia in 170 A.D.[4] But nothing exactly resembling the distance-slabs of the *Vallum* of Antoninus Pius has been found in any other part of the Roman world[5].

Boundary-stones

Of boundary-stones (*cippi terminales*), the earliest are the two found at Venusia declaring certain places *aut sacrom aut poublicom locom ese*[6]. Next come the *cippi* marking out the *ager Campanus* for division among the plebs under the authority of Gaius Gracchus and his two colleagues, *tres viri agris iudicandis adsignandis*, with the lines and angles of the *cardo* and the *decumanus*[7]. We also have boundary-stones between different communities, for example, three inscriptions of 141—136 B.C., fixing the boundaries between Ateste and Patavium on the one hand[8], and between Ateste and Vicetia on the other. This last runs as follows:—

Sex. Atilius M. f. Saranus pro cos | ex senati consulto | inter Atestinos et Veicetinos | finis terminosque statui iusit[9].

[1] *Conspectus etc.* in James Macdonald's *Tituli Hunteriani*, in *Trans. of Glasgow Archaeological Society*, N.S. iv 49 ff. The conspectus in *C. I. L.* vii p. 193 is not quite accurate.

[2] *C. I. L.* vii 596.

[3] *ib.* 228, from Ribchester, now in the Library of St John's College, Cambridge, *coh*(*ortis*) X (*centuria*) *Titiana*. O(*pus?*) *p*(*edum*) XXVII. Cp. also 143, 144, 151, 213, 215, 630, 631 a, 780, 782, 789, 854.

[4] Dessau, i 2287, 2616, 2617.

[5] See esp. George Macdonald, *The Roman Wall in Scotland*, with map and plates, pp. 413, Glasgow, 1911; and cp. Haverfield in *Ephem. Epigr.* ix (1913) 622 f.

[6] *C. I. L.* i² 2, 402-3; Wilmanns, 863.   [7] *C. I. L.* i² 2, 639-42; Dessau, i 24 f.

[8] *C. I. L.* i² 2, 633-4; Dessau, ii 5944 f; Facs. in Ritschl, LVIII *a, b, c*.

[9] *C. I. L.* i² 2, 636; Dessau, ii 5945; Facs. in Ritschl, LV *b*.

In Rome there are the *termini ripae Tiberis*, beginning with 55 B.C.[1], and continuing in and after the Augustan age[2]. In that age we have a series of upright stones marking the boundary, and stating the distance of the next stone 'in a straight line' (*recto rigore*) in either direction :—

In front: Imp. Caesar divi f. | Augustus | pontifex maximus, | tribunic(ia) potest(ate) XVII, | ex s. c. terminavit.
On right side: r(ecto) r(igore) prox(imus) cipp(us) ped(es) XXIV.
On back: r(ecto) r(igore) prox(imus) cipp(us) ped(es) CCVI[3].

Cippi have also been found, in or near Rome, recording the *termini* of the *pomerium* of Claudius, and of Vespasian and Titus. In each case the inscription begins with the full name of the Emperor or Emperors, and ends with the phrase *auctis populi Romani finibus, pomerium ampliavit terminavitque*, or *ampliaverunt terminaveruntque*[4]. From the *Campus Martius* we have the following, of the time of Hadrian, 120 f A.D. :—

Ex s(enatus) c(onsulto) collegium | augurum, auctore | imp(eratore) Caesare divi | Traiani Parthici f(ilio), | divi Nervae nepote, | Traiano Hadriano | Aug(usto), pont(ifice) max(imo), trib(unicia) pot(estate) V, cos. III, procos. | terminos pomerii | restituendos curavit[5].

Near the bank of the Tiber, below the Aventine, a *cippus* has been found, recording the boundary between private and public property :—

(Imperator C)aesar Augustu(s) | ex privato in publicum | restituit, in partem dextram recta | regione ad proxim(um) cippum | ped(es) CLXXXII, | et in partem sinistram recta | regione ad proxim(um) cippum | ped(es) CLXXVIII[6].

We have similar *cippi* relating to the boundaries of *municipia* in Italy and the Provinces. When the colony of Capua was enlarged by Caesar, massive boundary-stones were set up along the line traced by the plough-share, with the inscription :— IVSSV·IMP·CAESARIS | QVA·ARATRVM·DVCTVM | EST[7]. At Pompeii, under the authority of Vespasian, a tribune announces on a *cippus* the fact that he has restored to public use certain

---

[1] *C. I. L.* i² 2, 766; Dessau, ii 5922 *a, b, c*; Facs. in Diehl, *Insc. Lat.* 8 *e*.
[2] *ib.* 5923 (8 B.C.).   [3] *ib.* 5924 *b*; 5932, *rect. rigore*.
[4] Dessau, i 213, 248.   [5] *ib.* 311.
[6] *ib.* ii 5936; cp. 5935—5943; 5946, ll. 8—9, *recta regione*; iii (2) 9376.
[7] Wilmanns, 858.

property, which had been encroached upon by private owners¹.
Many inscriptions as to *termini* have been found in the Provinces².
Similarly we have public notices as to private property, e.g. 'via
inferior | privatast | T. Umbreni C. f., | precario itur, | pecus
plostru | niquis agat'³.

In theatres, amphitheatres, and circuses, the Greek custom of
placing inscriptions on seats assigned to certain
officials or private persons, was adopted in many
parts of the Roman world⁴. Such inscriptions have
been found in the 'Flavian Amphitheatre', commonly called the
Colosseum, and in the Amphitheatres of Verona, Ariminum, Pola,
and Syracuse; also in those of Nîmes and Arles, Lyons and
Orange⁵.

Seats in theatres

The Fratres Arvales of Rome, in the minutes of one of their
meetings, specially record the places assigned to themselves in
the 'Flavian Amphitheatre' in 80 A.D.⁶

---

¹ Wilmanns, 864. ² Dessau, ii 5948—5986, iii (2) 9378—9387.
³ *ib.* 6012 ; cp. 5987—6041.
⁴ Wilmanns, 2740—2746.
⁵ Hübner, *Exempla*, p. xlix ; Dessau, ii 5654.
⁶ Dessau, ii 5049 ; *Facs.* in Hübner's *Exempla*, 996, and Ricci, *Tav.* lxi.

CHAPTER VIII

(v) INSCRIPTIONS ON PORTABLE OBJECTS

THE 'portable objects' here to be considered in connexion with inscriptions are usually classed in modern works under the heading of *instrumentum*. This is a general term including articles used in public or private life. They may be (i) articles of metal, such as (*a*) weights and measures, (*b*) *tesserae*, (*c*) armour and missiles, (*d*) vessels or other articles of gold, silver, or bronze, (*e*) pipes of lead, (*f*) stamps and seals; (ii) products of mines and quarries; (iii) tiles; and (iv) vessels of clay.

(i) (*a*) Weights and measures (*pondera et mensurae*) made of stone, lead or bronze, are generally marked with letters and numbers (either incised or raised in relief) denoting their size. Sometimes they bear **Weights and Measures** inscriptions giving the name of the place where they have been tested, e.g. *exactum ad Castoris*; or *iussu aed(ilium) exact(um) ad Artic(uleiana pondera) i(n) C(apitolio)*, Articuleius being one of the aediles of 47 A.D. The following is the inscription (of 72 A.D.) on the 'Farnese Congius', now in Naples:—IMP · CAESARE | VESPAS·VI | T·CAES·AVG · F · IIII COS[1] | MENSVRAE | EXACTAE IN | CAPITOLIO | P X (i.e. 10 pounds)[2]. After Trajan the weights and measures were tested by the praefect, e.g. *ex auc(toritate) Q. Iuni Rustici praef(ecti) urb(i)* (*c.* 162 A.D.)[3]. Weights belonging to a legion were stamped with the name of that legion[4].

For purposes of weighing, the Romans used a steelyard (*statēra*) of bronze, as well as a simple balance (*libra*). The

---

[1] 73 A.D.
[2] Dessau, ii (2) 8628; cp. 8629–36.   [3] *ib.* 8638.
[4] *C. I. L.* iii 784; Daremberg-Saglio, s.v. *Legio*, fig. 4406.

bar of the steelyard was graduated into several divisions, each subdivided into twelfths, representing pounds (*librae*) and ounces (*unciae*) respectively. The ounces were marked by notches, and the pounds by numbers incised in the bar, e.g. on the bar of a steelyard found in London (which can also be used as a foot-rule) the numbers marking the pounds are inscribed at distances of one foot from each other :—

X   IIIIV   IIIV   IIV   IV   V   IIII |[1]

(*b*) *Tesserae*, primarily used of small cubes of bone or ivory, is also applied to various kinds of tickets or tokens:—

Tesserae

(1) the *tesserae frumentariae*, entitling the holder to obtain a dole of corn. Thus, in the British Museum, we have a quadrangular bronze corn-ticket, with a tapering top, inscribed, on one side *Ant*(*oninus*) *Aug*(*ustus*), *Lib*(*eralitas*) II, and, on the other, *fruentatio* LXI, i.e. the 61st monthly distribution dating from the accession of Antoninus (Pius?, 138 A.D.)[2]. We have also certain leaden counters (*tesserae nummariae*) marked with some attribute of Annona, such as the *modius* or ears of corn, with or without an indication of the time and place of distribution.

(2) Various *tesserae*, or counters of bone, ivory, or lead, inscribed, on one side, with Alexandrian buildings, and, on the other, with two numbers, one in Latin and one in Greek, used to be regarded as *tesserae theatrales* entitling the holder to admission to the circus, or the theatre or amphitheatre. But they are probably a kind of *tesserae lusoriae* used like draughts in the *ludus duodecim scriptorum*[3].

(3) Another kind of *tesserae lusoriae* of ivory has a Roman number from I up to LX on one side, and, on the other, some abusive or complimentary word, such as *nugator, fur, fortunate, facete*[4].

[1] *C. I. L.* vii 1282; cp. Dessau, ii (2) 8631, and *British Museum Guide to --Roman Life*, 148—151.
[2] *Guide to—Roman Life*, p. 10; cp. Juvenal, vii 174, 'vilis tessera— frumenti'.
[3] Daremberg-Saglio, s.v. *Tessera*, fig. 6818.
[4] Cp. Hülsen, in *Röm. Mitt.* 1896, 227 f; Dessau ii (2) 8625; Daremberg-Saglio, fig. 6817.

(4) The so-called 'contorniates', or bronze discs resembling coins, with designs in relief on either side within a raised rim and a circular depression, many of which have subjects connected with the circus, were probably used as counters in a game played on an oblong marble board inscribed with six words of six letters each. Here are two examples:

(*a*) CIRCVS PLENVS   (*b*) LVDERE NESCIS
     CLAMOR INGENS   PERDIS PLORAS
     IANVAE TE(NSAE?)[1]   VINCIS GAVDES[2]

Each word was separated from that opposite by a flower within a circle.

(5) *Tesserae hospitales*, or tokens interchanged between host and guest, are mentioned by Plautus (*Poen.* 958, 1047). We have two examples of the bronze head of a ram[3], and two of a bronze fish[4], divided longitudinally into two parts, one of which

Fig. 38. Tessera hospitalis, found near the *lacus Fucinus*, 1895; reproduced by permission from Daremberg-Saglio, s.v. *Hospitium*, fig. 3909.

T(itus) Manlius T(iti) f(ilius) | hospes | T(itus) Staiodius N(umerii) f(ilius).

[1] *Guide to—Roman Life*, p. 198 f.   [2] Dessau, ii (2) 8626 *d*, iii (2) 9453.
[3] (*a*) *C. I. L.* i² 2, 1764; Ritschl, tab. ii A; (*b*) Barnabei, *Notizie degli Scavi*, 1895, pp. 85—93 (Fig. 38), now in the Museo Nazionale, Rome; cp. Paribeni's *Guida*, 1911, p. 123.
[4] *C. I. L.* i² 2, 611; Dessau, ii 6093; see Ruggiero, s.v. *Hospitium*.

S. L. I.

could be kept by each of the two persons taking a pledge of 'hospitality'[1]. One of the former includes the word *hospes* (see Fig. 38); in one of the latter (*hospitium*) *fecere* is restored.

These belong mainly to private life, and specimens have been preserved in Rome and Vienna. Similar tokens relating to public life, and forming a compact between one community and another, or between a community and a private person, were recorded on bronze tablets known as *tabulae patronatus et hospitii*, presented (in the latter case) by a community to its patron. This was often in the form of a *tabella fastigiata*, with holes enabling it to be hung on the walls of the *atrium* of the person so honoured. Thus, L. Domitius Ahenobarbus, the grandfather of Nero, was made patron of a *pagus* in Northern Africa[2]. The usual phrase in such cases is *hospitium fecit*[3]; but, on a tablet of 2 B.C. it is stated that a certain Spaniard *tesseram hospitalem fecit cum civitate Palantina sibi et filiis suis posterisque*[4]. Most of these tablets have been found in Spain or Africa. As forms of agreement between a person and a community, they are sometimes regarded as belonging to the class of legal compacts[5].

(6) The *tesserae gladiatoriae* are small oblong pieces of bone or ivory, less than two inches long, with a handle or a hole at one end, and with inscriptions distributed over the four long faces. The inscription has (1) the name of a person, whether slave or freedman, (2) that of his owner or trainer, (3) the word *spectavit* or the abbreviation *sp.*, *spe.* or *spect.*, (4) the month, with or without the day, and (5) the consuls of the year. This last item, which determines the date, has led to their being called *tesserae consulares*; they extend over the first century B.C. and the first A.D. Over sixty of them are earlier than 44 B.C. and seven of these have SPECTAVIT in full, (1) DIOCLES VECILI; (2) PILOMVSVS PERELI (both known to Ritschl); (3) PROTEMVS FALCI (in the British Museum); (4) GENTI(VS) PACONI T(ITI) S(ERVVS); (5) MENOPIL·ABI·L(VCII) S(ERVVS) C·VAL(ERIO)

---

[1] See, however, Wordsworth's *Early Latin*, p. 472.
[2] Dessau, ii 6095; facsimile in Hübner, *Exempla*, 863.
[3] Dessau, ii 6095, 6099, 6100, 6103, etc.
[4] *ib.* 6096; facsimile in Hübner, *l. c.* 865, cp. *ib.* 862—887.
[5] p. 157 *infra*.

M·HER(ENNIO) (consuls of 93 B.C.); (6) PILEMO·FVLVI·Q(VINTI)· S(ERVVS); (7) PAMPHIL·SOCIORVM[1]. Two of those with SP· belong to 63 B.C. M·TVL·C·ANT[2]. The subject of *spectavit* is the gladiator, who, on the date specified, received this ticket of discharge, and 'took his place as a spectator' on being released from the arena. In a single *tessera* from Arles (only preserved in MS) we have *Anchial(us) Sirti L(ucii) s(ervus) spectat. num. mense Febr. M. Tul(lio) C. Ant(onio) cos.* (63 B.C.). SPECTAT· NVM is interpreted by Mommsen as *spectat(or) num(erator)*, and by Ritschl as *spectatus munere*. The latter view would make it parallel to the phrase in Horace (*Ep.* i 1, 2), *spectatum satis et donatum iam rude*[3].

(7) The *tesserae conviviales* were tickets of admission to public banquets, marked with numbers which probably indicated the place reserved for the holder[4].

(8) A number of perforated leaden seals of circular or oval shape have been found in England, inscribed with abbreviations denoting cohorts or centuries of the Second Legion[5]. These are probably *bullae* or badges, worn either as countersigns, or as marks of military distinction. *Bullae?*

The above are only a few of the many varieties of inscribed Roman *tesserae*. The *tesserae plumbeae* in particular, or tokens of lead, were first classified by O. Benndorf in 1875[6]. An important advance was made, on the same general lines, by Rostovzev, who

[1] *C. I. L.* i² 2, 945, 950, 946, 948, 890, 949, 951.
[2] Henzen, *ib.* 204; *C. I. L.* i² 2, 907 and 909.
[3] *C. I. L.* i² pp. 564 ff; Ritschl, *Opusc.* iv 572—656, with many facsimiles in Atlas of plates, xx, xxi, xxii; Hübner, *Exempla*, 6 facsimiles, 1194–9; *British Museum Guide to—Roman Life*, p. 75, specimen belonging to 85 B.C.; Dessau, ii 5161, with literature on p. 310; Friedländer's *Sittengeschichte*, ed. 6, ii 524; Bursian's *Jahresb.* lvi (1888) 103 f; Egbert, p. 260. Names of gladiators are followed twice by *sp.* in Dessau, ii 5084. Fröhner, *Coll. Dutuit*, ii (1901) 162 f, 211 f, approved by Rostovzev, *Bleitesserae* (1905) 2 f, reads *spectat num(en)* in the *tessera* of Arles, and understands it of an *incubatio*. Herzog explains the *tesserae* as *nummulariae*, bankers' labels on sacks of silver. See *L'Ann. Épig.* 1920, p. 1.
[4] On *tesserae* in general, see esp. Daremberg-Saglio, s.v., 1912, where the Roman *tesserae* are reviewed under the following headings:—(1) *frumentariae*, (2) *spectaculorum*, (3) *collegiorum iuvenum*, (4) *collegiorum et sodalitatum*, (5) *balneorum et hospitiorum*, (6) *sportularum*, (7) *hospitales*, (8) *militares*.
[5] *C. I. L.* vii 1269.   [6] *Zeitschr. f. d. österr. Gymn.* 1875.

catalogued nearly 4000, in 1903¹. The *tesserae* discussed by him may be classified as follows : *I, tesserae publicae,* (1) *imperiales,* (2) *militares,* (3) *frumentariae* and *nummariae,* (4) *spectaculorum,* (5) *collegiorum iuvenum* ; *II, tesserae privatae,* (1) *hospitales,* (2) *collegiorum,* (3) *artificum,* (4) *negotiatorum*². *Tesserae frumentariae, spectaculorum, hospitales* and *militares* have already been mentioned above under the headings (1), (2), (5), and (8).

(*c*) *Armour.* The 'Sword of Tiberius', found at Mainz, and now in the British Museum³, was probably presented to an officer who served under Germanicus; it is inscribed FELICITAS · TIBERI and VIC · AVG, *Victoria Augusti.* The shield was sometimes marked with the name of the owner and that of his legion and cohort. Thus the *umbo* (or centre-plate) of the shield of a Roman legionary, adorned with two military standards, and figures of the four seasons and of Mars and an eagle and an ox, found near the mouth of the Tyne, is faintly inscribed:—*Leg*(*ionis*) *VIII Aug*(*ustae*); *c*(*enturiae*) *Iul*(*ii*) *Magni ; Iunii Dubitati*⁴.

Armour

Leaden sling-bolts (*glandes plumbeae*), oval in form and pointed at both ends, are inscribed with letters in relief denoting the name of the praetor, as in the bolt at Asculum used in the Social War of 90—88 B.C., inscribed *T. Laf*(*renius*) *pr*(*aetor*), (*C. I. L.* i² 2, 848). They may also be inscribed with the name of the people making war, as *Itali* (on the bolt just quoted); or the person, as *Cn. Mag*(*nus*) *im-p*(*erator*), on a bolt used in the war waged against Julius Caesar by Cn. Pompeius Magni filius (*C. I. L.* i² 2, 885); or the maker; or the corps of slingers. Sometimes they bear the word *feri*, or insulting messages to the foe : *em tibe malum malo ; fugitivi peristis ; pertinacia vos radicitus tollet*⁵. Many similar bolts are forgeries⁶.

Missiles

¹ *Tesserarum urbis Romae et suburbi plumbearum Sylloge*, with Atlas, St Petersburg, 1903 ; also new German ed., *Römische Bleitesserae*, with two plates, Leipzig, 1905, in *Klio, Ergänzungsband*, i (3).
² Cp. *Berlin. Philol. Woch.* 1903, pp. 1486 f; 1904, pp. 110 f, 146 f; 1905, p. 1511.
³ See Illustrations in *British Museum Guide to—Roman Life*, 102-4.
⁴ *C. I. L.* vii 495 ; Hübner's *Exempla*, 942 ; Schreiber's *Atlas*, xlv 5.
⁵ Ritschl, tab. viii—ix ; *C. I. L.* i² pp. 559—564, ix pp. 631—647, x 8063, 1—5 ; *Eph. Ep.* vi, 143 pp. with 13 plates. Bursian, *Jahresb.* lvi (1888) 107—113 ; Egbert, 262, 328.   ⁶ *C. I. L.* ix 35* ff.

(d) Among inscriptions on **gold**, the first place must be assigned to that on the very ancient *fibula* from Praeneste:—*Manios med fhefhaked Numasioi* (p. 38). **Gold** Inscriptions are found on gems and on the gold rings in which they are mounted. Thus AMO TE is found on the gem and on the gold of a ring from Aix (*C. I. L.* xii 5692 f).

The various portions of the **silver** plate from Hildesheim are stamped with the weight of each[1], and similarly with the silver *lanx* from Corbridge, marked on the **Silver** back as weighing 14 pounds, 3 ounces, and 2 scruples[2]. In many cases we find the name or initials of the owner. Among other inscriptions on silver may be mentioned the itinerary from Gades to Rome engraved on four cylindrical cups found at the warm springs of Vicarello (*Aquae Apollinares*) in Tuscany[3].

The silver mirrors and the **bronze** jewel-boxes (*cistae*) of Praeneste are inscribed with the names of Greek gods or heroes, and (in two or three examples) **Bronze** with the name of the maker or owner. Thus the celebrated *cista Ficoroniana* bears on the lid the inscription

NOVIOS·PLAVTIOS·MED·ROMAI·FECID
DINDIA·MACOLNIA·FILEAI·DEDIT

(*C. I. L.* i² 2, 561, xiv 4112; Dessau, ii (2) 8652.)

A dedication to 'Mater Mursina' occurs on the rim of a bronze strainer said to have been found near Cortona

SACRO·MATRE·MVRSINA[4]

(i.e. *sacrum Matri Mursinae*)

On a bronze cup found in Wiltshire there is a very short itinerary of some stations on or near Hadrian's Wall[5]. Among the inscriptions on the numerous bronze vessels exported from Italy, and found in various parts of Europe, may be mentioned those

[1] Dessau, ii (2) 8617.
[2] *C. I. L.* vii 1286; Haverfield in *Journal of Roman Studies*, iv 1—12.
[3] *C. I. L.* xi p. 496 f; Desjardins, *Géographie...de la Gaule Romaine*, iv 1—20, *les Vases Apollinaires de Vicarello*, with plates and maps.
[4] *C. I. L.* i² 2, 580, now in the museum of Johns Hopkins University; see Wilson in *A. J. Ph.* 1908, pp. 450 ff.
[5] *C. I. L.* vii 1291; Hübner's *Exempla*, 911.

on the handle of a bronze *patera* with the name of the maker stamped in relief in small characters, surrounded by another inscription formed by a series of dots ending with the abbreviation for *votum solvit libens merito*[1]. The collars of bronze worn by slaves bore inscriptions such as *tene me, ne fugiam, et revoca me in* ...[2]. Some of these are too small for a slave, and are probably dog-collars. We also find makers' marks on bronze objects, and bronze stamps for marking goods with letters[3].

(*e*) Lead water-pipes (*fistulae plumbeae aquariae*) bear inscriptions in relief dating from the age of Augustus to the end of the third century. The earliest have only the name of the emperor; those of the second century add that of the *procurator*, or other official, and that of the *officinator*, under whose direction the pipe was made, or of the slave who made it. In special cases the inscription gives the name of the owner of the house, or the capacity of the pipe[4].

Water-pipes

(*f*) Seals (*signacula*) for stamping inscriptions in relief on softer substances were mainly made of bronze. They include the name of the owner of the article stamped, and sometimes that of the slave employed. They were also used to stamp certain kinds of provisions, e.g. *C. I. L.* x 8058, 18, *inscriptio impressa pani*, found at Herculaneum. A *centuria* of the 14th legion is named on the four sides of a stamp, found at Mainz, which resembles a small brick, and was probably used to mark the four sides of every loaf of bread supplied to that *centuria*. See Daremberg-Saglio, s.v. *Legio*, fig. 4407. The passage of Pliny, *cibi quoque ac potus anulo vindicantur a rapina* (xxxiii 26), need only refer to the use of a signet-ring to seal up stores.

Stamps and seals

A special class of *signacula* or seals, with letters cut on each of the four outside edges of small rectangular tablets of steatite or slate, was used by oculists for stamping the packets containing the medicament prescribed. Each of the edges bears an inscrip-

---

[1] Hübner's *Ex.* 933.
[2] *C. I. L.* xv 7171–91; Dessau, ii (2) 8726–33.
[3] See p. 151 *infra*.
[4] Cp. Dessau, ii (2) nos. 8677–8705.

tion, usually in two lines, giving the name of the oculist, and the remedy, and the malady for which it is to be used. See Fig. 39.

Fig. 39. Impression produced by Oculist's Stamp found at Reims (from Hübner's *Exempla*, 1203).

D · GALL(I) SEST(I) (S)FRAG|IS AD ASPRITVDI(NES)
D · GALL(I) SEST(I) SFRA|GIS AD IMPET(VM) LIPPIT(VDINIS)
D · GALL(I) SESTI PE|NICILLE AD LIPP(ITVDINEM)
D · GALL(I) SESTI | DIYNV(M) AD ASP(RITVDINES)[1].

The following are the inscriptions corresponding to the stamps on a specimen, found in England, and now in the British Museum:—

M · IVL · SATYRI DIASMY(R)|NES POST IMPET(VM) LIPPIT(VDINIS)
M · IVL · SATYRI PENI|CIL(LVM) LENE EX OVO
M · IVL · SATYRI DIA|LEPIDOS AD ASPR(ITVDINES)
M · IVL · SATYRI DIALI|BANV(M) AD SVPPVRAT(IONES)[2].

On the sole of a bronze foot we have a stamp enabling the vendor of pieces of pottery to impress his wares with the words **VTERE FELIX** (Ricci's tav. lxv). Stamps were also used to impress inscriptions in relief on vessels of glass, as in the words **BIBE VIVAS MVLTIS ANNIS** running round the rim in letters of green on the opal ground of the beautiful bowl in the Museo Trivulzio at Milan[3]. Souvenirs of Baiae have been found in the

[1] *C. I. L.* xiii 3 (2) p. 573.
[2] Cp. Espérandieu in *C. I. L.* xiii 3 (2) p. 579; Hübner's *Ex.* p. 435; Dessau, ii (2) 8734–42; Ricci, p. 295 n.; *Brit. Mus., Roman Life*, p. 182.
[3] Guhl and Koner, E. T. fig. 453.

form of glasses bearing representations of the oyster-parks of that sea-side health-resort, and inscribed (*inter alia*) with *memoriae felicissime filiae*, and *anima felix vivas*[1].

(ii) Inscriptions are found on blocks of marble in ancient quarries (as those in Lebanon, and near Hadrian's Wall), or at the Roman emporium on the Tiber. They include the number of the block, the name of the quarry, the consuls of the year, the officials or slaves in charge, and the emperor to whom the quarry belongs (cp. Dessau, ii (2) 8713–25).

Products of quarries and mines

Pigs of lead, found in various parts of England, Spain and Sardinia, as well as in Italy, are stamped with the name of the emperor, and the place where the metal was obtained. At Wookey hole, near the Mendip hills, a block of lead belonging to 49 A.D. was found bearing the inscription:—*Ti. Claud(ius) Caesar Aug(ustus) p(ontifex) m(aximus) trib(unicia) p(otestate) VIIII imp(erator) XVI. De Britan(nicis)*. Others are inscribed *De Cea(ngis)* or *De Ceangi(s)*, (the *Cangi* of Tac. *Ann.* xii 32), or *metalli Lutudare(n)-s(is)*, from the Derbyshire mines of Lutudaron near Matlock[2].

(iii) Ancient tiles (*tēgŭlae*) have been found near Parma, Veleia and Placentia, bearing the names of consuls between 76 and 11 B.C.[3] In Rome the consuls are not named until the second century A.D. Tiles of the last century of the Republic, or the first of the Empire, bear rectangular stamps with the inscription in a single line. Two straight lines of lettering are found on the stamps from about 50 A.D., and several in the time of Trajan and Hadrian. Thus far, each of the letters is concave. From the former date onwards, we also have stamps, with the lettering in relief, which are either perfectly round, or are of a semicircular or crescent shape. The crescent is produced by leaving a small circle blank within the edge of the larger circle. In process of time, the size of the small circle diminishes, the result being that the lettered portion of the stamp

Tiles

[1] Daremberg-Saglio, s.v. *Vivarium*, figs. 7559 f. For inscriptions on glass, see also the works of Delville (1873) and Fröhner (1874).
[2] *C. I. L.* vii p. 220 f; *Eph. Ep.* ix p. 642–4; Hübner's *Ex.* 1204–13; Dessau, ii (2) 8706–11. In Tac. *l.c.* 'inde Cangos' is best read as 'in Decangos'; hence Haverfield rightly prefers *Deceangi(cum)*; cp. *C. I. L.* vii 1203, *Brit(annicum)*.
[3] *C. I. L.* i² pp. 571 ff. The letters of the stamps are in relief with the exception of those of one *figulus* C.M.

is of a crescent shape in 60—100 or 120 A.D.; the crescent increases between 100 and 180, and becomes an almost complete circle in 175—217[1]. The inscription runs round the circumference in two or three concentric bands. The following are examples:—e.g. *Opus doliare Dionysi Domitiae P. filiae Lucillae, Paeto et Aproniano consulibus* (123 A.D.)[2]; *ex fig(linis) M. Herenni Pollionis dol(iare) L. Sessi Succesi*[3]; *Op(us) dol(iare) ex pr(aediis) C. Fulv(ii) Plaut(iani) pr(aefecti) pr(aetorio),* || *C(larissimi) V(iri), Cos. II, fig(lina) Bucconia* (203-5, Fig. 40). This last has no smaller

OP l. 1

CV l. 2

Fig. 40. Stamps on a Roman tile in the Vatican Museum, 203-5 A.D. (from Marini's *Atti Arvali*, 1795, p. 544). Only part of the second stamp is here reproduced.

[1] Dressel, *Untersuchungen über die Chronologie der Ziegelstempel der gens Domitia*, Berlin, 1886, and *C. I. L.* xv (1) pp. 1—11. Cp. Egbert, 269 ff.
[2] Hübner's *Ex.* 1214.   [3] *Brit. Mus. Guide—Roman Life*, p. 154.

circle left blank within the circumference; but there is a second inscription running in two horizontal lines at the foot of the same tile :—*L. Numer(ius)*, divided by the palm-branch from *Iustus fec(it)* in the second line. It also has in the centre of the circle a helmeted female figure, seated on a trophy. Other tiles have in the centre a decorative figure by way of trade-mark, sometimes referring to the name of the owner of the kiln, e.g. a wolf for Lupus, a crown for Stephanus.

Tiles used by soldiers in building their quarters are stamped with the name of the cohort, legion, or army. The badge of the legion is sometimes added. Thus, a capricorn playing with a ball appears on a tile of the LEG(IO) XXII PR(IMIGENIAE) P(IAE) F(ELICIS), found on the borders of Raetia and Germania[1]. In Britain, the graves of Roman soldiers are marked by tiles bearing the names of their legions, such as LEG(IO) II AVG(VSTA), LEG(IO) VI VICT(RIX) P(IA) F(IDELIS), or LEG(IO) XX V(ALERIA) V(ICTRIX), Tiles have also been found, in Kent, inscribed CL · BR · (*classis Britannicae*)[2].

Roofing-tiles were stamped with a decorative trade-mark. Flange tiles have been found in London, inscribed P · P · BR · LON, that is, probably, *publicani provinciae Britanniae Londinienses*[3]. A tile inscribed with abbreviations equivalent to 'Nero Claudius Caesar Augustus Germanicus', i.e. the Emperor Nero, has been found at Silchester[4].

Vessels of clay

(iv) Vessels of clay, including lamps (*lucernae*), and jars of various sizes, ranging from the small *patellae* and *pelves* to the intermediate *amphŏrae*, and the huge *dōlia*, are stamped with the name of the maker, merchant, or owner. The inscriptions include abbreviations of the words *fecit*, *manu*, *officina* or *figlina*. The letters are either impressed or in relief. Lamps were sometimes used as inexpensive New Year's gifts; these were stamped with a figure holding a small disc inscribed with ANNO NOVO FAVSTVM FELIX TIBI SIT[5]. On the

---

[1] Copied in Cagnat[4], p. 343. [2] *C. I. L.* vii 1222–6.
[3] *C. I. L.* vii 1235; see, in general, H. B. Walters, *Ancient Pottery*, 1905, ii 340—365. The flange tile above mentioned is figured *ib.* p. 363.
[4] Haverfield, *Romanization of Roman Britain*, ed. 3, p. 49, n. 2.
[5] Daremberg-Saglio, fig. 7415.

wine-jars we find the name of the wine, and of the maker or merchant, and the consuls of the year (as implied in Horace, *C.* iii 21, 1; *Ep.* i 5, 4); e.g. in red letters below the neck of an *amphora* from the Esquiline:—*Ti. Claudio P. Quinctilio cos.* (13 B.C.), *a*(*nte*) *d*(*iem*) *XIII K*(*al.*) *Iun*(*ias*); *vinum diffusum quod natum est duobus Lentulis cos.* (18 B.C.), *autocr*(*atos*)[1].

[1] Cp. Athenaeus, 32 f; see Dessau, ii (2) 8580, and cp. 8578—8594, and, in general, Walters, *l. c.*, (lamps) ii 420–9, and (jars) 458—467.

CHAPTER IX

(II) DOCUMENTS

THE second great class of inscriptions consists of Documents (*acta* or *instrumenta*), incised on tablets of stone or metal. These fall into the following subdivisions:—

(1) Treaties (*foedera*)[1]. The only Italian treaty recorded in an extant inscription is that relating to the Oscan *civitas libera* of Bantia in Lucania, drawn up in 133—118 B.C., containing part of the concluding portion of an agreement in Latin and in Oscan, providing for the annual election of a *iudex*[2]. The phrase *lex plebeive scitum* implies that the Latin document may have been a *lex de foedere*[3]. The discovery of this inscription in 1790 led to the investigation of the Oscan dialect.

The oath sworn by the citizens of the *civitas foederata* of Aritium in Lusitania, on the accession of Caligula in 37 A.D., may be regarded as a *foedus*. Its terms are as follows:—

> Ex animi mei sententia, ut ego iis inimicus ero, quos C. Caesari Germanico inimicos esse cognovero, et si quis periculum ei salutique eius infert inferetque, armis bello internicivo terra marique persequi non desinam, quoad poenas ei persolverit, neque me neque liberos meos eius salute cariores habebo, eosque, qui in eum hostili animo fuerint, mihi hostes esse ducam; si sciens fallo fefellerove, tum me liberosque meos Iuppiter optimus maximus ac divus Augustus ceterique omnes di immortales expertem patria incolumitate fortunisque omnibus faxint[4].

---

[1] Cp. p. 3 f *supra*.
[2] Facsimile in Ritschl, tab. xix; *C.I.L.* i² 2, 582; ix 416; Allen, no. 103; Diehl, *Altlateinische Inschriften*, no. 226.
[3] Cp. Conway's *Italic Dialects*, i 22—24; Lindsay, 80—83; and Ernout, *Textes Latins Archaïques*, 85—89.
[4] Dessau, i 190. Cf. Mommsen in *Eph. Epigr.* v 154 f; *Ges. Schriften*, viii 461 f.

CHAP. IX] LAWS 157

The *tabulae patronatus et hospitii*, already noticed (p. 146 *supra*), are of the nature of legal compacts.

(2) Laws (including *leges* and *plebiscita*). (*a*) The earliest and most important of those preserved is the *lex Acilia repetundarum* (122 B.C.), inscribed on bronze plates about six feet broad in 90 lines of no less than 200—240 letters each[1].

On the back of the *lex Acilia* is (*b*), the *lex agraria* of 111 B.C., the last of the enactments made after the death of Gaius Gracchus with a view to annulling his agrarian laws[2].

(*c*) The *lex Cornelia de viginti quaestoribus*, being the eighth tablet of Sulla's legislation[3], referring to the appointment of additional quaestors.

(*d*) The *plebiscitum* of 71 B.C., confirming the autonomy of Termessus in Pisidia, one of four or five large plates[4].

(*e*) The *lex Rubria de civitate Galliae Cisalpinae* (49 B.C.). It is characteristic of Caesar's legislation that this document is drawn up in a more convenient form, in two columns, with numbered divisions, of which the extant bronze tablet is the fourth[5].

(*f*) The '*lex Iulia municipalis*' (45 B.C.), found near Heraclea in Lucania, on the reverse of a much older Greek decree of that place, and dealing with the distribution of corn, the duties of the aediles, and the rules of municipal government[6].

(*g*) A fragment of Caesar's general municipal institutions containing a curious passage relating to the promulgation of laws[7].

[1] *C. I. L.* i^2 2, 583; Ritschl, tab. xxiii—xxv; cp. Wordsworth, 176 f, 429 f; Lindsay, 84—88.

[2] *C. I. L.* i^2 2, 585; R. tab. xxvi—xxviii; Wordsworth, 189 f, 440 f.

[3] *C. I. L.* i^2 2, 587; R. tab. xxix; cp. Wordsworth, 205, 460; Allen, 49; Lindsay, 90 f; Ernout, 96—99.

[4] *C. I. L.* i^2 2, 589; Dessau, i 38; R. tab. xxxi, partly copied in Ricci, tav. xxxiv; Wordsworth, 209, 462.

[5] *C. I. L.* i^2 2, 592; R. tab. xxxii; cp. Wordsworth, 212, 463; Lindsay, 96 f.

[6] *C. I. L.* i^2 2, 593; R. tab. xxxiii f; Dessau, ii 6085; Wordsworth, 213 f, 464 f; Lindsay, 97 f; E. G. Hardy, J. Elmore, and J. S. Reid, in *Journal of Roman Studies*, iv—v (1914—5).

[7] *C. I. L.* v 15. See texts of all the above laws in Bruns, *Fontes Iuris Romani antiqui*, ed. 7, 1909, with Gradenwitz, *Simulacra*, 1912; cp. E. G. Hardy, *Six Roman Laws*, 1911.

Under the Empire *leges* assumed the form of *senatus consulta* and imperial *constitutiones*. It was as a *senatus consultum* that the *leges de imperio*, on the accession of an emperor, were promulgated, e.g. the *lex de imperio Vespasiani* (70 A.D.), recorded on a bronze tablet found in Rome, formerly in the Church of St John Lateran, and now in the Capitoline Museum[1].

The constitutions given to *civitates* were also called *leges*, e.g. (1) the *lex municipii Tarentini*, which was granted before 62 B.C.[2]; (2) the *lex coloniae Genetivae Iuliae Vrbanorum sive Vrsonis* (Osuna in Spain), which was granted in 44 B.C., and is partly preserved in three bronze tablets of the time of Vespasian[3]; (3) the *lex Salpensana*, and (4) the *lex Malacitana*, granted by Domitian in 81—84 A.D. to the *municipia* of Salpensa and Malaca in Spain[4]; and (5) the *lex metalli Vipascensis*, granted by one of the Flavian emperors to a mining settlement in southern Portugal[5].

(3) Of the *Senatus Consulta* of the Roman people the earliest preserved as a Latin inscription on bronze tablets is (*a*) part of the Latin portion of the *S. C. Lutatianum* of 77 B.C., declaring Asclepiades of Clazomenae and his comrades *amici populi Romani*[6]. We have also (*b*) fragments of decrees on the *ludi saeculares* of 17 B.C. and 47 A.D., preserved on a marble slab[7]; (*c*) fragments decreeing posthumous honours to Germanicus and the younger Drusus, as mentioned by Tacitus, *Ann*. ii 83 (of Germanicus), *honores... reperti decretique...*, and iv 9, *memoriae Drusi eadem quae in Germanicum decernuntur*[8]... (*d*) regulations against the demolition, and on the rebuilding, of houses in Rome (41—46 and 56 A.D.), on a bronze plate found at Herculaneum[9]; (*e*) a permit for a

---

[1] Dessau, i 244; Rushforth, *Lat. Hist. Inscr.*, no. 70; Facsimile of a few words in Hübner, *Exempla*, 802; cp. p. 21 *supra*, and Appendix IV (4) *infra*.
[2] *C. I. L.* i² 2, 590; Dessau, ii p. 500 f, no. 6086; Mommsen, *Ges. Schr.* i 146—161.
[3] *C.I.L.* i² 2, 594; Dessau, ii pp. 502—515, no. 6087; Hübner, *Exempla*, 805.
[4] Dessau, ii pp. 516—525, nos. 6088 f. For translation of (2), (3), (4) see E. G. Hardy, *Roman Laws and Charters*, 1912; cp. Gradenwitz, *Simulacra*, 1912.
[5] Dessau, ii pp. 682—685, no. 6891.
[6] *C. I. L.* i² 2, 588; R. tab. xxx; Wordsworth, 205 f, 460.
[7] *C. I. L.* vi 877, and 32323. For the *Acta* of the *ludi* of 17 B.C., see p. 176 f *infra*.   [8] *C. I. L.* vi 911 f; Orelli-Henzen, no. 5381.
[9] Dessau, ii p. 480, no. 6043.

IX] MUNICIPAL DECREES 159

market in the *saltus Beguensis* in Northern Africa[1]; (*f*) a *Senatus Consultum* on Cyzicus, of the time of Antoninus Pius (138—161 A.D.) now in the British Museum[2]; (*g*) a *Senatus Consultum* of 176—177 A.D., *de sumptibus ludorum gladiatoriorum minuendis*, found in 1888, now in Madrid. This forms a large part of a speech delivered by a senator, after a message from M. Aurelius and his son and colleague, Commodus, had been read to the Senate. It is with reference to this enactment that Iulius Capitolinus writes in his *M. Antoninus Philosophus*, 11, 4, 'gladiatoria spectacula omnifariam temperavit', and 27, 6, 'gladiatorii muneris sumptus modum fecit'[3].

The *Senatus Consulta, de Bacchanalibus*, and *de Tiburtibus*, are embodied in letters, and are noticed at a later point (p. 161 f).

(4) The municipal decrees, now extant, are far more numerous, and are in a more or less complete form.

(*a*) The earliest is the *lex operum Puteolana II*, described in the document itself as *lex parieti faciendo*. The date corresponds to 105 B.C., but, as the lettering is more graceful than in other inscriptions of that date, the inscription is supposed to have been restored under the Empire; but, as it is of the nature of a specification for a particular building, it is difficult to understand why it should be restored at any later date than that which it bears. The form, however, of the letters shows that it was 'recut in imperial times' (Wordsworth, p. 476). See next page, Fig. 41.

<small>Municipal decrees</small>

(*b*) The two *decreta Pisana* were passed by the Senate. of Pisa, in 3—4 A.D., prescribing funeral rites in honour of Lucius and Gaius Caesar, the adopted sons of Augustus, being the sons of Agrippa and Iulia, the only child of Augustus. Lucius had died on his way to Spain, 2 A.D., and Gaius in Lycia, 4 A.D. The memory of Lucius was to be honoured by an altar, and that of Gaius by a triumphal arch with a statue above it, between equestrian statues of both brothers[4].

[1] Wilmanns, 2838; Facsimile in Cagnat, ed. 1914, pl. xii 1.
[2] *C. I. L.* iii 7060 *bis*.
[3] Dessau, ii p. 310 f, no. 5163; Mommsen, *Ges. Schriften*, viii 499—531.
[4] Dessau, i 139, 140; Wilmanns, 883; Hübner's *Exempla*, 1063-4.

(c) A *decree of Lanuvium* belonging to 136 A.D., laying down the rules for a funeral club[1]. A single sentence, addressed to any prospective applicant for admission, may be worth quoting :—

Tu qui novos in hoc collegio intrare vole(s, p)rius legem perlege et sic intra, ne postmodum queraris aut heredi tuo controver(si)am relinquas.

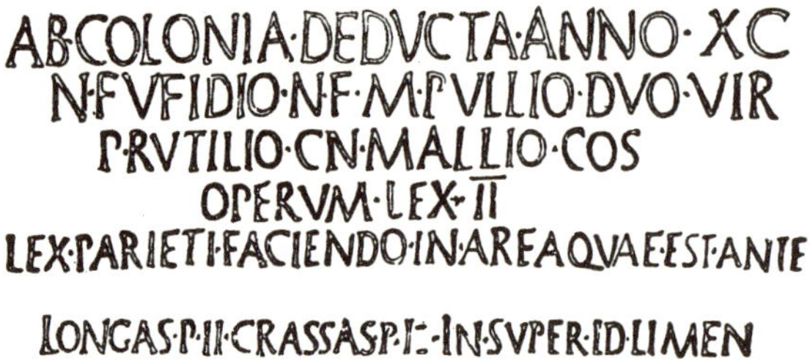

ABCOLONIA·DEDVCTA·ANNO·XC
N·F·VFIDIO·N·F·M·P·VLLIO·DVO·VIR
P·RVTILIO·CN·MALLIO·COS
OPERVM·LEX·II
LEX·PARIETI·FACIENDO·IN·AREA·QVAE·EST·ANTE

LONGAS·P·II·CRASSAS·P·I≟·INSVPER·ID·LIMEN

Fig. 41. From the lex parieti faciendo, of Puteoli; see p. 159; (lines 1—5 and 13, from Hübner's *Exempla*, 1072.)

Ab colonia deducta anno XC, |
N(umerio) Fufidio N(umerii)
f(ilio), M(arco) Pullio duovir(is), |
105 B.C. P(ublio) Rutilio, Cn(eio) Mallio cos. | Operum lex II |
Lex parieti faciendo in area, quae est ante—
(13) longas p. II, crassas p. I ≟. Insuper id limen—

Complete facsimile in Ritschl, tab. lxvi; copied on small scale in Egbert, 378; text in *C. I. L.* i² 2, 698 (with architectural drawing of porch etc.), Dessau, ii 5317; Wordsworth, 222, 476 f; discussed by Wiegand, in *Jahrb. f. class. Phil.*, Suppl. XX (1894) 661 f. Cp. Gradenwitz, *Simulacra*, 1912, no. ix.

(d) A *decree of Tergeste* (Trieste), ordaining the erection of a statue in honour of L. Fabius Severus, an eloquent and public-spirited advocate, under Antoninus Pius (138—161)[2].

(e) A *decree of Puteoli*, c. 180 A.D., paying M. Laelius Atimetus the compliment of remitting the ground-rent (*sŏlarium*)[3] of a building he was erecting :—

IIII non(as) Septembr(es) in curia templi basilicae Augusti Annianae, scribundo adfuerunt Q. Granius Atticus, M. Stlaccius Albinus, A. Clodius Maximus, M. Amullius Lupus, M. Fabius Firmus.

Quod T. Aufidius Thrasea, Ti(berius) Claudius Quartinus IIviri v(erba)

---

[1] Dessau, ii (2) 7212; Wilmanns, 319; Hübner's *Exempla*, 1076.
[2] Dessau, ii (1) 6680; Hübner's *Exempla* 1079.
[3] Cp. p. 129 *supra*.

IX] MUNICIPAL DECREES 161

f(ecerunt) de desiderio Laeli Atimeti, optimi civis, Q · D · E · R · F · P·, D · E · R · I · C ·¹.

Cum M. Laelius Atimetus, vir probissimus et singulis et universis karus, petierit in ordine nostro, uti solarium aedifici, quod extruit in transitorio, remitteretur sibi ea condicione, ut ad diem vitae eius usus et fructus potestasque aedifici sui ad se pertineret, postea autem rei p(ublicae) nostrae esset: placere huic ordini tam gratam voluntatem optimi civis admitti, remittique ei solarium, cum plus ex pietate promissi eius res publica nostra postea consecutura sit.

In curia f(uerunt) n(umero) LXXXXII².

Among municipal inscriptions may be mentioned those of Pompeii³, including (*a*) monumental inscriptions cut in stone on public buildings, on pedestals, or on tombs; (*b*) public notices painted on the walls in bright red or in black, especially those recommending a particular candidate as *virum bonum*, V · B, urging his election in the phrase, *oro vos faciatis*, O · V · F, or making a personal appeal involving a pledge of future support, *Sabinum aed(ilem)*, *Procule, fac, et ille te faciet*; (*c*) notices of public buildings to let; (*d*) advertisements of animals or articles, lost or found; and (*e*) announcements of gladiatorial games with the special attraction, *venatio et vela erunt*, followed by the name of the painter,—the same enterprising person who puts up outside his house:— *Ae(mili)us Celer hic habitat*⁴.

<small>Pompeian inscriptions</small>

(5) Of the decrees of magistrates under the Republic the earliest extant example is a decree of L. Aemilius Paullus as praetor in Further Spain (in 189 B.C.), setting the Lascutani free from the control of their neighbours at Hasta. It is incised on a bronze plate (Fig. 42).

<small>Decrees under the Republic</small>

As an example of a document embodying a *Senatus Consultum* we have (*a*) the Letter addressed by the Consuls of 186 B.C. informing the Teurani in the Bruttian peninsula of the terms of the *Senatus Consultum de Bacchanalibus*⁵. The original bronze

<small>Documents embodying Senatus Consulta</small>

¹ *quid de ea re fieri placeret, de ea re ita censuerunt.* Cp. *App.* v (45).
² Dessau, ii (1) 5919; complete facsimile in Hübner's *Exempla*, 1084.
³ Dessau, ii (1) pp. 306—602.
⁴ Dessau, ii 5145, 6409 note; Mau, *Pompeii*, c. 55.
⁵ See text in Appendix IV (1), below; also text and notes in Dessau, i 18; Allen, no. 82; Lindsay, pp. 59—67; Ernout, pp. 58—68; cp. Livy, xxxix 8 f.

plate (called *tabola ahena* in the inscription) is now in Vienna[1]. While, in the above-quoted Decree of 189 B.C. (five years before the death of Plautus), there is no ablative in *d*, the present document, though three years later than the Decree, is more archaic in its form. But, in this document, the retention of the

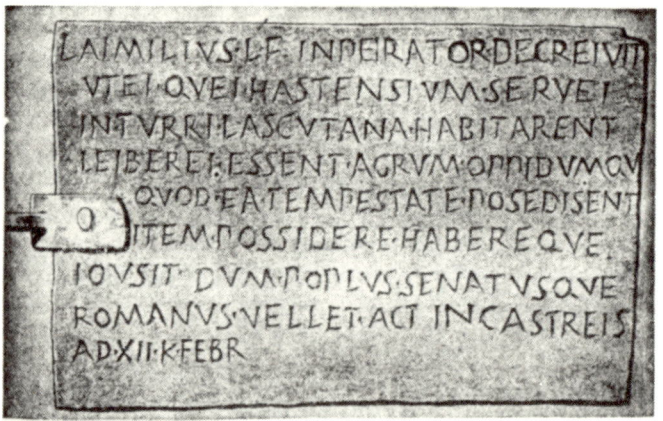

Fig. 42. Decree of L. Aemilius Paullus, 189 B.C.
(from *C. I. L.* ii 5041).

L. Aimilius L. f. inpeirator decreivit, | utei quei Hastensium servei | in turri Lascutana habitarent, | leiberei essent ; agrum oppidumqu., | quod ea tempestate posedisent, | item possidere habereque | iousit, dum poplus senatusque | Romanus vellet. Act. in castreis | a. d. XII k. Febr.[2]

old ablative in *d* (discarded in the decree of 189) is purely a piece of conservative spelling. Further, we have no doubled consonants, and *ai* is used throughout, except in l. 1, *aedem Duelonai.* On the other hand, we have *-us* and *-um*, not *-os* and *-om*. In the ancient notice hung up in the sacred grove at Spoletium the final *d* is sometimes added, but is sometimes dropped. Curious verbforms ending in *d* are found in a similar notice, from Luceria[3].

[1] Facsimile in Ritschl, tab. xviii, Gradenwitz, *Simulacra*, no. iii, and Diehl, *Inscr. Lat.* 5.

[2] *C. I. L.* i^2 2, 614; Dessau, i 15; Allen, p. 27; Wordsworth, 415 f; Lindsay, p. 57; Ernout, p. 57. Cp. Mommsen, *Hermes*, iii 261 f (*Ges. Schriften*, iv 56—62).

[3] Both notices quoted in (6) (*a*) (*b*) *infra*. Cp. Lindsay, 53, 56 f.

(*b*) The substance of a *Senatus Consultum* relating to the Tiburtes is embodied in a Letter from the praetor L. Cornelius (possibly of 156 B.C.). This was recorded on a bronze plate, found at Tibur[1].

(*c*) The award of the Minucii in a boundary-dispute between the Genuates and their tributaries belongs to 117 B.C. This is preserved on a bronze plate found near Genoa[2].

(6) As a 'sacred inscription' of the early republican period we have (*a*) the notice hung up in a sacred grove at Spoletium in Umbria:— <small>Sacred and public documents</small>

<small>honce loucom nequ(i)s violatod neque exvehito neque exferto quod louci siet, neque cedito, nesei quo die res deina anua fiet. eod die quod rei dinai cau(s)a (f)iat sine dolo ced(e)re (l)icetod. sei quis violasit, Iove bovid piaclum datod; sei quis scies violasit dolo malo, Iovei bovid piaclum datod et a(sses) CCC moltai suntod. eius piacli moltaique dicator(ei) (?) exactio est(od).</small>

Here *deina* and *dinai* stand for *divina, -ae*. The final *d* after a long vowel is sometimes written, sometimes dropped; double consonants are written single in *anua* and *violasit*; *n* is dropped before *s* in *scies*; *cedito* and *cedere* are dialectal for *caidito, caidere*[3].

(*b*) Several examples of the final *d* may be seen in the following similar notice from Luceria in Apulia:

<small>in hoc loucarid stircus ne(qu)is fundatid neve cadaver proiecitad neve parentatid. sei quis arvorsu hac faxit (in) ium quis volet pro ioudicatod n(ummum) (L) manum iniect(i)o estod. seive macisteratus volet moltare, licetod[4].</small>

(7) Among documents connected with religious worship may be noticed the *leges templorum*.

(*a*) One of these is the decree of 58 B.C. relating to the temple of Iuppiter Liber at the Sabine town of Furfo. The heading is clear enough; *L. Aienus L(uci) f(ilius), Q. Baebatius Sex(ti) f(ilius) aedem dedicarunt | Iovis Liberi Furfone a.d. III idus Quinctileis, L. Pisone, A. Gabinio cos., mense Flusare* (i.e. *Florali*).

---

[1] *C.I.L.* i² 2, 586; Dessau, i 19; Allen, no. 105; Wordsworth, 204, 459; Ernout, 68 ff.

[2] *C.I.L.* i² 2, 584; Ritschl, tab. xx; Ricci, tav. xxxiii; Gradenwitz, no. vi; text in Allen, no. 104; Wilmanns, 872; Dessau, ii 5946; Ernout, p. 89 ff.

[3] *C.I.L.* i² 2, 366; Dessau, ii 4911; cp. Lindsay, 53—56; Ernout, p. 38 f.

[4] *C.I.L.* i² 2, 401; Dessau, 4912; Lindsay, 56 f; Ernout, p. 47.

The colloquial forms for *alius* and *aliud*, namely *alis* and *alid*, found in Catullus (lxvi 28) and Lucretius (i 263), are exemplified in the phrase *alis ne potesto*; but the inscription in general, which fills about half a page of print, was denounced by Mommsen as the most corrupt inscription he had ever known[1].

(*b*) At Narbo, in Southern Gaul, we have an inscription of 11 A.D. (restored in the second century) dedicating an altar to Augustus, beginning with the date :—*T. Statilio Tauro | L. Cassio Longino | cos. x k(alendas) Octob(res) | numini Augusti votum | susceptum á plebe Narbonensium inperpetuom*[2]. On the side of the altar, the terms of the dedication are introduced as follows: (*plep*)*s Narbonesis a(ram) | numinis Augusti de(di)cavit... | legibus iis q(uae) i(nfra) s(criptae) s(unt)*, and, at a later point, we read *ceterae leges huic arae titulisq(ue) eaedem sunto, quae sunt arae Dianae in Aventino.* The formula for the dedication of the temple of Diana was apparently the oldest of which the Romans possessed any record. In accordance with that ancient precedent, the present dedication proceeds as follows: *hisce legibus hisque regionibus, sicuti dixi, hanc tibi aram...doque dedicoque, uti sies volens propitium*[3].

(*c*) At Salōnae in Dalmatia an altar is dedicated to 'Iuppiter optimus maximus' in 137 A.D., and the formula just quoted is there repeated[4].

(*d*) An 'ara incendii Neroniani' has been found in Rome on the Quirinal, with one of several upright stones (*cippi*) marking out the boundaries of the consecrated ground. The following is taken from the first half of the dedicatory inscription of 83 or 84 A.D.

haec area, intra hanc definitionem cipporum clausa veribus[5], et ara quae est inferius, dedicata est ab imp(eratore) Caesare Domitiano Aug(usto) Germanico ex voto suscepto, quod diu erat neglectum nec redditum, incendiorum arcendorum causa, quando urbs per novem dies arsit Neronianis temporibus. Hac lege dedicata est, ne cui liceat intra hos terminos aedificium exstruere, manere, nego(t)iari, arborem ponere aliudve quid serere,...[6].

[1] *C. I. L.* i[2] 2, 756; Wilmanns, 105; Dessau, ii 4906; Wordsworth, 224, 479 f; Lindsay, 93.
[2] Facsimile in Hübner's *Exempla*, 1099 (and Egbert, p. 371).
[3] sc. *numen*. Wilmanns, 104; Dessau, i 112; cp. p. 88, *supra*.
[4] Wilmanns, 103; Dessau, ii 4907. [5] For *verubus*. [6] Dessau, ii 4914.

Among minor examples of 'sacred inscriptions' we have the *sortes*, or small tablets bearing vague and commonplace admonitions, which were drawn out of an urn, and were regarded as oracular responses, e.g.

> LAETVS·LVBENS·PETITO·QVOD
> DABITVR·GAVDEBIS·SEMPER

C. I. L. i² 2, 2183.

Seventeen of these tablets were found near Padua, having probably been used at the *Fons Apŏnus*, a neighbouring seat of divination[1]. Others have been found near Parma[2]; while tablets with prescriptions, and with exhortations to prayers to Jupiter and Aesculapius, have been found at Pavia, e.g. *Obscura fati quaerella deum praesidio lenietur*; *esto cura cauta tu placa Iovem* etc.[3]

Foremost among documents belonging to the sacerdotal *collegia* are the *Acta collegii fratrum Arvalium*, an ancient corporation revived by Augustus. Their sole duty was to preside at the festival of the *Dea Dia* in May; and their place of worship was in the grove of that goddess on the old *Via Campana*, five miles from Rome. It was there that the marble tablets recording their meetings were found. These were collected and published first by Marini in his *Atti e monumenti de' fratelli Arvali* in 1795, and, finally, by Henzen in his *Acta fratrum Arvalium quae supersunt* in 1874. They form a most important group of epigraphic monuments. In a tablet discovered in 1778 their most ancient *carmen* has been preserved among the *acta* of 218 A.D. in an almost unintelligible, and probably corrupted, form

Acta Collegii Fratrum Arvalium

> enos Lases iuvate.
> neve lue rue Marmar sins incurrere in pleores.
> satur fu fere Mars limen sali sta berber.
> semunis alternei advocapit conctos.
> enos Marmor iuvato.
> triumpe.

[1] *C. I. L.* i² p. 689 f.   [2] *ib.* xi 1129 *a—c.*
[3] Hübner's *Ex.* 908—9.

Each of the first five lines is repeated thrice, and the final *triumpe* five times¹. The following version in ordinary Latin (only partially clearer than the original) has been suggested :—

(1) *nos, Lares, iuvate!* (2) *neve luem, ruem, Marmar, sine incurrere in plures.* (3) *satur esto, fere Mars; limen sali, siste verber.* (4) *semones alternatim advocabit cunctus.* (5) *nos, Marmor, iuvato.* (6) *triumphe.* *Marmor* (like *Mamers*) is a reduplicated form of *Mars*²; (1), (2), half of (3), and (5) are addressed to the gods; the rest of (3), and (4), and (6) to the brethren.

If, in the grove of Dea Dia, a fig-tree has to be uprooted from the roof of the temple, and the roof repaired; if an ancient branch falls to the ground, or, if any of the trees are struck by lightning, every one of these events calls for a sacrifice of expiation. These sacred rites are recorded in various *acta* extending from 14 to 224 A.D.³ In the *acta* of 80 A.D., the year in which Titus dedicated the *Amphitheatrum Flavianum*, the position and the exact dimensions of the places permanently assigned to the *Fratres Arvales* are carefully indicated⁴. The *acta* for 101 A.D. record the vows offered by the *collegium* to Iuppiter, Iuno, Minerva, Mars, Victoria, Fortuna redux, and other divinities, for the safe and victorious return of Trajan from his Dacian expedition, while they perpetuate the language of the prayer addressed to each :— *principem parentemque nostrum...feliciter incolumem reducem victoremque facias*⁵.

Among the *decreta collegiorum* may be noticed the *lex collegii salutaris Dianae et Antinoi* of 136 A.D.⁶; the *lex collegii Aesculapii et Hygiae* of 153 A.D.⁷; and the *lex collegii Iovis Cerneni* of 167 A.D., found in Dacia⁸.

Decrees of collegia

¹ *C. I. L.* i² 2, 2; Dessau, ii p. 276; facsimile in Ritschl, tab. xxxvi A (copied in Ricci, tav. xv); also in Hübner, 1024 (Ricci, tav. xii).

² Cp. Lindsay, pp. 1—26; Ernout, p. 107; also Mommsen's *History of Rome*, Book I, c. xv (i 287, ed. 1894); English version (and notes) :— Wordsworth, 385—395.   ³ Dessau, ii 5042—5048.

⁴ Dessau, ii 5049; Hübner, *Ex.* 996 (Ricci, tav. lxi); p. 142, *supra*.

⁵ Dessau, ii 5035. For the *Acta* in general, see Dessau, i 229, 230 (*Acta* of 58—59 A.D.), 241 (69 A.D.), 451 (213 A.D.), ii 5026—5049, and iii (2) 9522 (240 A.D.). Facsimile of about 50 lines of no. 229 in Diehl, *Inscr. Lat.* 25.

⁶ Dessau, ii (2) 7212; complete facsimile in Diehl, *Inscr. Lat.* 28 *a*.

⁷ Dessau, ii (2) 7213.

⁸ *C. I. L.* iii p. 924; Wilmanns, 321; Dessau, ii (2) 7215 *a*.

ACTA COLLEGIORUM

The 'public and sacred' documents include the *Fasti*, in both senses of the term, (1) the monthly, and (2) the annual calendar. Both of these calendars were comprehended under the name of *Fasti*, which strictly belonged only to the list of court days. The *pontifex maximus* combined the annual, with the earlier monthly, calendar, one of his duties being to keep 'an official record of the names of the chief annual magistrates'[1]. This is specially stated by Servius in his commentary on Virgil's *Aeneid*, i 377:—

> Ita annales conficiebantur; tabulam dealbatam quotannis pontifex maximus habuit, in qua praescriptis consulum nominibus et aliorum magistratuum, digna memoratu notare consueverat, domi militiaeque, terra marique gesta, etc.

Among the most important of the historical inscriptions of Rome are the *Fasti consulares* and the *Acta triumphorum*. By far the largest number of the fragments of these inscriptions was discovered in 1546, the number of the fragments of the *Fasti* and the *Acta* then discovered being 30 and 26 respectively, the corresponding totals being now 49 and 38. Almost all of these have been placed in the *Sala dei Fasti* in the *Palazzo dei Conservatori* on the Capitol; hence the name of *Fasti Capitolini*[2]. They have been elaborately edited in the first volume of the *Corpus Inscriptionum Latinarum*, in the first edition of 1863, and in the first part of the second edition of 1893[3].

Fasti consulares. Acta triumphorum

Most of the fragments were found in the north-eastern quarter of the Forum, between the temple of Antoninus and Faustina, and the temple of Castor. In that portion of the above space which lies immediately to the north of the temple of Vesta, and to the south of the Sacra Via, certain architectural remains have been discovered which have been identified with the foundations of the new *Regia*, or public office of the Pontifex Maximus[4]. The position, between the Sacra Via and the temple of Vesta,

---

[1] Mommsen, *H. R.* ii 101, E. T. ed. 1894.
[2] p. 25 *supra*.
[3] See pp. 1—54, with the plates at end of this part.
[4] F. M. Nichols, *Archaeologia*, vol. 50 (1887).

corresponds to that of the traditional site of the *Regia* of Numa, as described in Ovid's *Tristia* (iii 1, 26):—

Haec est a sacris quae via nomen habet,
hic locus est Vestae qui Pallada servat et ignem,
hic fuit antiqui Regia parva Numae.

After the conflagration of the old *Regia*, the new *Regia* was built by the pontifex maximus, Domitius Calvinus, on his triumphant return from Spain[1]. The site was a little to the east of the old Regia. The date of the new Regia was 718/36.

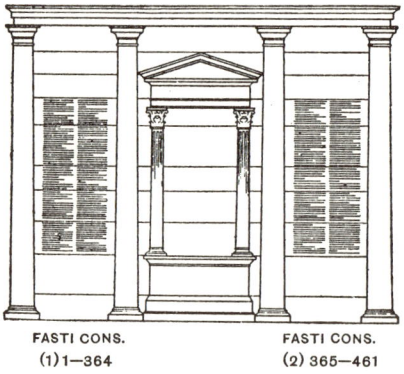

FASTI CONS. (1) 1—364   FASTI CONS. (2) 365—461

Fig. 43 (a). Elevation of the West End of the Regia, showing the probable position of the *Fasti Consulares* (1) and (2). Figs. 43 (a) and (b) are founded on a perspective view of Hülsen's restoration.

The *Fasti consulares* and the *Acta triumphorum* were placed on the outer walls of this *Regia*. They were inscribed, not on separate slabs, but on the actual blocks of marble, more than eighteen inches thick, of which the *Regia* was built. It was a small but costly building, gleaming with the marble of Luna, that was destined to receive the record of more than seven centuries of Roman rule and Roman triumph.

The building was oblong in shape, with its narrow ends facing east and west, and its broad sides facing north and south. The

[1] Dion Cassius, xlviii 42, τυχών τε τῶν ἐπινικίων...τὸ χρυσίον τὸ παρὰ τῶν πόλεων...τὸ μέν τι ἐς τὴν ἑορτὴν ἀνάλωσε, τὸ δὲ δὴ πλεῖον ἐς τὸ βασίλειον. κατακαυθὲν γὰρ αὐτὸ ἀνῳκοδόμησε καὶ καθιέρωσεν, ἄλλοις τέ τισι λαμπρῶς κοσμήσας καὶ εἰκόσιν κ.τ.λ. Coins of Calvinus, struck in Spain, name him as *imperator*, and include his insignia as *pontifex*.

IX] FASTI CONSULARES. ACTA TRIUMPHORUM 169

sunlit southern aspect was the most suitable for a long inscription, and it is practically certain that these inscriptions were begun on the west end and were completed on the south side. Apparently, the only external rectangle was at the south-west corner[1].

The *Fasti consulares* were divided into four tables in double columns. The first and second were on the west end, and the third and fourth on the south side, probably to the left and right of a central door. The *Acta triumphorum* were also divided into four tables, but all of these were on the south side, the third

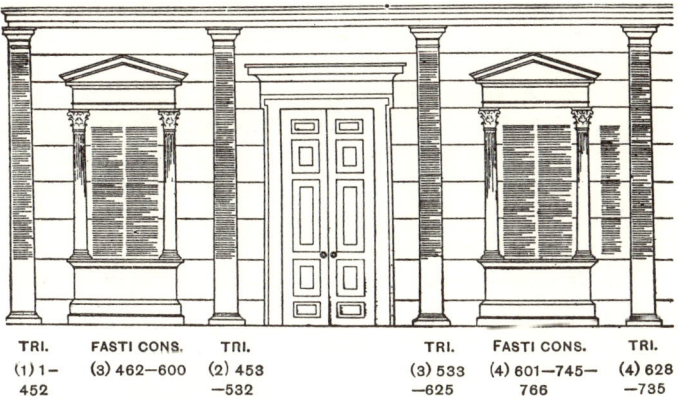

TRI.	FASTI CONS.	TRI.		TRI.	FASTI CONS.	TRI.
(1) 1– 452	(3) 462–600	(2) 453 –532		(3) 533 –625	(4) 601–745– 766	(4) 628 –735

Fig. 43 (*b*). Elevation of the South Side of the Regia, showing the probable position of the *Fasti Consulares* (3) and (4), and of all the four lists of the *Acta Triumphorum* (TRI.).

table of the *Fasti* being flanked by the first and second of the *Acta triumphorum*, and the fourth table of the *Fasti* by the third and fourth of the *Acta triumphorum*[2]. See Fig. 43 (*a*) and (*b*).

The *Fasti* record under each year, in chronological sequence, the names of the consuls, and (where necessary) the military tribunes with consular power, the dictators and *magistri equitum*,

---

[1] View of 'remains' and 'ground-plan' in Hülsen, *The Roman Forum*, E. T. (1906), 181 f.

[2] For architectural restoration, see Hülsen, in (1) *Jahrbuch des Instituts*, 1889, 228–253; (2) *C. I. L.* i² (1893) pl. ii; and (3) *The Roman Forum*, E.T. (1906), p. 184. All three represent a view taken in perspective from the S.W. angle of the building. Hülsen's corrections in *Beitr. z. alt. Gesch.* ii 255 ff. (Pauly-Wissowa s.v. Fasti, p. 2030) are incorporated in Fig. 43 (*a*).

and the censors. After every ten years they add in the left-hand margin the date from the foundation of Rome, according to the Catonian era, which was one year later than the Varronian subsequently in general use. The names of all the magistrates were inscribed in double columns. The height of tables I and II (on the west end) was probably 8 feet 6 inches (2·62 mètres); and that of III and IV (on the south side) 7 feet 10 inches (2·41 mètres). The corresponding Varronian years covered by the four tables were I, 1—364; II, 365—461; III, 462—600; and IV, 601—745, with a marginal continuation covering the years 746—766. The dates of certain *ludi saeculares* were added :—(1) to the left of table III, the date 518 A.V.C. (236 B.C.), and (2) and (3), below 766, the dates 737 and 841, for the *ludi* of Augustus (17 B.C.) and Domitian (88 A.D.) respectively. The number of lines in the double columns has been ascertained to have been originally 1300. In table III, which is less incomplete than the others, the number of lines extant is 187 out of 249, or, roughly, three-fourths.

The *Acta triumphorum*, inscribed on four pilasters of a single column only, were nearly 11 feet high (3·35 mètres), the years of Rome in each being I, 1—452; II, 453—532; III, 533—625; IV, 628—735 (= 19 B.C.). This last was the year in which L. Cornelius Balbus, the younger, who was proconsul in Africa, celebrated his triumph over the Garamantes. The total number of lines was 660. In II, which is better preserved than the rest, the number of lines extant is 139 out of 160, or about seven-eighths.

As to the date when the *Fasti* and the *Acta* were inscribed on the walls of the *Regia*, there have been two opinions.

(1) Borghesi[1], followed by Mommsen and Henzen in the first edition of vol. i of the *Corpus Inscriptionum* (1863), placed the date after 718/36 (the year of the building of the *Regia*), and before 724/30. The latter date was inferred from the fact that, in the *Fasti*, the name of the triumvir M. Antonius had been first erased, and subsequently restored, under the years 707/47 and 717/37, and similarly in the case of his grandfather,

---

[1] 1818; *Œuvres*, ix 1, p. 6.

IX]   FASTI CONSULARES.   ACTA TRIUMPHORUM   171

the orator, under 657/97. It was argued by Borghesi that the erasures must have been made in 724/30[1], after the triumvir's defeat at the battle of Actium, and that the *Fasti*, at any rate, were completed before that date. This assumes that the *Fasti* ended with the year 718/36, in the middle of the second column of the third table, and were afterwards continued to 766 or 13 A.D.

(2) While Borghesi, Mommsen and Henzen placed the date of the *Fasti* and the *Acta* between 718/36 and 724/30, Hirschfeld placed the date of both between 742/12 and 747/7. The former was the year in which Augustus became *pontifex maximus*[2]. In the second edition of the *Corpus* (1893), Mommsen and Henzen adhered to Borghesi's date for the *Fasti* (shortly after 36 B.C.), but placed the completion of the *Acta* between 736/18 and 742/12, and most probably in the latter year, thus accepting the earlier of Hirschfeld's dates for the *Acta* (*c.* 12 B.C.).

The following extract, relating to the beginning of the First Punic War, may serve as a specimen (on a reduced scale) of the style of the lettering adopted in the *Fasti*. It represents the first half of a few lines in the first column of the third table,

BELLVM·PVNICVM·
AP·CLAVDIVS·C·F·AP·N   CAVDEX
XC·M·VALERIVS·M·F·M·N ·MAXIMVS
QVI·IN·HOC·HONORE·MESSALLA·PPELLE
CN·FVLVIVS·CN·F·CN·N·MAXIM·CENT·

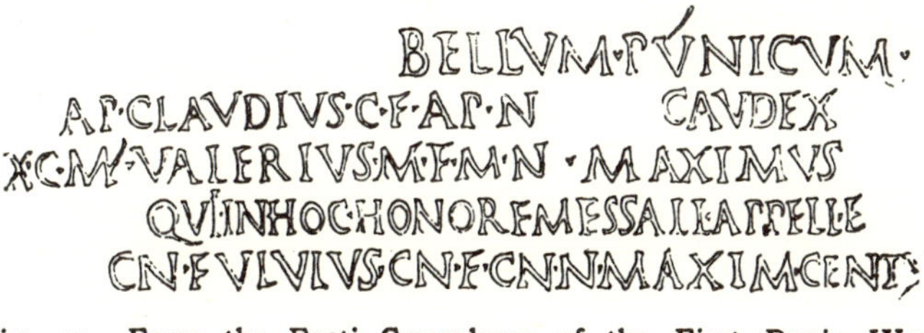

Fig. 44. From the Fasti Consulares of the First Punic War (reduced from Hübner's *Exempla*, col. 1 of no. 948 *c*), $\frac{1}{15}$ of original size.

Bellum Punicum (primum) Ap. Claudius, C. f(ilius), Ap. n(epos), Caudex | (CD) XC. M(anius) Valerius, M. f(ilius), M. n(epos), Maximus, | qui in hoc honore Messall(a) appell(atus) e(st) | Cn. Fulvius, Cn. f(ilius), Cn. n(epos), Maxim(us) Cent(umalus).

The *Acta triumphorum* begin with the triumphs of Romulus and Ancus Marcius[3], and they include, under the year 718/36,

[1] Dio Cassius, li 9.
[2] *Hermes*, iv (1875) 93—108, xi (1876) 154—163 (*Kl. Schr.* 330—352).
[3] Dessau, i 69.

the triumph of Cn. Domitius Calvinus, the builder of the *Regia*[1]. The following specimen, on a reduced scale, belongs to the year 493/261 f.

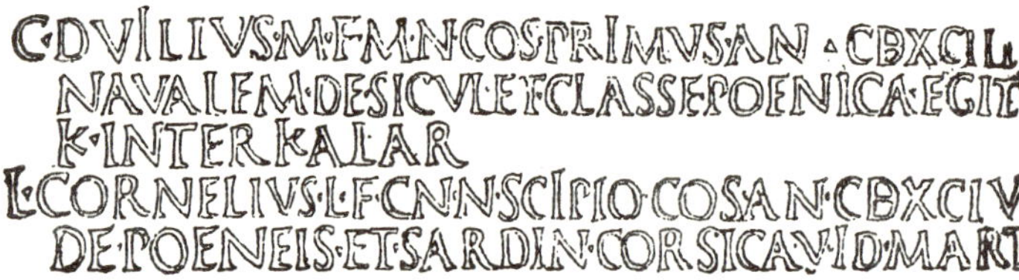

C·DVILIVSM·F·M·N·COSPRIMVSAN · CBXCIL
NAVALEM·DESICVLE·ECLASSEPOENICA·EGIT
K·INTER·KALAR
L·CORNELIVS·LF·CN·N·SCIPIO·COS·AN·CBXCIV
DE·POENEIS·ET·SA·RDIN·COR·SICA·V·IDMA·RT

Fig. 45. From the Acta Triumphorum (reduced from Hübner's *Exempla*, no. 949), about ¼ of original size.

C. Duilius M. f(ilius) M. n(epos) co(n)s(ul) primus an(no) CDXCIII
navalem (triumphum) de Sicul(is) et classe Poenica egit,
k(alendis) interkalar(ibus).

L. Cornelius L. f(ilius) Cn. n(epos) Scipio co(n)s(ul) an(no) CDXCIV
de Poeneis et Sardin(ia) Corsica V. id(us) Mart(ias).

(*C. I. L.* i 458; i² p. 47.)

We have also certain other *Fasti consulares* and *Acta triumphorum*, drawn up by priestly colleges and Italian municipalities, as records of public events. The battle of Actium is so recorded in the *Fasti* discovered at Amiternum[2].

The *Fasti anni Iuliani* are calendars arranged according to the Julian year[3]. About thirty of these have been found; they extend from the age of Augustus to that of Claudius, and have survived in a more or less fragmentary form[4]. The best known is the *Kalendarium Maffeianum*, which was in the Palace of the Maffei in the sixteenth century, and is now represented by a few fragments only[5]. These *Fasti* contain lists of all the days of each month in a series of

Fasti anni Iuliani

[1] Cp. G. Schön, *Das Capitolinische Verzeichnis der Römischen Triumphe*, Wien, 1893; Pauly-Wissowa, s.v. *Fasti*; Ett. Pais, *Fasti triumphales populi Romani*, Rome, 1920.

[2] *C.I.L.* i² p. 61; Hübner's *Exempla*, 952, copied in Egbert, p. 365.

[3] The most ancient Roman calendar known and the only one prior to the Julian reform was recently found at Antium and published in *Notizie degli Scavi*, 1921, pp. 73 ff. It dates from near the beginning of the first century B.C.

[4] *C. I. L.* i² pp. 206—279, ed. Mommsen.

[5] The whole is restored by Mommsen, *C. I. L.* i² pp. 222—228; Dessau, ii (2) pp. 987—991. Cp. p. 25 f *supra*.

columns, the first of which gives the sequence of the eight *litterae nundinales*, from A to H, with the several days marked C for *comitialis*, F or N or NP, for *fastus* or *nefastus* or *nefastus prior*[1], or (more probably) for *fas* or *nefas* or *nefas, feriae publicae*. The following is from the Maffeian calendar for March 23—31.

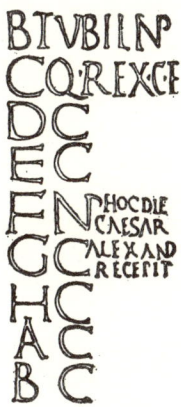

Fig. 46. Fasti anni Iuliani (Hübner's *Exempla*, no. 971), ⅓.

March 23. *Tubil(ustrium)*. *N(efas)*, *F(eriae) P(ublicae)*. The *Fasti Praenestini* add the note: *hic dies appellatur ita, quod in atrio sutorio tubi lustrantur, quibus in sacris utuntur*. Ovid, *Fasti*, iii 849, v 725.

March 24. *Q(uando) rex c(omitiavit), f(as)*. Cp. Ovid, *Fasti*, v 727.

March 27. *Hoc die Caesar Alexand(riam) recepit*, 707/47.

The *Fasti Praenestini* were set up in the Forum of Praeneste by Verrius Flaccus, the famous grammarian of the Augustan age. Cp. Suetonius, *de grammaticis*, 17, *statuam habet Praeneste, in inferiore fori parte circa hemicyclium, in quo fastos a se ordinatos et marmoreo parieti incisos publicarat*. Large marble slabs of these *Fasti* were found in the neighbourhood of Praeneste. They are more fully annotated than the other *Fasti*[2]. A fragment was

[1] This explanation was attacked by Mommsen (*C. I. L.* i² p. 289 f), who regarded NP as a corruption of an old form of N, denoting *Nefasti hilares*. With Wissowa, *Religion und Kultur der Römer* (1902), p. 371, and Reid, in *Companion to Latin Studies*, p. 97, I prefer Soltau's interpretation, *nefas, feriae publicae*, 'the abbreviation having undergone some distortion of form.' Hence, in Festus, s.v. *nefastus*, NEP should be N·F·P.

[2] Hübner, *Exempla*, 972, and Diehl, *Inscr. Lat.* 11.

published by Ursinus in 1577, and further fragments in 1771. In and after 1774, they were preserved in Rome, at the residence of one of the Cardinals[1].

Calendars were also prepared for the use of farmers. Two of these were discovered in Rome in the sixteenth century:—(1) the lost *Menologium Vallense*, which once belonged to the De la Valle family[2]; and (2) the *Menologium Rusticum*, discovered by Angelo Colocci, and now in the Naples Museum. The latter is engraved on the four upright sides of a cubical marble altar, 2 feet high, by $1\frac{1}{4}$ broad, with three months on each side. At the head of each month is a sign of the zodiac, followed by the name of the month, the number of days, the date of the nones, the number of hours in the day and the night, the name of the sign of the zodiac, and the agricultural *agenda* and the festivals of the month[3].

Menologia Rustica

The following is the complete text, as printed in *C. I. L.* i[2] p. 280 f (notes on details, *ib.* pp. 305—339).

capricornus	*aquarius*	*pisces*
MENSIS· IANVAR	MENSIS· FEBRVAR	MENSIS· MARTIVS·
DIES · XXXI	DIES · XXVIII	DIES · XXXI
NON · QVINT ·	NON QVINT	NON SEPTIMAN
DIES · HOR · VIIIIS	DIES · HOR · XS	DIES HOR · XII
NOX · HOR · XIIII ⁻⁻	NOX · HOR · XIII ⁻⁻	NOX · HOR · XII
SOL	SOL · AQVARIO	AEQVINOCTIM
CAPRICORNO	TVTEL · NEPTVNI	VIII · KAL · APR
TVTELA	SEGETES ·	SOL · PISCIBVS
IVNONIS	SARIVNTVR	TVTEL MINERVAE
PALVS	VINEARVM	VINEAE PEDAMIN
AQVITVR	SVPERFIC · COLIT	IN PASTINO
SALIX	HARVNDINES	PVTANTVR
HARVNDO	INCENDVNT ·	TRIMESTR SERITVR
CAEDITVR	PARENTALIA	ISIDIS NAVIGIVM
SACRIFICAN͞	LVPERCALIA	SACR · MAMVRIO
DIS	CARA COGNATO	LIBERAL QVINQVA
PENATIBVS	TERMINALIA	TRIA LAVATIO

[1] *C. I. L.* i[2] pp. 230—239. A new fragment, *Notiz. degli Scavi*, 1921, p. 277.
[2] Published from manuscript copies in *C. I. L.* vi 2306, and i[2] p. 280 f.
[3] Dessau, ii (2) pp. 994–6; complete facsimile in Egbert, 369 f; copies in bronze (not in exact facsimile) inscribed 'cast in Lauchhammer' (N. of Dresden) 'Ael. Rost.'

MENOLOGIA RUSTICA

aries	*taurus*	*gemini*
MENSIS APRILIS	MENSIS MAIVS	MENSIS IVNIVS
DIES · XXX	DIES · XXXI	DIES XXX
NONAE	NON · SEPTIM	NON · QVINT
QVINTAN	DIES · HOR · XIIIIS	DIES HOR · XV
DIES	NOX · HOR · VIIIIS	NOX HOR · VIIII
HOR · XIIIS	SOL TAVRO	SOLIS · INSTITIVM
NOX	TVTEL · APOLLIN	VIII · KAL · IVL
HOR · XS	SEGET RVNCANT	SOL · GEMINIS
SOL · ARIETE	OVES TVNDVNT	TVTELA
TVTELA	LANA · LAVATVR	MERCVRI
VENERIS	IVVENCI DOMAN	FAENISICIVM
OVES	VICEA PABVLAR	VIN//AE
LVSTRANTVR	SECATVR	OCCANTVR
SACRVM	SEGETES	SACRVM
PHARIAE	LVSTRANTVR	HERCVLI
ITEM	SACRVM MERCVR	FORTIS
SARAPIA	ET · FLORAE	FORTVNAE

cancer	*leo*	*virgo*
MENSIS IVLIVS	MENSIS AVGVST	MENSIS SEPTEMBER
DIES · XXXI	DIES · XXXI	DIES · XXX
NONAE	NON · QVINT	NON QVINT
sic SERTIMAN	DIES · HOR · XIII	DIES HOR · XII
DIES	NOX · HOR · XI	NOX HOR · XII
HORARVM	SOL · LEONE	AEQVINOCT
XIIII ⸗	TVTEL · CERER	VIII · KAL · OCT
NOX · HOR	PALVS · PARAT	SOL · VIRGINE
VIIIIS ⸗	MESSES	TVTELA
SOL · CANCR	FRVMENTAR	VOLCANI
TVTELA	ITEM	DOLEA
IOVIS	TRITICAR	PICANTVR
MESSES	STVPVLAE	POMA · LEGVNT
HORDIAR	INCENDVNT	ARBORVM
ET FABAR	SACRVM · SPEI	OBLAQVIATIO
APOLLINAR	SALVATI · DEANÆ	EPVLVM
NEPTVNAL	VOLCANALIA	MINERVAE

libra	*scorpio*	*sagittarius*
MENSIS	MENSIS	MENSIS
OCTOBER	NOVEMBER	DECEMB
DIES · XXXI	DIES · XXX	DIES · XXXI
NONAE	NON QVINT	NON QVINT
SEPTIMAN	DIES · HOR · VIIIIS	DIES HOR · VIIII
DIES	NOX · HOR · XIIIIS	NOX HOR · XV
HOR · XS ⚊	SOL	SOL · SAGITT
NOX	SCORPIONE	TVTEL · VESTÆ
HOR · XIII ≡	TVTELA	HEMPS · ℏITIV
SOL	DEANAE	SIVE · TROPAE
LIBRA	SEMENTES	CHIMERIN
TVTELA	TRITICARIAE	VINEAS · STERC
MARTIS	ET · HORDIAR	FABA · SEᴋEɴES
VINDEMIAE	SCROBATIO	MATERIAS
SACRVM	ARBORVM	DEICIENTES
LIBERO	IOVIS	OLIVA · LEGENT
	EPVLVM	ITEM · VENAɴ̄
	HEVRESIS	SATVRNALIA

The marble slabs of the *Acta Sacrorum Saecularium* of 17 B.C.

Acta Sacrorum Saecularium were mainly discovered in 1890. They form an almost complete record of the proceedings on that memorable occasion. The arrangements were carried out by Augustus and Agrippa as members of the *collegium quindecim virorum*, who had the custody of the Sibylline books, and the duty of superintending any religious ceremony prescribed in them. In the *Monumentum Ancyranum* (§ 22) Augustus himself refers to the leading part which he played in this commemoration :—*pro conlegio xv virorum, magister conlegii, collega M. Agrippa, ludos saec⟨u⟩lares, C. Furnio C. Silano consulibus, ⟨feci⟩*. The official duties of the *collegium* on the same occasion are briefly touched upon by Horace in his *Carmen Saeculare* (l. 70): *Quindecim Diana preces virorum curat.*

The inscription, in its present form, begins with the letter from Augustus to the *Quindecimviri*, dated March 24, detailing the proposed arrangements for the commemoration on June 1—3. During those days all the law-courts were to be closed, and ladies in mourning were to lay aside that sign of grief. The *Quindecimviri* announce that, at four centres in the city, they would distribute torches, sulphur, and bitumen, for purposes of purification, on May 26, 27, 28, and wheat, barley, and beans on May 29, 30, 31. On May 23 the Senate meets, and passes two resolutions. As none of the living had seen, or would see, any similar commemoration, the prohibition against unmarried persons between the age of twenty and fifty attending ceremonies of state is removed; and two pillars are to be set up, one of bronze, and one of marble, recording the official report of the celebration. During the night of May 31, sacrifices are offered to the Fates[1], and other ceremonies performed on a wooden stage illuminated by lights and fires. In the pageant of June 1—3, the order of the procession is as follows: at its head is Augustus, as Emperor and Pontifex Maximus; next come the Consuls, the Senate, the *Quindecimviri* and other Colleges of priests; then follow the Vestal virgins, and, lastly, one hundred and ten matrons, corresponding to the number of the years of the *saeculum*. On the 3rd of June, Augustus and Agrippa sacrificed to Apollo and Diana on the Palatine; and, on the completion of the sacrifice, seven and twenty boys and girls of patrician descent, both of whose parents were living, sang the several portions of the *Carmen Saeculare*:—

SACRIFICIOQVE PERFECTO PVERI (X)XVII · QVIBVS · DE-
NVNTIATVM · ERAT · PATRIMI · ET · MATRIMI · ET PVELLAE ·
TOTIDEM |
CARMEN · CECINERVNT · EODEMQVE · MODO · IN · CAPITOLIO |
CARMEN · COMPOSVIT · Q · HOR(AT)IVS · FLACCVS | [2].

In 1890 many other fragments were discovered, which contain the record of the commemoration under Septimius Severus and Caracalla, in the year 204 A.D.[3]

[1] *Moerae*, the *Parcae* of Horace's *Carmen Saeculare*, 25.
[2] Cp. Mommsen in *Ephemeris Epigraphica*, viii 225—309 (1892), and in his *Gesammelte Schriften*, viii (1913) 567—626; Hülsen in *C. I. L.* vi 32323; Dessau, ii pp. 282-7; Lanciani, *Pagan and Christian Rome* (1892), pp. 73—82, with Mommsen's text in Appendix; and Lindsay, 102 f. Facsimile of lines 85—167 in Diehl, *Inscr. Lat.* 9 and 10.
[3] *C. I. L.* vi 32327; one extract in Dessau, ii 5050 *a*.

S. L. I.

On the walls of the temple of Augustus and Roma, at Ancyra (the modern *Angora*) in Galatia, we have, in the form of a 'sacred' inscription, the *Monumentum Ancyranum*, the best preserved copy of a secular document of the highest historical importance as to the life of Augustus. This is the *Index rerum a se gestarum*, originally incised on bronze tablets to be placed in front of his mausoleum in Rome[1]. The inscription at Ancyra, discovered and partly copied by Busbequius in 1555, was first published by Schott at Antwerp in 1579; the Greek translation was partly copied by W. J. Hamilton in 1836. Many further portions were discovered by Georges Perrot and E. Guillaume in 1861[2]; and in 1873 the whole was edited in the *Corpus Inscriptionum Latinarum*[3] by

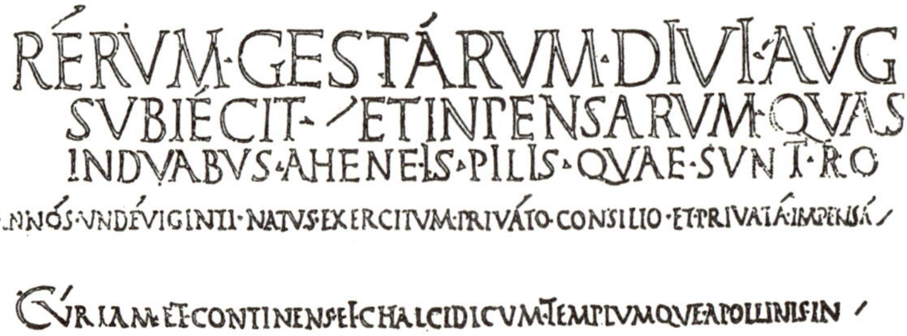

Monumentum Ancyranum

RERVM·GESTARVM·DIVI·AVG
SVBIECIT· ET INPENSARVM·QVAS
INDVABVS·AHENEIS·PILIS·QVAE·SVNT·RO
·NNOS·VNDEVIGINTI·NATVS·EXERCITVM·PRIVATO·CONSILIO·ET·PRIVATA·IMPENSA·

CVRIAM·ET·CONTINENS·EI·CHALCIDICVM·TEMPLVMQVE·APOLLINIS·IN

Fig. 47. From the Monumentum Ancyranum
(Hübner's *Exempla*, no. 1090), ⅔.

Rerum gestarum divi Augusti, quibus orbem terra[rum] imperio populi Rom(ani) | subiecit et inpensarum, quas in rem publicam populumque Ro[ma]num fecit, incisarum | in duabus aheneis pilis, quae su[n]t Romae positae, exemplar sub[i]ectum

§ 1. Annos undeviginti natus exercitum privato consilio et privata impensa | comparavi ...

§ 19. Curiam et continens ei Chalcidicum, templumque Apollinis in | Palatio cum porticibus...feci.

---

[1] Suet. *Aug.* 101.
[2] *Exploration archéologique de la Galatie*, 1872 ; view of remains of the temple (from Perrot) in Duruy's *Histoire de la Grèce*, iv 154 ; restoration of temple, *ib.* 155 ; facsimile of large part of the Latin text, *ib.* 163.
[3] *C. I. L.* iii (2) 769 f; followed by Bergk's ed. (Göttingen, 1873).

IX] MONUMENTUM ANCYRANUM 179

Mommsen, who also produced separate editions of this important document[1].

In Fig. 47 we see a reduced facsimile of the heading, and of two items. Here, as in Augustus' inscription on the obelisk from the Circus Maximus (Fig. 8), we have the tall I and the *apex* over other long vowels. The heading is in the *scriptura monumentalis*, and the rest in the *scriptura actuaria*.

The *Oratio* of Claudius (48 A.D.) on the admission of Gallic citizens to public office is engraved on large bronze tablets discovered at Lyons in 1528 (Dessau, i p. 52, no. 212; Lindsay, 107), being a copy of the original text of the speech reported by Tacitus as having been delivered before the Roman Senate (*Ann.* xi 24).

Decrees etc. under the Empire

TEMPVSESTIAMTICAESARGERMANICEDETEGERETEPATRIBVSCONSCRIPTIS
QVOTENDATORATIOTVAIAMENIMADEXTREMOSFINESGALLIAENAR
BONENSISVENISTI

Fig. 48. From a Speech of Claudius, 48 A.D.; preserved at Lyons.

(Hübner's *Exempla*, no. 799; Boissieu, *Inscr. ant. de Lyon*,
p. 132 ff), ⅙.

Tempus est iam, Ti. Caesar Germanice, detegere té patribus conscriptis, | quo tendat oratio tua; iam enim ad extremos fines Galliae Nar|bonensis venisti (cp. Bury's *Greek Historians*, 229). Here we have I for *i*, also an *apex*' in line 1, and in line 2 the point twice placed *within* the letter (to save space)[2].

The decrees of the imperial age include (1) the award of the proconsul, L. Helvius Agrippa (69 A.D.), on a boundary-dispute in Sardinia (Dessau, ii 5947); (2) the letter to the magistrates of Saepinum and Bovianum in Samnium from the *praefecti praetorio* of 166–9, to protect the farmers of the imperial sheep-walks; inscribed on a stone still to be seen at Saepinum near the present sheep-path, which passes through the gate to Bovianum (*C. I. L.* ix 2438; Wilmanns, 2841).

[1] 1865 and 1883; also by Cagnat and Peltier, 1886; and at the end of Shuckburgh's ed. of Suetonius, *Augustus*, 1896; small ed. by Diehl, 1908, 1910[2]; ed. by E. G. Hardy, Oxford, 1923; cp. Lindsay, 104–6; and see Appendix IV (2) *infra*.
[2] For the whole of the extant text, see Appendix IV (3).

12—2

180   LATIN INSCRIPTIONS   [CHAP.

Among the *Constitutiones* of the emperors may be mentioned (1) the edict of Augustus on the aqueduct at Venafrum [1]; (2) that of Claudius (46 A.D.) on the Civitas Anaunorum (in the *Val di Non*, north of Trent)[2]; and (3) the celebrated Latin and Greek edict of Diocletian (301 A.D.) *De pretiis rerum venalium*, promulgating a maximum price for provisions and other articles of commerce, and a maximum rate of wages[3]. There are also certain *decreta*, or judicial decisions, of the emperor in the form of a letter, such as those of Vespasian relating to disputed boundaries in Corsica[4] and Spain[5], and the *tabulae alimentariae* of Trajan, providing for the relief of the children of poor parents, as in the inscriptions relating to the Ligures Baebiani in Samnium[6] and to the inhabitants of Veleia near Parma[7]. These inscriptions give the details of the plan whereby the emperor lent large sums at low interest on the security of landed estates belonging to members of the municipality, while the interest was paid to the municipal chest for the relief of the children.

The *diplomata militaria* record the privileges as to *civitas* and *conubium* granted to veteran soldiers by nearly all
Military diplomas   the emperors from Claudius in 52 A.D. to Diocletian in 305.

These inscriptions are of special interest in connexion with the legal rights of the Roman army. Soldiers of foreign birth received the above privileges when they had completed their time of service, which usually extended to twenty years, that of the auxiliaries being twenty-five. For this purpose the emperor published a 'law' including a complete list of the veterans

[1] Wilmanns, 784; Dessau, ii p. 415 f, no. 5743; facsimile of three lines in Hübner's *Exempla*, 1062.

[2] Wilmanns, 2842; Dessau, i 206; facsimile of seven lines in Hübner's *Ex.* 800. Cp. Mommsen, *Ges. Schriften*, iv 291—311; Rushforth, 99—103; E. G. Hardy, *Three Spanish Charters* (1912), 119—132.

[3] *C. I. L.* iii p. 801 f (separate editions by Waddington, and by Mommsen and Blümner; selections in Dessau, i 642; *exordium* in Wilmanns, 1061, and, *infra*, in Appendix IV (6); facs. from three lines of copy at Aix in Hübner's *Ex.* 1097.

[4] *C. I. L.* x 8038; Orelli, 4031.   [5] *C. I. L.* ii 1423.

[6] Wilmanns, 2844; Dessau, ii p. 612 f (no. 6509); facsimile of about 60 lines in Diehl, *Inscr. Lat.* 27.

[7] Wilmanns, 2845; Dessau, ii p. 640 (no. 6675).

entitled to these privileges at a given date. This law was not a *lex rogata*, but a *lex data*, and, as such, belongs to the class of *principum constitutiones*[1]. Even under the Republic the right of citizenship could be granted by *triumviri coloniis deducendis*[2], and by *imperatores*. Cicero[3] mentions a *tabula, in qua nomina civitate donatorum incisa essent*, and such *tabulae* were set up in the Capitol[4]. Hence it was in the Capitol that the imperial enactments, with regard to the grant of citizenship and other privileges to the veterans, were set up from the time of Claudius (52 A.D.) to that of Domitian (86 A.D.). Later in Domitian's reign, in and after 90 A.D., they were set up on the Palatine[5].

Each of the soldiers concerned was entitled to a copy of the enactment, followed by his own name. This copy is known as a military *diploma* because it was composed of two tablets of bronze folded together in the form of a diptych. All these diplomas include the same elements in the following order :—

(1) the full name and titles of the emperor. (2) the class of soldiers, or the special corps, to which the privilege is granted, and the name of their commander. (3) the number of years of service. (4) the formula *quorum nomina subscripta sunt*, followed, in documents before 145 or after 178, with the extension of the same privileges to their descendants. (5) the statement of the privileges conferred, namely *civitas* and *conubium* (or legal Roman marriage) on those already married or thereafter to be married :—*ipsis liberis posterisque eorum civitatem dedit et conubium cum uxoribus, quas tunc habuissent, cum est civitas iis data, aut, si qui caelibes essent, cum iis quas postea duxissent, dumtaxat singuli singulas*. As the foreign wife of a veteran obtained the right of Roman citizenship, the last clause above quoted limited this privilege to a single marriage, to prevent abuses arising from his marrying and divorcing a series of wives, and securing the privilege of citizenship for each wife and her offspring. (6) the date, day, month, and year (reckoned by consuls). So far all is a copy of the imperial enactment. (7) the name and nationality of the soldier, preceded by the name of his cohort and his commander, and his rank in the same. Lastly, (8), a certificate that the document was a correct copy of the original on the Capitol (or Palatine).

The diploma was engraved on two tablets of bronze of exactly equal size (about 6 inches by 5), which were folded together.

[1] Gaius, i 57.   [2] Cicero, *Pro Balbo*, 48.
[3] *Ad Fam.* xiii 36.   [4] *Phil.* ii 92.
[5] *in muro post templum divi Aug(usti) ad Minervam* (cp. Dessau, i 1998, note).

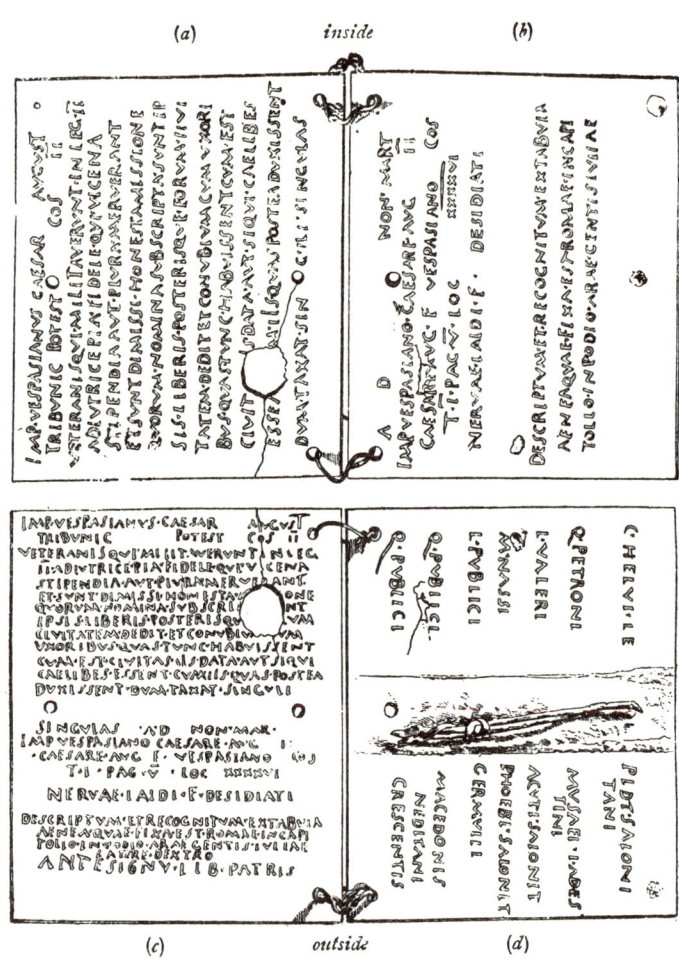

Fig. 49. Military diploma of Vespasian, 70 A.D. ½ of the original found at Resina, 1746, and now in the Naples Museum. Facsimile in *Museo Borbonico*, v (1767), pag. xliii f; reproduced in Marini, *Atti Arvali* (1795), 440 f; Platzmann, *Iuris Romani specimen* (1818); and Daremberg-Saglio, s.v. *Diploma* (1892), fig. 2452, here copied on a smaller scale.

IX]   MILITARY DIPLOMAS   183

Text of inner tablets (a) and (b), and also of outer copy (c).

IMP · VESPASIANVS · CAESAR · AVGVST · TRIBVNIC · POTEST · COS II[1]
VETERANIS · QVI · MILITAVERVNT · IN · LEG · II · ADIVTRICE · PIA · FIDELE ·
QVI · VICENA · STIPENDIA · AVT · PLVRA · MERVERANT · ET · SVNT · DIMISSI ·
HONESTA · MISSIONE · QVORVM · NOMINA · SVBSCRIPTA · SVNT · IPSIS · LIBE-
RIS · POSTERISQVE · EORVM · CIVITATEM · DEDIT · ET · CONVBIVM · CVM ·
VXORIBVS · QVAS · TVNC · HABVISSENT · CVM · EST · CIVITAS · IIS · DATA ·
AVT · SIQVI · CAELIBES · ESSENT · CVM · IIS · QVAS · POSTEA · DVXISSENT ·
DVM · TAXAT · SINGVLI · SINGVLAS.

A · D · NON · MAR · IMP · VESPASIANO · CAESARE · AVG · II · CAESARE · AVG ·
F[2] · VESPASIANO · COS[3].

T · I · PAG · V · LOC · XXXXVI[4] · NERVAE · LAIDI · F · DESIDIATI[5].

DESCRIPTVM · ET · RECOGNITVM · EX · TABVLA · AENEA · QVAE · FIXA · EST ·
ROMAE · IN CAPITOLIO · IN · PODIO · ARAE · GENTIS · IVLIAE · [6]LATERE · DEX-
TRO · ANTE SIGNV · LIB · PATRIS[6].

Text of tablet (d).

C · HELVI · LE		PIDI · SALONITANI
Q · PETRONI		MVSAEI · IADESTINI
L · VALERI	*locus sigillorum*	ACVTI · SALONIT
M · NASSI		PHOEBI · SALONIT
L · PVBLICI		GERMVLLI
Q · PVBLICI		MACEDONIS · NEDITANI
Q · PVBLICI		CRESCENTIS

All the witnesses, whose country can be identified, were Dalmatians.

Text in *C. I. L.* iii (2) p. 849; Rénier, 21; Wilmanns, 2864; Dessau, i 1989.

The text of the enactment was copied lengthwise on the two inner surfaces of the tablets ((*a*) and (*b*) in upper half of Fig. 49); it was also copied crosswise on the outer surface of one of them ((*c*) in lower half of Fig. 49). The tablets were perforated in two or more places, and were closed by a three fold wire which passed through the perforations. On the outer surface of the other tablet (*d*), the wire was sealed with the several seals of the

---

[1] 70 A.D.   [2] 'filio', Titus.
[3] 7 March, A.D. 70.
[4] T(abula) I, pag(ina) V, loc(o) xxxxvi.
[5] 'Desidiates populus Dalmatiae' (cp. Plin. iii 143).
[6-6] added in exterior copy (*c*).

seven witnesses whose names were added to certify the identity of the copy with the original. It was with a view to prevent forgery that this method had been adopted in legal documents in the time of Nero[1].

It was only in this way that the document had legal validity. A decision of the Senate on these details is recorded by the jurist Iulius Paulus, who became *praefectus praetorio* about 222 A.D.[2]

Originally, the text was copied only on one of the inner tablets, and one of the outer tablets contained the names of the witnesses; but only one *diploma* of this kind has survived[3]. At an early date it became customary to make a fresh copy of the text on one of the outer tablets, so that the contents of the diploma might be known without breaking the seals. Down to the time of Trajan the interior and the exterior copy were drawn up with equal care, but, under that emperor, the interior copy, which ought to have been of primary importance, was less carefully executed.

Most of the diplomas refer to the auxiliary cohorts; few to the navy; and still fewer to the praetorian or urban cohorts. In the last case, as the soldiers were already citizens, they only received the right of *conubium*. Few diplomas have been found in which privileges were granted to an ordinary legionary soldier[4]. The chief apparent exceptions are soldiers of the *legio prima adiutrix* and the *legio secunda adiutrix*, created by Nero and Vitellius respectively. But these were formed, not out of Roman citizens, but out of the naval forces of foreign birth, and they were therefore eligible for the special grant of citizenship. Such soldiers receive the grant in diplomas of 68 and 70 A.D.[5] The second of these is here reproduced (Fig. 49).

Down to 1872 the total number of *diplomata* recorded in the

---

[1] Suetonius, *Nero*, 17, *adversus falsarios tunc primum repertum, ne tabulae nisi pertusae, ac ter lino per foramina traiecto, obsignarentur.*

[2] *Sententiae*, v 25, 6, *Amplissimus ordo decrevit, eas tabulas, quae publici vel privati contractus scripturam continent, adhibitis testibus ita signari, ut in summa marginis ad mediam partem perforatae triplici lino constringantur, atque impositae supra linum cerae signa imprimantur, ut exteriores scripturae fidem interiori servent.* (Edd. for ʻexteriori scripturae fidem interior servetʼ.) *Aliter tabulae prolatae nihil momenti habent.*

[3] Late in 79 A.D. (Dessau, i 1994).

[4] See Lesquier, *L'armée romaine d'Égypte*, p. 312.   [5] Dessau, i 1988, 1989.

Corpus Inscriptionum was fifty-eight[1]; by 1884, twenty-two more had been published in the *Ephemeris Epigraphica*[2]: twenty-three have since been published[3], or one hundred and three in all. Facsimiles of twelve were published by Arneth (Vienna, 1843), engravings on thirty-seven plates by Renier (Paris, 1876); and specimens of the lettering of the first few lines of about fifty in Hübner's *Exempla* (Berlin, 1885). These have been found in many parts of the Roman world, but their ultimate *provenance* is always Rome, and they therefore supply evidence of the style of lettering there used for this purpose from the time of Claudian to that of Diocletian[4].

Among official documents we may here mention the *diptycha consularia*, or ivory tablets including the names and portraits of the consuls with representations of the public spectacles to which they invited the senators and other important personages. They extend from 406 to 541 A.D. A diptych of 487 A.D. bears a portrait of the father of Boëthius, with the following inscription:—*Nar*(*ius*) *Manl*(*ius*) *Boëthius v*(*ir*) *c*(*larissimus*) *et in*(*lustris*), *ex p*(*raefecto*) *p*(*raetorio*) *p*(*raefectus*) *u*(*rbi*) *sec*(*undo*), *cons*(*ul*) *ord*(*inarius*) *et patric*(*ius*)[5].

Diptycha consularia

(1) Private documents are represented by wills, such as that of Dasumius (109 A.D.), inscribed on two marble columns found in Rome in 1820 and 1830[6]. Another inscription, set up in honour of M. Meconius

Private documents. Wills

[1] *C. I. L.* iii (2) pp. 842—901; cp. Bursian, *Jahresb.* 23 (1880), 210—214.
[2] Conspectus in v (1884) pp. 101, 610 ff; cp. Bursian, 56 (1888), 83—86.
[3] Eleven in *C. I. L.* iii, Suppl. iii (1893) pp. 1955—2038; and five more in Pauly-Wissowa, s.v. (1903); also seven in Dessau, iii (2) 9052-8, cp. 9059.
[4] Cp., in general, Marini, *Atti Arvali* (1795), 448—468; Mommsen in *C. I. L.* iii pp. 842—901 (text), 902—919 (commentary); Wilmanns, 2863-9; Dessau, i pp. 389 f, nos. 1986—2010, iii (2) 9052-8; Cagnat, ed. 1914, pp. 302—306, with diploma of 128 A.D. on p. 307, and of 82 A.D. in Pl. ix, and ed. 1890, diploma of 98 A.D. on p. 269 (and Egbert, p. 357); also articles in Daremberg and Saglio (Thédenat) and Smith's *Dict. of Ant.* (L. C. Purser), and *British Museum Guide,...Roman Life*, p. 8. Among the *diplomas* in the British Museum is that granted by Trajan to the Spaniard Reburrus, one of the veterans, *qui...militant in Britannia* (*C. I. L.* vii 1193).
[5] Dessau, i pp. 288—292; Gori, *Thesaurus veterum diptychorum*, Florence, 1759; full list by Villefosse in *Gazette Archéologique*, 1884.
[6] Wilmanns, 314; Dessau, ii (2) 8379ᵃ.

Leo by the magistrates of Petelia among the Bruttii, includes (at his own request) a long extract from his will[1], which contains a clause relating to a vineyard of 'Aminean' vines[2].

(2) Among other private documents we have those written on waxed tablets in a cursive hand recording the business transactions of the Pompeian banker, L. Caecilius Iucundus, mainly for the years 52—62

Waxed tablets

Fig. 50. Receipt for a payment made by a Pompeian banker, 59 A.D., in Naples Museum (from *C. I. L.* iv 3340, cxliii)[3].

Cn. Pompeio Grospho, Grospho Pompeio Gaviano, II vir(is) iur(i) dic(endo), VI idus Iulias, privatus colonorum coloniae Veneriae Corneliae Pompeianorum ser(vus) scripsi me accepisse ab L. Caecilio Iucundo sestertios mille sescentos[4].

[1] Wilmanns, 696. [2] Cp. Virgil, *Georg.* ii 97.
[3] Further facsimiles in Diehl, *Inscr. Lat.* pp. xvi—xxvi; cp. Van Hoesen's *Roman Cursive Writing* (1915), p. 27; and Daremberg-Saglio, s.v. *Tabella*, fig. 6714.
[4] Cp. Mau-Kelsey, *Pompeii, its Life and Art*, c. 57.

A.D. On the opposite page is the first of the two tablets of a receipt belonging to 59 A.D. Here *e* is represented by two upright strokes, and *m* by four.

(3) The cursive hand of private documents is also exemplified in the waxed tablets of 131—167 A.D., discovered between 1786 and 1855 in Transylvania, in the mining district of Verespatak, corresponding to the ancient Alburnus maior in Dacia[1]. Like the military diplomas already mentioned[2], the Pompeian and Dacian documents contain the deed inside, and the sealed duplicate copy outside; but, while the diplomas are diptychs of bronze, the Dacian, and most of the Pompeian, documents are triptychs of wood[3]. The former are incised on both sides of the bronze plates. In the latter, the deed is begun on the back of the first tablet, and continued on the front of the second, and is then closed up, and concealed from view; the duplicate copy is visible on the back of the second tablet (which includes the seals), and on the front of the third. Only the interior surfaces are waxed. The front of the first tablet and the back of the third are unwaxed and are left blank; the two outer tablets thus serve to protect the inner waxed surfaces, and the seals on the back of the middle tablet[4].

(4) A rude cursive of an illiterate type is used in the maledictions written on tablets of lead or bronze devoting to destruction the personal enemies of the writer. **Exsecrationes** These were known as *exsecrationes, defixiones*, or *devotiones*[5]. A tablet, still preserved at Bath, invokes dire calamities on the head of one who has stolen a certain napkin[6]. A similar tablet is preserved at Lydney Park in Gloucestershire, together with two bronze plates recording the fulfilment of a vow[7]. Very few

---

[1] *C. I. L.* iii (2) pp. 921—960, with facsimiles, partly copied in Egbert, 382-5, Sir E. M. Thompson's *Introduction to Palaeography*, 316, and Daremberg-Saglio, s.v. *Tabella*, fig. 6715.

[2] p. 180 *supra*.

[3] Cp. 'Tabellae ligneae Aegyptiacae,' Dessau, iii (2) 9059.

[4] *C. I. L.* iii (2) p. 922, and Sir E. M. Thompson, *l.c.* p. 20.

[5] Tac. *Ann.* ii 69.   [6] Hübner's *Exempla*, 947 (Egbert, p. 386).

[7] *C. I. L.* vii 138-140; cp. in general, Dessau, ii (2) pp. 996—1000; esp. no. 8749, facs. in Ritschl, tab. xvii 30; also W. S. Fox, *Am. Journ. Philol.* no. 129 (1912), with bibliography; Jeanneret, *Rev. de Philol.* (1917) 599.

188   LATIN INSCRIPTIONS   [CHAP. IX

of such curses are engraved on stone, as that addressed to a Spanish form of Proserpine:—

Dea Ataecina Turi|brig(ensis) Proserpina, | per tuam maiestatem te rogo obsecro, | uti vindices quot mihi | furti factum est *etc.*[1]

Graffiti

(5) The cursive hand is also found in the 3500 *graffiti* scribbled on the walls of Pompeii[2]. Some of them record the prices of provisions, or the names of members of the praetorian guard. Among those of a distinctly literary interest, we find a phrase from Ennius, *Romulus in caelo*. We have also the opening words of Lucretius, *Aeneadum genetrix*; the first line of the first *Aeneid*, the beginning of the second, *conticuere omnes*[3] | *intentique*, and eleven other passages of Virgil[4]. Besides these, we have several reminiscences of Propertius[5] and Ovid[6], and of both combined[7]. In the quotation from the *Ars Amatoria*, i 475, *quid pote tan durum saxso aut quid mollius unda, dura tamen molli saxsa cavantur aqua*, our MSS have *quid magis est saxo durum, quid mollius unda*? In the amphitheatre, as well as in the *basilica*, the trivialities which are to be seen on every side have provoked the quotation of a couplet from an unknown poet:—

    Admiror, paries, te non cecidisse ruina,
     qui tot scriptorum taedia sustineas[8].

[1] Dessau, ii 4515.

[2] First partially collected by Chr. Wordsworth, *Inscriptiones Pompeianae* 1837; ed. 2, 1846, republished in *Conjectural Emendations &c.*, 1883; and finally edited by Zangemeister, in *C. I. L.* iv (1871), and by Mau, *ib.* Suppl. ii (1909).

[3] *Conticuere omnes* has also been found in England, on a tile from Silchester; facsimile in Haverfield's *Romanization of Roman Britain*, ed. 3 (1915), p. 30.

[4] *Ecl.* ii 56, iii 1, v 72, viii 70; *Aen.* i 135, 234; ii 148; v 461, 485; vii 805; ix 404.

[5] ii 5, 9 f; iii 16, 13 f; iv (v) 5, 47. Cp. p. 46 *supra*.

[6] *Amores*, i 4, 67; i 8, 77 (p. 46 *supra*), and *Ars Am.* i 475 f.

[7] Prop. i 1, 5, and Ovid, *Amores*, iii 11, 35 (Bücheler, *Carmina Epigraphica*, 354). Cp. in general, Diehl, *Pompeianische Wandinschriften...* (1910), esp. pp. 44—46; also Mau-Kelsey, *Pompeii, its Life and Art*, 1899, pp. 481—488, *The Graffiti*; and Bücheler, *l.c.*, 1785-7.

[8] *C. I. L.* iv 1904, 2487 (Bücheler, *l. c.*, 957).

CHAPTER X

LANGUAGE AND STYLE

It has been said of language, that 'the perfection of strength is clearness united to brevity; but' that 'to this combination Latin is utterly unequal; from the vagueness and uncertainty of meaning which characterises its separate words, to be perspicuous it must be full'[1]. Nevertheless the Latin of inscriptions can certainly be 'perspicuous' without being 'full', and, like the Roman legal and technical style, it commends itself by its 'clearness and precision'[2]. Even in modern times Latin continues to be the language of dedicatory inscriptions and of epitaphs. In Rome, in the sixteenth century, when 'the Bishop orders his tomb in St. Praxed's church', he requires for the epitaph 'choice Latin, picked phrase, Tully's every word'[3]. Of an English epitaph in the island of Skye, Dr Johnson said, 'the inscription should have been in Latin, as every thing intended to be universal and permanent should be'[4].

The language of a Latin inscription should be brief and perspicuous, and appropriate to its subject. Ancient inscriptions, or, at any rate, the best of them, and those belonging to the best times, are usually brief, simple, and severe in style, for example those on Pompey and Augustus recorded by the elder Pliny[5]. A higher degree of grandiloquence was characteristic of the inscriptions of Trajan, who, in restoring

[1] J. H. Newman on Cicero in *Enc. Metr.*, *Roman Lit.* p. 367 f, 1852.
[2] Mommsen, *R. H.*, Book II chap. ix (ii 114 ed. 1894).
[3] Browning, *Selections*, ed. 1884, p. 181.
[4] *Tour to the Hebrides*, 5 Sept. 1773.
[5] p. 9 f. *supra*.

the Circus Maximus, described it as worthy of the Roman people[1], and allowed the language of vague exaggeration to appear on the pedestal of his Column[2]. A still more pompous style may be observed in the inscriptions in honour of Aurelian, *perpetuo victoriosissimo indulgentissimo imperatori, restitutori orbis*[3]; Diocletian, *aeterno imperatori nostro, maximo optimoque principi*[4]; Constantius Chlorus, *piissimo ac fortissimo fundatori pacis, ac publicae libertatis auctori*[5]; and Constantine the Great, *restitutori humani generis, propagatori imperii dicionisque Romanae, fundatori etiam securitatis aeternae*[6].

As regards the order of words, adjectives used as epithets of divinities are usually placed *after* the name; for example, *Iovi optimo maximo, Minervae medicae, Herculi invicto*[7]; *deo sancto Apollini pacifero*[8]. But we occasionally find the epithet placed *first*, as in *sancto Silvano*[9], while both orders are combined in *virgini victrici, sanctae deae Nemesi*[10], and *sanctissimo Herculi invicto*[11]. Substantives in apposition to the na ̇es of deities are naturally placed *after* them, as *Herculi victori, Neptuno adiutori*. Genitive cases dependent on a word in apposition are placed *after* that word, as in *I·O·M· conservatori imp(eratoris)* ..., *totiusque domus divinae*[12], and *Herculi comiti et conservatori dominorum nostrorum*[13].

Order of words

In the case of other titles including a genitive case, the most natural order is adopted, and the governing noun precedes the genitive, e.g. *magister collegii fratrum arvalium*; *praefectus vigilum et armorum*; *procurator Augusti Alpium maritimarum*; also, in complimentary phrases, such as *parenti patriae*[14]; *conservatori orbis*

---

[1] Dio Cassius, lxviii 7, 2, οὕτω...καὶ μεγαλόφρων καὶ μεγαλογνώμων ἔφυ ὥστε καὶ τῷ ἱπποδρόμῳ ἐπιγράψαι ὅτι ἐξαρκοῦντα αὐτὸν τῷ ʼΡωμαίων δήμῳ ἐποίησεν, ἐπειδὴ διαφθαρέντα πῃ καὶ μεῖζω καὶ περικαλλέστερον ἐξειργάσατο. Cp. Pliny, *Paneg.* 51, 'digna populo victore gentium sedes'. Morcelli, *De stilo inscr. Lat.* ii 4, suggests an inscr. beginning with all the titles of the emperor, and ending ʼ circum maximum vetustate corruptum | operibus a solo ampliatis | immensique lateris ambitu exornato | parem populo Romano fecitʼ.
[2] p. 127 f, *supra*.   [3] Dessau, i 578.   [4] *ib.* 614.
[5] *ib.* 648.   [6] *ib.* 692.   [7] Dessau, ii 3407–9.
[8] *ib.* 3223.   [9] *ib.* 3543.   [10] *ib.* 3739.
[11] *ib.* 3446.   [12] Wilmanns, 1004.   [13] *C. I. L.* vi 305.
[14] Dessau, i 72 (of Julius Caesar), 101 (of Augustus); rarer than *patri patriae*.

terrarum; or *conservatori orbis*[1], or *patriae*[2], or *generis humani*[3]; or *propagatoris imperi*[4]; or *defensori pacis et conservatori imperii Romani*[5]. In inscriptions dedicated to Vespasian we find the normal order of words:—*conservatori caerimoniarum publicarum et restitutori aedium sacrarum*[6], and, elsewhere, *c. aedium sacrarum*[7], and *c. aedium publicarum et restitutori aedium sacrarum*[8]. These examples of the normal order throw suspicion on the inverted order adopted in an inscription in honour of the same emperor:—*sacrarum aedium restitutori et rituum antiquorum conservatori*[9]. Genitives, in general, are doubtless usually placed *after* the noun which governs them, as *memoriae suorum*; *constitutori collegi*, and *ex postulatione plebis*. Sometimes, however, they are placed before it, as *populi advocatio*; *suo et liberorum suorum nomine*; and *imitatus patris exemplum*.

Cases defining the duties of a public office are placed *after* the general name of the office, as *decemvir stlitibus iudicandis*; *triumvir aere*[10] *argento auro flando feriundo*; *curator pecuniae publicae exigendae et attribuendae in ludos*; and *quattuorviri aedilicia potestate*.

Participles are usually *preceded* by cases dependent on them, as, with *potens*:—*deo Marti, militiae potenti*[11]; and *Mercurio, lucrorum potenti et conservatori*[12]. Also, with passive participles, as *principi castrorum, equo publico exornato et donis donato ab impp...*[13]; *omnibus honoribus in patria sua functus*. But they are

[1] *ib.* 579; *restitutor orbis, ib.* 577 (of Aurelian).
[2] *C. I. L.* xi 3872 (of Tiberius), and iii 12333 (of Aurelian).
[3] Dessau, i 304 (of Trajan).
[4] Wilmanns, 989 (of Septimius Severus, in 205 A.D.).
[5] Dessau, ii 5827 (of Constantius II, 337—361 A.D.).
[6] *ib.* i 252; Wilmanns, 921 (*C. I. L.* vi 934).
[7] Gruter, p. 243, n. 7 (ex Panvinio).
[8] *ib.* p. 244, n. 7 (ex Roma Onufrii).
[9] *ib.* p. 243, n. 5 (ex Metelli schedis), Orelli, 746; possibly a modern variation of the inscr. in note 6.
[10] Old dative for *aeri*.
[11] Wilmanns, 147; Dessau, i 2296.
[12] Dessau, ii 3199.
[13] Wilmanns, 1595, followed by *ab Impp....*; *equo publico exornatus, ib.* 1200, 2380; or *honoratus*, 1821, 1825; less frequently *exornatus* (1828), or *honoratus* (2005), *equo publico*.

almost always *succeeded* by the dependent case, when the latter is the name of the emperor, as *curatori reipublicae—dato ab imp. Traiano*[1]; and *misso ab imp. Antonino Augusto Pio ad deducendas vexillationes in Syriam ob bellum Parthicum*[2].

A name denoting any honour or dignity (and, indeed, everything of the nature of a title) is commonly placed *after* the proper name, being regarded simply as an explanatory addition[3], e.g. *Cn. Domitius—Calvinus, pontifex, consul iterum, imperator*[4]; and, similarly, *C. Poplicio—Bibulo*, followed by *aedili plebis*[5], and *L. Cornelio Sullae*, by *dictatori*[6]. But the hereditary title, *rex*, is frequently placed *before* the name, as *regi Iubae, regis Iubae filio, regis Iempsalis n*(*epoti*), *regis Gaudae pronepoti, regis Masinissae pronepotis nepoti*[7]; *rex Antiochus*[8]; *rex magnus Samsigeramus*[9]; *de rege Ponti Mithridati et de rege Armeniae Tigrane*[10]. But, conversely, we sometimes find orders such as *Tigranis regis liberta*[11], and *cum Iugurtha rege Numidiae*[12]; also *Acrone rege Caeninensium*[13].

A complimentary epithet usually follows the noun, as in *patrono optimo; amico optimo; viro innocentissimo; feminae castissimae*. But we also find *optimo parenti; optimorum fratrum; magnificus vir*; and *rarissimae, nobilissimae, sanctissimae*, or *obsequentissimae ac pudicissimae feminae*. The superlative also comes *first* in the case of *Princeps* or *Caesar*, as *optimum Principem*[14]; *nobilissimus Caesar*[15]; *invictissimi Principes*[16].

[1] *ib.* 2167.
[2] Dessau, i 1076; cp. Wilmanns, 1828, *exornatus equo publico ab* —; or *honoratus equo publico ab* — (2005, cp. 1821); conversely, *ab eodem equo publico honoratus* (1825).
[3] Zumpt, *Latin Grammar*, § 796.
[4] Dessau, i 42.
[5] *ib.* 862; p. 105, *supra*.
[6] *ib.* 872.
[7] *ib.* 840.
[8] *ib.* ii (3) 9200 (cp. Wilmanns, 541).
[9] *ib.* 8958. Sampsiceramus in Cic. *ad Att.* ii 14—23.
[10] *ib.* i 60 (cp. Wilmanns, 2595, *de familia regis Mitredatis*).
[11] *ib.* 850.
[12] *ib.* 59.
[13] Wilmanns, 623.
[14] Dessau, ii 6680 (of Antoninus Pius); cp. *optimus maximusque princeps* (of Trajan, Hadrian, and Antoninus Pius).
[15] Dessau, i 488—491 (of Maximinus I, 235-8 A.D.).
[16] *ib.* 797 (of Arcadius and Honorius, 401 f, A.D.).

The epithet *follows*, when it serves to define a public office, or a trade or business; as *pontifex maximus*; *faber ferrarius*; or *negotiator frumentarius*; also when it defines the exact status of a citizen, as *vir clarissimus*, or *spectabilis*, or *perfectissimus* (V · P ·). This last is the true title of *Martianus V· P·* (*praeses provinciae Norici mediterr.*)¹, and not *Vrbi praefectus*², for the latter would have been expressed by *praefectus Vrbi* (*P · V·*).

Cicero, in his speeches, seldom mentions any man of mark, or even of ordinary respectability, without describing him as *vir clarissimus*³, or *amplissimus, fortissimus, nobilissimus, ornatissimus*. *Clarissimus vir* was mainly used of Senators, and, in the course of the first century⁴, it became a fixed epithet of senatorial rank⁵. Early in the second, the full phrase is reduced to the abbreviation C · V ·; members of a senatorial family may be called *c. i*(*uvenis*) or *c. p*(*uer*), and *clarissima puella* is applied to a girl who died at the age of a month and a half⁶. The title was, in the earlier age, *clarissimus vir*; in later times, *vir clarissimus* (V · C ·). When combined with other epithets, *clarissimus* regularly comes first. As a title, *vir clarissimus* immediately *follows* the name, unless the title has been won at a particular stage in the *cursus honorum*, e.g. during the transition from equestrian to senatorial rank. Down to the time of Marcus Aurelius, it was the only official title of the superlative degree; under Marcus, the equestrian officials were divided into three ranks, (1) the praetorian praefect was *vir eminentissimus*; (2) any of the other praefects of the highest rank⁷, or of the highest procurators, was *vir perfectissimus*⁸;

---

¹ Gruter, p. 283, n. 5.
² Muratori, *Anecd. Graec.* p. 5.
³ We find 22 examples of the various cases of *vir clarissimus*, and 96 of *clarissimus vir*.
⁴ For an early example of its use in inscriptions, cp. Dessau, ii 6043 (middle), *Hosidio Geta et L. Vagellio cos., clarissimis viris* (*c.* 45 f, A.D.). *T. Pomponium Bassum, clarissimum virum* (*ib.* 6106) is found in 101 A.D. The earliest certain examples in literature are probably those in Pliny's *Epp.* ix 13, 19; *Paneg.* 90; *ad Traianum* 56, 77. But Lentulus, in Cic. *Epist.* xii 1, has 'M. Brutus V. C.'
⁵ Cp. Friedländer, *Sittengeschichte*, vol. i, Appendix to Section iii.
⁶ *C. I. L.* vi 1334.   ⁷ See p. 227.   ⁸ First found in 201 A.D.

S. L. I.

(3) any other procurator was *vir egregius*. *Eminentissimus* and *perfectissimus* were epithets personally applied to an equestrian official, without being extended to members of his family. In an inscription of the fourth century, the son of a *v(ir) p(erfectissimus)* is called, in full, *puer egregius*. The abbreviations *p(uer) e(gregius)* and *e(gregia) f(emina)* are very rare; *iuvenis egregius* seems to have been avoided; *vir egregius* appears for the last time in 321 A.D. *Vir eminentissimus* was properly confined to the praefect of the praetorian guard, but, in the third century, it was extended to the *praefecti vigilum*. The equestrian titles of rank continued until 323. Under Gratian (367—383), *eminentissimus* had lost its distinctiveness as an equestrian title; for it was then combined with the senatorial epithet *clarissimus*. In 384 there were three classes of *perfectissimus*, and the title was even given to the clerks of the treasury; meanwhile the *praesides* and *duces* were promoted to the title of *clarissimi*. By 412 the title *perfectissimus* had vanished; it never appears in Cassiodorus, whose official letters (collected in 538 A.D.) teem with laudatory titles. After the reforms of Constantine, *vir clarissimus* long remained the sole title of the highest officials, but, under his successors, two new titles for these officials were introduced,—*inlustris* and *spectabilis*. The former is first found in 354; the latter was probably introduced by Valentinian I (364—375), who (as stated in the Theodosian code) *singulis quibusque dignitatibus certum locum meritumque praescripsit*[1]. The first certain example of *spectabilis* is dated 378 A.D. In the age of Isidore[2] (*ob.* 636) the three ranks of Senators were, in descending order, (1) *illustres*, (2) *spectabiles* and (3) *clarissimi*. The latest example of a *v(ir) c(larissimus)* in an inscription belongs to the year 629[3].

The *legio*, the *cohors*, and the *ala* are always *followed* by their distinctive numbers, or epithets, as *legio II adiutrix pia fidelis*; *cohors II Gallorum Macedonica*; *ala I Tungrorum Frontoniana*. The number of times that any one has held office is placed *after* the title, as COS · III; and the number of years of any one's life

[1] Cod. Theod. vi 5, 2.
[2] *Etym.* ix 4, 12.
[3] Cp. in general O. Hirschfeld, *Die Rangtitel der römischen Kaiserzeit* (1901), in *Kleine Schriften* (1913), 646—681.

is placed *after* VIXIT ANNIS, and similarly with months and days.

As regards conjunctions, the successive epithets of any single divinity are not introduced by *et*. Thus we have *Herculi victori pollenti potenti invicto*[1]. But, if several divinities are mentioned, the conjunctions may be either omitted, as in *Sanctae Isidi, numini Sarapis, sancto Silvano, Laribus*[2]; or inserted, as in *Silvano sancto et Mercurio et Libero patri sacrum*[3]. In enumerating a series of military or civil offices held by the same man, the conjunction is generally omitted, but the full title of each office is set forth, even if part of the title is the same in all: as *praefecto annonae, proc(uratori) a rationibus, proc. provinciarum Lugdunensis et Aquitanicae, proc. hereditat., proc. Hispaniae*..., *proc. Alpium maritimarum* etc.[4] Similarly we find *proc(uratori)* at the beginning of each of six lines relating to T. Statilius Optatus[5].

When an adjective is in agreement with a substantive governed by *ob, pro, propter*, or the like, the adjective generally precedes the substantive, as *ob insignem in cives amorem et singularem erga patriam adfectionem*[6]; *ob eximiam benignamque erga omnes cives suos adfectionem, sinceramque et incomparabilem innocentiam eius*[7]; *pro singulari eius circa se amore* ...[8]; *propter eximiam pietatem et affectionem fraternam quam circa se et liberos exhibet*[9].

On the 'language' of inscriptions, compare, in general, Zell's *Handbuch* (1852), pp. 65—81, and, on their 'style', pp. 135—138. See also Morcelli, *De stylo inscriptionum Latinarum*, vol. ii pp. 250—303, ed. 1820.

[1] Dessau, ii 3434, cp. 3436.
[2] Wilmanns, 1263.
[3] Gruter, p. 62, 4.
[4] Dessau, i 1342.
[5] *ib.* ii (2) 9011; Papers of British School at Rome, iv 85 (pl. iii, fig. 1); see also Mommsen, *Comm.* on *Res gestae divi Augusti, De iteratione legationum*, pp. 179—182.
[6] Wilmanns, 1636.
[7] *C. I. L.* xi 6362; Dessau, ii (2) 7364.
[8] Dessau, i 1278.
[9] *ib.* ii 6822.

CHAPTER XI

RESTORATION AND CRITICISM OF INSCRIPTIONS

MANY of the extant inscriptions are mutilated and fragmentary. Before they can be adequately published, or profitably used as evidence, they often require to be restored by means of conjectural criticism. The first requirement is a completely accurate copy of the original taken by the best mechanical means available. The usual method is that of paper 'squeezes'. These are made by wetting sheets of thick unsized white paper and pressing them into the indentations of the inscription by means of a brush with short stiff bristles. Rubbings may also be made with black lead; and, in the case of very small articles, such as gems, impressions can be taken in wax[1].

<small>Copies of inscriptions</small>

Errors may arise from an inaccurate transcript. Thus, the last six letters of Q·CONSTANTIS·F·HE QVE were interpreted by Muratori as *f(ilii) he(redes)que*, but a more accurate copy of the original has FEL· OVF·, *Fe(licis) Ouf(entina) (tribu)*. The transcript DE·CARNVNT· led Fabretti[2] to imagine the existence of a *Deus Carnuns*, whereas the inscription really reads DEF·CARNVNTI, *defuncto Carnunti*[3].

<small>Sources of error</small>

Errors of interpretation may be due to a misunderstanding of the special meaning of certain abbreviations in some particular context. Such was the error of one who inferred the existence at Lyons of no less than three hundred augurs from an inscription

---

[1] Cp. Hübner, *Ueber mechanische Copieen von Inschriften*, 1870, '80; S. Reinach, *Conseils aux voyageurs archéologues* (1886), 36—42.

[2] *Inscr. Ant.* (1702), p. 258, 86.

[3] Wilmanns, 256. Cp. in general, Zaccharia, *Istituzione*, 346, and Zell, *Anleitung*, 346.

CHAP. XI]　　　SOURCES OF ERROR　　　197

in Spon[1] including the letters C · C · C · AVG · LVG ·, the true interpretation of which is the full official title of the city, *Coloniae Copiae Claudiae Augustae Luguduni*[2]. In an inscription ending with the words *qui vixit annis* LXXXVII V · V · V · *aliquando securus sum*, V · V · V · was dubiously interpreted by Mommsen as meaning *vixi vitam vexatam*[3], an interpretation supported by no precedent. A more probable solution is *vale, vale, vale*, which is ordinarily said by the living to the dead[4], but may also be the reply of the dead to the living as in *vale viator* and *viator vale*[5].

Errors may be due to the original carver of the inscription, and are, in some cases, corrected by the carver himself. Thus, in Fig. 35 (p. 132 *supra*), a mistake in the numbers of the miles in lines 6, 7 and 9 is corrected by punching out a square space, and thus removing the erroneous endings of the numerals.

Among other errors are the following. On a distance-slab of the Antonine Vallum in Scotland, among the symbols for *millia passuum tria*, P · III is wrongly repeated: M · P · III P III CCCIV[6]. In a Roman inscription, *h(eredem) nostrum sequetur* is substituted for *h(eredem) non sequetur*[7]; and, in an inscription of Ostia, Q · Q · for 'q(uin)q(uennali)' has been set out in full as QVOQVE[8]. In provincial inscriptions, *pater patriae* is sometimes allowed to stand as an indeclinable nominative, in the midst of several datives[9]. In epitaphs, datives and accusatives are occasionally combined in the statement of the duration of the life of the deceased, as *vixit annis* VII *mens.* VII *dies* XII[10]. Mistakes may arise from similarity in the shapes of various letters, such as

---

[1] Spon, *Misc.* (1685) 170, 3 and 173, 2; cp. R. de la Blanchère, *Hist. de l'épigr. rom.* (1887), p. 46.

[2] Orelli, 194; cp. Wilmanns, 120, 121, 122; Dessau, ii 4132-4.

[3] *C. I. L.* vi 10251ᵃ; Dessau, ii (2) 7348 (taken from Rome to Verona).

[4] Servius on Virgil, *Aen.* ii 644, 'dici mortuis solet, *vale, vale, vale*'. This interpretation, that of Maffei (*Mus. Ver.* 96, 5), was accepted by Orelli, 2389, and is entered in Cagnat's list of abbreviations.

[5] *C. I. L.* iii 405; i 1027 (Wilmanns, 1641; 556 = Dessau, ii (2) 7602); cp. i 2555, *tu qui legis vale*.

[6] *C. I. L.* vii 1126.

[7] vi (2) 9138.　　　[8] xiv 418.　　　[9] ii 2054.

[10] xiii 2140. Cp. H. A. Seydel, *Observationum Epigraphicarum capita duo*, Breslau, 1880; Dessau, iii (2), *Indices*, p. 873 f, 'scripturae vitia.'

I and L, E and F, B or P and R. Thus we have AQVIER for *Aquilifer*[1], FOPVM for *eorum*[2], and AVG · LIR · SIR for *Aug(usti) lib(erti) ser(vi)*[3]. When the surface of the stone has been much rubbed, the horizontal strokes of letters such as E, L, T are often worn away, leaving nothing but the vertical stroke, I[4]. Words are sometimes wrongly divided, as SVPERVM PONITVR for *superimponitur*[5]. Occasionally, owing to local peculiarities of pronunciation, consonants of similar sound are interchanged, as B and V, e.g. *bixit* for *vixit*; *vene* for *bene*; and even *veneficium* for *beneficium*[6].

In restoring *lacunae*, the general principles of textual criticism are the same in the case of an inscription as in the case of a manuscript. But inscriptions are subject to more rigid rules than literary texts, and leave less room for the exercise of the imagination. From the length of the lines, and the size of the letters, we ascertain the exact number of letters missing. To restore an inscription we are not at liberty to assume any abbreviation we please. Certain words are seldom, if ever, abbreviated, while in others the abbreviated forms are frequent. The restoration of an incomplete inscription may be suggested or confirmed by a more complete inscription on the same subject or by a parallel passage from a classical author.

Restoration of inscriptions

A knowledge of the history and chronological development of the Roman name; and a familiarity with the sequence of the *cursus honorum*, and with the successive names and titles of the Emperors, are an important aid towards the restoration of *lacunae*; and the same may be said of a knowledge of the customary legal *formulae*. In the case of the *cursus honorum* and the titles of the Emperors, this may be illustrated by Mommsen's restoration

[1] v 2495. [2] vi 13016. [3] v 8247.
[4] Hagenbuch in Orelli, ii p. 362.
[5] On *errata fabrilia*, cp. Hagenbuch, *l. c.* p. 366 § 44; also Hübner's *Exempla*, p. xli f, and his index to *C. I. L.* i[1] p. 646, and Dessau, iii (2) p. 873 f.
[6] *Eph. Ep.* ix, no. 776, 27, 'propter quod veneficium statuam eidem— collocarunt' (at Praeneste). Cp. *History of Classical Scholarship*, i[2] 268, 475; Cagnat[4], 412 f, B(eteranus) for *veteranus*; also Diehl, *Vulgärlateinische Inschriften*, nos. 419, 498, *vene* combined with *bixit* and *habe* (for *ave*), and many other references in index, p. 162 f.

```
C · PLINIVS · L · F·OVF · CAECILIVS  secundus  cos
AVGVR · LEGAT · PRO PR · PROVINCIAE · PON  ti     bithyniae
CONSVLARI · POTESTAt · IN · EAM · PROVINCIAM · Ex  et  ab
IMP · CAESAR · NERVA · TRAIANO · AVG · GERMANico  s.  c. missus
CVRATOR · ALVEI · TIberIS · ET · RIPARVM · Et     dacico  p. p
PRAEF · AERARI · SATVRNI · PRAEF · AERARI · MIL·it.  cloacar.  urb
QVAESTOR · IMP · SEVIR · EQVITVM              pr.  trib.  pl
TRIB · MILIT · LEG · iii·GALLICAe                  romanorum
                                                   xvir stli
TIB · IVDICANDO · THERMas ex iis       ADIECTIS ·       IN
ORNATVM · HS · CCC      · · · · · et eo ampLIVS · IN · TVTELAm
HS · CC · T · F · I   item in alimenta  LIBERTOR · SVORVM · HOMIN · C
HS · |XVIIi| LXVI ÐCLXVI · REI p.  legavit, quorum  incREMENT · POSTEA · AD · EPVLVM
pLEB · VRBAN · VOLVIT · PERTINere · · · item vivus S · DEDIT · IN · ALIMENT · PVEROR
ET · PVELLAR · PLEB · VRBAN · HS d  item bybliothecam e IN TVTELAM · BYBLIOTHE
CAE · HS · C
```

Inscription recording the career of the younger Pliny.

Gaius Plinius, Luci filius, Oufentina, Caecilius Secundus; consul, augur, legatus pro praetore provinciae Ponti et Bithyniae consulari potestate, in eam provinciam ex senatus consulto missus ab imperatore Caesare Nerva Traiano Augusto Germanico Dacico, patre patriae; curator alvei Tiberis et riparum et cloacarum urbis, praefectus aerari Saturni, praefectus aerari militaris, praetor, tribunus plebis, quaestor imperatoris, sevir equitum Romanorum, tribunus militum legionis tertiae Gallicae, decemvir stlitibus iudicandis; thermas ex sestertiis..., adiectis in ornatum sestertium tercentum millibus...et eo amplius in tutelam sestertium ducentum millibus, testamento fieri iussit, item in alimenta libertorum suorum, hominum centum, sestertium decies octies centena et sexaginta sex millia cum sexcentis sexaginta sex reipublicae legavit, quorum incrementum postea ad epulum plebis urbanae voluit pertinere; item vivus dedit in alimenta puerorum et puellarum plebis urbanae sestertium quingenta millia; item bybliothecam, et in tutelam bybliothecae sestertium centum millibus.

of the celebrated inscription, formerly at Como, now in Milan, recording the career of the younger Pliny[1].

The date of an inscription may be determined (1) by its *form*, in respect to (*a*) the shapes of the letters, or (*b*) the spelling of the words; and (2) by its *subject-matter*.

Date determined by lettering

(1*a*) The date of an inscription belonging to the *Roman Republic* may be partly determined by the character of the letters. Under the Republic, forms of A, such as Λ, ⋀, or ⋀, which are never constant, cease altogether about 184—174 B.C., and the same is true of the sibilant letter Ƨ, and of those forms of O which are open at the top or the bottom. The acute-angled ⌐ (for L) ceases about the same date. The rectangular form of ⌐ (for P) ceases in 114 B.C. In process of time the triangular-headed R and R become the round-headed R and R. The tall I is not found before the age of Sulla (dictator in 80 B.C.), or the *apex* (or accented vowel) before that of Caesar (dictator in 48). Y is hardly ever found before 55 B.C. Z, which had appeared after 273 B.C. on an ancient coin of Cosa, was finally borrowed solely for the spelling of Greek words containing that letter, and was placed at the end of the Latin alphabet.

The characteristic shapes of the other letters of the alphabet (1) in the last quarter of the fifth century of Rome (279—254 B.C.) and (2) in the sixth century (253—154 B.C.), have been stated in a tabular form on a previous page[2]. The archaic forms of the letters were gradually superseded by the normal and regular alphabet, as it finally appeared in the *monumental* and in the *documental* style of the Augustan age, and a specimen of each (1) from an important monument, and (2) from a public record, has already been given[3], as well as the corresponding alphabet[4]. The lettering of the later alphabets of Claudius[5], Nero, the Flavian emperors, Trajan, Septimius Severus, and Constantine, as set forth in Hübner's *Exempla*, shows very little change.

---

[1] *Hermes*, iii (1869), p. 112, *Ges. Schr.* iv 366—468; *C. I. L.* v 5262; Dessau, i 2927.
[2] Fig. 15, p. 48, *supra*.   [3] (1) Fig. 8 (p. 43); (2) Figs. 44, 45 (p. 171 f).
[4] Figs. 9, 10*a* (p. 43 f).   [5] Fig. 10*b* (p. 44).

Inscriptions of nearly the same date may have a different style in their lettering, a fact that prompted Maffei's remark, *fallax et ambigua scripturae coniectura*[1]. The painstaking epigraphist, Fabretti[2], was led by the inferior lettering of the last two lines of an inscription to assign it to a later time. The superior lettering ends with C · SEPTIMI and the inferior begins with O · GEMELLO; so that, on this view, the *praenomen* and nearly the whole of the *nomen* would belong to one age, and its last letter, and the *cognomen*, to another!

The correct shape of the letter R is an important criterion in determining the date of a dedication to Iuno Sospita by a former slave of Cn. and Aulus Caecilius, and of Q. Flaminius. An inscription in the following terms was discovered by Ritschl at Basel. It was carved on a perfectly faultless tablet of slate, with a central point, made by a pair of compasses, still visible in every circular O and Q, and in every semicircular C:—

Q · CAECILIVS · CN · A · Q
FLAMINI · LEIBERTVS
IVNONE · SEISPITEI
MATRI · REGINAE

This was condemned by Ritschl on the ground of the shapes of the letters, especially that of the thrice repeated R, with its unduly large head and its curiously curved tail. Mommsen defended the substance of the inscription, and even regarded the lettering as of the ordinary late Republican type[3]. Meanwhile, an inscription in the same terms had been seen somewhere in the Campagna by the Roman architect, Canina, who had mentioned it to Henzen[4]. It was ultimately traced to the famous seat of Juno's worship at Lanuvium, where the whole of the inscription was found extending in a long line on the architrave of an ancient temple of the goddess, with the letter R appearing

---

[1] *Ars Critica Lapidaria* (1765), col. 165.
[2] *Inscr. Antiquae* (1699), pp. 150, 721.
[3] *Bullettino dell' Instituto*, 1853, p. 170 f, translated with additions in *Rhein. Mus.* ix (1854), 450 f, 639.
[4] Orelli-Henzen (iii) 5659 a.

in a perfectly regular form[1]. Thus Ritschl was right in condemning the lettering of the Basel copy, and Mommsen in defending its substance. Both of these eminent epigraphists were justified, in different ways, by the discovery of the lost original at Lanuvium.

(1 *b*) Turning to questions of spelling, we find that, in the final syllable of the inflexions of nouns and verbs such as *tribunŏs, pocolom, donom, sacrom, dederont, coiraveront, o* is superseded by *u* about 234 B.C. (though *o* survives after *u* and *v*, as in *mortuŏs* and *vivŏs*). Similarly unaccented *ĕ* (e.g. *meretod*) is superseded by *i*. *E* for *ei* as in *Iove, Hercole* (datives) ceases about 200 B.C. The final *d* of the ablative and imperative falls out of use about the same time, though it is retained in the *Senatus Consultum de Bacchanalibus*[2] (186 B.C.). *ae* for *ai* occurs once in that document and becomes established by the latter half of the second century. The first instance of *xs* for *x* occurs in the same document (*exstrad*) and the spelling is common in the time of the Gracchi and subsequently in the Augustan age and later. Double consonants are not found before the time of Ennius (d. 169); examples of their presence or absence are about equal in number from 174 to 134 B.C.; from 134 B.C. they become more common, and they are practically constant from 114 B.C.[3]. Double vowels are confined to the sixty years between 134 and 74 B.C.[4] *ei* begins to pass into *i* about the middle of the second century and during the latter half of this century an original long *ī* is not infrequently spelt *ei*. The omission of final *s* and *m* ceases about 130 B.C. in carefully written inscriptions, but is common in later times in vulgar Latin. The change of *oi* to *u* begins as early as 200 B.C., but *oi* and *oe* continue to be used and occur up to the time of Cicero. *u* replaces the older *ou* about 100 B.C. but instances of *u* are found earlier. About the same date old declension forms, such as *eis* or *is* in the nominative plural of *o*-stems (as in *leibereis, magistreis, hisce*

Spelling

---

[1] Ritschl, in *Rhein. Mus.* 1858, *Opusc.* iv 335—354, with facsimile of the Basel copy, and of the original, in taf. xii and xi, and in *P. L. M. E.* tab. lxi and lxii A respectively. The former alone is reproduced by Ricci, tav. ix. Text in *C. I. L.* i² 2, 1430, xiv 2090; Dessau, ii 3097.

[2] p. 161 f *supra*.   [3] p. 36 *supra*.   [4] p. 36 *supra*.

ministris) and *us* in the genitive singular of consonant stems (as in *nominus, Venerus*) become obsolete. Towards the beginning of the first century B.C. the aspirated consonants *ph, ch, th* are introduced to represent φ, χ, θ. In earlier times these sounds are represented by *p, c, t,* as in *Pilotimus, Antiocus, Corintus,* and the older spelling continues fairly frequent till about the middle of the first century[1].

(2) The date may also be determined by the subject-matter, by the mention of consuls or other officials, whose date is exactly or approximately known. In imperial inscriptions the details of the titles borne by the emperor are generally conclusive[2]. References to consulships, and to imperial titles, are often found in honorary inscriptions. Epitaphs are rarely dated by consulships[3], and it is very exceptional to find an epitaph in which the successive dates in a centurion's career are recorded in terms of imperial titles[4]. The *lex parieti faciendo* of Puteoli is dated *ab colonia deducta anno XC*[5], the year of the foundation of the colony being 194 B.C. An Umbrian monument of 32 A.D. in honour of Tiberius is dated 704 years from the foundation of Interamna[6]; and the 'restoration of liberty' by Nerva on the death of Domitian in 96 A.D. was commemorated on the Capitol in an inscription dated in the year of Rome, 848[7]. Such dates are generally confined to *tituli sacri,* and are very rare in Italy. But they are common in Asia, and are also found in Mauretania, where some public baths were dedicated in 'the year of the province 157,' i.e. 196 A.D.[8], and where a priest is described as having died at the age of 105 ('more or less') 'in the year of the province 363,' or 402 A.D.[9]

---

[1] For further details see index to Diehl's *Altlateinische Inschriften,* 2nd ed., 1911, and Dessau, iii (2) 802—875, *Grammatica quaedam*.
[2] Appendix III, *infra.*
[3] Wilmanns, 179, 207, 234, 1285, 1999.
[4] Dessau, i 2118, quoted, p. 117 *supra.*
[5] *C. I. L.* i² 2, 698; p. 160 *supra.*
[6] Wilmanns, 64 a; Dessau, i 157.
[7] Wilmanns, 64; Dessau, i 274, and iii (1) p. 347 f.
[8] Dessau, ii 6876.
[9] *ib.* ii (2) 8083, and iii (1) p. 348 f. On dating inscriptions cp. C. Bone's *Anleitung,* pp. 50—82.

Modern criticism of Latin inscriptions began when the forgeries of Pirro Ligorio (who died about 1586)[1] were detected by Maffei[2] and Olivieri[3]. Inscriptions produced solely to glorify a particular family, or to support a particular opinion, are always liable to suspicion[4]. An inscription supporting the view that *Basilice* is on the site of the Samnian town *Murgantia* is discredited by the illegitimate formation of the adjective in *populus Murgantius*, instead of *Murgantinus* or *Murgantiensis*, and (less strongly) by the unidiomatic use of the demonstrative in *basilicam hanc*[5].

Forgeries

With this we may contrast Dessau, ii 5527, 'M. Nonius...Balbus procos. | basilicam, portas, murum pecunia sua'. The demonstrative, is, however, occasionally found in inscriptions: see p. 88 *supra*.

Among modern forgeries we have the epitaph of Paulus Aemilius :—

Annibal Pauli Aemilii Romanorum consulis apud Cannas trucidati conquisitum corpus inhumatum iacere passus non est; summo cum honore Romanis militibus mandavit sub hoc marmore reponendum et ossa eius ad urbem deportanda[6].

Caesar's favourable reception of Cicero, on their meeting between Tarentum and Brundisium in September, 47 B.C.[7], finds expression in the following forgery :—

C. Caesar M. T. Ciceronem ob egregias eius virtutes singularesque animi dotes per universum orbem virtute nostra armisque perdomitum salvum et incolumem esse iubemus[8].

The daughter of Marius is commemorated in a forged inscription at Arles, ascribed to the middle of the seventeenth century :—

D M (separated by two palm-branches) | Calphur|niae | Cai Marii | cons. filiae | piissimae—Cimbror(um) | victrici[9].

---

[1] p. 28 n. 4, *supra*.
[2] *Ars Critica Lapidaria*, 1765 (p. 28 *supra*).
[3] *Esame della iscrizione di L. Antidio Feroce*, Ravenna, 1764 (quoted in Orelli's *Inscr. Lat. Select.* i 43—54).
[4] Cp. *C. I. L.* x 91*, 109*, 110*, 607*, 711*; xii 188* (Egbert, p. 12).
[5] *C. I. L.* ix 147*; Cagnat, 390[4] f.
[6] *C. I. L.* ix 99*. [7] Plutarch, *Cic.* 39. [8] *C. I. L.* vi 81*.
[9] *C. I. L.* xii 112*; facsimile in Hübner's *Ex.* p. 445, 10*.

As it was known that Cicero intended to set up a temple, either at Arpinum or across the Tiber, in memory of his daughter Tullia[1], there was an obvious temptation to forge an inscription in her honour. Abela, in his *Malta Illustrata*, describes her epitaph as having been found at Malta, of all other places, in the following form:—Tulliola M. Tullii F.[2] An altar in Florence bears the inscription:—D · M · | Tulliolae | v · c | cineres[3]. Again, when the body of a young girl was found in 1485, in an ancient tomb, six miles from Rome on the Appian Way, it was declared that it was the tomb of Tullia, the young wife of Dolabella, and the phrase *nihil unquam peccavit nisi quod mortua est* was stolen from a genuine epitaph[4] to enrich a forgery in her memory:—Tulliola filia mea unica | quae nunquam peccavit | nisi quod mortua fuit | infelix pater posuit M · T · Cicero[5].

In the celebrated epitaph of Iulia Alpinula, founded on the fate of Iulius Alpinus of Aventicum, as recorded in Tacitus, *Histories*, i 68, the name Alpinula was doubtless derived from that of 'Alpinia Alpinula' in a genuine inscription of Baden in Switzerland[6]. The forgery, which was among the inscriptions supplied to Lipsius by Paulus Gulielmus[7], deceived Johann Müller, the historian of Switzerland, and also Lord Byron, who alludes to it in *Childe Harold* (iii 66). The epitaph is as follows:—

Iulia Alpinula hic iaceo | infelicis patris infelix proles | Deae Avent(icae) sacerdos. | exorare patris necem non potui. | male mori in fatis illi erat. | vixi annos XXIII[8].

[1] *Ad Att.* xii 18, 19, 21.
[2] Forsyth's *Cicero*, p. 402, note (ed. 1867).
[3] *C. I. L.* vi (5) 3465*; v. c. is probably meant for 'viri clarissimi (filiae).'
[4] *C. I. L.* vi (4), 20634.
[5] *ib.* vi (5) 3593*; Lanciani, *Pagan and Christian Rome*, 300 f.
[6] Orelli, 457.
[7] Orelli, i p. 40.
[8] Orelli, 400*, where Byron is quoted as saying *je ne connois point de composition humaine plus touchante que cette inscription*. The same inscription is the theme of a poem by "N." (i.e. J. N. Simpkinson) in *The Rugby Magazine*, no. 1, July 1835, p. 78, and reprinted in Holden's *Foliorum Silvula*, i (1866) no. 637 (with note), beginning "'Tis past—the struggle now is o'er | Which I have borne for thee; | A daughter's prayers can bend no more | Those hearts of cruelty'.

The inscriptions from Nennig near Trier[1], and many of the sling-bolts of Asculum[2], are also forgeries[3]. Genuine inscriptions have sometimes been wrongly regarded as fabrications. Even certain of the epitaphs of the Scipios were suspected by Gori and Maffei; the *decreta Pisana*, by Scaliger; and the *lex regia Vespasiani*, by others[4]. An inscription, once described as a forgery[5], has since been discovered in the sanctuary of Fortuna Primigenia at Praeneste[6]. Among the *inscriptiones falsas urbi Romae attributas* collected in 1885, *C. I. L.* vi (5), nearly 3000 were recorded by Ligorio, but more than fifty of them are accepted as genuine in the *Corrigenda*, four of these being still extant in Rome, Perugia, Florence, or Paris. Another inscription, which was first transcribed in 1674, afterwards disappeared, and was regarded as a forgery[7], partly because it referred to the Census of Quirinius. In 1880, about half of the inscription was discovered at Venice, and it was afterwards admitted by Mommsen to be genuine[8]. On this subject in general he modestly said in the early part of his great career as one of the founders of Latin epigraphy,

Omnino nobis modeste confitendum est, in hac quaestione de vera titulorum fucatave antiquitate multum dandum esse testium honestati et oculorum auctoritati[9].

[1] Hettner, *Röm. Steindenkmäler*, Trier, 1893, p. 221.
[2] p. 148 *supra*.
[3] Cp., in general, Hübner's *Ex.*, pp. 412–416; Cagnat, 388–395[4]; Waltzing, *Recueil général des inscr. latines...*, 23—29.
[4] Cp. Orelli, i p. 63, and Zell, 353.
[5] *C. I. L.* vi 696*.   [6] xiv 2907.   [7] v 136*.
[8] *Eph. Ep.* iv p. 537; *C. I. L.* iii *suppl.* 6687; Rushforth, *Lat. Hist. Inscr.* no. 23; Dessau, i 2683.
[9] *Inscr. Neap.*, *Praef.* p. xi.

APPENDIX I

ROMAN NAMES

Plurimum Epigraphicae Romanae debere nominum rationem consentaneum est. Hübner, *Quaestiones Onomatologicae Latinae* (1854), p. 5.

OUR knowledge of Roman names depends largely on Latin inscriptions. In every kind of inscriptions, except copies of Roman laws, Roman names are frequent. Epitaphs necessarily include the name of the deceased; dedicatory inscriptions, the name of the dedicator; honorary inscriptions, the name of the person honoured: while names form a no less important feature of the *Fasti Consulares* and the *Acta Triumphorum*, and of lists like those from the Caelian hill, each of them recording the names of one thousand soldiers[1].

The knowledge of Roman names, derived from inscriptions which have been perfectly preserved, often makes it possible to restore inscriptions which have come down to us in a mutilated or otherwise illegible form.

It was believed by Varro that, in ancient Italy, each individual bore a single name. In support of this opinion he pointed out that Romulus and Remus, and Faustulus, had apparently no *praenomen* or *cognomen*. It was urged, however, in reply, that the mother of Romulus and Remus bore the double name of Rea Silvia, and their grandfather that of Silvius Numitor; that an early Alban king was named Agrippa Silvius, and a later Alban general, Mettus Fufetius; that the Sabines claimed the names of Titus Tatius, Numa Pompilius, and Mettus Curtius; and the Etruscans, that of Lars Porsena. Hence it was sur-

[1] Wilmanns, 1499; Dessau, i 2157.

mised that it was from the Alban and the Sabine peoples that the Romans derived the custom of having more than one name[1]. When a single name was used, the individual was distinguished by the addition of the name of the father, the husband, or the master, in the genitive case. 'Marcus, son of Marcus', was at first expressed by *Marcus Marci*. Hence arose the fuller form *Marcus Marci f(ilius)*, in which *f(ilius)* follows, instead of preceding, the father's name. At a later date we have *Caecilia Metella* described as *Q. Cretici f(ilia)* and as *Crassi (uxor)*[2]. Among ancient names of slaves were *Marcipor* and *Lucipor*, for *Marci* and *Lucii puer* (i.e. *servus*).

As a general rule, all free-born Romans had three names, the *praenomen*, the *nomen*, and the *cognomen*, e.g. M(arcus) *Tullius Cicero*. These are the *tria nomina* of Juvenal (v 127). The *praenomen* was the personal name given to a boy on the ninth day after his birth[3]; but, according to Scaevola, this name was not officially recognised, until he had assumed the *toga virilis*. In inscriptions a boy's *praenomen* is sometimes mentioned, and sometimes omitted. Its mention became more common owing to an ordinance of Marcus Aurelius (161—180), by which every citizen, in Rome and in the provinces, was required to report the birth of a son, within thirty days of his birth, *nomine imposito*[4]. If a son has died before coming of age, he is described as an infant, under the name *Pupus*, which is placed first, in the same position as any *praenomen*, e.g. *Pup(o) Pontio, T(iti) (Pontii) f(ilio), Vol(tinia tribu) Proculo, an(norum) tredecim*[5].

In inscriptions, when a *praenomen* stands by itself, it is given in full; when it is prefixed to another name, it is abbreviated, the ordinary form of the corresponding abbreviation being the initial letter or letters here printed in capitals before the parenthesis:

A(ulus), AP(pius), C for Gaius, CN for Gnaeus, D(ecimus), K(aeso), L(ucius), M(arcus), N for Manius, N(umerius), P(nblius), Q(uintus), Ser(vius), Sex(tus), S or SP for Spurius, TI or TIB for Tiberius, T(itus), and V(ibius)[6].

[1] *Liber de praenominibus*, appended to editions of Valerius Maximus.
[2] P. 42, fig. 7, *supra*.   [3] Macrobius, i 16, 36.
[4] Capitolinus, *Vita Marci*, 9.
[5] *C. I. L.* ix 2789; Wilmanns, 2697.   [6] Cp. p. 60 *supra*.

Varro recognised thirty *praenomina*[1]. Of the eighteen above mentioned, Kaeso, Manius, Servius and Spurius are comparatively rare. Among still rarer *praenomina* are Agrippa, MAM(ercus), Paullus, POST(umus), and VO(piscus). Spurius is often found in the *Fasti Consulares*, and in ordinary inscriptions, as a *praenomen* of Postumii and Albini. But Spuri f. and Sp. f. are also used to denote illegitimate sons or daughters, being sometimes combined with further epithets, which show that the above phrases are only used to conceal an indefinite paternity, e.g. *C. Asinius Spuri f. spurius*, and *C. Mamercius Sp. f. Ianuarius ...filius naturalis*[2].

Certain *gentes*, or subdivisions of *gentes*, confined themselves to a particular group of *praenomina*. Thus the *gens Claudia* used only Appius, Gaius, Decimus, Publius, and Tiberius; the Claudii Nerones, only two:—Tiberius and Decimus; the Cornelii Scipiones, only three, Gnaeus, Lucius, and Publius; and the Manlii:—Aulus, Gnaeus, Lucius, Publius, and Tiberius. In distinguished families certain *praenomina* fell out of use, as Lucius among the Claudii, owing to the condemnation of two who bore that *praenomen*[3], and Marcus among the Manlii[4], and the Antonii[5]. In 20 A.D. Cn. Piso, the son of a conspirator, was compelled to change his *praenomen*[6].

In the earliest times *praenomina* were given to women. This is proved by legendary names, such as Acca Larentia, and by the testimony of Varro, who cites names derived from the colour of the hair or eyes, such as *Rutila*, *Caesellia*, and *Rodacilla*. Accordingly, in the Sabine region near the birth-place of Varro, we find inscriptions bearing the names of *Rutila*[7], and *Gavia Caesidia*[8]. *Gavia* is an old form of *Gaia*, which is mentioned by Varro, with *Lucia*, *Publia*, and *Numeria*, among female names formed from the *praenomen* of the husband; *ceterum Gaia usu super omnes celebrata est*[9]. *Gaia*, in particular, in its old spelling *Caia*, the form in use before the introduction

women

---

[1] *De Praen.* § 3.
[2] *C. I. L.* ix 2696; x (1) 1138.
[3] Suet. *Tib.* 1.
[4] Livy, vi 20, 14; Cicero, *Phil.* i 22.
[5] Plutarch, *Cicero*, 41.
[6] Tacitus, *Ann.* iii 17.
[7] *C. I. L.* ix 4298, 5124.
[8] *ib.* 3621.
[9] *De Praen.* 7.

of the letter G, was the typical *praenomen* of a wife, as is proved by the inquiry in Plutarch's *Quaestiones Romanae* (30):—

'Wherefore do they at Rome, when they bring a newly espoused bride home to the house of her husband, force her to say these words unto her spouse, ὅπου σὺ Γάϊος, ἐγὼ Γαΐα'? (Here Plutarch is simply translating the Latin *formula*:—*ubi tu Gaius, ego Gaia.*) To this Plutarch answers: 'it implieth as much as if she should say, 'where you are lord and master, I will be lady and mistress.' Now these names they used as being common, and such as came first to hand...like as the lawyers use ordinarily these names *Caius, Seius, Lucius,* and *Titius*[1].

This use of Gaia as a typical woman's name is humorously described by Cicero as leading to the fancy of the lawyers that every woman, who entered into a kind of legal contract, called *coëmptio*, bore the name of *Gaia*[2]. A certain number of these *praenomina*, including *Gaia* and *Lucia*, are found in inscriptions of the Roman Republic[3]. They have no civic importance, and are rarely found under the Empire, as in the epitaph of *Ser(via) Cornelia Sabina*, a *liberta* of *Ser(vius) Cornelius*[4].

Of two sisters, the elder and the younger are distinguished in inscriptions by the prefix of *maio(r)* and *mino(r)*[5], while the eldest is described as *maxuma*. The ages of a series of sisters are distinguished by *Prima, Secunda, Tertia,* etc.

Among female *praenomina* we find *Pola*, the oldest form of *Paulla*, and of the later *Paula*, and of the more rustic *Polla*; and, in the same sense, *Pusilla*. We also find *Pupa*, the feminine of *Pupus*.

It is only rarely that women have *praenomina* corresponding to those of men, and similarly abbreviated, e.g. *Ap(pia)* (as in *Ap(pia) Aurelia Aurelii f. Lupercilla* in Spain[6]); also *Gaia* and *Gnaea*, as well as *Lucia, Publia, Ser(via), Sex(ta),* and *T(ita)*.

nomen
The *nomen* proper is the *nomen gentilicium* or *gentile*, common to all members of the same *gens*, men or women, clients and freedmen. Varro held that the number

---

[1] Philemon Holland's transl.
[2] *Pro Murena*, 27. Cp. Quint. i 7, 28.
[3] Similarly we have M'. Curia and Pola Livia in an ancient dedication to Iuno at Pisaurum (*C. I. L.* i² 2, 379, xi 6301). Cp. also Hübner, in *Handbuch*, 664², and Cagnat⁴, 47, note 4.   [4] *C. I. L.* vi (3) 16450.
[5] Cp. Praenestine Epitaphs, *C. I. L.* i² pp. 391—402.   [6] *C. I. L.* ii 3372.

of such names was one thousand[1]. The ancient *nomen* of the patrician and the older plebeian families was most frequently formed by adding to the stem a suffix *ius*, as Gell-ius and Helv-ius, or *aius, aeus, eus, eius*, as Ann-aeus and Pomp-eius[2]. The addition of further suffixes led to the formation of names such as *Volc-acius, Sulp-icius, Alb-ucius; Auf-idius; Corn-elius; Licinius; Val-erius; Hor-atius; Hort-ensius; Vitr-uvius*.

There are also forms ending in *anus*, of Latin and also of Sabine or Umbrian origin, usually derived from names of places, as *Norb-anus*; with later forms in *anius*, as *Vips-anius*. Certain names of Sabine or Oscan origin end in *enus*, as *Alf-enus*; of Umbrian, in *as, anas, enas*, as *Maec-enas*: and of Etruscan in *arna, erna, enna, ina* and *inna*, as *Caec-ina* and *Spur-inna*[3].

In inscriptions most of the *nomina* are set forth in full. It is only those which are most frequent, owing to their passing from patricians to their clients or freedmen, or from emperors to their freedmen or soldiers, that are abbreviated, e.g.

AEL(ius), ANT(onius), AVR(elius), CL(audius), FL(avius), IVL(ius), POMP(eius), VAL(erius), and VLP(ius).

Nomina may be abbreviated, when the full form is easily inferred from the context, e.g. *M. Propertius Tert. et M. P. Q. f.*[4] They may also be abbreviated, or entirely omitted, in contiguous inscriptions referring to members of the same *gens*[5].

The *cognomen* was of later origin than the *praenomen* and *nomen*. It occurs in the *elogia* of the Scipios and in the *lex Repetundarum* (123 B.C.), but its use in important official documents dates from the time of Sulla. By the *lex Iulia municipalis* (45 B.C.) the officials charged with the *census* were enjoined to register the *cognomen* in addition to the other names[6]. The *cognomina* were, in some cases, originally derived from some personal peculiarity, e.g. *Barbatus, Capito, Longus, Nasica*. In the great families in particular, these *cognomina* soon became hereditary, thus serving to distinguish the various branches of

cognomen

---

[1] *De Praen.* 3.   [2] Cp. Hübner's *quaestiones onomatologicae*, Bonn, 1854.
[3] Hübner, *quaest. onomatol.* in *Eph. Epigr.* ii (1875) 25—92.
[4] Orelli, 482.   [5] Hübner, in *Handbuch*, 669².
[6] *C. I. L.* i² 2, 593, l. 146, 'censum agito, eorumque nomina, praenomina, patres aut patronos, tribus, cognomina...accipito'.

the same *gens*, as *Cornelii Balbi* and *Cornelii Scipiones*, or even the subdivisions of the same branch, as *Cornelii Scipiones Nasicae*. Sometimes we have even three *cognomina*, e.g. *Cornelius Scipio Nasica Corculum*.

A *cognomen ex virtute*, which was given by way of honour, such as *Africanus, Asiaticus, Creticus, Hispanus, Macedonicus*, became hereditary[1], but was possibly limited to the eldest son[2].

Under the early Empire several *cognomina* were often held by the same person, but from the second and third century their number was considerably increased[3]. It became customary to add the 'gentile name' of the mother, and the names of the maternal grandfather, and even of the adoptive father. In cases where a second *praenomen* was thus annexed, the original *praenomen* and *nomen* were followed by the new *praenomen, nomen*, and *cognomen*, e.g. *C. Antius A. Iulius Quadratus* (consul in 105 A.D.). When a new gentile name was annexed, it was generally placed immediately after the original name, e.g. L. *Aelius Aurelius* Commodus (the emperor); but it might also be placed at a later point, e.g. M. *Larcius* Magnus *Pompeius* Silo (consul in 82 A.D.). The multiplication of *cognomina* is well illustrated in the case of Q. Pompeius Priscus, consul in 169 A.D., who, in an honorary inscription at Tibur, boasts of more than thirty names, once supposed to be the names of fifteen or sixteen separate persons[4]:—

Q. Pompeio Q. f. Quir. Senecioni Roscio Murenae Coelio Sex. Iulio Frontino Silio Deciano C. Iulio Eurycli Herculaneo L. Vibullio Pio Augustano Alpino Bellicio Sollerti Iulio Apro Ducenio Proculo Rutiliano Rufino Silio Valenti Valerio Nigro Cl. Fusco Saxae [Am]yntano Sosio Prisco pontifici etc.

From his father he derives the names 'Q. Pompeio Roscio Murenae Coelio Silio Deciano Iulio Eurycli Herculaneo L. Vibullio Pio'; from his maternal grandfather, 'Senecioni' and 'Sosio'; from his great-grandfather, 'Sex. Iulio Frontino'; and from a consul of Trajan's time, 'Augustano Alpino Bellico Sollerti'[5].

In Latin literature, as in Latin inscriptions, the normal order of the *tria nomina* is *praenomen, nomen, cognomen*, and the best

[1] Cic. *de Rep.* vi 11.   [2] Mommsen, *Röm. Forsch.* i 53.
[3] A later name for such an additional *cognomen* was *agnomen*. *De praen.* 2.
[4] Cp. Orelli, 2761.   [5] Dessau, i 1104.

writers of prose, such as Cicero and Caesar, adhere to this order. Poets, however, for metrical convenience, often place the *nomen* before the *praenomen*, as in the epitaph of one of the Scipios, *Cornelius Lucius Scipio Barbatus* (page 66 f), while Ennius has *Aelius Sextus*; Lucilius, *Laelius Decumus*; and Horace, *Casellius Aulus*. The examples of the same inversion in Varro and Livy are due to corruptions in the text. The *praenomen* alone was used for relations and friends, and the *cognomen* alone in any other ordinary intercourse, with the *praenomen* prefixed in emphatic address, e.g. *O Marce Druse, patrem appello*[1]. In the language of literature, after Caesar's time, most writers place the *nomen* either before or after the *cognomen*. As, in inscriptions, we have the *cognomen* before the *nomen* in (*Pulcher Clau*)*dius et Rex Mar*(*cius*)[2], so, in Cicero, we have *Balbus Cornelius*[3], and *Ahala Servilius*[4]. The normal order, *nomen, cognomen*, is consistently used by Caesar; Livy and Tacitus[5] vary, while the younger Pliny reverts to the normal order of Caesar[6].

The Latin term for a distinctive sobriquet, or nickname, was *signum*. It is not found in inscriptions before 150 A.D., the earliest known example belonging to the time of Marcus Aurelius and Commodus. Some of these *signa* were borrowed from Greek, or from other foreign languages. They often ended in *ius*, in which case they were derived from an adjective, as *Gaudentius* from *gaudens*; *Eusebius* from εὐσεβής. Even when applied to women, the masculine termination -*ius* was retained in the genitive case, as 'Octavia Felicitas, *signo Leonti*'. The word *signo* or *signum* was usually prefixed, as *signum Aeaci, signum Olympi*, or *signo Concordiae*[7]. There were also introductory *formulae* such as *idem*, or *sive*, or *qui et*, or *qui et vocatur* or *dictus est*[8]. Such names were also placed at the beginning or the end of an inscription, either in the genitive or in the vocative, followed, in the latter alternative, by *vale* or *vivas*. Sometimes the name

margin note: signum

[1] Cic. *Orator*, 213.   [2] *C. I. L.* i² 2, 775.
[3] *Ad Att.* viii 19, 3.   [4] *Pro Mil.* 8.
[5] In *Ann.* ii he generally writes *Asinius Gallus*, and, less frequently, *Gallus Asinius*, or simply *Gallus*.
[6] Cp. Marquardt's *Privatleben der Römer*, ed. 1886, p. 9, and Smith's *Dict. of Antiquities*, ii 233 f.
[7] Wilmanns, 92, 2715.   [8] *ib. indices*, ii 406.

was common to several members of a family, or a society, such as a funeral-club. From Rome, under the Antonines, the custom spread to the provinces, and, by the fourth century, it had become frequent among the higher classes. Among the earliest examples are *Euhodi* and *Helvini* (200 A.D.). We also find *Asterii* applied to L. Turcius and his brother (346)[1]; *Phosphorii* to the father of Symmachus, the orator (377), and *Eusebii* to Symmachus himself (consul, 391)[2]. The prominence given to the familiar name by placing it at the head of the inscription ensured the ready identification of the person in whose honour the inscription was set up. Sometimes this familiar name was the only one mentioned in historical literature, as in the case of Clodius Celsinus ADELFIUS, *praefectus urbi* in 351, and of Iulius Festus HYMETIUS, proconsul of Africa in 362 A.D.[3]

Next to the *praenomen* and *nomen* was placed the father's abbreviated *praenomen* in the genitive case, followed name of father by F(ilius) or FIL(ius). This might be succeeded by the *praenomen* of the grandfather followed by N(epos), of the great-grandfather by PRON(epos), and even, sometimes, of the great great-grandfather by ABN(epos), e.g. C. Neratio C. FIL(io) C. N(epoti) C. PRON(epoti) C. ABN(epoti) Proculo[4]. Occasionally the *praenomen* of the father is superseded by his *cognomen*, e.g. Tito Mamilio Silonis Fil.[5] Sometimes the name of the mother is given (*a*) with or (*b*) without that of the father, as in Tuscan inscriptions of the time when the Etruscan language was giving way to Latin, e.g. (*a*) L. Pomponius L. F. Arsiniae gnatus, and (*b*) L. Gavius Spedo Septumia nat.[6] The latter is also exemplified in an *exsecratio*, where the absence of the father's name is part of the malicious character of the whole document, as it probably implies that the person in question is illegitimate[7].

[1] Dessau, i 1229.
[2] *ib*. 1257, 2946; cp. 1214, 1224–6, 1238–40, and Wilmanns, *indices*, ii 403.
[3] Ammianus Marc. xvi 6, 2; xxviii 1, 17. In the *indices* of Wilmanns, ii p. 369, and of Dessau, iii, p. 163, these are entered under *cognomina*, in the capital letters distinctive of the senatorial order. Elsewhere, they are sometimes included among *agnomina*, a late term of little authority (p. 212, n. 3, *supra*). [4] Dessau, ii 6485.
[5] *ib*. 6934 (in Spain). [6] Wilmanns, 155. [7] *ib*. 2749.

ROMAN NAMES

The *lex Iulia municipalis* enacted that the names of Roman citizens should be registered in the following order: *nomina, praenomina, patres aut patronos, tribus, cognomina*[1]. This is the order generally followed in inscriptions, except that, under the Empire, the *praenomen* is always placed first. The name of the father and that of the tribe were placed after the *praenomen* and *nomen*, and before the *cognomen*, e.g. *Q. Lollio M(arci) fil(io) Quir(ina tribu) Vrbico*[2]; *L. Minicio L(ucii) f(ilio) Gal(eria tribu) Natali*[3]. The name of the tribe may be given in full, either in the ablative or (rarely) in the genitive, or in an adjectival form. More frequently it is abbreviated. In any case the word *tribu*, or *tribus*, is omitted. The following are the names of the thirty-five tribes, with the most frequent abbreviation of each. It will be observed that the abbreviation generally consists of three letters.

name of tribe

AEM(ilia), ANI(ensis), ARN(iensis), CAM(ilia), CLA(udia), CLV(stumina), COL(lina), COR(nelia), ESQ(uilina), FAB(ia), FAL(erna), GAL(eria), HOR(atia), LEM(onia), MAEC(ia), MEN(enia), OVF(entina), PAL(atina), PAP(iria), POL(lia), POM(ptinia), PVB(lilia), PVP(inia), QVIR(ina), ROM(ilia), SAB(atina), SCAP(tia), SER(gia), STE(llatina), SVC for Suburana[4], TER(etina), TRO(mentina), VEL(ina), VOL(tinia), VOT(uria)[5].

The *patria*, or native town, if mentioned, is generally placed, in the ablative or genitive, or in an adjectival form, after the *cognomen*, e.g. *C. Aufidius C. fil. Arn(iensi) Restitutus* Karth(agine)[6]; and similarly with the province, or region, of birth or of nationality. The town of residence may be denoted by *domo* followed by a locative case. Several of these local indications may be combined, e.g. *domo Voltinia Philippis Macedonia*[7].

In the case of legitimate sons, the eldest generally received the same *praenomen* as his father. Sometimes the father's *praenomen* is borne by several of his sons; there are also cases in which the *praenomen* of the eldest son is different from that of his father.

Transmission of praenomen, and cognomen

---

[1] p. 211 *supra*. [2] Dessau, i 1065.
[3] Wilmanns, 1179. Cp. *Senatus Consultum* in Cic. *Epist.* viii 8, 5.
[4] Varro, *De L. L.* v 48: Quint. i 7, 28.
[5] Wilmanns, *indices*, ii 407 f; Cagnat⁴ p. 63.
[6] Wilmanns, 1500. [7] *ib.* 2095; *indices*, ii 409 f.

In the early Empire, the eldest son generally received the *cognomen* of his father; the second, that of his mother; and the third a *cognomen* in *-anus* derived from that of his father. Thus the eldest son of M. Cosinius Priscus and Tuccia Prima is named M. Cosinius *Priscus*; the second, M. Cosinius *Primus*; and the third, M. Cosinius *Priscianus*[1]. Similarly, the eldest son of Flavius Sabinus and Vespasia Polla is named T. Flavius Sabinus; and the second, T. Flavius Vespasianus, the emperor, whose *cognomen* is derived from the *gens* of his mother. Again, the eldest son of Vespasian and Flavia Domitilla is named T. Flavius Vespasianus (the emperor 'Titus'); and the second son, T. Flavius Domitianus (the emperor 'Domitian'), while their daughter takes her mother's name, Domitilla[2]. Occasionally the eldest son received the *praenomen* and *cognomen* of his paternal grandfather; and there was room for even further varieties in the names of the children, which, however, were generally in some sort suggested by the names of their ancestors[3].

Illegitimate children generally take the gentile name of their mother. Thus a son of Cn. Numidius Berullus, **names of natural sons** by his concubine Allia Nysa, appears as L. Allius L. f(ilius) Quartinus; it will be observed that he is called L(ucii) f(ilius), although his father's *praenomen* is Gnaeus. Again, P. Paccius Ianuarius and Mamercia Grapte dedicate an epitaph to their son, *C. Mamercio, Sp. F. Ianuario...filio naturali*, where *Sp. F.*, owing to its position in the series of names, is probably intended to be read *Spurii filio*, though it really means *spurio filio*[4]. This interpretation is confirmed by inscriptions in which the *praenomen* is given in full, — *Spuri f(ilius)*, e.g. *C. Asinius, Spuri f(ilius), Spurius*[5]. Such sons were often assigned to the *tribus Collina*, or *Suburana*, or *Esquilina*.

An adopted son, on passing into the *gens* of his adoptive **adoption** father, gave up his own *tria nomina* and took those of his adoptive father. Under the Republic, he added to these names a *cognomen* formed from the *gens* of his own father by expanding it into an adjective ending in *anus*.

[1] *C. I. L.* x 1506. [2] Suetonius, *Vesp.* 1 and 3.
[3] Cp. Cagnat, 67—72[4]. [4] *C. I. L.* x 1138; p. 209 *supra*.
[5] Cagnat, 73[4] f.

Thus a son of L. Aemilius Paullus, who is adopted by P. Cornelius Scipio, becomes P. Cornelius P. f. Scipio Aemilianus; a son of C. Octavius, adopted by C. Iulius Caesar, becomes C. Iulius Caesar Octavianus (the emperor Augustus); T. Pomponius Atticus, on his adoption by his uncle, Q. Caecilius, becomes Q. Caecilius Q. f. Pomponianus Atticus[1].

Under the Empire, the change of name was attended by some irregularities. Thus the younger Pliny, whose original name was P. Caecilius L. f. Ouf(entina) Secundus, on his adoption by his maternal uncle, the elder Pliny, C. Plinius Secundus, became C. Plinius L. f. Ouf. Caecilius Secundus. By his adoption he took the name of his adoptive father, while he lost his own *praenomen*, and placed his original gentile name *Caecilius* immediately before his *cognomen* Secundus; but he continued to describe himself as L. f., the son of his actual father, instead of C. f., the son of his adoptive father[2].

Under the Flavian emperors, it became customary to keep, in many cases, not only the former *praenomen*, but even some of the other original names. Thus T. Aurelius Fulvus Boionius Arrius Antoninus, on his adoption by P. Aelius Hadrianus (the emperor Hadrian), became T. Aelius Hadrianus Aurelius Antoninus (commonly called Antoninus Pius); and M. Annius Verus, on his adoption by the latter, became M. Aelius Aurelius Verus (commonly called M. Aurelius).

The same rule applies, if the person in question is adopted by a woman. Thus, Ser. Sulpicius Galba, the future emperor, on his adoption by his step-mother, Livia Ocellina, took her father's praenomen Lucius, and the gentile name Livius, and the *cognomen* Ocella[3]. In a Greek inscription his full name is equivalent to Lucius Livius Sulpicius Galba.

When a foreigner received the Roman citizenship, he generally took the *praenomen* and *nomen* of the person to whom he owed the citizenship; but he retained his original name in the form of a *cognomen*. Thus Caburus, who obtained the citizenship through C. Valerius Flaccus,

naturalised foreigners

---

[1] Cicero, *ad Atticum*, iii 20 superscr.
[2] Cp. Mommsen in *Hermes*, iii 70—77, *Ges. Schr.* iv 404—412.
[3] Suetonius, *Galba*, 3.

became C. Valerius Caburus[1]. In Gaul we have many who owed their citizenship to C. Iulius Caesar, and accordingly received names beginning with C. Iulius. Similarly, under the Empire, in and after the time of Claudius (41 f), naturalised foreigners generally took the gentile name of the emperor to whom they owed their citizenship. Thus Alexander, on receiving the citizenship from T. Flavius Vespasianus, became T. Flavius Quir(ina tribu) Alexander[2].

Not only foreigners, but even foreign towns raised to the rank of Roman cities, were assigned to a particular tribe by the emperor to whom they owed that privilege. In the case of the Julian emperors, the towns in the East, with all the newly adopted citizens, were assigned to the *tribus Fabia*; towns in Spain, to the *Galeria*; those in Gallia Narbonensis, to the *Voltinia*; those in Dalmatia, to the *Sergia*. Under Claudius, the towns in Mauretania were assigned to the *Quirina*, those in the rest of the Empire to the *Claudia*; under Nero and the Flavian emperors, the tribe was the *Quirina*; under Hadrian, the *Sergia*; under Antoninus Pius, the *Voltinia*; and, under M. Aurelius and Septimius Severus, the *Papiria*.

Foreigners enrolled in the Roman legions frequently took the *praenomen* and *nomen* of the emperor under whom they were enrolled. Roman citizens serving in the legions had not the right of contracting a legal marriage. Hence their sons were illegitimate, and, if enrolled in the legions, did not receive the gentile name of the emperor, but that of their father, and were assigned to the *tribus Pollia*.

Foreigners who were not naturalised sometimes assumed the name of a Roman *gens*, and added their own name as a *cognomen*, thus usurping the privileges of Roman citizens. This was carried so far that Claudius forbade their use of the gentile names of Rome[3]. Foreign kings, allied to the Roman empire, often adopted the name (usually the gentile name) of the reigning emperor, as in the case of the British king, *Ti. Claudius Cogidubnus*[4].

[1] Caesar, *B. G.* i. 47.
[2] *C. I. L.* iii 6785.
[3] Suetonius, *Claud.* 25.
[4] *C. I. L.* vii 11; *Cogidumnus* in Tac. *Agr.* 14.

Slaves usually bore a single name, followed by the name of their master in the genitive of possession, with or without the addition of *servus* or of its abbreviation *S*. [slaves] In many cases they have double names. Some of these are aliases or nicknames, e.g. *Speratus, Caesiae s., Mus*; and *Philadelphus, qui et Polydapanus*[1]. Many more are examples of *servi publici*, or of slaves of emperors, with second names in *anus* derived from those of their former masters.

Under the Empire, freedmen usually bore three names corresponding to the *praenomen, nomen*, and *cognomen* of a free Roman. For the *praenomen* and *nomen* [freedmen] they took those of the master to whom they owed their liberty; and, for their *cognomen*, their former slave-name. This is the point of the passage in Persius (v 78 f), 'momento turbinis exit Marcus Dama'[2]. In inscriptions a freedman usually inserts between his former master's *praenomen* and *nomen*, and his own former name, the genitive case of that master's *praenomen* followed by L. (or LIB.) for *libertus*, e.g. *C. Iulius C. lib(ertus) Hermes*. When the former master is an emperor, the *praenomen* is replaced by *Aug(usti)* or *Caes(aris) n(ostri)*. *Liberti* not unfrequently use a different *praenomen* and occasionally a different *nomen* from that of their former master[3].

A slave, enfranchised by a woman, takes the gentile name of the woman, preceded by that of her father, e.g. Menophilus, a former slave of Livia Augusta, daughter of M. Livius Drusus, receives the name of *M. Livius Aug(ustae) l(ibertus) Menophilus*[4].

In inscriptions the fact that a *libertus* owes his freedom to a woman is denoted by Ɔ·L, i.e. *G(aiae) libertus, Gaia* being a typical name conventionally used of any woman[5], and the inverted C being its regular symbol[6]. This interpretation of the inverted C is confirmed by the fact that its place is sometimes taken by

---

[1] Wilmanns, 1945, 2640.
[2] The *Quintus* (or *Publius*) *Dama* of Horace, *Sat.* ii 5 18, 32, whose sensitive ears *gaudent praenomine*, is clearly a wealthy *libertus*.
[3] Willmanns, *indices*, i 404.
[4] *C. I. L.* vi 3939.   [5] pp. 60, 210 *supra*.
[6] Quintilian, i 7, 28, 'Gaius C littera notatur, quae inversa mulierem declarat'.

the word *mulieris*, either written in full, or abbreviated, or represented by an inverted M or W[1].

If the *libertus* has been the slave of two masters bearing the same *praenomen* and *nomen*, he takes the *praenomen* and *nomen* of both, e.g. *Q. Cornelius, Q. Q. l(ibertus), Saturninus*[2], where *Q. Q.* stands for *Quintorum*.

If he has been the slave of more than one master, with the same gentile name, but with different *praenomina*, he places one of the *praenomina* before the gentile name, and all of them (in the genitive) before the abbreviation for *libertus*. Thus Philomusus Mus, a former slave of Marcus and Publius and Vibius Decumius, becomes *P. Decumius*, M. P. V. l(ibertus), Philomusus Mus[3].

If his former masters have different *praenomina* and different gentile names, he takes either the *praenomen* and *nomen* of one of them; or the *praenomen* of one, and the *nomen* of the other; and similarly in the case of three former masters. Thus a *libertus* of Cn. Caecilius and of Aulus and Quintus Flaminius may be called *Q. Caecilius, Cn. A. Q. Flamini leibertus*[4].

The former *servi publici* of a *municipium*, or a *colonia*, take, as *liberti*, either (*a*) the gentile name *Publicius*, formed from *publicus*, e.g. *M. Publicius Coloniae l(ibertus) Philodamus*[5];

or (*b*) a gentile name occurring among the *cognomina* of the town in question, e.g. *Ti. Claudius, municipii Celeiani libertus, Favor*, the name of Celeia being the *municipium Claudium*[6];

or (*c*) a name derived from the name of the town, e.g. from Venafrum, *Q. Venafranius, col(oniae) l(ibertus), Felix*[7].

A *libertus* often takes his name from the trade followed by the college, or colleges, to which he formerly belonged, e.g. *Cresimus* (sic), a *libertus* of two *collegia* of *Fabri* and *Centonarii*, becomes *Fabricius Centonius, collegiorum lib(ertus), Cresimus*[8].

Slaves, who rose to high rank, sometimes completely concealed their original names under a new designation derived from the gentile name of one of their former masters. Thus the

---

[1] Wilmanns, 2674 f.   [2] *C. I. L.* vi (3) 16307.
[3] *ib.* 16771 *a*.   [4] p. 201 *supra*
[5] Wilmanns, 2665 (cp. Hübner, in *Eph. Epigr.* ii 89).
[6] *ib.* 2668.   [7] *ib.* 2666.   [8] *ib.* 2670.

former slave Icelus, whose name, as a *libertus* of Ser. Sulpicius Galba, would naturally have been Ser. Sulpicius Icelus, assumed, in place of his former slave-name, that of Marcianus, implying probably that he had been transferred to Galba by a former master named Marcius[1].

[1] Tacitus, *Hist.* i 13.
On Roman Names in general cp. Lahmeyer, in *Philologus* (1865) 469 ff.; Mommsen, *Röm. Forschungen*, i (1864) 1—68; Marquardt, *Das Privatleben der Römer*, ed. 2 (1886) 7—27; Hübner, *Handbuch*, 653—680[2]; Cagnat, 37—87[4]; Egbert, 82—102; and, for illustrative inscriptions, Orelli, i pp. 472—487; Wilmanns, ii 197—208; and esp. Egbert, 103—113. See also Dessau, iii (2), *Indices*, 920—929, 'Nominum ratio'.

APPENDIX II

TITLES OF ROMAN OFFICIALS

CURSUS HONORUM

Gerendorum honorum non promiscua facultas est. Digest, iv 14, 5.

In Chapter VI, on Honorary Inscriptions, the general rules as to the *cursus honorum*, or the order in which public offices were held, have been briefly set forth, together with certain peculiarities in the way in which those offices are enumerated in Latin inscriptions. The offices may be enumerated either in the *direct* or in the *reverse* order, while, occasionally, there is a combination of both methods[1].

Tabular lists of the various offices concerned have been reserved for the present Appendix, which also sets forth the ordinary abbreviations for each office.

Senatorial Cursus Honorum

Preliminary minor offices, held for one year

(1) *Vigintiviri* XX VIRI

(a) *decemvir stlitibus iudicandis,* X · VIR · STL · IVD; member of civil court.

(b) *quattuorvir viarum curandarum,* IIII · VIR · VIAR · CVR; supervisor of city streets.

(c) *triumvir capitalis,* III · VIR · CAP(KAPIT); superintendent of capital sentences.

(d) *triumvir monetalis,* III · VIR · MON,— *aere argento auro flando feriundo,* III · VIR · A · A · A• F · F; officer in charge of coinage.

(Under Severus Alexander (222—235), the *vigintiviri* disappeared.)

[1] pp. 110—117 *supra.*

(2) *tribunus militum laticlavius*, TR(IB)· LAT · (or L·C·) M(IL), or T·L·C, for at least one year.

List of Senatorial Magistracies (in ascending order)

I. Quaestor . . . . . Q, QVAE, QVAEST, QVAIST (archaic)
  „ pro praetore . . . PR(O) · PR(AET)
  „ (provinciae—) . . . — (PROVINC)
  „ urbanus . . . . — VRB
  „ Augusti, Caesaris, Imperatoris — AVG, CAES, IMP

II. Aedilis . . . . . . AED, AEDIL
  „ curulis . . . . — CVR
  „ plebis . . . . — PL(EB)
  „   „ cerealis . . . — — CERIAL

or II. Tribunus plebis . . . . TR, TRIB, PL

III. Praetor . . . . . PR
  „ peregrinus . . . — PER
  „ urbanus . . . — VRB
  „ tutelarius . . . — TVTEL
  „ aerarii . . . . — AER

IV. Consul . . C (rare), COS (later CON, CONS)

Priesthoods open to the Senatorial Order

Augur . . . . AVG
  „ publicus populi Romani Quiritium — PVB · P · R · Q(VIR)
Fetialis . . . . . . *not abbreviated*
Flamen Dialis . . . . . FL, FLAM, DIALIS
  „ Quirinalis . . . . — — QVIR
  „ Augustalis . . . . — — AVG
  „ Claudialis . . . . — — CLAVD
Frater Arvalis . . . . . FR · ARV (*rarely*
Pontifex . . . . . . PONT [*used*)
  „ maximus . . . . . PONT · MAX
Quindecimvir sacris faciundis . . XV VIR · S(ACR) · F(AC)

Salius	SAL (rare)
Septemvir epulonum	VII VIR · EPVL(ON)
Sodalis Augustalis	SOD · AVG
„ „ Claudialis . .	— — CL(AVD)
„ Hadrianalis, Marcianus, Aurelianus etc.[1]	
Virgo Vestalis	V · V

Officials appointed out of the Senatorial Order

Censitor (or legatus Augusti censibus accipiendis) assigned to *consulares* or *praetorii*	CENS or (LEG · AVG · CENS · ACC)
Comes—Augusti (assigned generally to *praetorii*)	COMES · —AVG
Corrector (*consulares* or *praetorii*) .	CORR
Curator actorum senatus (*quaestoricii*)	CVR(AT) · AB · ACT · SENAT
Curator alvei Tiberis et riparum et cloacarum urbis (*consulares*) . .	CVR(AT) · ALV · TIB · ET · RIP · ET · CLOAC · VRB
Curator operum publicorum (*consulares* or *praetorii*) . . .	CVR(AT) · OPER · PVB
Curator aquarum et Miniciae (*consulares*)	— AQVAR · ET · MIN
Curator Miniciae (cp. Wilmanns, 1202, n. 4)	— MIN
Curator viarum (*praetorii* or *consulares*)	— VIAR
Curator rei publicae—(*praetorii* or *quaestoricii*)	— R · P
Iuridicus per Italiam regionis—(*consulares*)	IVR, IVRID
Iuridicus, legatus iuridicus provinciae —(*consulares* or *praetorii*) . .	LEG · IVR, IVRID—
Legatus Augusti pro praetore provinciae—	LEG · AVG · PR · PR · PROV—
Legatus proconsulis, or pro praetore provinciae (*quaestoricii*) . .	LEG · PROCOS, PR · PR · PROV
Legatus legionis (*praetorii*) . .	LEG · LEG

[1] Dessau, i 1160.

Praefectus	P, PF, PR, PRAE, PRAEF
„ aerarii militaris (*praetorii*)	— AER · MIL(IT)
„ aerarii Saturni (*praetorii*)	— AER · S(AT)
„ alimentorum (*praetorii* or *consulares*)	— ALIMENT(OR)
Praefectus frumenti dandi ex senatus consulto (*praetorii* or *aedilicii*) .	— F · D · EX · S · C
Praefectus urbi (urbis), (*consulares*) .	— V, VRB
Praeses provinciae[1]— . . .	P(RAES) · P(ROV)—
Proconsul (*consulares*, of Asia or Africa; *praetorii*, of other senatorial provinces)	PROCOS

Equestrian Cursus Honorum

Under the Empire the ancient body of eighteen centuries of *equites*, known as *equites Romani equo publico* EQ · R(OM) · EQ · P or PVB(L), was reorganised. The preliminary qualifications for admission to this body were free birth, and the possession of property amounting to not less than 400,000 sesterces. To be enlisted in the equestrian troop, it was further necessary for a duly qualified applicant to be recognised by the emperor's presentation of a knight's horse. The recipient was described as *equo publico donatus*, or *exornatus*[2]. From this body officials were appointed to represent the emperor, and to be promoted in due course from the lower grade of *procuratores* to the higher grade of *praefecti*.

I. *Preliminary services*, (a) *military*

(a) The three forms of preliminary military service, instituted by Claudius, were, according to Suetonius[3], (1) *praefectura cohortis*, (2) *praefectura alae*, (3) *tribunatus legionis*; but we learn from inscriptions that, until early in the second century, one or more tribunates in the army or one of the three tribunates in the city,— that of the *tribunus cohortis vigilum* or *urbanae* or *praetoriae*, might be substituted for the *praefectura*

[1] Mommsen, *Staatsrecht*, ii
[2] Wilmanns, 1595; Dessau, i 2667.
[3] *Claudius*, 25.

From the time of Septimius Severus the centurionate became the first military office, leading up through the primipilate, and the *praefectura legionis*, to the procuratorship, the higher positions in the latter being generally reserved for those who had filled the city tribunates above mentioned[1].

(*b*) From the time of Hadrian various grades of civil service were recognised as avenues to the position of *procurator* or *praefectus*.

II. *Procuratores*. The *procurator* was an imperial agent charged with minor administrative duties. Originally, he was generally one of the emperor's *liberti*, but, ultimately, he was always appointed from among prominent members of the equestrian order.

From the time of Hadrian there were four classes of *procuratores*, whose rank may be determined by their salaries, rising from 60 to 100, 200, or 300, thousand sesterces, and described as *sexagenarii, centenarii, ducenarii*, and *trecenarii* respectively.

The *sexagenarii* were mainly composed of the assistants and subordinates of the *procuratores* and *praefecti*. Thus there is definite evidence that they included the assistants in the state-council, the *adiutores studiorum*, the provincial directors of the post, the district directors of alimentation, the *procurator ad annonam Ostiis*, and (in the second century) the *procurator bibliothecarum*. They also included the lower district-officials of the *ratio privata*, of the *xx hereditatium* (with the *promagister* in Rome), the superintendents of the provincial gladiatorial schools, the sub-praefects of the fleet in Italy and probably some of those in the provinces, the sub-procurators in the provinces, the assistants of the *praefectus annonae* in Rome and the provinces, the *adiutores ad census* in Rome, and the *advocati fisci*.

The *centenarii* included the *procuratores alimentorum, aquarum, bibliothecarum* (in the earlier time), *hereditatium patrimonii privati, ludi magni, monetae, operum publicorum, patrimonii*, and *portus* ; the *subpraefecti annonae* and *vigilum* ; a *praefectus vehiculorum* ; an imperial *consiliarius* ; the *magister vicesimarum* in Rome; the *procuratores* of important mines in the provinces; the *procurator rationis privatae* ; the *iuridicus Alexandreae*, the *procurator Pelusii* ; and the *praefectus classis* in Italy (in the first two centuries).

The *ducenarii* included the *procurator* or *praeses* of certain provinces ; the *procurator stationis hereditatium* ; the *praefectus vehiculorum viae Flaminiae* ; and the president of the Museum of Alexandria.

The *trecenarii* included the *procurator a rationibus* or *rationalis*; the *procurator rationis* (or *rei*) *privatae*; the *procurator a censibus, a cognitionibus*,

[1] Egbert, in *Studies in honour of H. Drisler*, New York (1894), 16—23.

ab epistulis Latinis, a libellis, a memoria, a studiis; and the *magister summarum rationum*[1].

The details of the above classification of officials rest on the authority of inscriptions. Thus we have an inscription in memory of Sex. Varius Marcellus, the father of 'Heliogabalus,' describing him as *proc(uratori) aquar(um)* $\overline{C}$ (= *centenario*), *proc. prov(inciae) Brit(anniae)* $\overline{CC}$ (= *ducenario*), and *proc. rationis privat(ae)* $\overline{CCC}$ (= *trecenario*)[2]. We have also an inscription in honour of the *praefectus praetorio*, C. Caelius Saturninus, dedicated to him as *ducenario a consiliis ⟨sacris⟩, sexagenario a conciliis sacris*, and *sexagenario studiorum adiutori*[3].

III. *Praefecti.* These important officials held the following rank, in ascending order:—

(1) Praefectus classis (praetoriae, at Ravenna and Misenum), PRAEF·CLASS —: (2) — vigilum, — VIG, VIGIL; (3) — annonae, — ANN; (4) — Aegypti, — AEG; (5) — praetorio, — PRAET.

The *priesthoods* held by *equites* were those of Haruspex, HAR; Lupercus, LVPERC; (Sacerdos) Laurens Lavinas, L·L or LAVR·LAVIN; and tubicen sacrorum populi Romani Quiritium, TVB·SAC·P·R·QVIRIT.

Offices open to the Third Class

The official positions open to persons below the senatorial and equestrian orders were very numerous, and comparatively unimportant. In the *indices* of the *Corpus Inscriptionum*, members of this third class are arranged as follows:—

(1) Apparitores et Officiales Magistratuum et Imperatoris et Vectigalium.

(2) Officia Militaria et Classiaria.

(3) Honorati et Principales Coloniarum et Municipiorum.

(4) Principales Collegiorum.

---

[1] O. Hirschfeld, *Verwaltungsbeamten* (ed. 1905), *die procuratorische Laufbahn*, 410—465, esp. 432—441.

[2] Dessau, i 478.

[3] *ib.* 1214. Cp. Mommsen, *de Cael. Saturnini titulo* in *Nuove Memorie dell' Instituto* (1865), 298—332, and, in general, Liebenam, *die Laufbahn der Procuratoren* (1886), pp. 124 ff.

228   LATIN INSCRIPTIONS   [APP.

(1) Among *apparitores*, the following are those most frequently mentioned in inscriptions, with some of the more notable abbreviations:—

Accensus consulis or *patroni*; *lictor*; *scriba, viator*, or *praeco, decurialis* (who were members of the *decuriae*, or organised subdivisions of *scribae*, etc.). *arcarius*, ARK; *commentariensis*; *contra*(Ↄ or 7)*scriptor*, ↃSC or 7SC; *dispensator*; *tabellarius*; *tabularius rationis fisci* or *vigesimae hereditatum*,— XX HER.

(2) Subordinate officers of (a) the army or (b) the navy, including

(a) *actarius* (*legionis*), A, ACT; *aquilifer*; *beneficiarius*, BF; *centurio* Ↄ, 7,), Z, or CENT; *curator fisci*; *custos armorum*, C · A; *frumentarius*, FR, FRVM; *optio*, OP, OPT; *secutor tribuni*, S · T; *signifer*, SIG, SIGN, SIGNIF; *singularis consularis*, S, SING · COS; *speculator*, SPEC; *tesserarius*, TES, TESS; *tubicen*, TVB; *veteranus*, VET,—*honesta missione*, H · M, or—*honesta missione missus*, H · M · M; *vexillarius*, VEX, VEXILL.

The following is the order of the lower stages of the *cursus militaris*, which may be inferred from inscriptions recording promotions from rank to rank, ending with that of *centurio* :—

(1) *Secutor tribuni*; (2) *singularis*; (3) *beneficiarius tribuni*; (4) *tesserarius*; (5) *optio*; (6) *signifer* or *vexillarius* (*cohortis vigilum*); (7) *curator fisci*; (8) *cornicularius*; (9) *beneficiarius praefecti praetorio*; (10) *cornicularius praefecti annonae*; (11) *evocatus Augusti*; (12) *centurio*[1].

(b) Some of the more distinctive titles in the Roman Navy are *faber duplarius* (DVPL) or *duplicarius*; *navarchus*, N; *praefectus classis*, PR, PRAE, PRAEF·CL, CLAS, CLASS; *praepositus* (PRAEP) *classi*; *trierarcha* (*-us*), TR, TRIER.

(3) As a third class of subordinate officials we have the magistrates of the *coloniae* and *municipia*. The *municipes* consisted of three classes, (1) the *ordo decurionum*, or the local senate; (2) the *ordo Augustalis*, dating from the time of Augustus, and consisting of six persons entrusted with the duty of providing public entertainments at their own expense; and (3) the *plebs* or *populus*.

The magistrates of the *municipia* and *coloniae* were usually termed *duoviri* (or *quattuorviri*) *iure*[2] *dicundo*, II̅ (or II̅II̅)·V·I(VR)· D(IC), *aediles* (*duoviri* or *quattuorviri aediles*) and *quaestores*. The

---

[1] Cp. P. Cauer in *Eph. Epigr.* iv 355 f (quoted by Egbert, p. 183). Cp. the 19 grades of *militia urbana* in note to Wilmanns, 1499. On the *nomina et gradus centurionum*, cp. Mommsen, *Ges. Schriften*, viii (1913) 360–84, and, in general, Domaszewski, *Die Rangordnung des römischen Heeres*, in *Bonner Jahrbücher*, 278 pp., 1908.

[2] An old dat. for *iuri*.

title *quattuorviri* (*iure dicundo* or *aediles*), implying that the two magistrates *iure dicundo* and the two *aediles* formed one body, is usually found in the Italian *municipia*, that of *duoviri* in the *coloniae* and the provinces. The II *viri* or IIII *viri* elected every five years in the year of census were termed *quinquennales* and were of higher rank.

(4) There are also numerous officials in the various *collegia*, or corporations, in which the official *decuriones* and *honorati* are contrasted with the ordinary members, the *plebs collegii*. Among special epithets applied to individuals are BIS(ellarius)[1]; HON (oratus); IMM(unis); e.g. IMM·II·HON·III[2]; and *quinquennalis*, Q, QQ, or QVINQ, used especially of an official ordinarily elected for five years, who, if elected for life, became a *quinquennalis perpetuus*, QQ·PER[3].

For further details on Official Titles, see Mommsen, *Römische Staatsrecht*, vols. i³, ii³, iii¹ (1887 f), French transl.—1896; Otto Hirschfeld, *Untersuchungen auf dem Gebiete der römischen Verwaltungsgeschichte*, i (1877), and ed. 2, entitled *Die kaiserlichen Verwaltungsbeamten bis auf Diocletian* (1905); *Die Rangtitel der römischen Kaiserzeit*, in *Kleine Schriften*, 646-81; also Cagnat, 88—156⁴, or Egbert, 164—221, with Wilmanns, ii (*indices*) pp. 539—574 (*res publica Romana*), 575—609 (*res militaris*), 611—630 (*res municipalis*), and 631—644 (*collegia*), and Dessau, iii (*indices*) pp. 350—441 (*res publica populi Romani*), 442—506 (*res militaris*), 506-9 (*officia classiaria*), 665—709 (*res municipalis*), and 710—725 (*collegia*).

[1] Wilmanns, 2190, 'pater collegii bisellarius'; cp. p. 78 *supra*.
[2] *Ib*. 1739.
[3] *Ib*. 1726. On *collegia* in general, cp. Waltzing's *Étude historique*, 4 vols. 1895—1900; Liebenam, *Röm. Vereinswesen*, 1890; and Kornemann in Pauly-Wissowa, s.v., with the literature there quoted.

APPENDIX III

NAMES AND TITLES OF ROMAN EMPERORS

'Trajan erected many famous monuments and buildings, insomuch as Constantine the Great in emulation was wont to call him *Parietaria*, wallflower, because his name was upon so many walls.'

Bacon, *Of the Advancement of Learning*, I vii (cp. *Incerti auctoris Epitome de Caesaribus*, 41 § 13).

Names and titles

IN Latin inscriptions, whenever a Roman emperor is mentioned during his life-time, his *praenomen, nomen,* and *cognomen* (or *cognomina*), are followed by his official titles arranged in a fixed order. The following inscription in honour of Trajan may be taken as a typical example :—IMP · CAESARI DIVI NERVAE F · NERVAE TRAIANO AVG · GERMANICO DACICO PONTIFICI MAXIMO TRIBVNIC · POT · VII · IMP · IIII · COS · V · P · P etc.[1]

The following are the eleven names or titles here found in the dative case :—

(1) *Imperator* occurs twice, in an abbreviated form, (1) in the place usually filled by the *praenomen*, and (2) at a later point, where it denotes the number of times that the emperor has been saluted by that title, including the salutation on the occasion of his being proclaimed emperor.

(2) *Caesar*, a *cognomen* of the *gens Iulia*, is used by the emperors in lieu of the ordinary *nomen gentile*.

(3) *Divi Nervae filio* describes Trajan as the (adopted) son of the late emperor, the 'deified' Nerva, who gave M. Vlpius Traianus the rank of Caesar, and the names of Nerva and Germanicus.

(4) *Nerva Traianus* formed part of Trajan's name after his adoption, even before his accession.

(5) *Augustus*, a title of honour, implying sanctity, decreed to Octavian by the Senate[2], and assumed by all his successors as a *cognomen*. Trajan's

[1] A.D. 103; Dessau, i 286.
[2] Cp. Haverfield, in *J.R.S.* v (1915), 249 f.

APP. III] ROMAN EMPERORS 231

name, even before his accession, was *Imperator Caesar Nerva Traianus Augustus*.

(6) *Germanicus*, the title conferred on Trajan, as well as Nerva, in 97; *Dacicus* was added late in 102.

(7) *Pontifex Maximus*, president of the college of pontiffs, a priestly dignity held by Caesar, and by Augustus, and granted to all his imperial successors.

(8) *tribunicia potestate* (or *tribuniciae potestatis*) *VII*. The *tribunicia potestas*, received by Augustus in 23 B.C., as the chief feature in the prerogative of the Princeps[1], and conferred on all his successors immediately on their elevation to the imperial dignity. It was a perpetual title, but it was formally renewed annually, thus indicating the year of the emperor's rule. With the successors of Augustus, down to Nerva (inclusive), the imperial year began with the actual date of accession. Trajan succeeded Nerva on 27 Oct. 97 A.D., when he first received the *tribunicia potestas*. It was probably on 10 Dec. in the same year that he received it for the second time; and he certainly received it on that date in every subsequent year. Thus the year of his seventh *tribunicia potestas* begins on 10 Dec. 102, and ends on 9 Dec. 103. This arrangement was continued by Hadrian and his successors, until Diocletian made the second and subsequent receptions of the *tribunicia potestas* fall on Jan. 1.

(9) *Imperator IIII* refers to the fourth occasion when Trajan was saluted as *imperator*, namely in 102, the second and third salutations having been granted in the same year.

(10) *Consul V*. Trajan's fifth consulship began on 1 Jan. 103 (after he had been *Cos. designatus V* for the whole or part of the previous year). This item determines the date of the inscription to be later than 1 Jan. 103, while item (8) shows that it is earlier than 10 Dec. 103. It was not until 112 that Trajan accepted the consulship for the sixth time.

(11) *Pater patriae*, a title accepted by Augustus in 2 B.C., and assumed by all succeeding emperors, except Tiberius, and Galba, Otho, Vitellius. It was accepted by Trajan after some slight delay[2]. In the latter part of the time of Domitian, it became customary to place this title last in the list[3].

The title of *censor* was borne by Claudius, Vespasian, and Titus; and that of *censor perpetuus* by Domitian. That of *proconsul* was occasionally taken by Trajan, Hadrian, and the Antonines, especially when they were absent from Italy, while

[1] Suet. *Aug.* 27, 'tribuniciam potestatem perpetuam recepit' (with Shuckburgh's note).
[2] Suet. *Aug.* 58; cp. Pliny, *Pan.* 21.
[3] Cp., in general, Mommsen, *Staatsrecht*, ii³ 763—785; Cagnat, 157—165[4]; Liebenam, *Fasti Consulares* (1910), pp. 101-3.

it was almost always used by Septimius Severus and his successors, even when they were residing in Rome[1].

The title of *divus* was conferred, after death, on those of the emperors whose memory it was desired to honour. It was conferred first on Iulius Caesar, and afterwards on the fifty-five emperors mentioned below:—

Augustus, Claudius I, Vespasian, Titus, Nerva, Trajan, Hadrian, Antoninus Pius, Lucius Verus, Marcus Aurelius, Pertinax, Commodus, Septimius Severus, Geta, Caracalla, Severus Alexander, Gordian I, II, III, Philip I, II, Traianus Decius, Herennius Etruscus, Valerian I, Piso Frugi, Gallienus, Victorinus, Claudius II, Aurelian, Probus, Carus, Numerian, Maximian I, Diocletian, Constantius I, Maximian II (Galerius), Constantine I, Constans, Constantius II, Iulian II, Iovian, Valentinian I, Valens, Gratian, Valentinian II, Theodosius, Arcadius, Constantius III, Honorius, Theodosius II, Valentinian III, Leo I, II, Zeno, Anastasius.

The same title was conferred on eleven, and that of *diva* on sixteen, members of the imperial house[2].

On the other hand, the names of certain persons were erased on monuments, in accordance with a decree of the Senate abolishing their memory. Such were the following emperors:—

Caligula, Nero, Domitian, Commodus, Albinus, Geta, Macrinus, Diadumenianus, 'Heliogabalus' (under the name of Antoninus), Severus Alexander, Maximin I, Maximus I (these two names were never erased in Spain, and were restored in Africa), Gordian III (in *C. I. L.* iii 4644), Philip I, II, Traianus Decius, Herennius Etruscus, Hostilianus, Aemilianus, Gallienus, Aurelian (very rarely), Probus, Carus, Carinus, Numerianus, Diocletian (in Africa and Spain), Maximian I, II (Galerius), Flavius Severus, Maximin Daia, Maxentius, Licinius I, Constantine II, Constans I, Magnentius, Maximus II.

The names of twenty other persons were similarly erased, on account of their connexion with certain of the emperors, whose memory had been formally condemned[3].

date

The date of an inscription, which includes the names and titles of a Roman emperor, may be determined by noticing the number of the *tribunicia potestas*, and of the consulship, and of the imperial salutations, and also

[1] Wilmanns, 940, n. 3.
[2] List in Cagnat, 171[4] f. Cp. Mommsen, *l. c.* 817 f.
[3] List in Cagnat, 173[4] f. For erasures in the names of private persons, see *ib.* 175 f, and cp. in general the monograph of Zedler, *De memoriae damnatione* (1884), and Pauly-Wissowa, s.v. *Damnatio memoriae*.

the *cognomina* assumed in consequence of a victory. The following is an inscription found at Herculaneum :—

IMP CAESAR VESPASIANVS AVG PONTIF MAX TRIB POT VII IMP XVII P P COS VII DESIGN VIII TEMPLVM MATRIS DEVM TERRAE MOTV CONLAPSVM RESTITVIT (Dessau, i 250).

The year of Vespasian's seventh *tribunicia potestas* extended from 1 July 75 to 30 June 76; and he became *consul* for the seventh time on 1 Jan. 76. Hence the date of the inscription is between 1 Jan. and 30 June 76, probably late in the half-year, as he was saluted *imperator* three times (XVI, XVII, XVIII) in the course of the year. See p. 239 *infra*.

The following inscription is in memory of Lucius Verus, 'brother' and colleague of Marcus Aurelius :—

divo Vero Parth(ico) max(imo), fratri imp(eratoris) Caesaris M. Aureli Antonin(i) Aug(usti), Armeniac(i) Medic(i) Germ(anici) Parthic(i) max(imi), tribunic(iae) potestatis XXVI, imp(eratoris) V, p(atris) p(atriae), cos. III, procos. etc. (Dessau, i 370).

Lucius Verus had died in the winter of 169; his 'brother', Marcus Aurelius, assumed the title of Germanicus in 172, which was also the year of his 26th *tribunicia potestas*. Hence the date of the inscription is 172. All the other titles refer to earlier years. See p. 245 *infra*.

LIST OF ROMAN EMPERORS,

with examples of dated inscriptions relating to them.

AUGUSTUS (23 B.C.—14 A.D.)

C. Octavius, called after his adoption by C. Iulius Caesar, *C. Iulius Caesar Octavianus*, generally designated in inscriptions as IMP·CAESAR·DIVI F· AVG. Cp. Suet. *Aug.* 97, p. 12 f *supra*.

Imperator, 15 April, 43 B.C.; II Dec. 40; III 38?; IV 36; V 34 or 33; VI 31; VII 29; VIII 25 (for IX—XXI, see table).

Consul (1), 43 B.C.; (2), 33 B.C.; (3)—(11), annually, 31—23 B.C.; (12), 5 B.C.; (13), 2 B.C.

Augur, in or before 37 B.C.

XV vir sacris faciundis, between 37 and 34 B.C.

Augustus, 16 January, 27 B.C.

Tribunicia potestas, 1 July, 23 B.C.; II 1 July 22—30 June, 21; III 1 July 21—30 June, 20.

VII vir epulonum, before 16 B.C.

Pontifex maximus, 12 B.C.

Pater patriae, 2 Feb. 2 B.C.

B.C. 23 1 Jan. .... COS · XI IMP. VIII
       1 July I TRIB · POT
   20 1 Jan. IX
       1 July IV
   15 1 Jan. X
       1 July IX
   13 1 Jan. .... Tiberius COS
       1 July XI
   12 1 Jan. .... XI PONT · MAX
       1 July XII
   11 1 Jan. XII
       1 July XIII
    9 1 Jan. XIII   Tiberius IMP
       1 July XV
    8 1 Jan. XIV   Tiberius IMP · II
       1 July XVI
    7 1 Jan. ....   Tiberius COS · II
       1 July XVII
    6 1 Jan. .... 27 June, Tiberius TR · P
       1 July XVIII
    5 1 Jan. .... COS · XII
       1 July XIX
    2 1 Jan. .... COS · XIII P(ater) P(atriae) Tiberius TR · P · V
       1 July XXII
A.D. 2 1 Jan. XV
       1 July XXV
    4 1 Jan. .... XVI (?)
       1 July XXVII .... Tiberius TR · P · VI
    6 1 Jan. XVII   Tiberius TR · P · VIII
                                               IMP · III
       1 July XXIX
    8 1 Jan. XVIII   Tiberius TR · P · X
       1 July XXXI
    9 1 Jan. XIX   Tiberius TR · P · XI
                                               IMP · IV
       1 July XXXII
   11 1 Jan. XX   Tiberius TR · P · XIII
                                               IMP · V?, VI
       1 July XXXIV
   14 1 Jan. XXI   Tiberius TR · P · XVI
                                               IMP · VII
       1 July XXXVII
   14 19 Aug. Death of Augustus.

The following example is taken from a milestone near Arles:—
Pater patriae | Imp. Caesar divi f. | Augustus pontifex | maxumus, cos. XII, | cos. designatus XIII, | imp. XIIII, tribunic. | potest. XX. Dessau, i 100.

Pater patriae 2 B.C.; cos. XII 5 B.C.; cos. designatus XIII = the year before cos. XIII 2 B.C. = 3 B.C.; imp. XIIII from 8 B.C.; trib. pot. XX = 4 B.C.

Here the decisive item is 'cos. designatus XIII' = 3 B.C. Hence the date of the 'trib. pot.' must be corrected into XXI, and 'pater patriae' must have been prefixed in the following year, in a separate line at the head of the inscription.

TIBERIUS (14—37)

Ti. Claudius Nero; after his adoption, *Ti. Iulius Caesar*; in inscriptions the correct form is TI · CAESAR · AVG, Tiberius having declined the official title of *Imperator*, though he was so saluted first in 9 B.C., II in 8 B.C., III in 6 A.D., IV in 9 A.D., V in 10—11, VI in 11, VII in 14, VIII in 21. He was Consul in 13 and 7 B.C., and in 18, 21, and 31 A.D. He declined the title of Pater Patriae.

From A.D. 4 onwards, the tribunicial dates of Tiberius are always two numbers in advance of the year A.D.; hence, to find the year A.D., we must always deduct *two* from the tribunicial date of this emperor.

A.D. 14	19 Aug. Princeps	A.D. 21	1 Jan. COS · IIII · IMP · VIII
15	10 March PONT · MAX		1 July TRIB · POT · XXIII
	1 July TRIB · POT · XVII	31	1 Jan. COS · V
18	1 Jan. COS · III		1 July TRIB · POT · XXXIII
	1 July TRIB · POT · XX	37	16 March. Death of Tiberius.

The following inscription is from the copy at Puteoli of the colossus erected in Rome by the cities of Asia in gratitude for their restoration by Tiberius after the earthquakes of A.D. 17, 23, 29; cp. Tacitus, *Ann.* ii 47, and iv 13.

Ti. Caesari divi | Augusti f(ilio), divi | Iuli n(epoti) Augusto | pontif(ici) maximo cos. IIII, | imp. VIII, trib. potestat. XXXII, | Augustales; | res publica | restituit. Dessau, i 156.

'Cos. IIII, imp. VIII' places the date of the inscription after 1 Jan. 21 A.D., and 'trib. potest. XXXII' points to the second half of 30 A.D., before the 5th consulship of Tiberius, which began on 1 Jan. 31 A.D.

'CALIGULA' (37—41)

C. Iulius Caesar, son of Germanicus, and grandson of Drusus (I), the younger brother of Tiberius; commonly called *C. Caesar*; nicknamed *Caligula* (Suet. *C. Caligula* 9); called in inscriptions C · CAESAR AVG · GERMANICVS (with or without AVG ·). He was the adopted son of his father's elder brother, Tiberius, while Tiberius was the adopted son of his step-father, Augustus.

A.D. 37	18 March IMP ·, PONT · MAX ·, TRIB · POT		
	1 July COS · I (Claudius COS · I)		
38	Jan. P(ater) P(atriae)	A.D. 40	1 Jan. COS · III
	18 March TRIB · POT · II		18 March TRIB · POT · IIII
39	1 Jan. COS · II	41	1 Jan. COS · IIII
	18 March TRIB · POT · III		24 Jan. Death of Caligula

Inscription on a milestone at Cordova.

C. Caesar Germanicus, Germanici | Caesaris f(ilius), Ti(berii) Aug(usti) n(epos), divi Aug(usti) pron(epos), divi | Iuli abn(epos), Aug(ustus), pat(er) patr(iae), | cos. II, imp(erator), trib(unicia) potestate II, pontif(ex) max(imus), a Baete et Iano Augusto | ad Oceanum | ......Dessau, i 193.

Caligula received the title of *pater patriae* about January, 38 A.D., the *tribunicia potestas* for the second time on 18 March in the same year, and entered his second consulship on 1 Jan. 39. Hence the date of the inscription is between 1 Jan. and 18 March, 39, when he received the *tribunicia potestas* for the third time.

CLAUDIUS (41—54)

Ti. Claudius Drusus (Suet. *Claud.* 2), or *Ti. Claudius, Drusi Germanici f(ilius), Nero Germanicus*; in inscriptions (as emperor), TI · CLAVDIVS DRVSI F · CAESAR AVGVSTVS GERMANICVS, with or without DRVSI F. He was the younger son of Drusus (I), and the younger brother of Germanicus.

A.D. 41	25 Jan. IMP · PONT · MAX TRIB · POT*	A.D. 47	1 Jan. COS · IV · IMP · XIV, XV
	IMP · II	48	CENSOR, IMP · XVI
42	1 Jan. COS · II	49	IMP · XVII, XVIII
	6—12 Jan. P(ater) P(atriae)	50	IMP · XIX—XXI
	IMP · III		Adoption of Nero.
43	1 Jan. COS · III	51	1 Jan. COS · V
	IMP · IV · VIII		IMP · XXII—XXV
45	IMP · IX—XI	52	IMP · XXVI, XXVII
46	IMP · XII	54	13 Oct. Death of Claudius.

* Renewed in each year on this date.

Inscription on the aqueduct of the *aqua Claudia* above the *porta Praenestina* (p. 130 *supra*).

Ti. Claudius Drusi f(ilius) Caisar Augustus Germanicus pontif(ex) maxim(us), | tribunicia potestate XII, cos. V, imperator XXVII, pater patriae etc. Dessau, i 218.

Claudius was cos. V from Jan. 1 of 51 A.D., and, in 52 A.D., attained his 27th salutation as *imperator*, a number also attained by Constantius II. (337—361), son of Constantine the Great.

NERO (54—68).

L. Domitius Ahenobarbus, on his adoption by Claudius, added to the name of his adoptive father, Ti. Claudius Caesar, that of his maternal great-grandfather, Nero Drusus Germanicus, and thus became *Ti. Claudius Nero Drusus Germanicus Caesar*[1]. In 50 A.D. he appears once as *Ti. Claudius... Nero Caesar*[2]. He is also called in 51—53 *Nero Claudius Caesar Drusus Germanicus* (with or without *Drusus*)[3].

In inscriptions, his name is, generally, **NERO CLAVDIVS CAESAR AVGVSTVS GERMANICVS**. Occasionally, the *praenomen* Nero is preceded by the praenominal use of IMP· for *imperator*, as in an inscription *c.* 66 A.D. (Dessau, 233).

The date of Nero's accession was 13 Oct. 54 A.D., and, on that date in each year, from 54 to 59 inclusive, he received the *tribunicia potestas*; but, on 4 or 11 Dec. 59, he assumed it for a second time in the same year, and thenceforth reckoned his tribunicial year as beginning in December[4]. We thus arrive at the following dates for the beginning of his later tribunicial years, 13 Oct. 59 (VI); 4—11 Dec. 59 (VII); Dec. 60 (VIII); Dec. 61 (IX); Dec. 62 (X); Dec. 63 (XI); Dec. 64 (XII); Dec. 65 (XIII); Dec. 66 (XIV); Dec. 67 (XV).

A.D.			A.D.		
54	13 Oct.	IMP PONT· MAX	60	1 Jan.	COS · IV
55	1 Jan.	COS IMP· II	60		IMP· VII
55	(late in year)	P(ater) P(atriae)	61		IMP· VIII · IX
57	1 Jan.	COS· II	66		IMP· X, XI
57		IMP· III, IV, V	67		IMP· XII
58	1 Jan.	COS· III	68	1 Jan.	COS· V
58		IMP· VI	68	9 June.	Death of Nero.

[1] Zonaras, xi 10 ; Wilmanns, 901 n.
[2] Dessau, i 224.   [3] *ib.* i 222 (4), ii 5025.
[4] Cp. Mommsen in *Hermes*, ii (1867) 56 f; *Staatsrecht* (ii³ 798 note) ; Cagnat, 186⁴; Egbert, 127. Stobbe, however, places his first *trib. pot.* on 4 Dec. 54, and makes him continue it on that day in each year down to 59.

On a military diploma of Nero, now in Vienna.

Nero Claudius divi Claudi f(ilius), Germanici Caesar(is) n(epos), Ti. Caesaris Aug(usti) pron(epos), divi Aug(usti) abn(epos), Caes(ar) Aug(ustus) Germ(anicus), pont(ifcx) max(imus), trib(uniciae) pot(estatis) VII, imp(erator) VII, cos. IIII etc. (Dessau, i 1987. All the three numerical data point to 60 A.D.)

GALBA (9 June 68—15 Jan. 69)

Servius Sulpicius Galba; *Lucius Livius Ocella Galba* (Suet. *Galba*, 4); *Lucius Livius Sulpicius Galba* (cp. *C. I. G.* 4957); in his military diplomas, **SER · GALBA IMPERATOR CAESAR AVGVSTVS** (Dessau, i 1988).

OTHO (15 Jan.—25 April 69)

Marcus Salvius Otho; in the *Acta* of the *fratres Arvales*, 69 A.D., **IMP · M · OTHO CAESAR AVGVSTVS** (Dessau, i 241 *passim*).

VITELLIUS (2 Jan.—20? Dec. 69)

Aulus Vitellius; **A · VITELLIVS L · F · IMPERATOR** (Dessau, i 242); **VITELLIVS GERMANICVS IMP ·** (*ib.* 241, 85). Suetonius, *Vit.* 8, 'cognomen Germanici delatum ab universis cupide recepit, Augusti distulit, Caesaris in perpetuum recusavit'; cp. Tac. *Hist.* i 64, ii 62, 90, and Wilmanns, 916 n. **COS · PERP** (Dessau, i 242).

VESPASIAN (69—23 June 79)

T. Flavius Vespasianus; in inscriptions, **IMP · CAESAR VESPASIANVS AVG**, or (less frequently) **IMP · VESPASIANVS CAESAR AVG**.

The years of Vespasian's rule were reckoned from 1 July, 69, when he was proclaimed *imperator* by his soldiers[1], and his *tribunicia potestas* was renewed in each year on that day. On 1 July, 71, his son Titus was associated with him in the empire, and their tribunicial dates run parallel, the dates of Titus being always two years behind those of his father[2].

The first consulship of Vespasian was in Nov. Dec. 51. The title of *pater patriae*, offered 22 Dec. 69, was not accepted until April 71.

---

[1] Tacitus, *Hist.* ii 79.

[2] Egbert, p. 129. On the years 69 to 81 A.D., see esp. H. C. Newton, in *Cornell Studies*, xvi, *The epigraphical evidence for the reigns of Vespasian and Titus*, pp. 140 (Ithaca, 1901).

ROMAN EMPERORS

		VESPASIAN	TITUS	DOMITIAN
A.D. 69	1 July	IMP · CAES TRIB · POT		
	22 Dec.	IMP · II CAES · AVG PONT · MAX		
70	1 Jan.	COS · II IMP · III, IV, V	COS 2 Sept. IMP	
71	1 Jan.	COS · III, IMP · VI (with Nerva, COS · I)	[TR · P	March—June, COS · I
	1 July	IMP · VII, VIII	IMP II, PONT	
72	1 Jan.	COS · IV IMP · IX, X (?)	COS · II IMP · III, IV	
73	1 Jan.	IMP · XI	IMP · V	COS · II
	April	CENSOR	CENSOR	
74	1 Jan.	COS · V IMP · XII—XIV	COS · III IMP · VI, VII, VIII	
75	1 Jan.	COS · VI IMP · XV (?)	COS · IV IMP · IX	COS · III
76	1 Jan.	COS · VII IMP · XVI—XVIII	COS · V IMP · X, XI, XII	COS · IV
77	1 Jan.	COS · VIII IMP · XIX (?)	COS · VI	COS · V
78		IMP · XX	IMP · XIII, XIV	
79	1 Jan.	COS · IX	COS · VII IMP · XV	
	23 June	Death of Vespasian		

Inscription on an oblong pedestal, which formerly supported three busts, (1) Vespasian in the middle, (2) Titus to the left, and (3) Domitian to the right.

(1) Imp. Caesar Vespasiano Aug(usto), pontif(ici) max(imo), tr(ibuniciae) pot(estatis) IIII, imp. VIIII, p(atri) p(atriae), cos. IIII.

(2) T. Caesari Vespasiano imp. III, pontif(ici), tr(ibuniciae) pot(estatis) II, cos. II.

(3) Caesari Aug(usti) f(ilio) Domitiano, cos. destinato II, principi iuventutis, etc. Dessau, i 246.

On 1 Jan. 72, Vespasian was *consul* IIII, and Titus *consul* II, and on 1 Jan. 73, Domitian was *consul* II. On 1 July 72, Vespasian received the *trib. pot.* IIII. Hence the date is between 1 July and 31 Dec. 72.

TITUS (79—81)

T. Flavius Vespasianus; in inscriptions, generally, IMP · T · (or TITVS) CAESAR VESPASIANVS AVG.

On 1 July, 71, Titus was associated in the empire with Vespasian, received the *tribunicia potestas*, and renewed it on that day in each year, attaining the *trib. pot.* VIII during the life of Vespasian. The corresponding numbers in his own reign were A.D. 79 (trib. pot. ix); 80 (trib. pot. x); 81 (trib. pot. xi).

A.D. 79   24 June   Sole Emperor, AVG
                    PONT · MAX, P · P
     80   1 Jan.   COS · VIII   Domitian, COS · VII
                    IMP · XVI, XVII
     81   13 Sept. Death of Titus.

Inscription near the thirteenth milestone of the *Via Aurelia*. Imp. Titus Caesar Vespasianus Aug. pontifex maximus, tribunic(ia) potestate VIIII, imp. XIIII, p(ater) p(atriae), cos. VII, designatus VIII, censor fecit. Dessau, i 262.

Titus was censor for the first time in April 73; 'cos. VII' corresponds to 79 A.D.; and 'trib. pot. VIIII' begins on 1 July in that year.

DOMITIAN (81—96)

T. Flavius Domitianus; the name on the monuments is generally IMP · CAESAR DOMITIANVS AVG, or, less frequently, IMP · DOMITIANVS CAESAR AVG. In the *lex municipii Salpensani* (before A.D. 84), the former title is found four times, but the latter occurs once, and also IMP. CAESAR AVG. DOMITIANVS (Dessau, ii 6088). In and after the first half of 84 the name ends with AVG · GERMANICVS.

Domitian takes the *tribunicia potestas* on his accession, 14 Sept. 81, and on that day in each year, ending with TR · P · XVI on 14 Sept. 96.

A.D. 81 14 Sept. IMP·AVG   A.D. 85 1 Jan. COS · XI
                  PONT · MAX, P· P   IMP · VIII, IX
     82 1 Jan.   COS · VIII   5 Sept. CENSOR
                  IMP · II, III   IMP · X, XI
     83 1 Jan.   COS · IX   86   1 Jan. COS · XII
                  IMP · IV, V   IMP · XII—XIV
     84 1 Jan.   COS · X   87   1 Jan. COS · XIII
                  GERMANICVS   88   1 Jan. COS · XIV
                  IMP · VI, VII   IMP · XV—XVIII

III] ROMAN EMPERORS 241

A.D. 89   IMP · XIX—XXI   A.D. 95 1 Jan. COS · XVII
90 1 Jan. COS · XV (Nerva, II)   96 18 Sept. Death of Domitian.
91 1 Jan. Trajan, COS · I
92 1 Jan. COS · XVI
           IMP · XXII

Inscription from a milestone at Cordova.

Imperator Caesar divi Vespasiani f. Domitianus Aug. Germanicus, pontifex maxsumus, tribuniciae potestatis VIIII, imp. XXI, cos. XV, censor perpetuus, p(ater) p(atriae), ab arcu, unde incipit Baetica, viam Aug(ustam) *restituit.* Dessau, i 269.

The evidence of coins shows that the title *Germanicus* was taken by Domitian in 83 or 84 A.D., at the end of which year the *consulship* was decreed to him for ten years. 'cos. XV' points to 90 A.D. He had become 'censor perpetuus' 17 Feb. 86 A.D.

NERVA (96—98)

M. Cocceius Nerva; in inscriptions generally IMP · NERVA CAESAR AVG, or, less frequently, IMP · CAESAR NERVA AVG. The title GERMANICVS was added in October or November 97.

Nerva's first *tribunicia potestas* extended from 18 Sept. 96 to 17 Sept. 97, and the second would normally have extended from 18 Sept. 97 to Nerva's death. Hence some inscriptions combine 'trib. pot. II' with 'cos. IIII', early in 98 A.D. (Dessau, i 279).

But there is reason to believe that, like Nero, Nerva altered the date of the *tribunicia potestas* from the anniversary of his accession (18 Sept.) to that of the beginning of the tribunicial year under the Republic (10 Dec.). Hence his second *tribunicia potestas*, strictly speaking, only lasted from 18 Sept. to 9 Dec. 97. Accordingly, 'trib. pot. III' may be combined with 'cos. III' (as in Dessau, i 278), to denote a date between 10 Dec. and 31 Dec. 97; or with 'cos. IIII' (as in Dessau, i 280) to denote a date between 10 Dec. 97 and the death of Nerva on 25 Jan. 98.

A.D. 96   18 Sept. IMP · CAESAR · AVG, PONT · MAX, TR · P, P(ater)
                    P(atriae)
     97   1 Jan.   COS · III
                    IMP · II
          18 Sept. TR · P · II
          27 Oct.   Trajan, CAES · IMP, TR · P
                    GERMANICVS   „   GERMANICVS
          10 Dec.   TR · P . III
     98   1 Jan.   COS · IIII   „   COS · II
          25 Jan.   Death of Nerva.

From a milestone of the *Via Appia*, now in the Vatican Museum.

Imp. Nerva Caesar Augustus Germanicus pontifex maximus,

tribunicia potestate II, cos. III, designatus IIII, pater patriae, faciundum curavit. Dessau, i 277. The title *Germanicus* (with the other items) makes it probable that the date is Nov. 97.

TRAJAN (98—117)

M. Vlpius Traianus; in inscriptions, generally, IMP · CAESAR NERVA TRAIANVS AVGVSTVS GERMANICVS; sometimes—NERVA CAESAR TRAIANVS — —, or — NERVA TRAIANVS CAESAR — —.

Under Trajan the custom of computing the tribunicial year from a date in December (already begun by Nero and resumed by Nerva) became general. Trajan was invested with the tribunicial power by Nerva on 27 Oct. 97, but he counted TR. P. II as beginning on 10 Dec. in the same year, and TR. P. III on 10 Dec. 98.

A.D.			A.D.		
98	25 Jan.	IMP · CAES · AVG PONT · MAX, P(ater) P(atriae)	106 112 114	1 Jan.	IMP · VI COS · VI OPTIMVS
100	1 Jan.	COS · III			IMP · VII
101	1 Jan.	COS · IIII			IMP · VIII, VIIII
102		IMP · II, III, IIII	115		IMP · X, XI
	By end of Aug.	DACICVS	116		PARTHICVS
103	1 Jan.	COS · V			IMP · XII, XIII
105		IMP · V	117	*c.* 10 Aug.	Death of Trajan.

On a bridge of the *Via Flaminia* crossing the Metaurus.

Imp. Caesar, divi Nervae f., Nerva Traianus, Optimus, Aug(ustus), Ger(manicus), Dacicus, tribunic(iae) potest(atis) XIX, imp. XI, cos. VI, p(ater) p(atriae), faciundum curavit. Dessau, i 299.

The date of the title ' Germanicus' is Oct. or Nov. 97 (before his accession); that of 'Dacicus' is late in 102; cos. VI corresponds to 112; 'Optimus' to July or Aug. 114; 'imp. XI' to 115; while 'trib. pot. XIX' places the inscription between 10 Dec. 114 and 9 Dec. 115.

Even before 114, we find *optimi cognomen* in Pliny's *Panegyricus*, 2, 88 (100 A.D.); *optimus princeps* on coins and in inscriptions, from 105; and *optimus* in an inscription of 112 (Dessau, i 1293). Pliny, *ib.* 54, alludes to the 'ingentes arcus excessurosque templorum fastigium titulos' of Trajan's predecessors, and says, of Trajan himself, 'non trabibus aut saxis nomen tuum, sed monumentis aeternae laudis inciditur'. He adds, *ib.* 59, 'cum arcus, cum tropaea, cum statuas deprecaris, tribuenda est verecundiae tuae venia: illa enim sane tibi dicantur'. The date of the small 'triumphal arch' bearing his name at Alcántara, on the Tagus, is 104 A.D. (see p. 120 *supra*, and Baumeister, *Denkmäler*, iii, Tafel lxxxi 1); those of the arches erected in his honour at Beneventum and Ancona are 114 and 115 A.D. (p. 125 *supra*).

HADRIAN (117—138)

P. Aelius Hadrianus; in inscriptions almost always **IMP·CAESAR TRAIANVS HADRIANVS AVG**.

Hadrian received the *tribunicia potestas* on the death of Trajan in August 117, and renewed it on 10 December in the same year, and in all subsequent years.

In the summer of 136 he adopted L. Ceionius Commodus, who took the name of L. Aelius Commodus Verus, and appears in the monuments of 136—137 as **L. AELIVS CAESAR**. After the death of the latter on 1 Jan. 138, Hadrian adopted T. Aurelius Fulvus Boionius Arrius Antoninus, under the name of T. Aelius Caesar Antoninus, best known as **Antoninus Pius**.

Antoninus Pius thereupon adopted, as his ultimate joint successors, (1) his nephew, M. Annius Verus, who took the name of M. Aelius Aurelius Verus, best known as **Marcus Aurelius**, and (2) the son of L. Aelius Caesar abovementioned, named L. Ceionius Commodus, who took the name of L. Aelius Aurelius Commodus, but is best known as **Lucius Verus**.

A.D. 117	11 Aug.	**IMP·CAES·AVG, PONT·MAX, TR·P**	
118	1 Jan.	**COS·II** (108 **COS·I**)	
119	1 Jan.	**COS·III**	
122			
128	21 April	**P**(ater) **P**(atriae)	
135		**IMP·II**	
136	1 Jan.		Aelius, **COS**
			„ **CAES, TR·P, PONT**
137	1 Jan.		„ **COS·II**
138	1 Jan.		Death of Aelius.
	25 Feb.		Antoninus, **CAES, TR·P, PONT**
	10 July	Death of Hadrian.	

Inscription from Arrabona in Pannonia superior (*Raab in Hungary*).

Imp. Caes(ari) Traiano Hadriano Aug(usto), p(atri) p(atriae), trib(uniciae) pot(estatis) XXI, cos. III, imp. II, L. Aelius Caes(ar) fil(ius), trib(unicia) potes(tate), cos. II, procos., xvvir sacris faciund(is). Dessau, i 319.

Hadrian's 'trib. pot. XXI' was from 10 Dec. 136 to 9 Dec. 137. 1 Jan. 137 was the beginning of the second consulship of L. Aelius Caesar, 'Pannoniis dux ac rector impositus' (*Vita Aeli*, 3) *cum imperio proconsulari*.

ANTONINUS PIUS (138—161)

T. Aurelius Fulvus Boionius Arrius Antoninus, on his adoption by Hadrian, became *Imp. T. Aelius Caesar Antoninus*. In inscriptions he is usually named **IMP·CAESAR T** (or **TITVS) AELIVS HADRIANVS ANTONINVS AVG·PIVS**.

	Antoninus Pius	M. Aurelius	L. Verus
A.D. 138 25 Feb.	IMP·CAES, TR·P		
10 July	AVG, PONT·MAX		
139 1 Jan.	COS·II (120 COS·I)		
	P(ater) P(atriae)	CAES	
140 1 Jan.	COS·III	COS	
142	IMP·II		
145 1 Jan.	COS·IIII		
146 10 Dec.		COS·II	
147 25 Feb.		TR·P	
		PONT	
154 1 Jan.			COS
161 1 Jan.		COS·III	COS·II
7 March	Death of Antoninus Pius		

Epitaph of Antoninus Pius, including all his titles; formerly in the Mausoleum Hadriani.

Imp. Caesari Tito Aelio Hadriano Antonino Aug. Pio, pontifici maximo, tribunic(iae) pot(estatis) XXIIII, imp. II, cos. IIII, p(atri) p(atriae). Dessau, i 346.

'Trib. pot. XXIIII' began 10 Dec. 160.

MARCUS AURELIUS (161—180). LUCIUS VERUS (161—169).

M. Annius Verus, on his adoption by his uncle, Antoninus Pius, 25 Feb. 138, became *M. Aelius Aurelius Verus*. The name *Caesar* was added 5 Dec. 139. After his accession in 161, he is usually designated on inscriptions, IMP·CAESAR M·AVRELIVS ANTONINVS AVG. He took the title *Armeniacus* in 164; *Parthicus Maximus*, and *Medicus*, in or after March, 166; *pater patriae*, in the middle of 166; *Germanicus*, in 172; and *Sarmaticus* in 175. On the death of his first colleague, Lucius Verus, in 169, he abandoned the general use of the first three of these titles.

Lucius Verus, the other adopted son of Antoninus Pius, was known, in his adoptive father's life-time, as *L. Aelius Aurelius Commodus*. After his accession, as the colleague of Marcus Aurelius, he is generally designated IMP·CAES·L·AVRELIVS VERVS AVG. He received the *tribunicia potestas* on his accession on 7 March, 161; his TR·P·II began 10 Dec. 161, and so on, in each subsequent year. He attained the title *Armeniacus* in 163, *Parthicus Maximus* in 165, *Medicus* in 166, and *pater patriae* at the end of 166. He died in 169.

Meanwhile Commodus, son of M. Aurelius, had been named a *Caesar* by his father in 166. He was named *Germanicus* in 172, *Sarmaticus* in 175. He received the *tribunicia potestas* on 27 Nov. 176; his TR · P · II began 10 Dec. 176; and so on in each subsequent year. On his father's death in 180, he became Sole Emperor.

For his successive titles, see below, under COMMODUS.

	M. AURELIUS	L. VERUS	COMMODUS
A.D. 161 7 March	IMP· AVG,P· M	IMP· AVG, P· M,TR· P	Born 31 Aug.
163	IMP · II	ARMENIACVS,IMP· II	
164	ARMENIACVS		
165	IMP · III	PARTH · MAX, IMP · III	
166	PARTH · MAX MEDICVS	MEDICVS, IMP · IV	12 Oct. CAES
	IMP . IV P(*ater*) P(*atriae*)	P(*ater*) P(*atriae*)	
167 1 Jan.		COS · III	
	IMP · V	IMP · V	
169 midwinter		Death of Verus	
170 or 171	IMP · VI		
172	GERMANICVS		GERMANICVS
174	IMP · VII		
175	SARMATICVS IMP · VIII		SARMATICVS
176 27 Nov.			IMP, TR · P
177 1 Jan.			COS
	IMP · IX		IMP · II AVG P· M, P · P
178			IMP · III
179 1 Jan.			COS · II
	IMP · X		
180			IMP · IV
17 March	Death of M. Aurelius		

Inscriptions of M. Aurelius and L. Verus, placed side by side, in columnar form, on one pedestal at Hydruntum (*Otranto*).

Imp. Caes. M. Aurelio Antonino Aug., trib. pot. XVI, cos. III, divi Antonini f(ilio), divi Hadriani nep(oti), divi Traiani Parthic(i) pro(nepoti), divi Nervae abnepot(i), publice d(ecreto) d(e-curionum).

Imp. Caes. L. Aurelio Vero Aug., trib. pot. II, cos. II, divi Antonini f(ilio), divi Hadriani nep(oti), divi Traiani Parthic(i) pron(epoti), divi Nervae abnepoti, publice d(ecreto) d(ecurionum). Dessau, i 359.

The *tribunicia potestas* in both cases begins on 10 Dec. 161 A.D.

COMMODUS (176—192), sole emperor, 180—192

L. (Aelius?) Aurelius Commodus appears on the monuments first as L·AVRELIVS COMMODVS CAES. (*c.* 166—175); next, as IMP·CAES· L·AVRELIVS COMMODVS AVG. 177—180; as IMP·CAESAR M·AV- RELIVS COMMODVS ANTONINVS AVG. 180—190; and, lastly, once more as IMP·CAESAR L·AELIVS AVRELIVS COMMODVS AVG. He was *Pater patriae* and *Pontifex maximus* in 177; *Pius* in 183; *Britannicus* in 184; *Felix* in 185; and *Invictus Romanus Hercules* in 192.

A.D.			A.D.		
180	17 March	Sole Emperor	185		FELIX
181	1 Jan.	COS·III	186	1 Jan.	COS·V
					IMP·VIII
182		IMP·V	190	1 Jan.	COS·VI
183	1 Jan.	COS·IV	192	1 Jan.	COS·VII Pertinax,
		IMP·VI, PIVS P·M			COS·II
184		IMP·VII, BRITAN- NICVS		31 Dec. Death of Commodus.

Epitaph formerly in the Mausoleum Hadriani.

Imperatori Caesari divi Marci Antonini Pii Germanici Sarmatici filio, divi Pii nepoti, divi Hadriani pronepoti, divi Traiani Parthici abnepoti, divi Nervae adnepoti

L. Aelio Aurelio Commodo Augusto Sarmatico Germanico maximo, Brittanico, pontifici maximo, tribuniciae potestat. XVIII, imperat. VIII, consuli VII, patri patriae (193 A.D.). Dessau, i 401.

PERTINAX (193)

P. Helvius Pertinax, designated on the monuments IMP·CAES·P· HELVIVS PERTINAX AVG, succeeded Commodus 1 Jan., died 28 March, 193.

DIDIUS IULIANUS (193)

M. Didius Scverus Iulianus; described, on coins only, as IMP·CAES· M·DID·SEVER·IVLIAN·AVG; suceeeded Pertinax 28 March 193, died 1 June, 193.

SEPTIMIUS SEVERUS (193—211)

L. Septimius Severus, usually styled in inscriptions IMP·CAES·L· SEPTIMIVS SEVERVS PERTINAX AVG · (TR. P. 1, May (?)—9 Dec. 193; TR. P. II 10 Dec. 193—194, etc.). He assumed the titles *Pertinax* 193, *Pater patriae* 194, *Pius, Arabicus, Adiabenicus* (both preceded by *Parthicus*) 195, *Parthicus maximus* 198, *Britannicus maximus* 210.

By 3 May, 198, his elder son, *Septimius Bassianus* (Caracalla), was made joint-emperor under the title IMP·CAESAR·M·AVRELIVS[1]·ANTONI- NVS·AVG (TR. P. autumn—9 Dec. 198; TR. P. II 10 Dec., 198—199, etc.); and, in Sept. or Oct. 209, his younger son, *L. Septimius Geta*, as IMP· CAES·P·SEPTIMIVS·GETA·AVG (TR. P. —9 Dec. 209; TR. P. II 10 Dec. 209—210, etc.). Geta had, before his accession, been the first to receive the title NOBILISSIMVS CAESAR.

		SEVERUS	CARACALLA	GETA
D. 193	May?	IMP · CAES · AVG PONT·MAX		
194	1 Jan.	COS·II, IMP·II IMP·III·IV, P(*ater*) P(*atriae*)		
195		PIVS (?) PARTHICVS ARABICVS ADIA- BENICVS IMP·V, VI, VII		
196		IMP·VIII	CAES	
197		IMP·IX, X	PONTIFEX	
198		PARTHICVS · MAXI- MVS, IMP·XI, XII?	IMP·AVG, TR·P	CAES
199			PARTHICVS · MAXI- MVS	
200			PIVS·FELIX	
202	1 Jan.	COS·III	COS	
205	1 Jan.		COS · II P(*ater*) P(*a- triae*)	COS
207			IMP·II	
208	1 Jan.	IMP·XII?	COS·III	COS·II
209		BRITANNICVS IMP·XV? (Dessau, 431)		AVG, TR·P PIVS
210		BRITANNICVS MAX· IMP·XIII (*ib.* 8917)	BRITANNICVS	BRITANNI- CVS
211	4 Feb.	Death of Severus		

[1] Also AVRELLIVS before and after his accession.

'CARACALLA' (198—217).—GETA (209—212).

	CARACALLA	GETA
A.D. 211 4 Feb.	PONT · MAX, BRITANNICVS · MAXIMVS	IMP, P(*ater*) P(*atriae*)
212 27 Feb.		Death of Geta
213 1 Jan.	COS · IV	
Oct.	IMP · III GERMANICVS · MAXIMVS ARABICVS ADIABENICVS	
214	IMP · IV	
217 8 April	Death of Caracalla	

The inscription on the Arch of Septimius Severus, in the Roman Forum, originally included the name of Geta ('et P. Septimii Getae nobilissimi Caesaris') as well as those of Septimius Severus, and Caracalla, who caused Geta to be put to death in 212, and ordered his name to be erased from all public monuments—(cp. p. 126 *supra*).

MACRINUS (11 April 217—8 June 218)

M. Opellius Macrinus appears on the monuments as IMP · CAES · M · OPELLIVS SEVERVS MACRINVS (with or without PIVS · FELIX) AVG · and his son, *Diadumenianus*, as M. OPELLIVS ANTONINVS DIADVMINIANVS NOBILISSIMVS CAESAR PRINCEPS IVVENTVTIS. (Cp. Dessau, i 461-5.)

'HELIOGABALUS' (218—222)

'Heliogabalus'[1] was the nickname of *Varius Avitus*, who was saluted by the soldiers as *M. Aurelius Antoninus*. On the monuments his name is IMP · CAESAR M · AVRELIVS ANTONINVS AVG. Henceforward all the emperors assume, on their accession, the titles *Pius, Felix, Aug.* (or *Invictus, Aug.*).

The *tribunicia potestas I* of 'Heliogabalus' ended on 9 Dec. 218; TR. POT. II etc. began on 10 Dec. 218, etc.

A.D. 218 16 May IMP · CAES · AVG, PONT · MAX, COS P(*ater*) P(*atriae*)
219 1 Jan. COS · II
220 1 Jan. COS · III
221 10 July   Severus Alexander, CAES
222 1 Jan. COS · IV   Severus Alexander, COS
     11 March   Death of 'Heliogabalus'.

[1] or 'Elagabalus.'

SEVERUS ALEXANDER (222—235).

Alexianus Bassianus, adopted by 'Heliogabalus', 10 July 221, as Caesar and joint-emperor, appears first as M. Aurelius Alexander Caesar, and, after his accession, as IMP·CAES·M·AVRELIVS SEVERVS ALEXANDER AVG· (TR. P. 11 March—9 Dec. 222; TR. P. II etc. 10 Dec. 222—9 Dec. 223 etc.).

A.D. 222 11 March, IMP· AVG, PONT· MAX, TR· P, P(*ater* P(*atriae*); 226 1 Jan. COS·II; 229 1 Jan. COS·III; 231 proconsul; 235, 18 or 19 March, death of Severus Alexander.

MAXIMINUS (235—238)

C. Iulius Maximinus is styled, on his accession, IMP· CAES· C·IVLIVS VERVS MAXIMINVS AVG. *Germanicus Maximus* 236; *Sarmaticus Maximus, Dacicus Maximus*, 236 or 7; TR. P. I *c.* 25 March—9 Dec. 235; TR. P. II etc. 10 Dec.—9 Dec. 236 etc. Died June 238.

PUPIENUS (238)

M. Clodius Pupienus Maximus ruled for 99 days with Balbinus (1 March—mid. June 238). He appears on monuments as IMP· CAES.M· CLODIVS PVPIENIVS (on coins, PVPIENVS) MAXIMVS AVG. Died June 238.

BALBINUS (238)

D. Caelius Calvinus Balbinus, as joint ruler for 99 days with Pupienus, is styled IMP· CAES· D·CAELIVS CALVINVS BALBINVS AVG. Died June 238.

GORDIANUS I AND II (238)

M. Antonius Gordianus, and his son of the same name, ruled for 20—22 days in Feb. and March, as IMP·CAES·M·ANTONIVS GORDIANVS SEMPRONIANVS ROMANVS AFRICANVS AVG. The father alone was 'Pontifex Maximus'. Both died in March(?) 238. (On the chronology of 238, see *Gibbon* i 179, 456 ed. Bury 1896, and Pauly-Wissowa i 2623.)

GORDIANUS III (238—244)

M. Antonius Gordianus is styled, on his accession in June(?) 238, IMP· CAES·M·ANTONIVS GORDIANVS AVG. TR. P. June—9 Dec. 238; TR. P. II etc. 10 Dec. 238—9 Dec. 239 etc. Died Feb. or March 244.

PHILIPPUS (244—249)

M. Iulius Philippus is styled on monuments IMP·CAES·M·IVLIVS PHILIPPVS AVG. TR. P. March—9 Dec. 244; TR. P. II etc. 10 Dec. 244—

250   LATIN INSCRIPTIONS   [APP.

9 Dec. 245 etc.; cos. 245, 247, 248. *Persicus Maximus, Parthicus Maximus,* 244; *Carpicus Maximus* 247 or 248, *Germanicus Maximus* 248.

His son, of the same name (247—249), was styled *Caesar* in 244, *Augustus* in August (?) 246, and *Germanicus* and *Carpicus* in 248. There are two ways of reckoning his TR. P, beginning either with that of his father, or with his own nomination as *Augustus*. Father and son died between 29 Aug. and 10 Oct. 249.

DECIUS (249—251)

C. Messius Decius is styled, on his accession, IMP · CAES · C · MESSIVS QVINTVS TRAIANVS DECIVS AVG. His sons Herennius and Hostilianus are styled (1) IMP · CAES · Q · HERENNIVS ETRVSCVS MESSIVS DECIVS AVG. and (2) IMP · CAES · C · VALENS HOSTILIANVS MESSIVS QVINTVS AVG. The father reckoned his first TR. P, either from the acclamation by the soldiers, or from his recognition by the Senate; the dates of renewal were on 1 Jan. Decius and his two sons had all died by the end of 251.

GALLUS (251—253)

C. Vibius Trebonianus Gallus is styled IMP · CAES · C · VIBIVS TREBONIANVS GALLVS AVG.; and his son, IMP · CAES · C · VIBIVS AFINIVS GALLVS VELDVMNIANVS VOLVSIANVS AVG. The father's TR. P. I is probably Nov.—Dec. 251; TR. P. II, 252; TR. P. IIII (instead of III), 253; TR. P. III is only found on coins (cp. Liebenam, *Fasti Cons.* s.v. p. 114). Father and son both died before 22 Oct. 253 (possibly in Sept.).

AEMILIANUS (June—Sept. 253)

M. Aemilius Aemilianus is styled IMP · CAES · M · AEMILIVS AEMILIANVS AVG.

VALERIAN (253—259).—GALLIENUS (253—268)

P. Licinius Valerianus is styled IMP · CAES · P · LICINIVS VALERIANVS AVG. TR. P. I Sept.—9 Dec. 253; TR. P. II 10 Dec. 253—9 Dec. 254. Captured by Sapor, 259.

His son GALLIENUS (*Caesar* in 253), who shared his rule from 253 to 259, and was sole emperor in Rome until March 268, is styled IMP · CAES · P · LICINIVS EGNATIVS GALLIENVS AVG.

Each of them is called *Germanicus Maximus*, in 256 or 257, and Gallienus is also called *Dacicus Maximus* in 257, *Parthicus Max.* in 264, and *Persicus Max.*

EMPERORS IN GAUL (258—273)

POSTUMUS (258—268); VICTORINUS (268—270); TETRICUS (270—273).

(1) *M. Cassianus Latinius Postumus* is styled IMP · CAES · M · CASSIANVS LATINIVS POSTVMVS AVG.
(2) *M. Piavonius Victorinus*, IMP · CAES · M. PIAVONIVS VICTORINVS AVG.
(3) *C. Esuvius Tetricus Pius*, IMP · CAES · C · PIVS ESVVIVS TETRICVS AVG.

CLAUDIUS II (268—270)

Before Sept. 268 *M. Aurelius Claudius* succeeded Gallienus as IMP · CAES · M · AVRELIVS CLAVDIVS AVG. He was entitled *Germanicus Maximus* early in 269; *Gothicus Maximus*, 269; *Parthicus Maximus*, 270. He ceased to be emperor before 29 Aug. 270.

QUINTILLUS (270)

The son of Claudius II, *M. Aurelius Claudius Quintillus*, ruled in August, 270, as IMP · CAES · M · AVRELIVS CLAVDIVS QVINTILLVS AVG.

AURELIAN (270—275)

L. Domitius Aurelianus ruled as IMP · CAES · L · DOMITIVS AVRELIANVS AVG. His titles were *Germanicus Maximus*, 270 or 271; *Gothicus Max.*, 271 or 272; *Parthicus Max., Carpicus Max.*, 272. He was occasionally described as *Arabicus, Dacicus, Britannicus, Sarmaticus, Palmyrenicus, Max.* This last (found in Dessau, i 579) commemorated his victory over Zenobia, queen of Palmyra; but the epithet is irregular, as Palmyra was part of the Roman Empire. In memory of the same victory, he is more correctly called *Arabicus* and *Parthicus* (*ib.* 576 f) by reason of the foreign forces (Persians and Saracens), which fought on the side of Palmyra. Of these two epithets, *Parthicus* has the better authority; it appears in inscriptions of 272-4 (Homo, *Aurélien*, p. 105 n. 2).

His tribunicial years correspond approximately to (1) 270; (2) 271; (3) 272; (4) 273; (5) 274; etc. so that (6) is 275. TR. P. VII on an inscription of Orleans (*ib.* 581) is possibly an error, as Aurelian probably died in August, 275. His consular years begin on 1 Jan. (1) 271; (2) 274; and (3) 275. Hence TR. P. V rightly corresponds to COS. II = 274 (Dessau, 578), and TR. P. VI to COS. III = 275 (*ib.* 580); but we have other inscriptions in which TR. P. III (272), IV (273), V (274) are wrongly combined with COS. III = 275 (*ib.* 576, 577, 579).

His death in 275 was followed by an *interregnum* of possibly a month and a half (cp. Pauly-Wissowa, v 1358). Homo, *Essai sur le règne de l'empereur Aur.* Paris, 1904, discusses the date on pp. 337—340; and quotes inscriptions of this reign on p. 340 f, and pp. 350—361.

TACITUS (275—276)

In the autumn of 275 (about 25 Sept.) *M. Claudius Tacitus* became emperor under the style of IMP· CAES· M· CLAVDIVS TACITVS AVG. His second consulship and his second tribunicial year correspond to 276. Before his death, early in the April of that year, he attained the title of *Gothicus Maximus*.

FLORIANUS (276)

M. Annius Florianus succeeded as IMP· CAES· M· ANNIVS FLORIANVS AVG·, and died in July, after a reign of two months and twenty days.

PROBUS (276—282)

M. Aurelius Probus is styled IMP· CAES· M· AVRELIVS PROBVS AVG. His TR. P. begins in July 276, TR. P. II etc.=10 Dec. 276—9 Dec. 277 etc., so that TR. P. VII=10 Dec. 281 to his death in the autumn of 282. His consulships are (1) 277, (2) 278, (3) 279, (4) 281, (5) 282. In this reign, TR. P, not followed by any number, is sometimes combined with the consular years 277 or 279, thus ceasing to record any definite tribunicial date. There are coins of Probus bearing the inscription VICTORIA GOTHIC. and VICTORIA GERM.; and inscriptions with the titles *Gothicus* (277; *C. I. L.* xii 5467) and *Germanicus Maximus* (279; *ib.* viii 11931). The following inscription of 280 from Valentia, in Spain, implies that he deserved these honours:—

⟨pie⟩tate iustitia fortitudine ⟨insigni⟩ et pleno omnium virtutum principi, ver⟨o Gothi⟩co veroque Germanico, ac victoriarum omnium nominibus inlustri, M. Aur. ⟨Pr̥ob̥o̥⟩, p(io) f(elici) invict(o) Aug., Pont. Max., trib. p(ot.) v, P(atri) P(atriae), cos. III, procos., Allius Maximus V(ir) C(larissimus) Leg(atus) iur(idicus) prov(inciae) Hisp(aniae) Tarraconens(is) maiestati eius ac numini dicatissimus. Dessau, i 597.

Here 'trib. pot. V'=10 Dec. 279—9 Dec. 280, and 'cos. III' covers 279 and 280, as his fourth consulship did not begin until 1 Jan. 281; hence the date is 280. As Probus was a blameless emperor, the mutilation of his name was probably due to some partisan in the western rebellion of Proculus and Bonosus. Cp. p. 18 *supra*, and Crees, *Probus* (1911), p. 126.

III]   ROMAN EMPERORS   253

CARUS AND HIS SONS (282—285)

M. Aurelius Carus is styled IMP · CAES · M · AVRELIVS CARVS AVG · (Oct.? 282—Aug. 283). In 283 he was entitled *Germanicus*, and *Persicus, Max.*

His elder son A. CARINVS ruled from 283 to the summer of 285, and his younger son NVMERIVS NVMERIANVS from 283 to 29 Aug. 284. Besides sharing their father's titles in 283, each of them had the further title of *Brittannicus* (sic) *Max.* (Dessau, i 608).

DIOCLETIAN AND MAXIMIAN (284—305)

IMP · CAES · C · (or M ·) AVRELIVS VALERIVS DIOCLETIANVS AVG
IMP · CAES · M · AVRELIVS VALERIVS MAXIMIANVS AVG
   M · (or C ·) FLAVIVS VALERIVS CONSTANTIVS NOBILISSIMVS
   CAES
   C · GALERIVS VALERIVS MAXIMIANVS NOBILISSIMVS CAES

Diocletian became emperor on 17 Nov. 284, and was joint-emperor with Maximian from 1 April 286 to 1 May 305, from which date they were called for a short time *Seniores Augusti*. Under their joint-rule Constantius (Chlorus) and Galerius were *Caesares* from 1 March 293, and became *Augusti* on the abdication of Diocletian in 305. Constantius died in July 306, and Galerius in May 311.

Diocletian and Maximian assumed the titles *Brittannicus Max.* in 285-8, and 296; *Germanicus Max.* seven times in 285—302; *Sarmaticus Max.* four times in 289—299; *Persicus Max.* in 288, 297; and *Carpicus, Armeniacus, Medicus, Adiabenicus, Max.* in 297. The same titles were shared by the *Caesares*, Constantius and Galerius, in 293 ff.

Beginning with Diocletian, the numerals following the imperial title, IMP, cease to denote acclamations decreed in consequence of victories, but simply record the successive years of the reign. These numerals now become identical with those of the *tribunicia potestas*, which, in the case of Diocletian, begins on 17 Sept. (or Nov.) 284, and is continued on 1 Jan. in each later year, while in that of Maximian it begins in 285. The consulships of Diocletian are (1) 284, (2) 285, (3) 287, (4) 290, (5) 293, (6) 296, (7) 299, (8) 303, (9) 304; and those of Maximian (1) 287, (2) 288, (3) 290, (4) 293, (5) 297, (6) 299, (7) 303, (8) 304.

Diocletian assumed the short title IOVIVS, also used by Galerius, Maximinus Daia, and Licinius; similarly Maximian assumed that of HERCVLIVS, also used by Constantius (Chlorus). Cp. Appendix v (26, 28) *infra*.

The title *dominus* was forbidden by Augustus and Tiberius (Suet. *Aug.* 53, *Tib.* 27); that of *dominus et deus noster* was assumed by Domitian (*Dom.* 13). Pliny, in his Letters, addresses Trajan as *domine*, but, in his Panegyric, c. 2, he says of that emperor, 'non de domino sed de parente loquimur'. The

254   LATIN INSCRIPTIONS   [APP.

title *dominus noster* is applied to 'Heliogabalus' (Dessau, i 2188, 2411, 2442);
it was forbidden by his successor, Alexander Severus (Lampridius, c. 4), but is
found in inscriptions in his honour (Dessau, i 485 etc.). It becomes common
under Diocletian and Maximian (*ib.* 628 f, 644); cp. Aur. Victor, *de Diocletiano*, 'primus post Caligulam et Domitianum dominum palam dici passus est, et adorari se appellarique uti deum'.

The edict of Diocletian *de pretiis rerum venalium* (301 A.D.) records the names and titles of the two *Augusti* and the two *Caesares* in the exordium, which is partially preserved only in the copy found in Egypt, and removed to Aix in Provence in 1807:—

⟨imp. Caesar C. Aurel. Val. DIOCLETIANVS, P. F. inv. Aug., po⟩nt. max., Germ. max. VI, Sarm. max. IIII, Persic. max. II, Britt. max., Carpic. max., Armen. max., Medic. max., Adiabenic. max., trib. p. XVIII, coss. VII, imp. XVIII, p. p., procoss.

et imp. Caesa⟨r⟩ M. Aurel. Val. MAXIMIANVS, P. F. inv. Aug., pont. max., Germ. max. V, Sarm. ⟨max. IIII, Persic. max. II, Britt. max., Carpic. max., Armen. max., Medic. max., Adiabenic. max., tri⟩b. p. XVII, coss. VI, imp. XVII, p. p., procoss.

et Fla. Val. CONSTANTIVS, Germ. max. II, Sarm. Max. II, Persic. max. II, Britt. max., ⟨Carpic.⟩ max., Armenic. max., Medic. max., Adiaben. max., trib. p. VIIII, coss. III, nobil. Caes(ar)

et G⟨ALERIVS⟩ Val. Maximianus, Germ. max. II, Sarm. ⟨max. II, Persic. max. II, Britt. max., Carpic. max., Armenic. max., Medic. max., Adia⟩b. max., trib. p. VIIII, coss. III, nobil. Caes(ar) dicunt (Dessau, i 642). For part of the preamble see Appendix IV (6) *infra*.

The tribunicial years of the two *Augusti* and the two *Caesares* above mentioned correspond to 301 A.D. On the dates of their several titles, see Wilmanns, no. 1061, and Mommsen, *Ges. Schriften*, ii 300 f.

CARAUSIUS (286—293) and ALLECTUS (293—296) claimed the empire in Britain. FLAVIUS SEVERUS was emperor in 306—307; MAXIMINUS DAIA in 305—313; MAXENTIUS in 307—312; and LICINIUS (*Sarmaticus* and *Germanicus max.* 316) in 308—324.

CONSTANTINUS I (306—337)

(*C.* or *L.* or *M.*) *Flavius Valerius Constantinus* became *Caesar* on 25 July, 306, and *Augustus* on 31 March (?) 307. As emperor he is styled IMP·CAES·C·FLAVIVS VALERIVS CONSTANTINVS AVG. He assumed the title *Maximus Augustus* on 29 Oct. 312; *Germanicus Max.* by 310, also in 314 f, 318; *Sarmaticus Max.*, 314; *Gothicus Max.*, 314 f; *Medicus, Britannicus, Adiabenicus, Persicus, Max.* 315; *Armeniacus Max.* 318; and *Carpicus Max.* 318 or 319. (Cp. Ferrero, *I titoli di vittoria di Costantino, in Atti d. R. Accad. di Torino*, 32 (1897) 657 ff.)

His consulships belong to the following dates :—(1) 307 or 309; (2) 312; (3) 313; (4) 315; (5) 319; (6) 320; (7) 326; (8) 329.

His tribunicial years do not begin at a uniform date. Stobbe, *Philol.* 32 (1873) 88 ff makes I and II begin 25 July, 306-7; III—XII, 11 Nov. 307—316; XIII—XIX, 1 March, 317—323; XX—XXIX, 8 Nov. 323—332, XXX—I, 25 Dec. 333 f; XXXII—III, 18 Sept. 335 f. Maurice, *Numismatique Constantienne*, makes II and all subsequent tribunicial years begin on 10 Dec. 306 etc.

The following inscription was found at Sitifi in Mauretania :—

Magno et invicto principi d. n. imp. Caesari
Flav. Val. Constantino pio felici semper Aug.
pont. maximo, Sarmatico max., Germ. max., Got. max.
trib. pot. X, cons. IIII, imp. VIIII, p. p., proconsuli, *etc.*

Here 'trib. pot. X', and 'cons. IIII', correspond to 315 A.D. (Dessau, i 695).

For the rest of the Roman Emperors, we confine ourselves mainly to those who assumed titles from victories over foreign foes :—

CONSTANTINUS II (337—340)

IMP · CAES · FLAVIVS CLAVDIVS CONSTANTINVS IVNIOR AVG.

Entitled (as *Caesar*) *Alamannicus Max.* 331; and *Germanicus* or *Gothicus*, 332.

CONSTANS (337—350)

IMP . CAES · FLAVIVS IVLIVS CONSTANS AVG. *Sarmaticus*, late in 338.

CONSTANTIUS II (337—361)

IMP · CAES · FLAVIVS IVLIVS CONSTANTIVS AVG.

(As *Caesar*), *Germanicus Alamannicus Max.*, *Germanicus Max.* 323—332; *Gothicus Max.* 332; *Sarmaticus Max.* 335.

(As *Augustus*), *Adiabenicus Max.* 338; *Persicus* (*Max.*) between 338 and 340; *Sarmaticus Max.* II, 358.

JULIAN (361—363)

Caesar, 6 Nov. 355; proclaimed *Augustus* in Gaul in the winter of 360; succeeded Constantius II as emperor, 3 Nov. 361. **IMP·CAES·FLAVIVS CLAVDIVS IVLIANVS AVG.**

His victorious progress from the West to the East is commemorated in an inscription of 362 found at Ancyra :—

Domino totius orbis Iuliano Augusto ex Oceano Britannico vis (=viis) per barbaras gentes strage resistentium patefactis adusque Tigridem una aestate transvecto, Saturninus Secundus v(ir) c(larissimus) ⟨praefectus⟩ praet(orio), ⟨d⟩(evotus) n(umini) m(aiestati)⟨q⟩(ue). (Dessau, i 754.)

In the same year he is entitled

Pontifex maximus, Ger. maximus, Alaman. maximus, Fran. maximus, Sarm. maximus, imperator ⟨v⟩II, consul III, pater patriae, proconsul (*ib*. iii 8945).

An inscription, found near Pergamum, is dedicated to him as *filosophiae magistro* (*ib*. i 751), and another, in Numidia, as *restitutori libertatis et Ro*⟨*manae*⟩ *religion*⟨*is*⟩ (*ib*. i 752).

VALENTINIAN (364—375)

IMP· CAES· FLAVIVS VALENTINIANVS AVG.

Germanicus Max. 366–8; *Alamannicus Max., Francicus Max.* 368; *Gothicus Max.* 369.

THEODOSIUS THE GREAT (379—395)

Theodosius, who subdued the Goths in 382, derived no special title from that conquest, but he is described, in general terms, as *dominus noster invictissimus* (Dessau, i 780). On his death in 395, the Empire was divided between his two sons, ARCADIUS ruling in the East (395—408) and HONORIUS in the West (395—423). Both of these are conventionally described as *invictissimi principes* (Dessau, i 794, 797). The 'Western Empire' ended with ROMULUS AUGUSTULUS in 476.

Among the Latin Inscriptions of the Emperors of the East, which have been found in the West, is the latest of those of Justinian (527—565), describing the Gothic victory of Narses, *vir gloriosissimus,...libertate urbis Romae ac totius Italiae restituta*, as having been won *imperante domino nostro piissimo ac triumphali semper Iustiniano perpetuo Augusto* (Dessau, i 832).

For Names and Titles of Roman Emperors, see Wilmanns, i pp. 276—350, with Index, ii pp. 499—537; Dessau, i pp. 22—187, with Index, iii (1) pp. 257—317; Liebenam, *Fasti Consulares Imp. Romani*, esp. pp. 101—124; also esp. Cagnat, 157—250[4], and Egbert, 114—163, with select inscriptions.

APPENDIX IV

SIX HISTORICAL INSCRIPTIONS

(1) Senatus Consultum de Bacchanalibus, communicated to the Teurani in the Bruttian peninsula by the Consuls of 186 B.C. (see p. 161 f *supra*). Cp. Livy, xxxix 14; Cicero, *de legibus*, ii 37.

⟨Q.⟩ Marcius L. F., S.[1] Postumius L. f., cos.[2], senatum soluerunt N. Octob. apud aedem Duelonai[3]. Sc. arf.[4] M. Claudi[5] M. f., L. Valeri[5] P. f., Q. Minuci[5] C. f.

De Bacanalibus, quei[6] foideratei esent, ita exdeicendum censuere:

'Neiquis[7] eorum (B)acanal[8] habuise velet. Seiques[9] esent quei sibei deicerent necessus ese Bacanal habere, eeis[10] utei ad pr(aitorem) urbanum Romam venirent, deque eeis rebus, ubei eorum ver⟨b⟩a audita esent, utei senatus noster decerneret, dum ne minus senator⟨i⟩bus C adesent, ⟨quom e⟩a res cosoleretur[11]. Bacas vir nequis adiese[12] velet ceivis Romanus neve nominus[13] Latini neve socium[14] quisquam, nisei pr(aitorem) urbanum adiesent[15], isque de senatuos[16] sententiad[17], dum ne minus senatoribus C adesent, quom ea res cosoleretur, iousisent[18]. Censuere.

Sacerdos nequis vir eset. Magister neque vir neque mulier quisquam eset; neve pecuniam quisquam eorum comoinem[19] habuise velet; neve magistratum neve pro magistratu(d)[20] neque

---

[1] An old abbreviation for 'Spurius'. Cp. p. 208.
[2] 186 B.C. [3] Bellonae. [4] Scribendo adfuerunt.
[5] For Claudius, Valerius, Minucius. [6] sc. eeis (iis) qui.
[7] Ne quis. [8] Not a festival, but a shrine of Bacchus.
[9] Si qui. [10] ii. [11] consuleretur.
[12] adiisse. [13] nominis. [14] sociorum. [15] adiissent.
[16] senatus. [17] sententia. For final *d*, see below *passim*.
[18] Mommsen reads 'iousiset'. [19] communem.
[20] magistratu.

S. L. I.

virum ⟨neque mul⟩ierem qui(s)quam[1] fecise velet. Neve posthac inter sed[2] conioura⟨se[3] nev⟩e comvovise neve conspondise neve conpromesise[4] velet, neve quisquam fidem inter sed[2] dedise velet. Sacra in oquoltod[5] ne quisquam fecise velet; neve in poplicod[6] neve in preivatod neve exstrad[7] urbem sacra quisquam fecise velet, nisei pr(aitorem) urbanum adieset, isque de senatuos sententiad, dum ne minus senatoribus C adesent, quom ea res cosoleretur, iousisent[8]. Censuere.

Homines plous[9] V oinvorsei[10] virei atque mulieres sacra ne quisquam fecise velet, neve inter ibei[11] virei plous duobus, mulieribus plous tribus arfuise[12] velent, nisei de pr(aitoris) urbani senatuosque sententiad, utei suprad scriptum est'.

Haice[13] utei in coventionid[14] exdeicatis ne minus trinum noundinum, senatuosque sententiam utei scientes esetis, eorum sententia ita fuit: 'sei ques esent, quei arvorsum[15] ead fecisent, quam suprad scriptum est, eeis rem caputalem faciendam censuere.' Atque utei hoce[16] in tabolam ahenam inceideretis, ita senatus aiquom[17] censuit; uteique eam figier ioubeatis, ubei facilumed gnoscier potisit[18]; atque utei ea Bacanalia, sei qua sunt, exstrad quam sei quid ibei sacri est, ita utei suprad scriptum est, in diebus X, quibus vobeis tabelai[19] datai erunt, faciatis utei dismota sient.

In agro Teurano[20].

Facsimile in Ritschl, tab. 18, Gradenwitz, no. 3, and Diehl, tab. 5; text in *C. I. L.* i[2] 2, 581; Dessau, i 18; with notes in Allen, pp. 28—31; Lindsay, 60—67; Ernout, 58—68.

(2) Res gestae divi Augusti, as recorded mainly in the Monumentum Ancyranum (*Anc.*), 14 A.D. (see p. 178 *supra*).

The inscription is divided into 35 unnumbered sections, and the Latin portion fills six columns.

The inscription is also divided into three parts; (1) the titles and honours conferred on Augustus; (2) his various gifts, and

[1] qui | quam inscr.   [2] se.   [3] coniurasse.   [4] compromisisse.
[5] occulto.   [6] publico.   [7] extra.
[8] Mommsen reads 'iousiset'.   [9] plus.   [10] universi.
[11] interibi.   [12] adfuisse.   [13] Haec.
[14] contione.   [15] adversum.   [16] hocce.   [17] aequum.
[18] utique eam figi iubeatis, ubi facillime nosci possit.   [19] tabellae.
[20] The archaic final *d*, retained in the body of the legal document, is omitted in the address.

IV] (1) DE BACCHANALIBUS (2) RES GESTAE DIVI AUG. 259

the buildings he restored and founded; (3) his acts, or *res gestae*. For topographical[1], as well as historical purposes, this inscription is of special value. It has been destribed as 'the queen of Latin inscriptions'[2], the *titulus inter Latinos primarius*, 'the incomparable monumentum Ancyranum, which is as unique as the man, whose honours...it records'. The inscription, originally incised on two columns of bronze in front of the Mausoleum of Augustus, is a document which defies any ordinary epigraphical classification. It has been variously viewed as an epitaph on a grand scale, or a sepulchral *elogium*[3]; as a formal statement of benefits received and conferred in a long-standing account between the Roman emperor and the Roman people[4]; as a political testament[5]; and even as a preliminary justification for an ultimate *apotheosis*[6]. On the whole, it may be fairly regarded as a posthumous political manifesto in the retrospective form of a dignified narrative of the emperor's public career.

The text is mainly that of Mommsen's second separate edition (1883), with some suggestions by Bormann (1884, 1895), Seeck (1884)[7], J. Schmidt (1885–7), Wölfflin (1886, 1896), and Geppert (1887), partly recorded by Cagnat and Lafaye (ed. 1902–6)[8], and

[1] Cp. Middleton's *Remains of Ancient Rome*, i 384–7.
[2] Mommsen, *Hist. Zeitschrift* (1887), 385; ed. 1883, p. xxxviii. Cp. Teuffel, *Rom. Lit.* § 220, 4; Merivale, *H. R.*, iv (1865) 359 f.
[3] *Grabschrift*, or *elogium sepulcrale*; Bormann, (1) *Bemerkungen zum schriftlichen Nachlasse des Kaisers Augustus*, Marburg, 1884; (2) *Verhandlungen der 43 Philol. Versammlung...in Köln* (1895), pp. 184 ff; supported by J. Schmidt in *Philologus* (1885) 442–70, (1886) 393—410, (1887) 70 ff, and H. Nissen in *Rheinisches Museum* (1886) 481–99; and opposed by O. Hirschfeld in *Wiener Studien* (1885), reprinted in *Kleine Schriften* (1913) 829–34, by Mommsen, *Der Rechenschaftsbericht des Augustus*, in *Hist. Zeitschrift* (1887) 385–97 (*Ges. Schriften*, iv 247–58), and by Hübner, in Iwan Müller's *Handbuch*, (1892) 688². See, in general, Gardthausen's *Augustus*, i 1279–95, ii 874–880.
[4] Wölfflin, in *S.-Ber.* of Munich Academy (1886) 280, *Rechnungsbuch, tabulae accepti et expensi*.
[5] O. Hirschfeld, in *Wiener Studien* (1881) 264.
[6] Wilamowitz, in *Hermes* (1886) 623–7, supported by Norden, *Die antike Kunstprosa* (1898) 268.
[7] *Wochenschrift f. cl. Philol.* (1884) 1473–81.
[8] Pp. 65—95 of the separately sold *fasciculus* i (1902) of vol. III (1906) of *Inscr. Graecae ad res Romanas pertinentes*, with bibliography on p. 65. For Bormann and Schmidt, see note 3, *supra*; for Wölfflin, note 1, p. 260.

by Diehl (ed. 1908, '10). In the notes, M stands for Mommsen. The Greek version is not here reprinted except where the Latin original is entirely lost. The Latin and Greek texts have been reprinted and translated into English, with accurate notes, in a pamphlet of 91 pages, by Dr William Fairley, Philadelphia, 1898[1].

There was also a copy of the Greek version at *Apollonia* in Pisidia, unimportant portions of which have been identified[2], but with these we are not here concerned.

In June, 1914, a number of very small fragments of the original Latin text was discovered by Sir W. M. Ramsay at *Antioch* in Pisidia. This new evidence is quoted in the notes to §§ 8, 10, 22 as 'ANT.' For my first knowledge of this discovery I am indebted to Dr J. S. Reid and, for all details, to Sir W. M. Ramsay, whose article forms part of the *Journal of Roman Studies*, vol. vi, 1919.

I RERVM GESTARVM D|V| AVGVST| QVIBVS ORBEM TERRARVM |MPERIO POPVLI ROMANI subiecit et inpensarum quas in rem publicam populumque Romanum fecit, incisarum in duabus aheneis pilis, quae sunt Romae positae, exemplar subiectum[3].

(1) Annos undeviginti natus exercitum privato consilio et

23 Sept. 44 B.C. privata impensa comparavi, per quem rem publi-
Early career   cam (do)minatione factionis[4] oppressam in liber-
43 B.C.   tatem vindica(vi. Quas ob res[5] sen)atus decretis honorificis in ordinem suum m(e adlegit C. Pansa A. Hirti)o

[1] On the language of the document, see esp. Wölfflin, in *S.-Ber.* of Munich Academy (1886) 253–77, (1896) 160–83. On the theory of the successive stages of its composition, Kornemann, in *Beiträge zur alten Geschichte*, ii (1902) 141 f, iii (1903) 74 f, iv (1904) 88 f, v (1905), 317 f; Wilcken, in *Hermes* (1903) 618 f; and Gardthausen, *Augustus*, i 3 p. 1290 f. On the general literature of the subject, Schanz, *Röm. Litt.* II i (1899 etc.) § 212; Haug, in Bursian's *Jahresbericht*, lvi (1890) 87—103: and Besnier, in *Mélanges Cagnat* (1912) 119—151. Some restorations have since been proposed in a pamphlet by R. Wirtz, Trier, 1912, reviewed in *Wochenschrift f. kl. Philol.* 1913, p. 12 f.

[2] Mommsen, ed. 1883, p. xxxiv, and Domaszewski, in *Philologus*, 1911 p. 569 f.

[3] *Divi Augusti*, in line 1, shows that this heading was prefixed after the emperor's death. For facsimile, see p. 178 *supra*.

[4] Thát of Antonius.

[5] 'Quas ob res' Wölfflin (1886), cp. Cic. *Phil.* iii 37, viii 33, ix 15, and esp. v 46 'ob eas causas' etc.; also § 4 l. 5 *infra*, 'ob res a (me)—gestas— decrevit senatus': 'Ob quae' M; 'Propter quae' Borm., Schm.

consulibus, consularem locum s(ententiae dicendae[1] simul dans[2], et im)perium mihi dedit. Res publica n(e quid detrimenti caperet, me) pro praetore simul cum consulibus pro(videre iussit. Populus) autem eodem anno me consulem, cum (cos. uterque bello[3] ceci)disset[4], et trium virum rei publicae constituend(ae creavit).

(2) Qui parentem meum (interfecer)un(t eo)s in exilium expuli iudiciis legitimis ultus eorum (fa)ci(nus, e)t   Lex Pedia
postea bellum inferentis rei publicae, vici b(is   Philippi
a)cie.   42 B.C.

(3) Bella terra et mari c(ivilia exter)naque toto in orbe terrarum s(aepe gessi)[5] victorque omnibus (veniam petentib)us[6] civibus peperci. Exte(rnas) gentes, quibus tuto (ignosci pot)uit, conservare quam excidere m(alui). Millia civium Roma(norum adacta) sacramento meo fuerunt circiter (quingen)ta.
Ex quibus dedu(xi in coloni)as aut remisi in muni-   Wars
cipia sua stipen(dis emeri)tis millia aliquant(o[7] plura   Veterans
qu)am trecenta et iis omnibus agros a(dsignavi) aut pecuniam pro p(raemiis mil)itiae[8] dedi. Naves cepi sescen(tas praeter) eas, si quae minore(s quam trir)emes fuerunt.

(4) (Bis) ovans triumpha(vi[9], tris egi c)urulis[10] triumphos[11] et appella(tus sum viciens se)mel imperator. (Cum   Honours
autem[12] plu)ris triumphos mihi se(natus decrevisset[13],   received
iis su)persedi. L(aurum de fascib)us[14] deposui in Capi(tolio,

[1] Cic. *Phil.* v 46, i 15, vii 15.
[2] 's. d. simul dans' Diehl;—'mihi dans' Borm., Wölf.; 's(imul dans sententiae ferendae)' M².   [3] 'consul uterque' Bormann (1895).
[4] Hirtius and Pansa, at the battle of Mutina, 43 B.C.; 'cum cecidit fato consul uterque pari' (Tibullus ii 5, 18 and Ovid, *Trist.* iv 106).
[5] Bormann (1895); 's(uscepi)', Mommsen (1883).
[6] Hirschfeld, Seeck, Schm.: '(superstitib)us' M.   [7] 'aliquant(um' M.
[8] 'a(dsignavi)—p(raemiis mil)itiae' Bergk, Borm., cp. § 16: 'a (me emptos)—p(raediis a) me' M.
[9] Cp. *Acta Triumphorum*, 714/40, 'ovans quod pacem cum M. Antonio fecit', and, 718/36, 'iterum ovans ex Sicilia' (*C. I. L.* i² p. 50).
[10] *-is* for *es*, as in *tris* and *pluris*.
[11] Suet. *Aug.* 22, 'Delmaticum, Actiacum, Alexandrinum, continuo triduo omnes' (13—15 Aug. 725/29).
[12] Borm.: 'deinde' M.   [13] Or 'dedisset' M; 'decerneret' Schm.
[14] Wehofer, a pupil of Bormann (1895); 'I(tem saepe laur)us,' or 'I(s ex bellis laur)us' M. After 'deposui' *Anc.* has a mark of punctuation, which is best placed after 'Capitolio'.

votis, quae) quoque bello nuncu(paveram, solu)tis. Ob res a (me aut per legatos) meos auspicis[1] meis terra m(ariqu)e prospere gestas qu(inquagiens et quin)quiens decrevit senatus supp(lica)ndum esse dis immo(rtalibus. Dies autem, pe)r quos ex senatus consulto supplicatum est, fuere DC(CCLXXXX. In triumphis meis) ducti sunt ante currum meum reges aut regum lib(eri novem.

2 B.C. Consul fuer)am terdeciens, cum (scribeb)a(m) haec,
14 A.D. (et agebam se)p(timum et trigensimum annum[2] tribu)niciae potestatis.

(5) (Dictatura)m et apsent(i et praesenti mihi oblatam[3] ab

Dictatorship   universo populo et senatu, M. Marce)llo et Ar-
declined   (runtio consulibus, non accepi. Non recusavi in
22 B.C.   summa frumenti p)enuria curationem an(nonae,

qu)am ita ad(ministravi, ut intra perpaucos die)s[4] metu et peric(lo praesenti[5] populu)m univ(ersum privata impensa[6] liberarem). Con(sulatum mihi obla)tum[7] annuum e(t perpetuum non accepi).

(6) (Consulibus M. Vinucio et Q. Lucretio, et postea P.) et
19 B.C.   Cn. L(entulis, et tertium Paullo Fabio Maximo et
18 B.C.   Q. Tuberone, senatu populoq)u(e Romano con-
11 B.C.   sentientibus), [8]ἵν(α ἐπιμε)λητὴς τῶν τε νόμων καὶ τῶν
τρόπων ἐ(πὶ τῇ με)γίστῃ (ἐξ)ουσ(ίᾳ μ)ό(νο)ς χειροτονηθῶ, ἀρχὴν
         οὐδεμ(ία)ν πα(ρὰ τὰ πά)τρ(ια) ἔ(θ)η διδομένην ἀνεδε-
Morum   ξάμην· ἃ δὲ τότε δι' ἐμοῦ ἡ σύνκλητος οἰκονομεῖσθαι
regimen
ἐβούλετο, τῆς δημαρχικῆς ἐξο(υ)σίας ὧν ἐτέλε(σα. κ)αὶ ταύτης αὐτῆς τῆς ἀρχῆς συνάρχοντα (αὐτ)ὸς ἀπὸ τῆς συνκλήτου π(εν)- τάκις αἰτήσας (ἐλ)αβον.

[1] For -iis. Cp. § 3, 7, 'stipendis'.
[2] 'scribebam—, et agebam—annum' M: '— — et eram—trigensimum' Bergk, Borm., Schm., Cagnat, καὶ ἤμην (without ἔτος), cp. middle of § 15; 'scripseram—eramque—annum' Diehl.
[3] Wölfflin, διδομένην, Suet. Aug. 52, 'dictaturam offerente populo': 'datam a' M; '—ab universo' Diehl.
[4] 'intra perpaucos dies' (Haverfield) fills the space better than 'intra paucos dies' Seeck, Schm., Wölf.; '..... paucis diebu)s' M, 'paucissimis diebus' Borm., ἐν ὀλίγαις ἡμέραις.
[5] M[1]; 'quo erat' M[2]; τοῦ παρόντος φόβου.
[6] Wölf., cp. § 1, 1: 'meis impensis' M; 'meis sumptibus' Schm.
[7] Haug, τότε διδομένην; 'tum datum' M.
[8-8] ἵνα—δέκα. Preserved in the Greek translation only.

(7) τριῶν ἀνδρῶν ἐγενόμην δημοσίων πραγμάτων κατορθωτὴς συνεχέσιν ἔτεσιν δέκα[8]. (Princeps senatus[1] fui usque ad eum diem, quo scrips)eram (haec, per annos quadraginta. Pontifex maximus[2], augur[3], quindecimviru)m sacris (faciundis[4], septemvirum epulonum[5], frater arvalis, sodalis Titius, fetiali)s[6] fui.

Offices held

II (8) Patriciorum numerum auxi, consul quintum, .iussu populi et senatus[7]. Senatum ter legi. [et][9] In consulatu sexto censum populi, conlega M. Agrippa, egi. Lustrum post annum alterum et quadragensimum feci. Quo lustro civium Romanorum censa sunt capita quadragiens centum millia et sexaginta tria millia. (Iteru)m consulari cum imperio lustrum solus feci, C. Censorin(o et C.) Asinio cos. Quo lustro censa sunt civium Romanoru(m capita) quadragiens centum millia et ducenta triginta tria m(illia. Tertiu)m consulari cum imperio lustrum, conlega Tib. Cae(sare, filio meo[10], feci), Sex. Pompeio et Sex. Appuleio cos. Quo lustro ce(nsa sunt civium Ro)manorum capitum quadragiens centum mill(ia et nongenta tr)iginta et septem millia. Legibus novi(s latis, et multa[11] e)xempla maiorum exolescentia iam ex nost(ro usu revocavi[12], et ipse) multarum rer(um exe)mpla imitanda pos(teris tradidi).

29 B.C.
28 B.C.
8 B.C.
14 A.D.

(9) (Vota pro valetudine mea suscipere[13] per cons)ules et sacerdotes qu(into) qu(oque anno senatus decrevit. Ex iis) votis

[8-8] ἵνα—δέκα. Preserved in the Greek translation only.
[1] 28 B.C.   [2] 12 B.C.   [3] 41 or 40 B.C.
[4] 37—34 B.C.   [5] Before 16—15 B.C.   [6] 32 B.C.
[7] Cp. Mommsen, *Ges. Schriften*, iv 57 f.   [9] om. Mommsen.
[10] added by Schm. (Diehl), μου.
[11] *et multa* Bormann, πολλά: *multa* M[1]; *complura* M[2] (usually translated by πλεῖστα); ANT. has M at beginning of line, implying that the line began with *multa*, not *-mplura*.
' (reduxi multa e)xempla m. ex. iam ex nost(ra civitate, et ipse proposui)—pos(teris)' M[1]; ' (multa revocavi e)xempla m. ex.—(ra civitate, et ipse de me)—pos(teris tradidi) ' Bergk; ' (complura e)xempla m. ex. iam ex nost(ro usu reduxi, et ipse)—pos(teris tradidi) ' M[2]; 'nost(ro)' is confirmed by ANT., which has RO at the beginning of the line.
[12] Bergk, Schm., Cagnat, Diehl; or *restitui* (Haug) or *reduxi* (M); διωρθωσάμην, followed by καὶ αὐτὸς (' et ipse ' is therefore indispensable).
[13] Borm., ἀναλαμβάνειν; *suscipi* M.

saepe fecerunt vivo me (ludos, interdum [1] sacerdotu)m quattuor amplissima colle(gia[2], interdum[1] consules. Privat)im etiam et municipatim univer(si cives uno animo continente)r[3] apud omnia pulvinaria pro vale(tudine mea sacrificaverunt).

(10) (Nomen meum senatus consulto inc)lusum est in Saliare carmen[4] et, sacrosan(ctus ut essem perpetuo[5], et, q)uoa(d) viverem, tribunicia potestas mihi (esset, per legem sanctum[6] est. Pontif)ex maximus ne fierem in vivi (c)onle(gae locum, populo id sace)rdotium deferente mihi, quod pater meu(s habuerat[7], recusavi.   [8]Quod) sacerdotium aliquod[9] post annos, eo mor(tuo demum[10] qui tumultus[8] o)ccasione occupaverat, cuncta ex Italia (ad comitia mea[11] coeunte tanta mu)ltitudine, 12 B.C.   quanta Romae nunquam (antea fuisse narratur[12], suscepi,) P. Sulpicio C. Valgio consulibus.

Sacred offices

[1] *interdum—interdum* Wölfflin, τότε μὲν—τότε δὲ : *aliquotiens—aliquotiens* M.
[2] Pontifices, augures, xv viri sacris faciundis, vii viri epulonum.
[3] (*uno animo continente*)*r—sacrificaverunt* Wirtz, cp. Cicero, *pro Fonteio*, 46, '*uno animo*', and Fügner, *lex. Liv.* p. 1124 (11 exx.); also *Auctor ad Herennium*, 21, 'uno spiritu continenter multa dicere'; ὁμοθυμαδὸν συνεχῶς ἔθυσαν: (*sacrificia concordite*)*r—*(*fecerunt*) Borm.; (*sacrificaverunt sempe*)*r* M.
[4] Tac. *Ann.* ii 83 (of Germanicus), 'ut nomen eius Saliari carmine caneretur'.
[5] For *in perpetuum* (Bergk, Schm., cp. Oros. vi 18, 34), filling the space of at least eleven letters, Nitsche, in *Berl. Phil. Woch.* 1884, 1251, proposes *perpetuo*, eight letters (with ἵνα ⟨ἀεὶ⟩ ἱερὸς ὦ in the Greek; cp. Appian, *B. C.* v 132, ἐς ἀεί). But Mommsen leaves space for only seven. This suggests *semper* (before *essem*), M being equivalent to two letters. Haverfield introduces 'ipse' before 'essem', implying ⟨αὐτὸς⟩ in the Greek, as in §§ 8 and 24; this makes good sense, but does not account for more than four letters.
[6] (*lege sanctum*) M, cp. Cicero, *de Off.* iii 69 etc., νόμῳ ἐκυρώθη; (per lege)M S(anctum) ANT., a probably unprecedented construction.
[7] *habuerat* Bormann,—AT ANT., (ἐσχ)ήκει ; *habuit* M.
[8-8] (*Quod*)—*eo mor*(*tuo suscepi, qui id tumultus*) Bormann (1884); (*cepi id*)—*eo mor*(*tuo qui civilis motus*) M ; (ἥ)ν—ἐν πολιτικαῖς ταραχαῖς, ἀνείληφα.
[9] For *aliquot*.
[10] VO D ANT. (or B or P or R, not S, or Q). For 'mortuo demum' (J. S. Reid) cp. Suet. *Aug.* 31, 'Pontificatum maximum, quem numquam vivo Lepido auferre sustinuerat, mortuo demum suscepit.'
[11] M : 'propter mea comitia', or 'comitiorum caussa', Borm. (the latter is preferred by Haverfield) ; 'coeunte' is placed next by Seeck, Schm., Haug.
[12] Diehl, who has no equivalent (such as *cepi* or *suscepi*) for ἀνείληφα; *memoriae proditur* Seeck ; *fertur, coeunte* M ; *fertur, suscepi* Wirtz.

(11) (Aram Fortunae Reducis[1] iuxta ae)des Honoris et Virtutis ad portam (Capenam pro reditu meo se)natus consacravit[2], in qua ponti(fices et virgines Vestales anni)versarium sacrificium facere (iussit eo die[3], quo, consulibus Q. Luc)retio et (M. Vinuci)o, in urbem ex (Syria redieram[4], et diem Augustali)a ex (c)o(gnomine nost)ro appellavit.

Sacred honours

(12) (Senatus consulto eodem tempor)e pars (praetorum et tri)bunorum (plebi cum consule Q. Lucret)io et principibus (viris ob)viam mihi missa e(st in Campan)ia(m, qui) honos (ad hoc tempus) nemini praeter (m)e e(st decretus. Cu)m ex H(ispa)nia Gal(liaque, rebus in his p)rovinciis prospere (gestis), R(omam redi[5]) T. Nerone P. Qui(ntilio consulibu)s, aram (Pacis A)u(g)ust(ae senatus pro) reditu meo co(nsacrari[6] censuit) ad cam(pum Martium, in qua ma)gistratus et sac(erdotes et virgines) V(est)a(les) (anniversarium sacrific)ium facer(e iussit).

19 B.C.

13 B.C.

(13) (Ianum) Quirin(um, quem tum[7] cl)aussum[8] ess(e maiores nostri voluer)unt, (cum p)er totum i(mperium po)puli Roma(ni terra marique es)set parta vic(torii)s pax, cum, pr(ius quam) nascerer, (a condita) u(rb)e bis[9] omnino clausum fuisse prodatur m(emori)ae, ter, me princi(pe, senat)us claudendum esse censuit.

Peace

29, 25, 2 (?) B.C.

III (14) (Fil)ios meos, quos iuv(enes mi)hi eripuit for(tuna)[10], Gaium et Lucium Caesares, honoris mei caussa senatus populusque Romanus annum quintum et decimum agentis consules designavit, ut eum magistratum inirent post quinquennium. Et ex eo die, quo deducti sunt in forum, ut interessent consiliis publicis

Gaius and Lucius

5, 2 B.C.

---

[1] Bormann: *reduci* M.
[2] 19 B.C.
[3] Bormann (1884), ἐκέλευσεν ἐν ἐκείνῃ τῇ ἡμέρᾳ; *iussi die* M, *iussit die* al.
[4] 12 Oct. 19 B.C. *redieram*, Bormann (1884), ἐπανεληλύθειν; *redi* M.
[5] For *redii*.
[6] Dedicated 30 Jan. 9 B.C.
[7] *tum* added by Schmidt to fill the total space of eleven letters.
[8] For *clausum* (l. 4); cp. *caussa* (§ 14, 3) and *causa*.
[9] Under Numa, and, after the First Punic War, 235 B.C.
[10] 2 and 4 A.D. Cp. p. 159 *supra*.

decrevit senatus. Equites autem Romani universi principem iuventutis utrumque eorum parmis et hastis argenteis donatum appellaverunt.

(15) Plebei Romanae viritim HS trecenos numerari ex testa-
44 B.C. mento patris mei, et nomine meo HS quadringenos
Benefactions ex bellorum manibiis consul quintum dedi, iterum
29 B.C.
autem in consulatu decimo ex patrimonio meo HS
24 B.C. quadringenos congiari viritim pernumeravi, et consul
23 B.C.
undecimum duodecim frumentationes frumento privatim coempto emensus sum, et tribunicia potestate duodecimum
12 B.C. quadringenos nummos tertium viritim dedi. Quae
mea congiaria pervenerunt ad (homi)num millia nunquam minus quinquaginta et ducenta¹. Tribuniciae potestatis
duodevicensimum, consul XII, trecentis et viginti
5 B.C.
millibus plebis urbanae sexagenos denarios viritim
29 B.C. dedi². In colonis³ militum meorum consul quintum ex manibiis viritim millia nummum singula
dedi; acceperunt id triumphale congiarium in colonis³ hominum
2 B.C. circiter centum et viginti millia⁴. Consul tertium
decimum, sexagenos denarios plebei, quae tum frumentum publicum accipiebat, dedi; ea millia hominum paullo plura quam ducenta fuerunt⁵.

(16) Pecuniam (pro) agris, quos in consulatu meo quarto et
30 B.C. postea, consulibus M. Cr(asso e)t Cn. Lentulo
14 B.C. Augure, adsignavi militibus, solvi municipis³. Ea
Veterans
(s)u(mma sest)ertium circiter sexsiens milliens fuit⁶,
quam pro Italicis praed(is)³ numeravi, et circiter bis milliens et sescentiens⁷, quod pro agris provincialibus solvi. Id primus

---

¹ He distributed (1) to *at least* 250,000 citizens, (*a*) 300 HS apiece,= 75,000,000 sesterces; (*b*), (*c*), (*d*), 400 HS apiece, on three occasions,= 300,000,000.
² To 320,000 citizens, 60 *denarii*=HS 240 apiece,=76,800,000.
³ For -*iis*.
⁴ To 120,000 colonists, at 1000 HS,=120,000,000.
⁵ To 200,000 citizens, 60 *denarii*=240 HS=48,000,000.
⁶ 600,000,000.
⁷ 260,000,000.

IV (2)] RES GESTAE DIVI AUGUSTI 267

et solus omnium, qui deduxerunt colonias militum in Italia aut in provincis[1], ad memoriam aetatis meae feci. Et postea, Ti. Nerone et Cn. Pisone consulibus, itemque, C. Antistio et D. Laelio cos., et C. Calvisio et L. Pasieno consulibus, et L. Le(ntulo et) M. Messalla consulibus, et L. Caninio et Q. Fabricio cos., milit(ibus, qu)os emeriteis stipendis[1] in sua municipi(a dedux)i[2], praem(ia n)umerato[3] persolvi, quam in rem seste(rtium) q(uater m)illien(s li)b(ente)r impendi[4].

7 B.C.
6 B.C.
4 B.C.
3 B.C.
2 B.C.

(17) Quater (pe)cunia mea iuvi aerarium, ita ut sestertium milliens et quing(en)t(ien)s[5] ad eos, qui praeerant aerario, detulerim. Et, M. Lepido et L. Arruntio cos., in aerarium militare, quod ex consilio m(eo) co(nstitut)um est[6], ex quo praemia darentur militibus, qui vicena (aut plu)ra sti(pendi)a emeruissent, HS milliens et septingenti(ens ex pa)t(rim)onio m(e)o detuli[7].

Aerarium

6 A.D.

(18) (Inde[8] ab eo anno, q)uo Cn. et P. Lentuli c(ons)ules fuerunt, cum deficerent (vecti)g(alia[9], tum) centum millibus h(omi)num, t(um pl)uribus [10](mul)to, fru(mentarias et n)ummа(ria)s t(esseras ex aere) et pat(rimonio) meo (dedi)[10].

18 B.C.

---

[1] For *-iis*.   [2] (*dedux*)*i* Haug, κατήγαγον : *remis*(*i* M.
[3] 'In ready money'.   [4] 400,000,000.
[5] 150,000,000.   [6] Suet. *Aug.* 49 ult.
[7] 170,000,000. Total recorded in §§ 15—17, = 2199,800,000 sesterces.
[8] *Iam inde* Wölfflin.
[9] (*vecti*)*g*(*alia*) M (Cagnat, Diehl), but M himself admitted that the sole surviving letter (which is almost impossible to find in the *facsimile*) resembles C rather than G : (*opes publi*)*c*(*ae*) Bergk ; (*publi*)*c*(*ani*) Seeck ; (*publi*)*c*(*a*...) Schmidt. The position of *c*, and the order of the Greek, αἱ δημόσιαι πρόσοδοι, point, I think, to (*publi*)*c*(*ae opes*), or (*publi*)*c*(*i reditus*).
[10-10] Schmidt (1887) ; i(nl)ato fru(mento vel ad n)umma(rio)s t(ributus ex agro) et pat(rimonio) m(e)o (opem tuli) M ; σειτικὰς καὶ ἀργυρικὰς συντάξεις ἐκ τῆς ἐμῆς ὑπάρξεως ἔδωκα. Rostovzev (quoted in *Berl. Phil. Woch.* 1904, 151) prefers *gratuito* to *multo* in the following form of the text :—'(mul)to fru(mentum et aes per n)umma(ria)s t(esseras ex agris)—dedi'. Cp. Suet. *Aug.* 41, 'frumentum...in annonae difficultatibus saepe levissimo, interdum nullo pretio viriliter admensus est tesserasque nummarias duplicavit'. This passage led Bergk (in 1873) to introduce the phrase 'ad frumentarias tesseras'; it also

268   LATIN INSCRIPTIONS   [APP.

IV (19) Curiam[1] et continens ei Chalcidicum, templumque
Buildings   Apollinis in Palatio[2] cum porticibus, aedem divi Iuli,
Lupercal, porticum ad circum Flaminium, quam
sum appellari passus ex nomine eius, qui priorem eodem in solo
fecerat[3], Octaviam, pulvinar[4] ad circum maximum, aedes in Capitolio Iovis Feretri et Iovis Tonantis[5], aedem Quirini[6], aedes
Minervae[7] et Iunonis Reginae[8] et Iovis Libertatis[9] in Aventino,
aedem Larum[10] in summa sacra via, aedem deum Penatium in
Velia[11], aedem Iuventatis[12], aedem Matris Magnae[12] in Palatio
feci.

(20) Capitolium[13] et Pompeium theatrum[14] utrumque opus
impensa grandi refeci sine ulla inscriptione nominis mei. Rivos
aquarum compluribus locis, vetustate labentes, refeci[15], et aquam,
quae Marcia appellatur, duplicavi fonte novo in rivum eius inmisso[16].
Forum Iulium et basilicam[17], quae fuit inter aedem Castoris et
aedem Saturni, coepta profligataque opera a patre meo, perfeci, et
eandem basilicam consumptam incendio, ampliato eius solo, sub
titulo nominis filiorum m(eorum i)ncohavi et, si vivus non per-

led Wölfflin to suggest (in 1886) 'i(nl)ato fru(mento atque n)umma(rii)s
t(esseris divisis) ex pat(rimonio) m(e)o (subveni)'. Schmidt (in 1887), agreeing that *nummaria tessera ea tantum dici potest, qua tradita quis pecuniam
accipiebat*, proposed 'frumentarias et nummarias tesseras', which has been
accepted by Cagnat and Diehl, and in the text.

[1] Dedicated 29 B.C.   [2] 28 B.C.
[3] Cn. Octavius, conqueror of Perseus, king of Macedonia, 168 B.C.
[4] The imperial box, Suet. *Aug.* 45 init.
[5] 22 B.C.   [6] 16 B.C.
[7] Ovid, *Fasti*, vi 728 (19 June).
[8] Originally dedicated by Camillus.
[9] Possibly the *aedes Libertatis* founded in 238 B.C. by the father of Tib.
Gracchus (consul of 215, 213 B.C.), Livy, xxiv 16 § 19. Cp. Dessau, 3067,
curatores Iovi Libertati, and *Iovi Libero* in the 'Fasti anni Iuliani', 1 Sept.
[10] Ovid, *Fasti*, vi 791.
[11] Livy, xlv 16 § 5.
[12] Dedicated by the duumvir C. Licinius Lucullus in 191 B.C., and subsequently destroyed by fire.
[13] Restoration begun in 28 B.C.
[14] *Theatrum Aug(ustum) Pompeianum*, 55 B.C.
[15] Frontinus, *de aquis*, 125.
[16] *ib.* 12. Cp. p. 131 *supra*.
[17] Restored 12 A.D.

tecissem, perfici ab heredib(us iussi). Duo et octaginta templa deum in urbe, consul sex(tum, ex decreto) senatus refeci, nullo praetermisso, quod e(o) temp(ore refici debebat); consul septimum, viam Flaminiam¹ a(b urbe) Ari(minum et pontes in ea²) omnes praeter Mulvium et Minucium. 28 B.C.

27 B.C.
Via Flaminia

(21) In privato solo Martis Vltoris templum³ forumque Augustum⁴ (ex mani)biis feci. Theatrum ad aede*m* Apollinis in solo magna ex parte a p(r)i(v)atis empto feci, quod sub nomine M. Marcelli, generi mei, esset⁵. Don(a e)x manibiis in Capitolio et in aede divi Iuli et in aede Apollinis et in aede Vestae et in templo Martis Vltoris consacravi, quae mihi constiterunt HS circiter milliens⁶. Auri coronari⁷ pondo triginta et quinque millia, municipiis et colonis⁸ Italiae conferentibus ad triumphos meos, quintum consul remisi, et postea, quotienscumque imperator a(ppe)llatus sum, aurum coronarium non accepi, decernentibus municipiis et colonis⁸ aeque benigne atque antea decreverant.

Buildings

29 B.C.

¹ p. 121 *supra*.
² 'viam Flaminiam—Ari(minum feci et pontes) omnes' M (Diehl); but Augustus only repaired the *via Flaminia*, and the summary of this chapter (§ 3, p 276 *infra*) begins with *refecit* and ends with *viam Flaminiam*. Hence, after *Ariminum*, we must here understand *refeci* from the previous sentence, and fill the space with 'et pontes in ea' (Wölfflin, followed by Cagnat). This corresponds closely to the Greek version, γεφύρας τε τὰς ἐν αὐτῇ πάσας ἔξω δυεῖν τῶν μὴ ἐπιδεομένων ἐπισκευῆς ἐπόησα (probably meaning ἐπεσκεύασα, which is possibly avoided owing to the preceding word, ἐπισκευῆς). After 'Minucium', instead of understanding *refeci*, Hoeing adds 'munivi', *Cl. Philology*, 1908, p. 87 f. (cp. Suet. *Aug.* 50, and p. 121 *ult.*); but the facsimile shows that, at the end of this §, a space of more than 20 letters is left entirely blank.

³ Dedicated 1 Aug. 2 B.C.   ⁴ p. 97 *supra*.
⁵ Dedicated 11 B.C.   ⁶ 100,000,000 HS; Suet. *Aug.* 30.

⁷ 'Vetusto more civitates, ad quas victoria aliqua pertineret, imperatori triumphaturo ex auro coronas offerebant....Sed a coronis a certis civitatibus imperatori oblatis differunt coronae oblatae imperatori triumphaturo a populo universo tributim, qui honor primum habitus est L. Antonio triumphanti a. 713 (41 B.C.)...ut eidem posuerunt statuam "quinque et triginta tribus patrono"...Id ipsum rursus decretum esse, cum instaret triumphus Actiacus, summa auri clare ostendit, oblatis scilicet a singulis tribubus auri pondo singulis milibus. Hanc collationem et tum et postea Augustus recusavit, de reliquo auro coronario nihil mutans' (Mommsen).   ⁸ For *-iis*.

(22) T(e)r munus gladiatorium dedi meo nomine et quinquens (*sic*) filiorum meorum aut nepotum nomine;

Spectacles

quibus muneribus depugnaverunt hominum circiter decem millia. Bis athletarum[1] undique accitorum spec(ta)c(lum[2] po)pulo pra(ebui meo) nomine et tertium nepo(tis) mei nomine.

Ludi

Ludos feci m(eo no)m(ine) quater, aliorum autem m(agist)ratu(um) vicem ter et viciens. (Pr)o conlegio xv virorum magis(ter conl)e(gi)i, collega M. Agrippa, lud(os

17 B.C. s)aecl(are)s, C. Furnio C. (S)ilano cos., (feci).

2 B.C. (C)on(sul xiii), ludos Mar(tia)les pr(imus feci), qu(os) p(ost i)d tempus deinceps ins(equen)ti(bus ann)is (senatus consulto mecum[3] fecerunt co)n(su)les. (Ve-n)ati(o)n(es) best(ia)rum Africanarum meo nomine aut filiorum meorum et nepotum in circo aut in foro aut in amphitheatris popul(o d)edi sexiens et viciens, quibus confecta sunt bestiarum circiter tria millia et quingentae.

(23) Navalis proeli spectaclum populo de(di tr)ans Tiberim, in quo loco nunc nemus est Caesarum, cavato (solo)[4] in longitudinem mille et octingentos pedes, in latitudine(m mille) et ducenti (*sic*). In quo triginta rostratae naves triremes a(ut birem)es, plures autem minores, inter se conflixerunt. Q(uibus in) classibus pugnaverunt praeter remiges millia ho(minum tr)ia circiter.

(24) In templis omnium civitatium pr(ovinci)ae Asiae victor ornamenta reposui, quae spoliatis tem(plis is[5]), cum quo bellum gesseram, privatim possederat. Statuae (mea)e

Statues, offerings

pedestres et equestres et in quadrigeis[6] argenteae steterunt in urbe xxc circiter, quas ipse sustuli, exque ea pecunia dona aurea in aede Apollinis meo nomine et illorum, qui mihi statuarum honorem habuerunt, posui.

[1] Suet. *Aug.* 43.

[2] Ant. here has (spec)TACVLV(m); cp., however, 'spectaclum', below, in § 23, 1, and 'saeclares' in § 22, 9.

[3] Adopted in Willemsen's *Lat. Inschr.* 1913, p. 35; (*s. c. mecum*) approximately fills the space of 9 letters in the Latin, and δ(όγματι συνκλήτου σὺν ἐ)μοί that of 20 letters in the Greek (proposed by Wirtz, 1912).

[4] 2 B.C.; Tac. *Ann.* xii 56, xiv 15; Suet. *Aug.* 43, 'circa Tiberim cavato solo'; (solo) is confirmed by Ant., which has (S)OLO.

[5] sc. *Antonius*; cp. Plin. *H. N.* xxxiv 58.

[6] (quad)RIGIS Ant.

IV (2)]   RES GESTAE DIVI AUGUSTI   271

V (25) Mare pacavi a praedonibus. Eo bello servorum, qui fugerant a dominis suis et arma contra rem publicam ceperant, triginta fere millia capta dominis ad supplicium sumendum tradidi. Iuravit in mea verba tota Italia sponte sua, et me be(lli), quo vici ad Actium, ducem depoposcit. Iuraverunt in eadem ver(ba provi)nciae Galliae Hispaniae Africa Sicilia Sardinia. Qui sub (signis meis tum) militaverint, fuerunt senatores plures quam DCC, in ii(s [1]consulares et qui pos)tea[1] consules facti sunt ad eum diem quo scripta su(nt haec, LXXXIII, sacerdo)tes circiter CLXX.

Pirates Slaves 36 B.C.

Actium 31 B.C.

(26) Omnium prov(inciarum populi Romani), quibus finitimae fuerunt gentes, quae n(on parerent imperio nos)tro, fines auxi. Gallias et Hispanias provi*n*cia(s, item Germaniam, qua clau)dit[2] Oceanus, a Gadibus ad ostium Albis flum(inis pacavi[3]. Alpes[4] a re)gione ea, quae proxima est Hadriano mari, (ad Tuscum pacificav)i[5], nulli genti bello per iniuriam inlato. Cla(ssis mea per Oceanum) ab ostio Rheni ad solis orientis regionem usque ad fi(nes Cimbroru)m navigavit, quo neque terra neque mari quisquam Romanus ante id tempus adit[6], Cimbrique et Charydes et Semnones et eiusdem tractus alii Germanorum populi per legatos amicitiam meam et populi Romani petierunt. Meo iussu et auspicio ducti sunt (duo) exercitus eodem fere tempore in Aethiopiam et in Arabiam[7], quae appel(latur) eudaemon, (maxim)aeque hostium gentis utriusque copiae caesae sunt in acie et (c)om(plur)a oppida capta. In Aethiopiam usque

Frontiers secured

Foreign wars 22 B.C. 24 B.C.

[1-1] Schmidt (Cagnat); (*qui vel antea vel pos*)*tea* M (Diehl).

[2] *item—claudit* Wölfflin (Cagnat), ὁμοίως δὲ καὶ —περικλείει; *et—includit* M (Diehl).

[3] Expeditions of Augustus against the Gauls and the Cantabri (27—25 B.C.), of C. Carrinas against the Morïni (28), and of M. Messalla against the Aquitani (27), besides several expeditions against the Germani.

[4] Cp. the *Tropaeum Augusti* in Plin. iii 136 (pp. 10, 19, 122, *supra*).

[5] Wölfflin (Cagnat); εἰρηνεύεσθαι πεποίηκα, *pacari feci* M (Diehl).

[6] For *adiit*.

[7] The expedition of C. Petronius against queen Candace the Ethiopian in 24—20 B.C., and that of Aelius Gallus against Arabia in 25—24 B.C. (Hor. *Carm.* i 29).

ad oppidum Nabata perventum est, cui proxima est Meroë. In Arabiam usque in fines Sabaeorum pro(cess)it exercitus ad oppidum Mariba.

(27) Aegyptum imperio populi Romani adieci. Armeniam maiorem, interfecto rege eius Artaxe, cum possem facere provinciam, malui maiorum nostrorum exemplo regnum id Tigrani regis Artavasdis[1] filio, nepoti autem Tigranis regis, per T(i. Ne)ronem[2] tradere, qui tum mihi privignus erat. Et eandem gentem postea d(esc)iscentem et rebellantem domitam per Gaium[2] filium meum, regi Ario(barz)ani, regis Medorum Artaba(zi)[1] filio, regendam tradidi, et post e(ius) mortem filio eius Artavasdi[1]. Quo (inte)rfecto (Tigra)ne*m*, qui erat ex regio genere Armeniorum oriundus, in id re(gnum) misi. Provincias omnis, quae trans Hadrianum mare vergun(t a)d orientem, Cyrenasque, iam ex parte magna regibus eas possidentibus, et antea Siciliam et Sardiniam[3], occupatas bello servili, reciperavi.

Egypt 30 B.C.
Armenia 20 B.C.
1 A.D.

(28) Colonias in Afri(ca Sicilia M)acedonia, utraque Hispania, Achaia Asia Syria, Gallia Narb(onensi, Pisidia) militum deduxi. Italia autem XXVIII (colo)nias, quae vivo me celeberrimae et frequentissimae fuerunt, me(is auspicis[4]) deductas habet.

Colonies

(29) Signa militaria complur(a per) alios duces am(issa), devicti(s hostibu)s, re(cipe)ravi ex Hispania et (Gallia et a Dalm)ateis[5]. Parthos trium exercitum[6] Romanorum spolia et signa[7] re(ddere) mihi supplicesque amicitiam populi Romani petere coegi. Ea

Standards recovered 23 B.C. 20 B.C.

---

[1] See *Addendum* on p. 285.
[2] Tiberius, in 20 B.C.; Gaius Caesar, in 1 A.D.; Tac. *Ann.* ii 3 f.
[3] In 36 and 38 B.C. respectively.
[4] For *-iis. me*(*a auctoritate*) Wölfflin.
[5] The standards lost in Dalmatia during the Civil War by Gabinius (48 B.C.) and Vatinius (44), and surrendered to Augustus (23). Other standards were recovered from the Cantabri, and in Gaul.
[6] A rare contraction for *exercituum*, as in *C. I. L.* vi 414, and *v.l.* for 'duorum exercituum' in Livy, x 44, 3; xxviii 25, 6 (Neue-Wagener, *Form.* i 548). Cp. Dessau, iii (2), p. 850, *gen. pl.*
[7] The standards lost by Crassus in 53 B.C., and Antonius in 40 and 36, and recovered in 20 by Augustus, or rather by his legate Tiberius.

IV (2)] RES GESTAE DIVI AUGUSTI 273

autem si(gn)a in penetrali, quod est in templo Martis Vltoris, reposui.

(30) Pannoniorum gentes, quas ante me principem populi Romani exercitus nunquam ad(i)t¹, devictas per Ti. (Ne)ronem², qui tum erat privignus et legatus meus, imperio populi Romani s(ubie)ci protulique fines Illyrici ad r(ip)am fluminis Dan(u)i³. Citra quod (D)a(cor)u(m tr)an(s)gressus exercitus meis a(u)sp(icis⁴ vict)us profligatusque (est, et) pos(tea tran)s Dan(u)vium ductus ex(ercitus me)u(s) Da(cor)um gentes im(peria populi Romani perferre⁵ coegit).   Illyricum 12—9 B.C.

Daci
12—9 B.C.
6—9 A.D.

(31) Ad me ex In(dia regum legationes saepe missae sunt, nunquam antea visae) apud qu(em)q(uam) R(omanorum du)cem. Nostram am(icitiam petierunt) per legat(os) Bastarn(ae Scythae)que et Sarmatarum q(ui sunt citra flu)men Tanaim (et) ultra reg(es, Alba)norumque rex et Hiber(orum et Medorum).   Envoys from India, etc.

(32) Ad me supplices confug(erunt) reges Parthorum Tirida(tes⁶ et postea) Phrat(es)⁷, ‖ regis Phrati(s filius); Medorum
VI   (Artavasdes⁸; Adiabenorum A)rtaxares; Britan-

¹ For *adiit*.
² 'privignus' in 12-9 B.C.; 'filius' during the Pannonian rebellion of 6-9 A.D.
³ After a trace of part of **D**, the *Mon. Ancyranum* has ·AN·I, for which Mommsen prints *Dan(u)i*, the short form of the normal prose genitive *Danuvi* (*C. I. L.* iii suppl. 13813 d). *Danuvi* (*ib.* x 3553) is also found as the genitive of the name of a trireme in the Roman navy, which is elsewhere called *Danuio* (*ib.* x 3508), as well as *Danuvio* (*ib.* x 3546; xi 67). Similarly, *Pacuvi* is sometimes written *Pacui* or *Pacvi* (Neue-Wagener, *Form.* i 149). In inscriptions **V** normally stands for *u* as well as *v*.
⁴ For *-iis*.
⁵ ὑπομένειν, *accipere* Wölf., *sustinere* Schm.; with *perferre* (M), cp. Caesar, *B.G.* i 17, 'Romanorum imperia perferre', and v 54, 'a populo Romano imperia perferrent'.
⁶ Hor. *Carm.* i 26, 5.
⁷ *ib.* ii 2, 17.
⁸ 30 B.C., after the defeat of Antonius. See *Addendum*, p. 285 *infra*.

S. L. I.

274 LATIN INSCRIPTIONS [APP.

norum Dumnobellau(nus)[1] et Ti*n*(commius)[2]; (Sugambr)orum[3]
Maelo; Marcomanorum Sueboru(m Tudmerus[4]).

Royal clients

(Ad me rex) Parthorum Phrates[5], Orodis filius,
filios suos nepot(esque omnes misit) in Italiam, non bello supe-
ratus, sed amicitiam nostram per (liberorum) suorum pignora
petens. Plurimaeque aliae gentes exper(tae sunt p. R.[6]) fidem me
principe, quibus antea cum populo Roman(o nullum extitera)t[7]
legationum et amicitiae commercium.

(33) A me gentes Parthorum et Medoru(m per legatos) principes earum gentium reges petitos acceperunt Par(thi Vononem,
regis Phr)atis filium, regis Orodis nepotem[8]; Medi Ar(iobarzanem),
regis Artavazdis[9] filium, regis Ariobarzanis nep(otem).

[1] *Dubnovellaunos* on coins.
[2] *et Tim* M, followed by a space for six (or seven) letters (ed. 1883, p. 135).
ET TIM rests solely on the authority of Chishull's copy (1728) of one of
Tournefort's transcripts of the *Mon. Ancyr.*, confirmed by ΚΑΙ Τ in the subsequently deciphered Greek version. The person meant is almost certainly
TINCOMMIVS, Commi filius. Commius is known to us from Caesar's *B. G.*
iv 21, vii 76, and Dio, xl 42 f, as a chieftain in Gaul and South Britain.
(Sir) John Evans, *Coins of the Ancient Britons* (1864) 158—170, and *Supplement*
(1890) 496—507, figures and discusses at least 15 coins, found mainly near the
coast of Sussex, and bearing legends such as TINC COMMI F, or TINCOM,
or TINCOM COMMI. One of these closely resembles a small brass coin of
Augustus (Cohen, ed. 2, no. 29). The evidence in the *Supplement* was
necessarily unknown to Mommsen, when he published his final edition of the
Mon. Ancyranum in 1883. See the present editor's paper in *Numismatic
Chronicle*, 1918 (2), pp. 97—110, with Plate IV.
[3] Tac. *Ann.* ii 26; xii 39; Suet. *Aug.* 21.
[4] .....*rus* (M), -*pos* in the Greek: (*Segime*)*rus* Wölf.; (*Tudme*)*rus* Vigfússon,
Oxf. Philol. Soc. Trans. (1885) 32 f. He also proposed in Tac. *Germ.* 42,
'Marcomanis Quadisque—reges manserunt nobile Marobodui et Tud(me)ri
genus'. But Tud(me)rus was apparently king of the *Quadi*, while the king
of the *Marcomani* was Maroboduus (Strabo, p. 290; Velleius, ii 108—119).
Hence we cannot assume that, in the text, any king of the *Marcomani* was named
Tudmerus. We may however accept the termination -*mērus*, often found in the
names of these German kings. We may even, provisionally, accept *Tudmerus*.
The king of the Quadi may have besought Augustus as head of a Romanising
faction among the neighbouring Marcomani.
[5] Phraates IV, 10 B.C.; Tac. *Ann.* ii 1.   [6] *populi Romani*.
[7] M: *fuerat* Bergk, Schm.   [8] Tac. *Ann.* ii 1.   [9] Cp. p. 285 *infra*.

(34) In consulatu sexto et septimo, b(ella ubi civil)ia[1] exstinxeram, per consensum universorum (potitus rerum omn)ium, rem publicam ex mea potestate in senat(us populique Romani a)rbitrium transtuli[2]. Quo pro merito meo senatu(s consulto Augustus appe)llatus sum[3], et laureis postes aedium mearum v(estiti[4] publice coronaq)ue civica super ianuam meam fixa est, (clupeusque aureu)s in curia Iulia positus, quem mihi senatum (populumque Romanu)m dare virtutis clem(entia)e iustitia(e pietatis caussa[5] testatum) est pe(r e)ius clupei (inscription)em. Post id tem(pus praestiti omnibus dignitate, potest)atis au(tem n)ihilo ampliu(s habui quam[6] qui fuerunt m)ihi quoque in ma(gis)tra(t)u conlegae.

28, 27 B.C.

Augustus

Principatus

(35) Tertium decimum consulatu(m cum gerebam, senatus et equ)ester ordo populusque Romanus universus (appellavit me patrem p)atriae[7], idque in vestibu(lo a)edium mearum inscriben(dum esse et in curia e)t in foro Aug.[8] sub quadrigis, quae mihi (ex) s.c.[9] pos(itae sunt, decrevit.

2 B.C.
Pater patriae

Cum scri)psi haec, annum ageham septuagensu-
(mum sextum).

14 A.D.

Here follows a summary written in inferior Latin by some provincial Greek:—

(1) Summa pecuniae, quam ded(it in aerarium vel plebei Romanae vel di)missis militibus; denarium se(xi)e(ns milliens)[10].

---

[1] M² (*cum* preferred to *ubi* by Geppert): *p*(*ostquam bella civili*)*a* M¹, Schm. exceeds the space of 14 letters, for which M's friends suggested *b*(*ella civilia qu*)*ia exstinxeram*. The first letter is either P or part of B.
[2] Tac. *Ann.* iii 28.
[3] 16 Jan. 27 B.C.; Ovid, *Fasti*, i 587. *Augustus* Schm. but there is no room for the full name: *Aug.* 'potest faber in eo compendio admittendo—errasse' M.
[4] +*sunt* Schm.: *v*(*elati*) Wölf.; Livy, xxx 36, 'velata—ramis oleae navis'.
[5] *caussa*, § 14 *supra*, 'lex Iulia municipalis' passim (Dessau, 6085, *Indices* iii (2) 804); *causa* casu, ut videtur, M.
[6] *iis* Geppert. [7] Suet. *Aug.* 58.
[8] *Augusto.* [9] *Senatus consulto.*
[10] 600,000,000 denarii = 2400,000,000 sesterces. The sums in §§ 15—17 amount to 2199,800,000 sesterces.

276   LATIN INSCRIPTIONS   [APP.

(2) Opera fecit nova, aedem Martis, (Iovis Tonantis et Feretri, Apollinis,) divi Iuli, Quirini, Minervae, (Iunonis Reginae, Iovis Libertatis,) Larum, deum Penatium, Iuv(entatis, Matris deum, Lupercal, pulvina)r ad circum, curiam cum Ch(alcidico, forum Augustum, basilica)m Iuliam, theatrum Marcelli, (p)or(ticus .¹, nemus trans T)iberim Caesarum.

(3) Refecit Capito(lium sacra)sque aedes (nu)m(ero octoginta) duas, thea-(t)rum Pompei, aqu(arum rivos, vi)am Flamin(iam).

(4) Impensa (praestita in spect)acul(a scaenica et munera) gladiatorum at(que athletas et venationes et naum)ach(iam) et donata pe(c)unia a² (⁴municipis³, oppidis in provinciis⁴ ter)rae motu incendioque consumpt(is) a(ut viritim) a(micis senat)oribusque, quorum census explevit, in(n)umera(bili)s.

Ed. Mommsen in *C. I. L.* iii (2) 769—799 (1873), and separately in 1865 and (with eleven facsimile plates) in 1883; also by Cagnat and Lafaye, *Inscr. Graecae ad res Romanas pertinentes*, in fasc. i (1902) of vol. iii (1906) 65—95, and by Diehl (1908, '10). For other editions, see p. 179 n. 1, and p. 259.

(3) SPEECH OF CLAUDIUS IN THE SENATE in 48 A.D., on the admission of Gallic citizens to public office (p. 179 *supra*). 'This genuine transcript of the emperor's words' may be compared with 'the paraphrase of Tacitus, *Ann.* xi 24' (Merivale, *History of the Romans under the Empire*, c. 49, vol. vi, p. 120 n.). See also H. Pelham in *Classical Review*, 1895, 441–3, and *Essays*, 1911, 152–7; E. G. Hardy, *Three Spanish Charters* (and *Roman Laws and Charters*), 1912, 133—154; and J. S. Reid, *The Municipalities of the Roman Empire*, 1913, 189—192.

Claudius was advised by Livy to attempt historical composition⁵, and the present speech resembles, in certain points, that of Canuleius in favour of granting *conubium* to the *plebs*⁶.

I   *Lacuna* at the beginning of column i

Equidem primam omnium illam cogitationem hominum quam maxime primam occursuram mihi provideo, deprecor, ne quasi novam istam rem introduci exhorrescatis, sed illa potius cogitetis, quam multa in hac civitate novata sint, et quidem statim ab origine

---

¹ (21 letters) in Palatio, et in Flaminio? στοαὶ ἐν Παλατίῳ, στοὰ ἐν ἱπποδρόμῳ Φλαμινίῳ. Cp. § 19, ll. 2—3.
² Possibly a mark of punctuation.   ³ For *-iis*.
⁴⁻⁴ (28 letters) Diehl; ἀποικίαις πόλεσιν ἐν Ἰταλίᾳ, πόλεσιν ἐν ἐπαρχείαις; the most obvious equivalent, *coloniis in Italia, oppidis in provinciis* (in M's note) exceeds the space of about 27 letters.
⁵ Suet. *Claud.* 41.   ⁶ Livy, iv 3—6.

urbis nostrae in quod¹ formas statusque res p(ublica) nostra diducta sit.

Quondam reges hanc tenuere urbem, nec tamen domesticis² successoribus eam tradere contigit. Supervenere alieni et quidam externi, ut Numa Romulo successerit ex Sabinis veniens, vicinus quidem, sed tunc externus; ut Anco Marcio Priscus Tarquinius. (Is) propter temeratum sanguinem³, quod patre Demaratho C(o)rinthio natus erat et Tarquiniensi matre, generosa, sed inopi, ut quae tali marito necesse habuerit succumbere, cum domi⁴ repelleretur a gerendis honoribus, postquam Romam migravit, regnum adeptus est. Huic quoque et filio nepotive eius—nam et hoc inter auctores discrepat⁵—insertus Servius Tullius, si nostros sequimur, captiva natus Ocresia⁶, si Tuscos, Caeli quondam Vivennae sodalis fidelissimus omnisque eius casus comes, postquam varia fortuna exactus cum omnibus reliquis⁷ Caeliani exercitus Etruria excessit, montem Caelium occupavit et a duce suo Caelio ita appellita(vit)⁸, mutatoque nomine—nam Tusce Mastarna ei nomen erat⁹—ita appellatus est, ut dixi, et regnum summa cum rei p(ublicae) utilitate optinuit. Deinde postquam Tarquini Superbi mores invisi civitati nostrae esse coeperunt, qua ipsius qua filiorum ei(us), nempe pertaesum est mentes regni, et ad consules, annuos magistratus, administratio rei p(ublicae) translata est.

Quid nunc commemorem dictaturae hoc ipso consulari imperium valentius repertum apud maiores nostros, quo in a(s)perioribus bellis aut in civili motu difficiliores uterentur? aut in auxilium plebis creatos tribunos plebei? quid a consulibus ad decemviros translatum imperium, solutoque postea decemvirali regno ad consules rusus¹⁰ reditum? quid in (pl)uris distributum consulare impe-

---

¹ i.e. *quot*. 'How many different forms of constitution our state has successively undergone'.

² Members of their own royal family, in contrast with *alieni—externi* below.

³ Tainted, or mixed, origin; his parents having belonged to two different states. Livy, i 34 f.

⁴ At Tarquinii.

⁵ Ovid, *Fasti*, vi 627; Plin. *N. H.* xxxvi 204. ⁶ Livy, i 46, 4.

⁷ i.e. *reliquiis*. ⁸ Niebuhr for *appellitatus*.

⁹ Claudius wrote a work in twenty books on *Tyrrhenica*, Suet. *Claud.* 42.

¹⁰ i.e. *rursus*.

rium tribunosque mi(lit)um consulari imperio appellatos, qui seni et saepe octoni crearentur? quid communicatos postremo cum plebe honores, non imperi solum, sed sacerdotiorum quoque?

Iam si narrem bella, a quibus coeperint maiores nostri, et quo processerimus, vereor, ne nimio insolentior esse videar, et quaesisse iactationem gloriae prolati imperi ultra Oceanum[1]. Sed illoc potius revertar. Civitat(em)...[*lacuna* at end of col. i followed by (po)test near the end of line 1 of col. ii.]

II Sane novo m(ore) et divus Aug(ustus), av)onc(ulus m)eus, et patruus Ti. Caesar[2] omnem florem ubique coloniarum et municipiorum, bonorum scilicet virorum et locupletium, in hac curia esse voluit. Quid ergo? non Italicus senator provinciali potior est? Iam vobis, cum hanc partem censurae meae[3] adprobare coepero, quid de ea re sentiam, rebus ostendam. Sed ne provinciales quidem, si modo ornare curiam poterint, reiciendos puto.

Ornatissima ecce colonia valentissimaque Viennensium[4], quam longo iam tempore senatores huic curiae confert! Ex qua colonia inter paucos equestris ordinis ornamentum L. Vestinum[5] familiarissime diligo et hodieque in rebus meis detineo[6], cuius liberi fruantur quaeso[7] primo sacerdotiorum gradu, post modo cum annis promoturi dignitatis suae incrementa; ut dirum nomen latronis taceam[8], et odi illud palaestricum prodigium, quod ante in domum consulatum intulit, quam colonia sua solidum civitatis Romanae benificium consecuta est. Idem de fratre eius possum dicere,

---

[1] Tacitus, *Ann.* xii 31 f; and inscr. in honour of Claudius 'quod...gentes barbaras trans Oceanum primus in dicionem populi Romani redegerit' (Dessau, i 216).

[2] Claudius was the son of Drusus, the younger brother of Tiberius, stepson of Augustus.

[3] Claudius was censor in 48 A.D. (Tacitus, *Ann.* xi 25—27).

[4] This eulogy, which is preserved in the present inscription of Lyon, is still a source of pride to her ancient rival, Vienne on the Rhone.

[5] Entrusted by Vespasian with the restoration of the Capitolium in 70 A.D., Tac. *Hist.* iv 53.

[6] As procurator.

[7] A modest form of request; the members of the priestly colleges were really nominated by the emperor.

[8] Valerius Asiaticus of Vienna, who had been 'twice consul' (Tac. *Ann.* xi 1—3; Merivale, vi 154 f).

miserabili quidem indignissimoque hoc casu, ut vobis utilis senator esse non possit.—

Tempus est iam, Ti. Caesar Germanice, detegere te patribus conscriptis, quo tendat oratio tua; iam enim ad extremos fines Galliae Narbonensis venisti[1].

Tot ecce insignes iuvenes[2], quot intueor, non magis sunt paenitendi senatores, quam paenitet Persicum[3], nobilissimum virum, amicum meum, inter imagines maiorum suorum Allo· brogici[4] nomen legere. Quod si haec ita esse consentitis, quid ultra desideratis, quam ut vobis digito demonstrem, solum ipsum ultra fines provinciae Narbonensis iam vobis senatores mittere, quando ex Luguduno[5] habere nos nostri ordinis viros non paenitet? Timide quidem, p(atres) c(onscripti), egressus adsuetos familiaresque vobis provinciarum terminos sum, sed destricte iam Comatae Galliae[6] causa agenda est, in qua, si quis hoc intuetur, quod bello per decem annos[7] exercuerunt divom Iulium, idem opponat centum annorum[8] immobilem fidem obsequiumque multis trepidis rebus nostris plus quam expertum. Illi patri meo Druso Germaniam subigenti tutam quiete sua securamque a tergo pacem praestiterunt, et quidem cum a[9] census novo tum opere et inadsueto Gallis ad bellum advocatus esset; quod opus quam arduum sit nobis, nunc cum maxime, quamvis nihil ultra, quam

---

[1] These words are generally assigned to Claudius himself; but Mommsen (*Eph. Ep.* vii 394; *Ges. Schriften*, viii 506) ascribes them to the senators. This opinion is, however, refuted in *Bull. Corr. Hell.* 1896, p. 342, n. 3, by Th. Reinach, who quotes Pliny, *Paneg.* 75.

[2] Probably youths from Gaul, who may have formed part of a deputation applying for the *ius honorum*.

[3] Paullus Fabius Persicus, consul in 34 A.D.

[4] Q. Fabius Maximus, the conqueror of the Allobroges; consul in 121 B.C.

[5] The birth-place of Claudius, founded as a Roman military colony in 43 B.C.

[6] The *Tres Galliae*, contrasted with *Gallia Togata*, the latter including *Gallia Cisalpina* and the *Provincia Narbonensis*.

[7] 58—50 B.C.

[8] 50 B.C. to 48 A.D. The rebellion of Florus and Sacrovir in 21 A.D. (Tac. *Ann.* iii 40) is here ignored.

[9] The inscription has *ad*. Cp. Tac. *Ann.* i 31, 'regimen summae rei penes Germanicum [son of Drusus, and younger brother of Claudius], agendo Galliarum censui tum intentum'.

ut publice notae sint facultates nostrae, exquiratur, nimis magno experimento cognoscimus.

C. I. L. xiii 1668; Dessau, i 212.

The above speech was delivered in the Senate House of Rome, and the large bronze tablet containing the local transcript of the same was preserved at Lugudunum near the altar of Rome and Augustus, the most important public site in the three provinces of ancient Gaul. Facsimile in Boissieu, *Inscr. ant. de Lyon*, p. 132 ff, and in Allmer et Dissard, *Musée de Lyon*, i (1888) facing p. 70.

---

(4) LEX DE IMPERIO VESPASIANI, 70 A.D. Formerly in the Church of St John Lateran (pp. 21, 158, *supra*), now in the Capitoline Museum, Rome. *Facsimile* in Gradenwitz, *Simulacra*, xvi.

This is the only extant example of the possibly single legal enactment, whereby the emperor was invested with his various constitutional powers. It has been assumed that the earlier clauses, which are now lost, conferred the *imperium* and the *tribunicia potestas*. The document, as a whole, is repeatedly described as a *lex*, but its several clauses are in the form of a *senatus consultum*, each of them being introduced by *uti*, dependent on *censuerunt*. See especially H. Pelham, 'On some disputed points connected with the *Imperium* of Augustus and his successors', *Journal of Philology* xvii (1888) 27—52, and *Essays*, 60—88; and G. McN. Rushforth, *Latin Historical Inscriptions* (1893), 82—87. It is now, however, generally agreed that Mommsen and some of his predecessors were right in holding that the *imperium* was conferred by a *senatus consultum* (or by the army, with the subsequent approval of the Senate); and the *tribunicia potestas* by what is nominally a *lex*, presented to a sham assembly (*Staatsrecht*, ii³ 789, 841 f, 874 f). The present *lex* gives proof of the gradual evolution of imperial authority by the accumulation of precedents (J. S. Reid).

(1) ...foedusve cum quibus volet facere liceat, ita uti licuit divo Aug(usto), Ti(berio) Iulio Caesari Aug(usto), Tiberioque Claudio Caesari Aug(usto) Germanico;

(2) utique ei senatum habere[1], relationem facere[2], remittere[3], senatus consulta per relationem discessionemque[4] facere liceat,

---

[1] Paragraphs 2 and 3 refer to the Emperor's rights as to holding meetings of the Senate.
[2] *relationem facere*, equivalent to *referre*.
[3] Tac. *Ann.* iii 10, '(Tiberius) integram causam ad senatum remittit'.
[4] The reference to the Senate (*relatio*) was a necessary preliminary to its dividing on the subject (*discessio*). See Mommsen, *Staatsrecht*, iii 983, n. 4.

LEX DE IMPERIO VESPASIANI

ita uti licuit divo Aug(usto), Ti(berio) Iulio Caesari Aug(usto), Ti(berio) Claudio Caesari Augusto Germanico;

(3) utique, cum ex voluntate auctoritateve iussu mandatuve eius praesenteve eo senatus habebitur, omnium rerum ius perinde habeatur servetur, ac si e lege senatus edictus esset haberetur-que;

(4) utique, quos magistrum potestatem imperium curationemve cuius rei petentes senatui populoque Romano commendaverit, quibusque suffragationem suam dederit promiserit, eorum comitis[1] quibusque extra ordinem ratio habeatur;

(5) utique ei fines pomerii proferre promovere, cum ex republica censebit esse, liceat, ita uti licuit Ti(berio) Claudio Caesari Aug(usto) Germanico[2];

(6) utique, quaecunque ex usu reipublicae maiestate divinarum humanarumque publicarum privatarumque rerum esse censebit, ei agere facere ius potestasque sit, ita uti divo Aug(usto), Tiberioque Iulio Caesari Aug(usto), Tiberioque Claudio Caesari Aug(usto) Germanico fuit;

(7) utique, quibus legibus plebeive scitis scriptum fuit, ne divus Aug(ustus), Tiberiusve Iulius Caesar Aug(ustus), Tiberiusque Claudius Caesar Aug(ustus) Germanicus tenerentur, iis legibus plebisque scitis imp(erator) Caesar Vespasianus solutus sit, quaeque ex quaque lege rogatione divum Aug(ustum), Tiberiumve Iulium Caesarem Aug(ustum), Tiberiumve Claudium Caesarem Aug(ustum) Germanicum facere oportuit, ea omnia imp(eratori) Caesari Vespasiano Aug(usto) facere liceat.

(8) utique, quae ante hanc legem rogatam acta gesta decreta imperata ab imperatore Caesare Vespasiano Aug(usto), iussu mandatuve eius, a quoque sunt, ea perinde iusta rataq(ue) sint, ac si populi plebisve iussu acta essent.

[1] i.e. *comitiis*; here *quibusque* is abl. of *quisque*; in the previous line it means *et quibus*.

[2] Claudius, 'auctis populi Romani finibus, pomerium ampliavit terminavitque' (Dessau, i 213). Tacitus (*Ann.* xii 23 *ult.*) says the same of Augustus, but this is not said, either in the text, or by Augustus himself in the *Monumentum Ancyranum*.

Sanctio[1]

(9) Si quis huiusce legis ergo[2] adversus leges rogationes plebisve scita senatusve consulta fecit fecerit, sive, quod[3] eum ex lege rogatione plebisve scito s(enatus)ve c(onsulto) facere oportebit, non fecerit huius legis ergo, id ei ne fraudi esto, neve quit[4] ob eam rem populo dare debeto, neve cui de ea re actio neve iudicatio esto, neve quis[5] de ea re apud se agi sinito.

C. I. L. vi 930; Wilmanns, 917; Dessau, i 244; Rushforth, no. 70; pp. 82—87.

(5) HADRIANI ADLOCUTIO AD EXERCITUM AFRICANUM.

From the speeches addressed by Hadrian to different contingents of the army in North Africa, during a visit paid in 128 A.D. in the course of one of his extensive tours in distant parts of the Roman Empire. The present passage commends certain soldiers for their prompt and energetic fortification of the camp, probably the temporary camp two kilometres west of the *praetorium* at Lambaesis. The speeches in question were found inscribed on a pedestal at the centre of the site of the temporary camp. The date is about July 1; cp. Cagnat, *L'Armée Romaine d'Afrique*, 2nd ed. (1913) 146, 149.

(Munitiones, quas) alii (per) plures dies divisis(sent, e)as uno die peregistis; murum lo(ngi) operis et qualis mansuris hibernaculis fieri solet, non (mul)to diutius exstrucxistis, quam caespite exstruitur, qui, m(o)dulo pari caesus, et vehitur facile et tractatur, et sine mo(les)tia struitur, ut mollis et planus pro natura sua : vos lapi(dibus) grandibus gravibus inaequalibus, quos neque vehere n(e)que attollere neque locare quis possit, nisi ut inaequa(lita)tes inter se conpareant. Fossam glaria[6] duram scabram(que) recte percussistis et radendo levem reddidistis. Opere pr(o)bato introgressi castra, raptim et cibum et arma cepistis ; equitem emissum secuti, magno clamore revertentem per (*portam excepistis*[7]).

Lambaesis (now in the Louvre), *C. I. L.* viii 2 (1881) 2532 p. 288, and Sup. ii (1894) 8042 p. 1725; Dessau, i 2487.

[1] Usually, 'a penal clause'; here, a proviso as to an existing penal enactment, and therefore, virtually, 'an exemption from penalty'. Cp. Cicero, *ad Att.* iii 23, 2 and Mommsen; *l.c.* iii 362, n. 1.

[2] 'In virtue of this law'.   [3] sc. *id quod*.

[4] i.e. *quid* (for *aliquid*).   [5] sc. *praetor*.   [6] i.e. *glarea*, 'gravel'.

[7] Here conjecturally added to complete the sense. Wilmanns, *C. I. L.* viii (2) p. 289, added nearly a whole line, 'per avia excepistis hostemque insequentem repressistis'.

IV] (5) ADLOC. HADRIANI (6) EDICTUM DIOCLETIANI 283

(6) DIOCLETIANI EDICTUM DE PRETIIS RERUM VENALIUM; 301 A.D. (p. 180, *supra*).

Under the rule of Diocletian it was ascertained that, notwithstanding plenteous harvests, prices and wages had gone up. Soldiers, in particular, being unable to purchase provisions out of their pay, were obliged to draw on their savings. Accordingly, an imperial edict was promulgated by Diocletian and his colleagues, fixing a maximum price for provisions and other articles of commerce, and a maximum rate of wages. Instead of being communicated in precise terms to the public officials, it is addressed in grandiloquent language to the provincials themselves. The articles mentioned in it include cereals, wine, oil, meat, vegetables, fruits, skins, leather, furs, foot-gear, timber, carpets, articles of dress; and the wages etc. range from those of the ordinary labourer to those of the professional advocate. The unit of money is the *denarius* of Diocletian, a copper coin worth either one farthing[1], or three-fifths of a penny[2]. The *absolute* equivalent is, however, difficult to determine; the modern interest of the list lies mainly in the *relative* values. The edict was only enforced for a few years, and, although ostensibly intended for the whole of the Empire (*universo orbi*), was, apparently, practically operative only in the provinces ruled directly by Diocletian. The result was that many traders were ruined[3].

Partial copies have been discovered in Egypt, and at Stratonicea in Caria, and, subsequently, at Plataea and Megalopolis (the last two by the American[4] and the British Schools respectively). The most complete editions of the text are those in *C. I. L.* iii (2), pp. 801—841 (1873) and Suppl., fasc. iii, pp. 1909—1953 (1893). A commentary on the details of the subject-matter is included in the separate editions of Waddington (1864), and of Mommsen and Blümner (1893). See also Blümner's article in Pauly-Wissowa, s.v. *Edictum Diocl.* v 1948—57 (1905), and his *Römische Privat-Altertümer* (1911), pp. 604-8, and the reprint of Mommsen's papers of 1851 and 1890 in *Ges. Schriften*, ii (1905), 252—322, and 323—340 respectively. The names of the

---

[1] So Blümner (in Pauly-Wissowa, v 1954), who infers from cap. 30, where one pound of fine gold is worth 50,000 *denarii*, that the *denarius* was then equivalent to 1·827 *Pfennig*. Cp. Mommsen, *Ges. Schr.* ii 331—340.

[2] Waddington made it equivalent to 6·2 *centimes*.

[3] Cp. Lactantius, *de mortibus persecutorum*, c. 7, Diocletianus, 'cum variis iniquitatibus immensam facere caritatem, legem pretiis rerum venalium statuere conatus est. Tunc ob exigua et vilia multus sanguis effusus, nec venale quicquam metu apparebat, et caritas multo deterius exarsit, donec lex necessitate ipsa post multorum exitium solveretur'. Cp. Appendix 23 at end of vol. i of Bury's Gibbon, ed. 1896. The edict promulgated for the same purpose at Antioch in 362 by Julian the apostate was equally unfortunate (see Ammianus Marcellinus, xxii 14, 1, and Gibbon, c. xxiv.

[4] J. C. Rolfe and F. B. Tarbell in *Papers of the American School*, v (1892), 233—247, with a translation of the Plataean portion of the preamble. Cp. W. Loring in *Journ. Hellen. Studies*, xi (1890), 299—342.

emperors at the head of the edict have been printed on p. 254, *supra*; the following passages are quoted from the preamble.

...Quis enim adeo optumsi[1] pectoris et a sensu humanitatis extorris[2] est, qui ignorare possit, immo non senserit in venalibus rebus, quae vel in mercimoniis aguntur, vel diurna urbium conversatione tractantur[3], in tantam se licentiam difusisse[4] pretiorum, ut effrenata livido[5] rapiendi nec rerum copia nec annorum ubertatibus mitigaretur?...

His omnibus, quae supra conprehensa sunt, iuste ac merito permoti, cum iam ipsa humanitas deprecari videretur, non praetia[6] venalium rerum—neque enim fieri id iustum putatur, cum plurima(e) interdum provinciae felicitate optatae vilitatis et velut quodam afluentiae privilegio glorientur—sed modum statuendum esse censuimus, ut, cum vis aliqua caritatis emergeret[7],—quod dii omen averterent!—avaritia, quae velut campis quada(m in)mensitate diffusis tener(i) non poter(at), statuti nostri finibus et moderaturae legis terminis string(e)retur. Placet igitur (e)a pretia, quae sub(di)ti brevis[8] scriptum designat, ita totius orbis nostri (o)bs(e)rvantia contineri, ut omnes intellegant egrediendi ea(d)em licentiam sibi esse praecisam, non inpedita utique in his locis, ubi copia rerum perspicietur afluere, vilitatis baeatitu(d)ine, (c)ui maxime providetur, dum praefinit(a) avaritia conpescit(u)r....

Quia igitur et apud maiores nostros hanc ferendarum legum constat fuisse rationem, ut praescripto metu conpescer(e)tur audacia—quod rarum admodum est humanam condicionem sponte beneficam deprehendi, et senper praeceptor metus iustissimus officiorum invenitur esse moderat(o)r—placet, ut siquis contra formam statuti huius conixus fuerit audentia[9], capitali periculo[10] subi(u)getur....

[1] i.e. *obtunsi* or *obtusi*. [2] 'estranged'.
[3] In wholesale or retail dealings.
[4] For *diffusisse*, cp. *afluentiae*, seven lines lower down.
[5] *Libido*. Cp. p. 198, *n*. 6, *supra*.
[6] Elsewhere correctly spelt *pretia* in the same document; cp. *baeatitudine* at end of paragraph.   [7] The Plataean portion ends with this word.
[8] 'The subjoined summary'.
[9] 'Shall have rashly disobeyed the terms of this statute'.
[10] Justinian, *Inst*. iv 18, 2, '(iudicia) capitalia dicimus, quae ultimo supplicio afficiunt, vel aquae et ignis interdictione, vel deportatione, vel metallo'.

IV (6) EDICTUM DIOCLETIANI

(Quae pr)etia (in singularum rerum venditionibus ex)cedere nemini licitum sit, (hic i)nfra oste(nditur).

C. I. L. iii (2) pp. 824–6, and Suppl. fasc. iii, pp. 1928 f; Dessau, i 642 (one and a half pages).

Here follow the maximum prices of cereals, wine, oil, meat, vegetables, and fruit. Next comes c. vii

de mercedibus oper(arior)um

Operario rustico (pasto diu)rni[1]	✶ vinginti quinque
lapidario stru(ctori ut supra diurni)	— quinquaginta
fabro intestin(ario .)	— quinquaginta
calcis coctor(i .)	— quinqua(ginta)
marmorario	— sexag(inta)
musaeario	— sexa(ginta)
(tessell)ario u(t) supr(a diu)rn(i)	— qu(inquaginta)
(picto)ri parietario u(t) supra diurni	— septuagin(ta quinque)
(pi)ctori imaginario ut supra diurni	— centum quinq(uaginta)

(followed by many other items of wages, and of prices).

Death, or deportation, is the ordinary alternative recorded in the *Sententiae* of Julius Paullus (*fl.* 222 A.D.), e.g. tit. xxi 2.

[1] 'For a farm-labourer, who also receives his food; for the day's work, 25 *denarii*'. The other labourers may be identified as 'stone-mason', 'joiner', 'lime-burner', 'worker in marble', 'worker in mosaic', 'tessellated pavement maker', 'wall-painter', and 'designer of wall-paintings'.

ADDENDUM
TO NOTES ON 'RES GESTAE DIVI AUGUSTI', pp. 272-4.

We have to distinguish between four kings named *Artavasdes*. A. I (§ 27, 4), son of the Armenian king Tigranes I (d. 54 B.C.), and father of Artaxes and of Tigranes II (whom Augustus made king of Armenia in 20 B.C.), and grandfather of Tigranes III. He deserted Antonius in 36, and was slain in 31 by Cleopatra, who sent his head to his enemy, the Median king, Artavasdes II. A. II (§§ 32, 33), called Artabazus in § 27, 9, son of Ariobarzanes I. In 30 B.C. he fled to Augustus, who made him king of Armenia (29—20), and his son and successor, the Median king, Ariobarzanes II, king of Armenia about 1 A.D., in succession to Tigranes III. A. III, son (?) of A. I, died *c.* 1 B.C., but is not named by Augustus. A. IV (§ 27, 10), son of Ariobarzanes II, was king of Media and Armenia, and died before 11 A.D. See Gardthausen's *Augustus*, ii 151, 166, and 469, 474.

APPENDIX V

SIXTY INSCRIPTIONS

EXEMPLIFYING ABBREVIATED PHRASES

La principale difficulté de l'épigraphie latine consiste dans les abréviations.
Salomon Reinach, *Manuel de Philologie Classique*, i 107.

IN Latin inscriptions, the initial letter is constantly used as an abbreviation for a single word in the case of *praenomina* in general, and of terms of relationship, such as *filius, nepos,* etc. (pp. 208, 214 *supra*). By an extension of this principle, a series of initial letters may be used instead of the successive words in certain conventional phrases. On abbreviations in general, see introduction to Appendix VI, *infra*.

The inscriptions given below are arranged under the first four customary classes, beginning in each class with the easier examples, and going on with the more difficult. For the full form of each phrase, see the subsequent *List of Abbreviations*.

(I) *tituli sepulcrales*

(1) D · M | HELIO · AFIN(IANO) | PVB · AVG | SEXTIA · PSYCHE | CONIVGI · B · M.
Wilmanns, 1334 a.

(2) D · M | OPTATO · FILIO | DVLCISS · V · A · I · M · II | D · XVIII.
ib. 471.

(3) D M S | LOLLIVS VIC|TOR LIBRATOR | LEG · III · AVG | STIPENDIOR | XI ANN XXXIII | MAT · F · F · CAR.
Lambaesi; *ib.* 1553.

(4) M · COMINIVS | L · F · POL · ASTA[1] | MILES · LEG · I | NA · AN · L · MIL | AN · XIII · H · S · E | H · EX · T · F · C.
Bonnae; *ib.* 1422.

[1] i.e. from Asta in Liguria.

(5) Q · FABIVS · Q · F · QVIRINA | FABIANVS · ILVRCONEN|SIS · IDEM · PA-TRICIEN|SIS · ANN · XXXXIII · PIVS | IN SVIS · H · S · E · S · T · T · L.
Hispali; *ib.* 184.

(6) CAESIA · (L) · F · CELSA | AN · LXV · H · S · E
TE ROGO PRAETERIENS DICAS | S · T · T · L · | Q · Q · V · L · P · XII.
In Hispania; *ib.* 586.

ABBREVIATED PHRASES 287

(7) L · M | FLAVIORVM | QQ · V · P · L.
Aquileiae; Dessau, ii (2) 8318.

(8) T · FLAVIVS | AVG · L · | CELADVS | TABVLARIVS | MARMORVM | LVNEN-
SIVM | V · A · XXXVII H · S · E | (*In angulis*) O · T · B · Q. (*Infra*) T · T · L · S.
Prope Romam: Dessau, i 1599.

(9) D M | SILIO VICTORI FILIO | ET · NAEBIAE AMOEBE | COIVGI · ET ·
SILIAE · VICTORIAE | FILIAE SVAE · P · SILIVS VICTOR | TRITOR · ARGEN-
TARIVS · F · S · ET S | L · L · POSTERISQVE · EO · RVM.
Wilmanns, 2574.

(10) L · CAESIVS · L · F | CAM · BASSVS | DOMO · PISAVRI | VET · LEG · VII · C ·
P · F | AN · LIII · STIP · XXXIII | H · S · E · T · F · I · H · P | IN · F · P · VI · IN · A ·
P · X.
Salonis; *ib*. 1438.

(11) D · M | FORTVNATO | IVLI · FRONTO|NIS · ACTORI | PATRATA CONIV(X) |
BENE MERENTI | ET FILI FECERVNT | IN F P XX IN AGR | P XXV | H M H N S.
Polae; *ib*. 280.

(12) M · ALLIO M · F · FESTO | FILIO | HOSTILIAE C · L · SEVERAE | N · F · F ·
N · S · N · C.
Patavii; Dessau, ii (2) 8164.

(13) (D) · M | ET · MEMORIAE · AETERNAE · | C · VLATTI · MELEAGRI · IIIIII ·
VIR · AVG · | C · C · C · AVG · LVG · PATRONO · EIVSDEM · | CORPOR · ITEM ·
PATRONO · OMNIVM · | CORPOR · LVG · LICITE · COEVNTIVM · | MEMMIA
CASSIANA · CONIVNX | SARCOFAGO · CONDIDIT · ET · S · A · D.
Lugduni; Wilmanns, 2226.

(14) Q · IVLIO | SERVANDO | SEVIR · AVG | C · I · P · C · N · M | LICINIA ·
PALLAS | MARITO · OPTIMO | INLATIS · ARCAE | SEVIR · OB · TVITIONEM |
STATVAE · HS · N · ∞ | L · D · D · D · SEVIR.
Narbone; *ib*. 195.

(15) C · MATIVS · AMPHIC · PATRONVS | PRAECO · EX · TRIBVS · DECVRIS |
QVI · COS · CENS · PR · APPARERE · SOLENT | APPARVIT · CAESARI · AVGVSTO |
MATIA · C · C · C · L · IVCVNDA · VXOR | C · MATIVS · VRBANVS · CONLIBERTVS |
ARBITRATV · C · MATI · VRBANI · CONLIBERTI.
Dessau, i 1933.

(II) *tituli sacri*

(16) CARMINIA · L · F | PRISCA | HISTRIAE · TERRAE | V · S · L · M.
In Histria; Wilmanns, 53.

(17) INCHOATVM EST SACRVM IIII | NONAS · MAIAS · CONSVMMA|TVM
NONIS · EISDEM | T · SEXTIO LATERANO · L · CVSPIO | RV(F)INO · COS | L D D D.
Lugduni; 197 A.D., *ib*. 122.

(18) Q · VIBIVS · L · F | DIANAE · V · S | EISDEM [1] · ARAM | D · S · F · C.
Naronae in Dalmatia; *ib*. 52; *C. I. L.* i² 2, 2288.

[1] idem.

(19) DIANAE AVG | P · IVLIVS LI|BERALIS SA|CERDOT(A)LIS P · A · II · VI(R) |
II · ET · QQ · P · I · D · IN | COL · THYS|DRITANA | F · P · NOMINE | FILIARVM |
SVARVM IV|LIARVM DE|DIT IDEMQ · DEDIC · D · D.
Thamugade; *ib*. 2358.

(20) IN · H · DD | SANCT · DIANAE · ARAM | CVM SIGNO AE|TETVS · AVGG |
N · N · LIB · PP · STAT · MA|IENS · XXXX · GALL · DE|DIC · ID · AVG · PRAE-
SENT(E) C [1].

[1] consule.

Tirol; 180 A.D.; *ib*. 1397.

(21) HERCVLES | (I)NVICTE SAN(C)|TE SILVANI NE|POS HIC ADVE|NISTI NE QVID | HIC FIAT MALI G · P · R · F.
Romae, in via Appia; Dessau, ii 3469.

(22) HERCVLI | INVICTO | P · LVCILIVS P · F | OVF · SVCCES|SOR · MEDIOLAN | QVOT¹ VOTVM | FECERAT CENTVRIO | P · P · SOL · L · M.
Tibure; *ib.* i 2642.
¹ quod.

(23) H · V · V · S | C · IVLIVS C · F | PAL · RVFVS | TRIB · MILITVM BIS | FANI CVRATOR | V · Q · AB AERARIO SATVRNI.
Tibure; *ib.* ii 3416.

(24) I · O · M · DOL · | Q · POBLICIVS MODESTINVS | (VI VI)R ET CLAVD · CENATORIVM P · S · F · | L · D · D · D.
Bononiae; *ib.* ii 4313.

(25) I · O · M · D | ET I · O · M · H | AVRELIVS DO|MITTIVS QV|M FL · CAS-TO|RE ET AVR · MAXIM|V FRATRIBVS E|X IVSO NVM|INIS V · S · L · M.
Laibach; *ib.* ii 4296.

(26) I O M ET | G · H · L · PRO | SALVTE DD | NN IOVIO | ET HERCVLIO | AVGG NN.
Sirmii in Pannonia; Wilmanns, 1059.

(27) I · O · M | ET · G · M · N | G¹ · VIB · POM · IA|NVARIVS | B · F · COS · LEG | I · ADI · V · S · L · M | II VIRIS · Q · Q · AVRR | MAXIMO · ET · ANNEO.
Novis in Dalmatia; *ib.* 66.
¹ Gaius.

(28) D · S · I · M | FAVTORI IMPERII SVI | IOVII ET HERCVLII | RELIGIOSIS-SIMI | AVGVSTI ET CAESARES | SACRARIVM | RESTITVERVNT.
Carnunti; Dessau, i 659 (p. 91 *supra*).

(29) M · D · M · I | ET ATTIDI MENO | TYRANNO CONSER|VATORIBVS SVIS CAE|LIVS HILARIANVS · V · C | DVODECIMBYR (sic) VRBIS ROMAE | P · S · ET HIEROCERYX | I · M · S · D · L · S · D | HECATE¹ | D · N · GRATIANO · AVG · | ET MEROBAVDE | CONSS · III · IDVS | MAIAS.
Romae in fundamentis basilicae Vaticanae, 377 A.D.; Wilmanns, 114.
¹ Hecatae.

(30) SALVTI EX VOTO | Q · PLAVTIVS IVSTVS AEDIL · ARIM | N · S · ET · CASSIAE · THREPTES · C · S · ET | Q · PLAVTI · VERECVNDI · F · S · AEDEM | S · A · DED | H · A · S · A · H · L · L · Q · D · R · IN A.
Arimini; *ib.* 102.

(III) *tituli honorarii*

(31) GENIO | M · CASSII | M · SATRIVS | VITVLVS · H · C.
Taurinis; Wilmanns, 239.

(32) L · SEPTIMIO | MANNO | C · V · | CONCILIVM | P · H · C.
Tarracone; *ib.* 656.

(33) CN · BAEBIO · CN · (F) | TAMPILO · VALAE | NVMONIANO | Q · PR · PRO · COS | III · VIR · A · A · A · F · F.
ib. 1117; Dessau, i 903.

(34) C · IVLIO C · F · CAESARI | IMP · TRIVMVIRO R · P · C · | PATRONO | D · D.
In Samnio; Dessau, i 76.

(35) LIBERTATI · AB · IMP · NERVA · CA(ES)ARE · AVG · ANNO · AB · VRBE CONDITA · DCCCXXXXIIX · XIIII · (K) · OC(T) · RESTITV(TAE) | S · P · Q · R.
Wilmanns, 64.

(36) M · AVRELO | CAESARI | D · D · P · P.
Thamugade; *ib.* 677.

ABBREVIATED PHRASES

(37) FORTISSIMO ET CLEMEN|TISSIMO IMP · CAES · M · AVR · CARO | IN-VICTO AVG · P · M · T · P · COS · II P · P · PROCONSVLI | M · AVR · VALENTINIA-NVS V · C · P · P · | HISP · CIT · LEG · AVGG · PR · PR · D · N · M · Q | EIVS.
Tarracone, 283 A.D.; Dessau, i 599.

(38) IMP · CAES | T · AELIO | HADRIANO | ANTONINO | AVG · PIO · P · P · | M · CAELIVS | M · F · HORATIA | SATVRNINVS | OB HONOR Q̄Q̄ | INLATA R · P · SVM | HONORARIA EX HS V̄ N̄ POSVIT | IDEMQ DED D D.
Thamugade; Wilmanns, 681.

(39) Q · POMPEIO · Q · F · QVIR · SENECIONI | —PRAEF | FERIARVM · LATI-NARVM · QQ · PATRONO | MVNICIPII · SALIO · CVRATORI · FANI · H · V · | S · P · Q · T.
Tibure; *ib.* 1194.

(40) MEMOR · P · TERENTI | L · F · CLA · AED · II VIRI | T · VETTIVS · GNE-SIVS | IN OPVS ORNAMENT | HS C̄C̄C̄C̄ DED X̄X̄ P R D.
Concordiae in Venetia; *ib.* 2141.

(41) Q · LARONIVS · Q · F · (AVGVR) | L · LIBERTIVS C · F · PONT · MAX | IIII V · I · D · Q · C · P · EX · S · C · CON · IIS—
Vibone; Dessau, ii 6463.

(42) CAMVRENAE | C · F · | CELERINAE | FLAM · FERON[1] | MVNICIPI · SEPTEM-P(EDANORVM) | MVNICIPES · ET · INCOLAE | TVF(ICENSES) VTRIVSQ · SEXVS | OB · MERITA · EIVS | H · A · I · R.
Tufici in Umbria; Wilmanns, 683.
[1] flaminicae Feroniae.

(43) L · AFILANO L · F · | AN · PROVINCIALI | EQVO P · ORNAT · | LVPERCO DESIG · | HVIC ORDO STATV|AM DECREVIT | L · AFILANVS VERECVN|DVS H · V · S · R.
Affile in Latio; Dessau, ii 4946.

(44) A · VETTIVM · FIRMVM | AED · O · V · F · D · R · P · O · V · F · PILICREPI · FACITE.
Pompeiis; Wilmanns, 1955 *g*.

(45) CALIBVS IN CVRIA TORQ(VATIANA) VITR(ASIANA) SCRIB · (ADF) · | TI · CL · FELIX TI · CL · CA(LE)NVS Q · SER · | PRISCVS
QVOD RECIT · EPISTVLA L · VITR(ASI) SILVEST(RIS) | L · MARCIVS VITALIO IIII VIR AD ORDIN(EM V · F) | Q · D · E · R · F · P · D · E · R · I · C
PLACER(E) · VNIVER · CONSCR · | L · VITRASIO SILVESTRI · PRO EIVS ERGA (NOS) | AMORE PVBLIC(E) GRATIAS AGI CVM IS ME(RCEDEM) | SVAM CVM R · P · N · SIT PAENE PARTITVS PE(RMIT)|TIQ EI INSCRIPTION · BASIS SVAE SICVT (EDI)|DER(IT) AMPLIARE QVOQ · MANIFESTIOR | CVNCT · MVNIC · N · LIBE-RALIT · EIVS EX(ISTAT) | EPIST · IIII VIR · SVB EDICT · SVO CELEBER · LOC(O) | PONEND · CVRENT V · D · P · R · L · P · C · C.
Calibus; *ib.* 695.

(IV) *tituli operum publicorum*

(46) ANSIA · TARVI · F | RVFA · EX · D · D · CIRC | LVCVM · MACER | ET · MVRVM · ET · IANV | D · S · P · F · C.
In Lucania; Dessau, ii 5430.

(47) EXCVBITORIVM · AD TVTEL | SIGNOR · ET IMAGIN · SACRAR | P · TVR-RAN · FIRMINVS VET · EX | CORNIC · LEG · II · ADI · ANTO|NINIANE[1] · P · S · A SOLO RES | SABINO II · ET · ANVLLINO · C.
Aquinci in Pannonia; 216 A.D.; Wilmanns, 736.
[1] Antoninianae.

(48) L · ANINIVS L · F · CAPRA IIII VIR ITER · | APOLLINIS AED · ET CIRCVM AEDEM | MVROS D · S · P · R · C.
Setiae; Dessau, ii 5397.

S. I. I. 19

(49) M · ACILIVS A · F · VOT · — — — | PRAEF · AERARI MILITAR · PONTIF · VOLCANI ET AEDIVM | SACRAR · P · C · CLVPEVM ARGENT · CVM IMAGINE AVREA D · D · L · D · D · D.
Ostiae; *ib.* 5451.

(50) M · LVVCIVS · M · F | C · VEIENVS · C · F | IIII · VIR · I · D · S · C | PONTEM · FACIV | CVR · PROBARVNTQ.
Spoleti; Wi!manns, 792; *C. I. L.* i² 2, 2107.

(51) CN · CORNELIVS | L · F · GAL · CINNA | II VIR | MVRVM LONG · P · CII | EX D · D · F · C · I · Q · P.
Carthagine nova in Hispania; Dessau, ii 5332.

(52) T · AIENVS · V · F · MED · (L) · BILLVCIDIVS · L · L · BILLO | Q · CAESI-ENVS · Q · (F) · POST · C · OP(I)SIVS · C · F · | M(AG) · (P)A(G)I · DE · V · S · F · C · I · Q · P.
Furfone in Vestinis; *C. I. L.* i² 2, 1804; Wilmanns, 705.

(53) C · FAESASIVS T · (F) · | P · APPAEDIVS P · F · | AQVILA CVR · FAN · | PORTICVM ALAM | D · PAG · S · F · C · ID · Q · P.
In Vestinis; Dessau, ii 5545.

(54) M · TERENTIVS · M · F | VARRO · LVCVLLVS | PRO · PR · TERMINOS | RE-STITVENDOS | EX · S · C · COERAVIT | QVA · P · LICINIVS | AP · CLAVDIVS | C · GRACCVS · III VIR | A · D · A · I · STATVERVNT.
Inter Pisaurum et Fanum; *C. I. L.* i² 2, 719; Dessau, i 26.

(55) IMP · CAESAR DIVI F | AVGVSTVS PONTIFEX MAXIMVS ' TRIBVNIC · PO-TEST · XVII | EX S · C · TERMINAVIT (*In latere dextro*) R · R · PROX · CIPP · PED · XXIV (*In postico*) R · R · PROX · CIPP · PED · CCVI.
Romae, in dextra ripa Tiberis, Dessau, ii 5924 *b*.

(56) IMP · CAES · DIVI HADRIANI F · ANTONINO AVG · PIO P · (P) | SEXTILIVS DEXTRI FIL · CELSVS ARCVM A FVNDAMEN(TIS) | CVM GRADIBVS ET STATVA S · P · F · ID · Q · DED | D · D.
In Africa; *ib.* ii 5569.

(57) IVNIA D · F · RVSTICA SACERDOS | .... PORTICVS .... D · P · S · D · D · STATVAS SIBI ET C · FABIO | IVNIANO F · SVO AB ORDINE CARTIMITANORVM DECRETAS | REMISSA IMPENSA ITEM STATVAM C · FABIO FABIANO VIRO SVO | D · P · S · F · D.
Cartimae in Baetica; *ib.* ii 5512.

(58) MELIA ANNIANA IN MEMOR · Q · LAEPICI Q · F · SERG · BASSI MARITI SVI | EMPORIVM STERNI ET ARCVM FIERI ET STATVAS SVPERPONI TEST · IVSS · EX HS DC · D · XX · P · R.
Zarae in Dalmatia; *ib.* ii 5598.

(59) CN · MELISSAEO CN · F · APRO M · STAIO M · F · RVFO II VIR · ITER · I · D · LABRVM EX D · D · EX P · P · F · C · CONSTAT IIS DCCL.
Pompeiis; *ib.* ii 5726.

(60) (*a*) NE QVIS IN OPPIDO COLON · IVL · AEDIFICIVM DETEGITO | NEVE DEMOLITO NEVE DISTVRBATO NISI SI PRAEDES | IIVIR · ARBITRATV DEDERIT SE RERAEDIFICATVRVM (*sic*) AVT | NISI DECVRIONES DECREVERINT DVM NE MINVS L AD|SINT CVM E · R · CONSVLATVR SI QVIS ADVERSVS EA FECE | Q · E · R · E · T · P · C · C · G · I · D · D · E · EIVSQ · PECVNIAE QVI VOLET PE|TITIO PERSECVTIOQ · EX H · L · ESTO.
(*b*) IVS IVRANDVM ADIGITO PER IOVEM DEOSQVE PENATES SESE PECV-NIAM PV|BLICAM EIVS COLON · CONCVSTODITVRVM RATIONES|QVE VERAS HABITVRVM ESSE V · Q · R · F · E · V · S · D · M · NE|QVE SE FRAVDEM PER LITTERAS FACTVRVM ESSE SC · D · M.
Lex coloniae Genetivae Iuliae; *ib.* ii 6087, §§ 75, 81; *C. I. L.* i² 2, 594.

APPENDIX VI

ABBREVIATIONS

THE brevity and the conventionality characteristic of Latin inscriptions are exemplified by the constant use of shortened forms for words of frequent occurrence. Abbreviations used in Roman laws are contained in a treatise by Valerius Probus (a grammarian of the first century of our era), first printed by Mommsen in 1853, and reprinted by him, with several similar treatises, in 1864[1]. It begins with the words : *est etiam circa perscribendas vel paucioribus litteris notandas voces studium necessarium*. Hence it has been supposed that it probably formed a part of a general treatise *De notis*. There were also special forms used in the superscriptions of letters[2].

These abbreviations were anciently known as *notae*[3], or *litterae singulares* (or *singulariae*[4]), and in later Latin as *siglae*, the term *sigla* being used in the nominative singular in the sense of *littera singula*. They usually consist of the first letter, or of the first two to five consecutive letters, of the word. Thus T stands for *Titus* TI or TIB for Tiberius ; and PR, PRAE or PRAEF for *praefectus*.

Originally there was no distinction of number, H stood for *heres* or for *heredes*. But, early in our era, it became customary to denote the plural of a *praenomen* by doubling it. Thus, under Tiberius, we have C·PEDANIVS·C·C·L, *Gaius Pedanius Gaio-*

---

[1] M. Valerius Probus de notis antiquis, *S.-Ber.* v 91—134, Leipzig, 1853, and separate ed. *ib.* 1855; reprinted (with similar treatises) in Keil's *Grammatici Latini*, iv (1864) 265—352; and, by itself, in Huschke, *Iurispr. Anteiust.* ed. 6 (1908) pp. 82 ff. Cp. Mommsen, *Ges. Schr.* vii (1909) 206—213, and on *notae iuris, ib.* 214-6, Teuffel, *Lat. Lit.* § 300, 4, and Schanz, § 478, 3.
[2] List in Roby, *Latin Grammar*, i 462.
[3] Festus, s.v....'litterae singulae aut binae'.
[4] Gellius, xvii 9, 1.

rum duorum libertus[1]. C·C soon became CC, and, in the second century, this reduplication was extended to the final consonant of the abbreviations for *Augustus* and *consul*, AVGG standing for *Augusti duo*, and COSS for *consules duo*. It was also extended to the titles and epithets of emperors, such as DD·NN for *domini nostri*, and IMPP, CAESS, AVGG for *imperatores, Caesares, Augusti*. Similarly AVGGG stand for *Augusti tres*, and even DDDD NNNN FFFF LLLL, for *dominis nostris Flaviis quattuor*, 'our four Flavian emperors'[2]. The same principle was sometimes carried still further[3].

Compound words may be expressed by the first letter (or letters) either of the whole word, or of each of its component parts. Thus *beneficiarius* may appear either as B, or as B·F, and *praepositus* as PRAEP or as P·P. For purposes of abbreviation, the enclitics *que* and *ve* are generally treated as separate words; *populusque* becomes P·Q. The above principles were maintained until about 300 A.D., when a certain amount of confusion was introduced by treating simple words as compounds; and by using non-consecutive letters for their abbreviations, as Q·D for *quondam*, PBL for *publicus*, and MCP for *municipii*[4].

Some abbreviations are in general use, those denoting *praenomina* being found in ordinary Latin literature. Others, which are seldom or never used in literature, are found in all classes of inscriptions, while some are characteristic of particular classes, or are confined to special regions[5]. Certain exceptionally ambiguous abbreviations of names of places (such as C·B and C·N) are only intended for local use[6]. But, for the most part, the same abbreviations are found in inscriptions representing widely distant districts of the ancient Roman world.

[1] *C. I. L.* vi 4397.
[2] *ib.* viii 27, cp. Dessau, iii (2) pp. 795 f.
[3] Cp. Jullian in *Bulletin Épigraphique*, iv (1884) 170–9.
[4] Mowat, in *Bulletin Épigraphique*, iv 127 f, v 30 f, vi 94 f, 194 f. Cp. Cagnat, 399—407[4].
[5] P·P, for *permissu proconsulis*, is only found in Africa, and is very doubtful, *ib.* 453[4] n.
[6] Cp. Mommsen, *l.c.*, 131 (*Ges. Schr.* vii 210), 'Formeln...die nur durch den Ort wo sie sich ursprünglich fanden, und auch dann nur für Eingeweihte verständlich waren.'

VI] ABBREVIATIONS 293

In Latin inscriptions, in general, the conventional element is peculiarly prominent. The same facts are usually stated in the same phrases or *formulae*, or expressed in brief by means of the same abbreviations. Thus, in epitaphs, we have the widely extended use of the same conventional phrase, *sit tibi terra levis*[1], and of the corresponding abbreviation, S·T·T·L[2]. This widely extended use of similar phrases, and similar abbreviations, suggests the probable existence of professional manuals for the guidance of makers of inscriptions[3].

Lists of abbreviations have been collected in Zell's *Handbuch der römischen Epigraphik*[4], Orelli-Henzen's *Inscriptiones Latinae*, in the *indices* of the several volumes of the *Corpus Inscriptionum*, and in the *Exempla* of Wilmanns[5]. One of the most complete lists in any single work is that supplied by Cagnat in his *Cours d'Épigraphie*[6], which has been followed by Egbert and by Ricci. The accompanying index, in which the practical needs of the student have been primarily kept in view, has been founded mainly on that of Wilmanns, with some necessary additions from Cagnat's list, and from that of Dessau[7]. It also includes references to abbreviations quoted in the course of the present work[8].

[1] Doubtless long in use in Latin, as in Greek (cp. Eur. *Alc.* 463), before its satirical application by Martial (ix 29, 11) which is imitated under Hadrian in *Anth. Pal.* xi 226; cp. Kaibel, *Ep. Gr.* 551, 4.

[2] This *formula* is frequently used either separately, or as part of a verse. In Bücheler's *Carmina Epigraphica* (1897) out of **34** examples of the latter, we find **7** in Rome (1040, 1269, 1456, 1460, 1462 f, 1537); **8** in the rest of Italy (1075, 1088, 1101, 1130, 1308, 1318, 1324, 1482); **11** in Spain (1103, 1123, 1193 f, 1316, 1451-4, 1457, 1566), where it is sometimes abbreviated; **4** in Germany (1082, 1100, 1104, 1461); and **4** in Africa (1328-30, 1455). On the other hand, O·B·Q, *ossa bene quiescant* (with its variations), is common in Africa, but rare elsewhere (Wilmanns, 186 n).

[3] Cagnat, in *Revue de Philologie*, 1889, 51—65.

[4] i (1850) 443-8, and ii (1852) 55-8, 142-5, 168 f, 176 f, 193-6.

[5] ii 710—737. The *litterae singulares et scripturae compendia* in Hübner's *Exempla*, p. lxxii f, are limited to the initial letters which are either inverted, or have lines drawn above or across them. (Cp. Cagnat[4], 405 f.)

[6] pp. 408-73[4], founded largely on the *Indices* of the *Corpus*.

[7] III ii (1916), pp. 752-851.

[8] References such as *App.* v 55 denote the numbers of the several inscriptions in Appendix v.

LIST OF ABBREVIATIONS

A

A (legio) adiutrix; ager; amicus; annus; as; Aulus; Aurelius; aurum
A · A Aquae Aponi; Auli duo
A · A · A · F · F (p. 222; *App.* v 33) aere argento auro (Cic. Epist. vii 13, 2; Dessau, i 1095), auro argento aere (*ib.* i 1069) flando feriundo; *aere* old dat. for *aeri*
AAGG Augusti (duo), **AAAGGG** Augusti (tres)
A B, BA, BAL a balneis
A BIB, BYB a bibliotheca
A · B · M amico(-is) bene merenti (-ibus), p. 63
ABN, ABNEP abnepos, p. 214
A · C aere collato; a commentariis
A CAD a caducis (Augusti libertus procurator), Dessau, i 1532
ACC accipiet, -iendus; accepit, -erunt; acc(ensus) cos (=consulis)
A · D ante diem
AD *vel* **ADI** adiutrix (*App.* v 27, 47); **ADI · P · F** — pia fidelis (legio)
A · D · A agris dandis adsignandis; **A · D · A · I** — iudicandis (*App.* v 54)
ADF adfuerunt (*App.* v 45); adfinis
ADIVT · TABVL adiutor tabulariorum
ADL (-LEC, -LECT) adlectus
ADN(EP) adnepos
AEC(VR) *vel* **AEQVOR** (dea) Aecurna *vel* Aecorna
AED aedes; aedilis, p. 223, — **CER** cerealis, — **COL** coloniae, — **CVR** curulis, — **LVSTR** lustralis, — **PL** plebis
AEDD · QQ aediles quinquennales
AED · P(OT) aedilicia potestate
AED · V · A · S · P · P · V · B · D · R · P · O · V · F aedilem viis, aedibus, sacris publicis procurandis, virum bonum dignum re publica oramus ut faciatis
AEG Aegyptus, -tius
AEL Aelius, -a
AEM Aemilia (tribu)
AER · COLL aere collato, — **P · P** proprio posuerunt
AER · MIL aerarii militaris; — **SAT** Saturni, p. 225

AET aeternus(-a), aeternitas
AF Afer; Africa
A · F · A · N Auli filius, Auli nepos
AG ager
AGR · DAND · ADTR · IVD agris dandis adtribuendis iudicandis
A · H · N · P ad heredem non pertinet, p. 64
A · I · A agris iudicandis adsignandis
AID · PL aidilis plebis, p. 134
A · L Augusti(-ae) libertus(-a); area lata
A · L · F animo libens fecit, — **P** posuit, *perscr.* Wilm. 1507
ALV · TIB alvei Tiberis, p. 224
AM · B · M amico bene merenti
A · M · C amicis memoriae causa
A MIL(IT) a militiis
AN(I) Aniensi (tribu), p. 215; *App.* v 43
A · N Augustus noster
AN anno, -os, -is; **ANN** annis, -os; annona
A · N · F · F annum novum faustum felicem
AN · P (A · P) anno provinciae
ANT Antonius
A · O · F · C amico optimo faciundum curavit
AP Apollinaris (legio); Appius; Aprilis
A · P · F (legio) adiutrix pia fidelis
A P(OP) a populo; **A · P** aram posuit; arca publica; argenti pondo; ager publicus
APP Appius
A · P · R aerarium populi Romani
A · P · R · C anno post Romam conditam (Dessau, i 466)
AQ aqua, aquarius, aquilifer
A · Q · E · R · P · P · R · L (ei) ad quem ea res pertinet pertinebit, recte liceto (Dessau, ii 8362)
A Q · P (*vel* **PR**) a quaestionibus praefecti
A RAT a rationibus
ARG argentum, argentarius, argenteus
ARG · P argenti pondo; **ARG · PVB** argento publico
ARK arca, arcarius, p. 228
ARN(IEN) Arniensi (tribu), p. 215

ABBREVIATIONS

A S   a solo, — **F** fecerunt; — **F·C** faciundum curavit, -verunt
A S   amico suo (*vel* sanctissimo); a sacris; a senatu
ASC   ascia
AV   augur; Augustus; Aulus; Aurelius; aurum
A·V   aediles vici; amphora vini; argenti unciae; ave (*vix* ave vale); agens vices, — **L** legati; — **P** praesidis
AVG   augur (p. 223), Augustalis (*App.* v 13), Augustus(-a), pp. 138, 140; Augustodunum
AVG·N   Augustus noster, p. 219, **AVGG·NN** Augusti nostri, Augustorum nostrorum (*App.* v 20)
AVR   Aurelius, **AVRR** Aurelii (*App.* v 27)

B

B   beneficia, beneficiarius; bonus
B·B   bonis bene (Dessau, ii 4452, 4493, 8137, *perscr.* 8428), — **M·M** malis male (*C.I.L.* viii 8739)
BBVV   boni viri, — **QQ** — quinquennales
B·D   Bona dea; — **R** Bona dea restituta *vel* -trix (Dessau, ii 3501 f)
B·D·S·M   bene de se merenti
B·F   beneficiarius (*App.* v 27); bonum factum; bona fortuna; bos femina
B·F·A·IVNCT   boves feminae auro iunctae
BIS·VI·AVG   bisellarius (pp. 78, 229) sevir Augustalis
B·M (*a*) bene merenti (p. 62, *App.* v 1), merito -ae; — **F** fecit; — **F·C** faciundum curavit; — **F·D·S** fecerunt de suo; — **M·C** memoriae causa; — **P** posuit; — **P·C** ponendum curavit
B·M (*b*) bona mens; bonae memoriae; (*c*) bos mas
B·Q   bene quiescat, p. 64
BR   Britannia, Britannicus, p. 154
BRIT(O)   Brittones, Britones
BRIT(T)   Brit(t)anicus
B·R·P·N   bono rei publicae natus
B·V   bene valeas, *perscr.* Dessau, ii 6156; bene vale
B·VIX   bene vixit
BV(C), BVCC(IN)   buccinator

B·V·V   balnea vina Venus (Dessau, ii 8157)

C

C   Caesar; Gaius, pp. 35, 60; Kalendae; candidatus; castra; censuere; centurio; cives, civitas; clarissimus, p. 117; Claudius -a; cohors; colonia; comitialis, p. 173; coniux; consule, *App.* v 20; curator, curavit -verunt, curante -tibus; curia
Ↄ   Gaia, pp. 60, 219; coniux, femina; centuria, centurio; contrascriptor
CA   candidatus; carissimus -a
C·A   colonia Agrippinensis (*Cologne*); curam agente; custos armorum, p. 228
C·A·A·M   colonia Aelia (?) Augusta Mediolanium (*Milan*)
C·A·AQ   colonia Aurelia Aquensium (*Baden-Baden*), p. 136
C·A·D·A·I   colonis agrorum dandorum adsignandorum ius
CAE(S)·N   Caesar noster, p. 219
CAM(IL)   Camilia (tribu), p. 215, *App.* v 10
C·A·N   colonia Augusta Nemausus (*Nîmes*)
C·A·V   centuria accensorum velatorum
CAP(IT)   capitalis
C·AQ   civis Aquensis
CAR·M   Carpicus maximus
C·B   colonia Beneventana
C·BEL   civis Bellovacus (*Beauvais*)
C·B·M   coniugi bene merenti, — **F** fecit, — **P** posuit
CC   Caesares; Gai duo
CC   ducenarius, p. 226
C·C   censuerunt cuncti (*App.* v 45); certa constans (legio); collegium centonariorum; colonia Claudia; (ex) conscriptorum consulto; (agens) curam carceris
C·C·A   colonia Caesaraugusta (*Saragossa*); cuius curam agit
C·C·A·A   colonia Claudia ara Agrippinensis (*Cologne*)
C·C·A·A·A   coloni coloniae Augustae Alexandrianae Abellinatium (*Abellinum*)
C·C·C   tres Gai, — **L** trium Gaiorum liberta (*App.* v 15); coire convocari cogi; colonia Copia

Claudia (*Lyon*); cum consilio collocutus, — D dixit
CCC trecenarius, p. 226
C · C · C · AVG · LVG(VD) colonia Copia Claudia Augusta Lugudunum, p. 197 (*Lyon*), *App*. v 13
C · C · C · IVL coloni coloniae Claritatis Iuliae (sc. Vcubitanorum in Hispania Baetica)
C · C · G · I(VL) (*App*. v 60) colonis coloniae Genetivae Iuliae, p. 158 (Urso, *Osuña*)
CC · II clarissimi iuvenes
C · C · I · K colonia Concordia Iulia Karthago
C · C · P coloni coloniae Patriciae (Corduba)
CC · PP clarissimi pueri
C · C · R coloni coloniae Romulensis (Hispalis (*Seville*)); curator civium Romanorum
CC · VV (*vel* C · C · V · V) clarissimi viri (*pl.*)
C · D compos dat; conscriptorum decreto; consulto decurionum
C · D · D cultor domus divinae
C · E coniux eius; curam egit
C · E · B · Q cineres eius bene quiescant
CEN(S), CES censor; CENS censuit, -uerunt
C · F Gai filius (filia); carissima filia; clarissima femina; coniux fecit
C · F · C coniux faciundum curavit; censores — curaverunt
CH, CHO, CHOR cohors
C · I clarissimus iuvenis, p. 193
C · I · F · S colonia Iulia Felix Sinope
C · I · K colonia Iulia Karthago
C · I · P · A colonia Iulia Paterna Arelate (*Arles*)
C · I · P · C · N · M colonia Iulia Paterna Claudia Narbo Martius (*App*. v 14 *Narbonne*)
C · L cives Latini; colonia Lambaesitana
CL clarissimus, p. 193 f; classis, p. 154; Claudius, -a (tribu), p. 215
C · L Gai libertus(-a) (*App*. v 12)
Ɔ · L mulieris libertus, — ⅃ — liberta
CLA (*App*. v 40) Claudia (tribu); classis
CL(AS) · PR classis praetoria; — M(IS) Misenatium
CLAVD (*App*. v 24) Claudialis
CL · BR classis Britannica

CL · F clarissima femina
CL · G · P · F classis Germanica pia fidelis
CL · PR(AET) classis praetoria
CL · V clarissimus vir, p. 193; CLV Clustumina (tribu), p. 215
C · M · V clarissimae memoriae vir; — F femina; — P puer
CN Gnaeus (pp. 35, 60, 208)
C · N Caesar noster; colonia nostra; — Nemausensium (*Nîmes*); civitas Nattabutum (Africa), Dessau, ii 6804
COD · TR codicillarius tribuni
COER coeravit, -averunt
COH cohors; COHH cohortes
COH · I · C · R cohors I civium Romanorum; COH · I · F(L) · D(AMAS) · ∞ · EQ · SAG cohors I Flavia Damascenorum milliaria equitata sagittariorum, Dessau, i 2585
COH · — PR cohors praetoria, — VIG vigilum; — VRB urbana
COIR coiraverunt
COL collega, collegium; Collina (tribu); colonia, p. 220; columbarium
COL · BEN colonia Beneventum, — DAC — Dacica, — FL · AVG — Flavia Augusta (Puteoli), — HEL — Heliopolitanorum, Helvetiorum, — Helvia (Lilybaeum), — IVL · G — Iulia Gemina (Accis *vel* Acci, Wilm. 1056, *Guadix*), — I · V · T — Iulia Victrix Triumphalis (Tarraconensis), — SAR(M) — Sarmizegetusa, — SARN · MILEV — Sarniensis Milevitana (Numidia), — SEP — Septimia (Africa), — SIP — Sipontinorum (Sipontum), — TARR — Tarraconensis, — VAL — Valentia, — VEN — Veneria (Rusicade, Cirta), — VEN · COR — Veneria Cornelia (Pompeii), — VLP · OESC — Vlpia Oescensis (in Moesia); COL · SER coloniae servus
COL · CENT collegium centonariorum; — FAB — fabrum
COL · HORR coloniae horrearius, — L(IB) — libertus(-a), p. 220
COLL Collina (tribu, p. 215); collegium, — AER — aerariorum, — CENT — centonariorum, — FAB(R) — fabrum; — S · S — supra scriptum
COM comes, — S · C — sacri consistorii; COM commentariensis,

— L commentariorum loco; COM commilitoni; C·O·M cum omnibus meis
CON constat (*App.* v 41); coniugi; — B·M — bene merenti, — KAR — carissimo(ae)
COND conductor, -ductio
CONL conlegium
CONS consul (cent. 3), — ORD — ordinarius; consularis, — MEM·V consularis memoriae vir; CONSS consule, consulibus (in or after Diocletian)
COR co(ho)rtis, -te
COR Cornelia (tribu, p. 215); -us; OOR Cornelia
COR corona, — AVR — aurea, — CLASS — classica, — MVR — muralis, — VALL — vallaris
COR(N) *vel* CORNIC (*App.* v 47) cornicularius, — PR — praefecti, — S·PR — subpraefecti, — TR(IB) — tribuni
CORP·CVST corporis custos
CORR corrector (p. 224)
COS consul (pp. 135, 194, 223), consulibus, consularis (*App.* v 27); COS·AMPL — amplissimus, — ORD — ordinarius; COS·A·A·S·E·V consul alter ambove si eis videretur; COSS consullbus
COS·AD·LEG·II·AD, (C·R cives Romani) consistentes ad legionem II adiutricem (Wilm. 2411)
C·P Castor (et) Pollux; castra peregrina; censoria potestate (*App.* v 41); clarissimus puer (p. 193); coniugi pientissimae
C·P·F (legio) Claudia pia fidelis (*App.* v 10)
C·P·P conductor publici portorii
C·R civis(es) Romanus(i), civitas Romana
C·R·M cives Romani Mogontiaci (*Mayence, Mainz*)
C·R·P curator rei publicae
CRV Crust- (*vel* Clust)umina (tribu)
C·S carus suis (p. 64); coniugi(s) suae (*App.* v 30); cum suis
C·S·O cum suis omnibus
C·T civitas Tolosa (*Toulouse*)
C·T(R) codicillarius tribuni; C·TR(E) civitas Treverorum (*Trèves, Trier*)
C·V clarissimus vir (p. 193, *App.* v 32); civitas (*vel* colonia) Viennensis; civitas Vlpia

CV (C·V) cura, curator
CVB (IC or ICV) cubicularius
CVR curavit, curaverunt, curante, curantibus, curator -tores (p. 224; *App.* v 53); curia
CVR·AER curator aerarii, — ALV·TIB alvei Tiberis, — ANN annonae, — IVV iuventutis, — MIN Miniciae, — P·P pecuniae publicae, — R·P rei publicae, — VIAR viarum (p. 120)
CVR·AG curam agente
CVST custos
C·V·T·P colonia Vlpia Traiana Poetovio (Pannonia superior, *Pettau*)
CYR Cyrene, Cyrenaia (legio)

D

D Dacia; Decimus; decreto; decuria, decurio(nes); dat, dedit, p. 86, dederunt, datum; defunctus; denarius; designatus; deus, dea; December; dies, die, diebus; dignus; discens; divus; dixit; Dolichenus; dominus; Domitius; domo; donum, donat, donatus; duplarius; dux
Ð defunctus; quingentaria (ala); dicit; dies; domo
D·A defunctus annorum ...; deae Augustae; deo aeterno
DAC Dacia, Dacicus; DA·M Dacicus maximus
DAT·COLL·S·S datum collegio supra scripto
D·C decreto conscriptorum; decurionum consulto (*vel* consensu); decurio civitatis, coloniae
D·C·R·MOC decurio civium Romanorum Mogontiaci; cp. C·R·M
D·C(OLL)·S de collegii sententia
D·C·S de conscriptorum (*vel* consilii) sententia
D·C·S·C de conscriptorum sententia curaverunt
DD dedicatum
D·D damnas damnates; dare debebit; dea Dia; dea Diana; decreto decurionum (p. 109; *App.* v 19, 34, 38, 46, 56, 59); dedit, dedicavit; dis deabus; donum (*vel* dono) dedit etc. (pp. 85 f); domini duo; domus divina (*App.* v 20): decreto decurionum *et* dono dat *in eodem titulo* Dessau, ii 5918

D·D·D datum decreto decurionum; deo donum dedit; domini tres; dono dedit dedicavit (p. 86); duplum dare debeto

D·D·D·ADL *vel* **ALLECT** decreto decurionum decurio adlectus

D·D·D·E·S dare damnas (damnates) esto (sunto), cp. *App.* v 60

DDDNNN domini nostri tres

D·D·H·C decreto decurionum hic consecravit

D·D·L·D·D·D dono dedit (*vel* dedit dedicavit) loco dato decreto decurionum (*App.* v 49)

D·D·L·M dono dedit libens merito

DDNN domini nostri duo

D·D·P decreto decurionum publice, — **P(EC)·P(VB)** pecunia publica (*App.* v 36); — **P·P** permissu proconsulis (?); p. 292, n. 5

D·D·Q dedicavitque

D·D·S de decurionum sententia; — **F·C** faciundum curavit

D·D·S·P dedit de sua pecunia

D·D·V·L·L·M dono dedit votum laetus libens merito (Wilm. 1572)

DEC· December; decessit; decreto; decuria, -alis; decurio, -ones, -onatus; **DECC** decuriones; **DEC· DEC** decurialis decuriae; decurionum decreto

DE CONL·SENT de collegii sententia

DE C·S de consilii sententia

DED dedit; **DED(IC)** dedicavit, dedicatus etc.

DED·XX·P·R·D (*App.* v 40) deducta vicesima populi Romani dedit

DEF defunctus (p. 196)

DEP depositus

DE PAG·SEN·FAC·COER (cp. *App.* v 53) de pagi sententia faciundum coerarunt

D·E·R de ea re, — **I·C** ita censuerunt

DES designatus

DE S·P de sua pecunia

DE S(EN)·S(ENT) de senatus sententia

D·F dare facere; decima facta; de figlinis; dulcissimae filiae; dabit fisco

DIC dicavit; **DIC·N·M·Q** dicatus numini maiestatique

DIC(T) dictator

DIF(F) diffusum (vinum) p. 155

DIG(N) dignus

D·I·M dis inferis Manibus

D·I(NV)·M deo invicto Mithrae (p. 91)

DIM dimidia

D·M dolus malus: — **A** abesto, — **ET·I·C** et ius civile, *perscr. C.I.L.* vi (2) 8862 = Bruns, *Fontes*, 141, 4 (Gradenwitz, *Simulacra*, xxxi *b*); *vel* iuris consultus, *perscr.* Dessau, ii 8365: domino meo (*collar. serv.*), Bruns, 159, 2 (Gradenwitz, xxxiv)

D(IS)·M(AN) dis Manibus (pp. 62, 64, 77); — **ET M** et memoriae; — **S** sacrum (p. 62, *App.* v 3)

DIS(P) dispensator; dispunctor

D·L dat libens

D·M·ID (mater) deum magna Idaea

D·N dominus noster, -na nostra

D·N·M(AI)·E *vel* **M(AI)·Q(VE)·E(IVS)** devotus numini maiestatique eius (p. 91, *App.* v 37)

DO domesticus; domino; donum, donatus

DOL doliaris; Dolichenus (p. 90)

DON donavit; **DON DON** donis donatus

D·P de praediis; de pecunia; dis penatibus; donum posuit

D·P·E devotus pietati eius

D·P·P de pecunia publica

D·P(AG)·S de pagi sententia (*App.* v 53)

D·P·S de pecunia sua (p. 88), — **D** dedit *vel* dedicavit, — **D·D** dono dedit, *vel* dedit dedicavit (*App.* v 57), — **F·D** factam dedit (*ib.*), — **P** posuit

D·Q decurio quaestor

D·Q·L·S·T·T·L dic qui legis: sit tibi terra levis (Spain and Africa, Wilmanns, 180 n); p. 293

D·R·P dignum rei publicae (*App.* v 44)

D·S de suo, — **D** dedit; — **D·D** dono (-num) dedit (*vel* dedicavit, *vel* dedit dedicavit); — **EX V·P** ex voto posuit; — **F** fecit, — **F·C** (*App.* v 18) faciundum curavit, — **L·L·M** laetus libens merito, — **P** posuit; — **L·D·D·D** loco dato decreto decurionum; — **R** restituerunt

D·S·I·M (p. 91; *App.* v 28) Deo Soli invicto Mithrae

D·S·P de sua pecunia; — **D** dedit, — **D·D** dono dedit; — **EX D·D** ex decreto decurionum; — **F** fecit,

— F·C faciundum curavit (*App.* v 46); — P posuit; — R·C reficiunda curavit (*ib.* 48)
D·S·S de senatus sententia; — F·C (cp. p. 118) faciundum curavit
D·T·S di te servent (Wilm. 2880)
D(VM)·T(AX) dumtaxat
D·V(IR)·I·D duo(um)vir iure dicundo; DVO·VIR duoviris (p. 160)
DVP(L) duplarius, duplicarius, p. 228
D·V·S·F·C·I·Q·P (*App.* v 52) de vici scitu (*vel* sententia) faciundum curarunt idemque probarunt
D·XX·P·R deducta vicesima populi Romani (*App.* v 58)

E

EE·QQ equites; — RR — Romani
E·F egregia femina (p. 194)
E·M ex monitu (? Dessau, ii 3545)
E(G)·M·V egregiae memoriae vir (cp. Wilmanns, 214 n)
E·H·L·IVS·POT ex hac lege ius potestasque esto; E·H·L·N·R eius hac lege nihil rogatum
EID Idus
EM·V eminentissimus vir
EN endotercisus (dies)
EQ eques, equestris, equitata; EQ·C·R (cohors) equitata civium Romanorum
EQ·P(VB) equo publico (cp. *App.* v 43); — EXOR exornatus (p. 191)
EQQ equites; EQ·R eques Romanus; — E(Q)·P(VBL) equo publico; EQ·R·S eques Romanus singularis, p. 75 f
E·R·A ea res agitur; — C consule(-a)tur (cp. *App.* v 60)
E R·P e re publica; — V videri
E S·C·R·C e senatus consulto reficiendum curavit
E·S·F·S·F·L ei sine fraude sua facere liceto
ESQ Esquilina (tribu, p. 215)
E·T ex testamento; — F fecit
E·V egregius vir
EV(OC) evocatus
EX A·C ex aere collato
EX(A)·AD·CAS(TO) exactum ad Castoris (p. 143)
EX AVC(T) ex auctoritate
EX C·C ex conscriptorum consulto
EX CC ex ducenario; — CCC trecenario (p. 226)

EX D·D ex decreto decurionum, — ORD ordinis; EX D·F·C (*App.* v 51) — faciundum curavit
EXER·PAN·INF exercitus Pannoniae inferioris
EX FIG(L) ex figlinis (p. 153)
EX IMP ex imperio
EX I·P ex imperio posuit
EX IV ex iussu (p. 88)
EX OF(F) ex officina (p. 153)
EX P·L ex pecunia legata
EX P·P ex pecunia publica; — F·C faciundum curavit, -erunt (*App.* v 59)
EX PR ex praediis; exceptor praefecti
EX R ex ratione; — VRB urbica
E(X) S·C ex senatus consulto, pp. 107, 109, 120, 131, 135, 141 (*App.* v 54, 55)
EX T(EST) ex testamento (p. 88)
EX V·DEC ex quinque decuriis
EX V·P ex voto posuit (p. 86); EX VOT·L·POS — libens posuit

F

F faciendum, faciunt, facto, fecit, fecerunt (pp. 86, 109); fastus (dies); feliciter; (legio) fidelis; figlinae; filius, -a, p. 214; fiunt; flamen; Flaviensis, Flavius; fundus
FAB Fabia (tribu, p. 215)
FAB(R) fabri; — CENT centonarii; — TIG(N) tignarii
FAC·COER faciundum coeravit, — COIR coiravit; F·C faciundum curavit, -erunt (pp. 86, 109; *App.* v 52 f)
FAL Falerna (tribu); Falernae (vites)
FAM familia; — GLAD gladiatoria
F·B·M filio bene merenti
F·C·I(D)·Q·P faciendum curavit idemque probavit, *App.* v 52 f, p. 118 f
F·D fecit, dedicavit; filio(-ae) dulcissimo(-ae)
F·D·S fecit (fecerunt) de suo
F·D·EX S·C (praefectus) frumenti dandi ex senatus consulto
F·D·S·S·C faciundum de senatus sententia curaverunt
FEB(R) Februarius
FEC fecit, fecerunt; FECErit (*App.* v 60)
FEL Felix (imperator *vel* legio)

FEL·IVL·OLIS Felicitas Iulia Olisipo, *perscr*. Wilm. 973 (*Lisbon*)
FER·LAT feriae Latinae
F·ET·F filii et filiae
F·F faustus felix; filius (filia) fecit, filii fecerunt; Flavia felix (legio); fiscus frumentarius
F·I(VS) fieri iussit
FID(EL) fidelis (legio)
FIG(L) figulus, figlinae (p. 153)
FL Flavius
FL(AM) flamen (p. 223); **FLAM·AVG** flamen Augustalis, *vel* flaminica Augustae (Wilmanns, 2209); — **CLAVD** flamen Claudialis, — **FERON** flaminica Feroniae (*App.* v 42), — **MART** Martialis, — **P(ER)P** perpetuus, — **QVIR** Quirinalis, — — **ROM·ET·AVG** Romae et Augusti
F·LOC faciundum locarunt
F·L·P funus locum publice, Dessau, ii 6473 (cp. Wilmanns, 296 n)
FORT·HORR Fortunae horreorum
F·P filius pientissimus; flamen perpetuus; frumentum publicum; funus publicum; Fortuna primigenia
F·P·C filius ponendum curavit
F·P·D·D Fortunae Primigeniae donum dant
F·P·VET fundus possessoris veteris
FR (*a*) frater, — **ARV** Arvalis (p. 223); (*b*) frumentarius
FR(ET) (legio) Fretensis
FRVM frumentum, -tarius
F·S (*App.* v 30) filii sui
F·S·A (ala) Flavia singularium Antoniniana
F·S·ET·S fecit sibi et suis, — **L·L·P·Q·E** libertis libertabus posterisque eorum (*App.* v 9)
FVL Fulvius
FVL·CON·P fulgur conditum publice
FVL(M)·C·C (legio) Fulminata certa constans
FVN funus

G

G Gaius (p. 89; *App.* v 27, Hübner in *C.I.L.* ii p. 715; Wilmanns, 66; Genius; (legio) Gallica; (legio) Gemina, **G·F** Gemina felix, **G·M·V** Gemina Martia victrix, **G·P·F** Gemina pia fidelis

GAL Galatia; Galeria (tribu, *App.* v 51); **GAL(L)** Gallia, Galliarum (*ib.* 20); **GALL** (legio) Gallica
GE(M) (legio) Gemina, — **P·F** pia fidelis; **SEV** Severiana
GEN Genius; **GEN·ET·HON** genio et honori (p. 109)
GER(M) *vel* **GERMAN** Germania, Germanicus
G·H·L Genius huius loci (*App.* v 26); **G·M** Genius municipii; **G·M·N** Genius municipii Novensium (*Bunovich*); **G·P·R** Genio populi Romani (p. 83); — **F** feliciter (*App.* v 21)
G·S Germania superior

H

H Hercules; heres, heredes; Hispana; homo, homines; hora
H·A haec ara (p. 64); h. aram, domus h. aeterna (Dessau, ii 8180, 8192)
H·ADQ (*vel* **AQ**) hic adquiescit
H·A·H·N·S haec ara heredem non sequetur
H·A·I·R (p. 110; *App.* v. 42) honore accepto impensam remisit, cp. Wilmanns, 301 n 2
H·A·S·A·H·L·L·Q·D·R·IN·A (*App.* v 30) habet aedes Salutis Augustae hoc loco leges quas Dianae Romae in Aventino; cp. p. 164
HAS·PR hastatus prior, — primus, **HAST·POS(TER)** hastatus posterior
H·B·M·F heres bene merenti fecit
H·B·Q hic bene quiescit
H·C hic conditus (*vel* cubat); Hispania citerior (*App.* v 32); honoris causa (p. 109; *App.* v 31); honore contentus, **H·C·I·R** — impensam remisit; **H·C·S·P·P** — sua pecunia posuit (p. 110), **H·C·E** hic conditus est; — **C·E·B·Q** — cineres eius bene quiescant
H·E·N·H heredem exterum non habebit, **H·E·N·S** — non sequetur, p. 64
HER heres, hereditates; **HER·B·M** heres bene merenti: — **P** posuit
H·E·S hic est situs...
H·E(X)·T·F heres ex testamento fecit, **H·E(X)·T·F·C** — faciundum curavit (*App.* v 4)

H·F heres fecit, H·F·C faciundum curavit; H·H·Q heres heredesque; H·P heres posuit, heredes posuerunt; H·P·C heres ponendum curavit
H·F honore functus; honesta femina
H·HQ heres heredesque
HIS(P) Hispana, Hispania
H·L hac lege (*App.* v 60); hic locus (p. 64), huius loci; H·L·D·M·A huic loco' dolus malus abesto (p. 64 f); H·L hic locus (*vel* H·L·ET M hic locus et monumentum, *vel* H·L·S hic locus sepulturae) H·N·S heredem non sequetur
H·L·I·R·Q hac lege ius ratumque (esto)
H·L·O (uti) hac lege oportebit
H·L·R (ante) hanc legem rogatam
H·M hoc monumentum, — A·H·N·P ad heredem non pertinet, — F·C faciundum curavit, — H·N·S heredem non sequetur (p. 64, *App.* v 11; cp. Wilmanns, 280 n; *paene perscr.* Dessau, ii 8401, cp. 8281), — H·E·N·S heredem exterum non sequetur, — S·S· H·N·S sive sepulcrum heredem non sequetur; H·M·D·M·A huic monumento dolus malus abesto; H·M·S·D·M hoc monumentum sine dolo malo: cp. Bruns, *Fontes*, 172, *iura sepulcrorum*, §§ 1—22
H·M·M honesta missione missus (p. 228)
H·N·S heredem non sequetur
HON honor; HON(OR) honoratus
HOR hora; Horatia (tribu, p. 215)
H·O·V·B·Q hic ossa vobis (*vel* volo) bene quiescant
H·P·R hostes populi Romani
H·R·I·R honore recepto impensam remisit; cp. H·A·I·R
H·S hic situs; H·S·B·Q hic situs bene quiescas; H·S·T·F·I hic situs testamento fieri iussit; H·S·E hic situs est (p. 60, *App.* v 4, 5, 6, 8, 10), — H·E(X)·T·F·C heres ex testamento faciundum curavit, — H·F heres fecit, — H·P heredes posuerunt, — O·T·B·Q ossa tua bene quiescant, — O·V· B·Q ossa volo bene quiescant, — S·T·T·L sit tibi terra levis, — T·F·I·H·F·C titulum fieri iussit,

heres faciundum curavit (*vel* H·P heres posuit)
HS sestertius, -os (pp. 55, 199)
H·S·D·M·A huic sepulcro dolus malus abesto
H·S·H·N·S hoc sepulcrum heredem non sequetur; H·S·N·S heredem secundum non sequetur
HS·N (*App.* v 14), or HS·N·V sestertium nummum
H·S·S hic siti sunt
H·T·B·Q hic tumulatus bene quiescas; H·T·H·N·S hic tumulus heredem non sequetur
H·T·F·C heredes testamento fieri curaverunt
H·V (*a*) Hercules Victor (*App.* v 39), H·V·V·S (*ib.* 23) Herculi Victori votum solvit; (*b*) honore usus, H·V·I·R — impensam remisit, — S·R sumptum remisit (*ib.* 43)

I

I invictus (Mithras), p. 91
I, IN, or INL industris (pp. 117, 185)
I·A(GR) in agro, I·A·P in agro pedes (p. 64; *App.* v 10, 11)
I·C·A ius civile (*vel* iuris consultus) abesto (Wilmanns, 271); cp. D·M·A
ID idus
I·D (*a*) iure (old dat. for *iuri*, Dessau, i 2227) dicundo (*App.* v 40, 59), I·D·Q·C·P iure dicundo quinquennalis censoriae potestatis, I·D·Q·Q iure dicundo quinquennalis
I·D (*b*) Iuppiter Dolichenus, I·D·D·D Iovi Dolicheno dono dedit ded(icavit), p. 90
I·D·P iure dicundo prae-est, -erit, -sunt, -erunt
I(D)·Q·P idemque probavit(-averunt) (*App.* v 51 ff), cp. pp. 118 ff
I·F in fronte; I·F·P in fronte pedes; p. 64
I·H·M·I·A·S·C·F in hoc monumentum itum aditum sacrorum causa facere; cp. Bruns, *Fontes*, 172, 45—53
I·L·H ius liberorum habens
I·M invictus Mithras; p. 91, *App.* v 29
IMA imaginifer; IM·C — cohortis
IMM immolaverunt; immunis (p. 229)

IM(P) (*a*) imperator; **IMP · P · Q · R** imperium populusque Romanus; (*b*) **IMP(ET)** impetum; (*c*) **IM · PP** immunis perpetuum
IN A(G) *vel* **AGR · P** in agro pedes
INC · FR · PVBL incisus frumento publico ('relatus in numerum eorum qui frumentum publicum accipiebant', Dessau, i 2163, ii 6065)
IN F(R) *vel* **FRONT · P** in fronte pedes (*App.* v 10, 11; Augustan, Wilmanns, 188 n; p. 64 *supra*)
IN H · D · D (p. 88, *App.* v 20) in honorem domus divinae
IN(L) industris (pp. 117, 185)
INV(I) *vel* **INVICT** invictus
I · O · D Iuppiter optimus Dolichenus
I · O · M Iuppiter optimus maximus (p. 83, *App.* v 26 f), — **CVL** Culminalis, — **D** Depulsor (Wilmanns 1406), Dolichenus (p. 90, *App.* v 24 f), — **FVLM · FVL** Fulminator Fulgurator, — **H** Heliopolitanus (*ib.* 25), — — **A** Augustus, — **S** Suessulanus; — **C · O · D · I** ceterique omnes di immortales
I · O · S · P · D Iovi optimo Soli praestantissimo digno, Dessau, ii 4320
I · S infra scriptus
I · S · M · R Iuno Sospes mater regina
IT item; **IT(ER)** iterum (*App.* v 48, 59)
IVD iudicans, iudex
I · V · E · E · R · P · F · S · V · E ita utei eis e re publica fideve sua videbitur esse
IVN · REG Iuno Regina
IVR iuridicus
IVS iussu

K

K (*a*) Kaeso; (*b*) calendae; (*c*) candidatus; (*d*) castellum
KAL calendae
KAR carissimus, -a; **K · S** carus suis (Spain and Africa, Wilmanns, 184 n)
K · K calumniae causa

L

L latum; legio; leuga; lex; libens; liberatus; libertus(-a) p. 74, 219 f; librarius; locus(-o); longum; Lucius; Lugdunum
L · A (Dessau, ii 3864) 'libens animo' *perscr. ib.* 3513, 3906, 4451, 4455; cp. **LIB · AN**
LAT(ICL), *vel* **LC** laticlavius, p. 223
LAVR · LAV(IN) Laurens Lavinas
L · D · D · C · F · C loco dato decreto collegii fabrum centonariorum;
L · D · D · D (pp. 64, 88, 112; *App.* v 17, 24) — decurionum (cp. Wilmanns, 50 n); **L · D · D · D · P** — decreto decurionum publice; **L · D · DEC · N · R** — nautarum Rhodanicorum
L · D · P loco dato publice, **L · D · P · P · D · D** — pecunia publica, decreto decurionum; **L · D · S · C** — senatus consulto
LEG legatus (p. 224); legavit; legio
LEG · AVG legatus Augusti, — **CENS · ACC** censibus accipiendis (p. 224), — **P(R) · P(R)** pro praetore; **LEG · IVR** legatus iuridicus; **LEG · LEG** legatus legionis (p. 224); **LEG · S · C** legatus senatus consulto; **LEG · S · S** legio supra scripta
LEG · COR lege Cornelia
LEM Lemonia (tribu, p. 215)
LIB libellorum; Liber; liberatus; libertus (p. 219 f); librarius; liburna
LIB · AN (Dessau, ii 3659), **LIB · ANIMO** *ib.* 3390 f, libens (*non* libenti) animo
LIBR libris; **LIBR · COMM** librarius commentariensis
L · L laetus libens; Laurens Lavinas (*vel* Laurentes Lavinates, p. 227); Lucii libertus; liberti libertus
L · L · M laetus libens merito
L · L · P · (*vel* P · Q·)E libertis libertabusque eorum posterisque eorum (p. 65, cp. *App.* v 9)
L · M libens merito (Plautus, *Persa*, ii 3, 1; *App.* v 22), — **V · S** — votum solvit: libertus meus; locus monumenti (p. 64); ludus magnus
LO(C) locus; **LOC · DAT · D · D** locus datus decreto decurionum; **LOC · EMPT** — emptus; **LOC · MONVM** — monumenti; **LOC · SEP** — sepulturae (p. 64); **LOC · ACCEP · D · D** loco accepto decreto decurionum; **LOC · D** loco dato;
L · PVB loco publico; **L(OC) · P(VBL) · P(ERSEQ)** locorum publicorum persequendorum
L · P · Q locus pedum quadratorum;
L · Q · P locus quadratus pedes —
L · S locus sepulturae

ABBREVIATIONS

L·S·PR librarius subpraefecti;
L·T(R) — tribuni
LV Lucius
LVC Lycia; LVC(IL) Lucilla
LVG(VD) Lug(u)dunum, -dunensis
L·V·M·S libens votum merito solvit

M

M (legio) Macedonica, Minervia; magister; maiestas; maiora; Marcus; mares; maximus; memoriae; menses, -ibus; metalla; miles; mille, millia; Mithras (*App.* v 28); modii; monumentum; mortua; muliebri; municipium; murmillo
M Manius (pp. 38, 60, 100 n. 1, 120, 171, 208), Mania
M·A·A municipium Aurelium Apulum, Wilm. 2419, Apulum in Dacia; M·A·C — Aelium Cetium, *ib.* 2462, Cetium in Noricum
MAC Macedonia; (*legio*) Macedonica
MAE(C) Maecia (tribu, p. 215)
MAG magister, -tri (*App.* v 52), -terium, -tratus; MAG·AVG magister Augustalis; MAG·COL magister collegii; MAGG magistri, -tratus; MAG·QQ (*vel* QVIN) magister quinquennalis; MAG·VIC magister vici
MAM Mamercus (p. 209)
MART·VICT (legio) Martia Victrix
MAT mater; MAT·F·F·CAR — fecit filio carissimo (*App.* v 3); MATR matri
MAV Mavortius
M·A·V municipium Aelium Viminacium (in Moesia)
MAVR·CAES Mauretania Caesariensis
MAX maximus
M·B (*a*) mihi bene (Mommsen in Dessau, ii 4493, *al.* malis bene, *propter errorem* (*ut videtur*) in *C.I.L.* viii 9182, b. b. et mal. b.; cp. B·B)
(*b*) municipium Bergomatium, Wilm. 2178 (*Bergamo*)
M·C mater castrorum; matri carissimae; Mauretania Caesariensis; memoriae causa; miles cohortis —; municipii cultoribus
M·D mater deum; M·D·M mater deum magna; M·D·M·I(D) mater deum magna Idaea (*App.* v 29)

MED Medicus; medicus; Mediolanum
MEM(OR) memoria, -am (*App.* v 58)
MEN(EN) Menenia (tribu, p. 215)
MEN mensa; mensor
MEN(S) *vel* MES menses -ibus
M·EQ milliaria equitata (cohors)
MER merita, merens, meritus
MET metalla
M·F miles factus; munere functus; municipium Flavium (e.g. Arva in Spain, Wilm. 2320)
M·H·M missus(i) honesta missione
MIL miles, militavit (*App.* v 4); MIL(L) millia
MIN (legio) Minervia; minister, -tri; minor; minus
MIN(IC) Miniciae, p. 224
MISS missio; missus, MISS·HON·M missus honesta missione
MM Marci duo; M·M malis male (cp. B·B); mater magna; municipes municipii
M·N millia nummum
MOD modii
MOG Mogontiacum, *Mayence*
MON monetalis; MON(V) monumentum (for synonyms, see Wilmanns, 211 n); MON·SAC monitor sacrorum
MONT·P·C (cohors) montanorum pia constans
M·P millia passuum (pp. 55, 138, 197); memoriam (monumentum) posuit; maior pars
M·P·F (legio) Minervia pia fidelis
M·V municipium Verulanum, Wilm. 2077, Verulae (Hernicorum)
M·VIC municipium Vicetinorum (*Vicenza*)
M·V·F monumentum vivus fecit, — uxori fecit; maritus uxori fecit
M·LIB mulieris libertus
MVL mulier
MVL·XX multis (votis) vicennalibus, Dessau, i 695 (cp. p. 127 *supra*)
MVN munere; municipium
MVR murmillo
MVT Mutinenses

N

N natalis; natione, natus; nauta; Nemausensis; nepos; niger; nomine; nonis; noster; numen;

Numerius (p. 160); numerus, numero; numerat; Numidia; nummus, -i, -ûm (*App.* v 14, 38)
NA(T) natus (*App.* v 4); natione
N·C Numidia Constantina, — Cirtensis
N·D·A·N·M(OR) nullum dolorem accepi nisi morte (cp. Orelli, 4640, *C. I. L.* ii 2994; cp. p. 205)
N·D·N·AVG numen domini nostri Augusti
NEG negotiator, — **FRV** frumentarius, — **PAENVL** paenularius, — **STIP·ARG** stipis argentarii
NEM Nemausus (*Nîmes*)
NEP Nepos
N·E·S·D numini eius semper devotus
N·F·(F·)N·S·N·C non fui, (fui,) non sum, non curo (*App.* v 12, Dessau, ii 8162 n)
N·MQ·E·D numini maiestatique eius dicatissimus (*perscr.* Dessau, i 570) *vel* devotus
NN nostri; **N·N** numerus noster
NOB·CAES nobilissimus Caesar; **NOBB·CAESS** nobilissimi Caesares; **NOB·FEM** nobilissima femina
NON nonae
Nᴾ ?nefas, feriae publicae, p. 173 n. 1
N·P nobilissima puella
N·R(HOD) nauta Rhodanicus
N·S (*App.* v 30) nomine suo
N·S·S numerus supra scriptus
N·S·S·I·M numini sancto Solis invicti Mithrae (Dessau, ii 4207), p. 91
NVM Numerius; numerus, -o; nummûm

O

O, **Θ**, **Ø**, **⊕** obiit, obitus (p. 62); *perscr.* obito, -ae, -is, Dessau, ii 8516, 7465, 7538
O officina; optimo; optio (p. 77); ostium; ovo
OB obiit
OB H(ON) ob honorem
O· (*vel* **O·E·**) **B·Q** ossa (eius) bene quiescant
O·C·S ob cives servatos
O·D opus doliare; **O·D·D·F·D·L** opus doliare de figlinis Domitiae Lucillae (p. 153)
OF officina; **OF·AVR** — Aureliana
OFEN Oufentina (tribu)

OFF officina (-nator); **OFF·PA(PI)** — Papiri: **OFF·RAT** — rationum
OFF·PVB officium publicum
O·H·S ossa hic sita; **O·H·S·S** — sunt
OL(L) olla; **OLL·D** ollas dedit
O·M ob memoriam; optime merito; optimus maximus
O·M·C·P·F·V·C·C·T·VE oppido, municipio, colonia, praefectura, foro, vico, conciliabulo, castello, territoriove (*lex Rubria*)
O·N·F omnium nomine faciundum
O·O(RN)·D(EC) ornatus ornamentis decurionalibus
OP(T) optio; **OP·CO** — cohortis; **OP·PR** — principis
OP·D(O) *vel* **DOL** opus doliare (p. 153)
OPER·PVB operum publicorum (p. 224)
OPT optimus, -a; optio
ORD ordinarius; **ORD·N** ordo noster
O·REST orbis restitutor (of Constantius, 305 f A.D.)
ORN ornatus, ornamenta; **ORN·DEC** ornamenta decurionalia
OST Ostiensis, -es
Ȯ·S·T·T·L opto sit tibi terra levis
O·T (*vel* **V**)·**B·Q** ossa tibi (vobis *vel* volo) bene quiescant (*App.* v 8)
O·V optimus vir; ornatus vir; oro vos; **O·V·F** oro vos faciatis (p. 161); **O·V·F·D·R·P** — dignum re publica (on Pompeian election placards, p. 161, *App.* v 44)
OVF (pp. 196, 215; *App.* v 22) Oufentina (tribu)

P

P pagus; passus (p. 138); pater; patronus; pecunia; pedes (pp. 131, 138, 160); periit; pius, pientissimus; pondo (p. 143); populus; posuit (p. 86), -uerunt; praefectus, p. 225; (legio) primigenia; procurator; provincia; publice, -us, -a; Publius; pugnarum
P·A (*App.* v 19) provinciae Africae
PAG pagus, pagani; pagina
PAL(AT) Palatina (tribu, p. 215, *App.* v 23); **PAL** palatium; pallium

PAN(N) Pannonia; PAN·INF — inferior
PAP Papiria (tribu, p. 215)
PAR parentes; Parentium; Parilia
PAR·M Parthicus maximus; PART(H) *vel* PARTHIC Parthicus
PAT (*a*) patricii; (*b*) patronus, PAT·COL — coloniae, PAT·ET CVR — et curator, PAT·MVN — municipii
PATR patronus, PATR O — centuriae, — COL coloniae, — COL·R·P·R coloniae rei publicae Riciniensis, — MVN municipii
PATRIC patricii
P·B·B·M·T·I patri bono bene merenti testamento iussus
P·B·P(R) principalis beneficiarius praefecti
P·C patres conscripti; patronus civitatis (*vel* coloniae, *App*. v 49); (legio *vel* cohors) pia constans; ponendum curavit (pp. 65, 109); potestate censoria; post consulatum
P·COL patronus coloniae
P·D·D publice decreto decurionum (p. 109)
P·D·D·E populo dare damnas esto
P·D·S posuerunt de suo
P·E puer egregius (p. 194); posteri eius
PEC (*vel* PEQ) pecunia
PED pedes; pedites, peditata (cohors)
P·E·Q·R·M patronus (eques Romanus) municipii
PER Percennius; peregrinus; permissu
PERP perpetuus
PERS(IC) Persicus
P·F (legio *vel* cohors) pia fidelis (p. 154); P·F·C·R (cohors) pia fidelis civium Romanorum; P·F pia felix (p. 154); P·F·F pia felix fidelis; P·F·F·AET — aeterna
P·F(EL) Pius Felix (imperator), Commodus, 'Caracalla', 'Heliogabalus' etc.
P·F·V Pius Felix Victor (imp.)
P·G·N provincia Gallia Narbonensis
PHAL phalerae
P·H·C (*App*. v 32) provinciae Hispaniae citerioris
P·H·O·ADQ·E·R·P·V placere huic ordini adque e re publica videri

PI pius, PI·F·F (legio) pia felix fidelis; P·I poni iussit; Pannonia inferior
PIC Picenum
P·I·D praefectus iure dicundo (*App*. v 19)
PIL pilus; PIL·POST pilus posterior
PIS Pisaurenses
P·I·S pius in suos (p. 64; Spain and Africa, Wilmanns, 184 n, cp. *App*. v 5)
P·K praetor candidatus
PL placuit
P·L provincia Lugdunensis
P·L·L posuit laetus libens
PL·M(IN) plus minus
PL(VE) SC plebei(ve) scita
P·M patronus municipii; plus minus, p. 63; pontifex maior *vel* maximus (*App*. v 37)
P·M·C provincia Mauretania Caesariensis
P·M·F patri merenti fecit
P·N provincia Numidia; P·N·C — Constantina
P·O princeps optimus
POB Poblilia (tribu), p. 215
POL Pollia (tribu), p. 215
POM Pomptina (tribu) (*App*. v 27)
PON·CENS *vel* CVR ponendum censuit *vel* curavit
PONT(IF) pontifex; PONT·MAX — maximus (p. 223); PONT·M·M — municipum municipii
POP populus; — S populi servus
PORT porticus; *raro* portus (COR Cornelii, Dessau, ii 8660)
POS posuit; POS·D·S posuerunt de suo
POST Postumus
P·P pater patriae (*App*. v 37, 38, 56); pater patrum; pecunia publica; permissu proconsulis; pendent pondo; praefectus praetorio (p. 185); praeses provinciae; populus Parmensis; primus pilus (*App*. v 22), primipilus, -laris; pro parte; pro pietate (p. 64); pro praetore; provincia Pannonia; publicum portorium
PP perpetuus; praepositus (*App*. v 20)
P·P·F (legio) primigenia pia fidelis
P·P·F·C pecunia publica faciundum curavit; P·P·F·D·D — fecerunt dedicarunt

P·P·L Publiorum duorum libertus; praeses provinciae Lusitaniae
P·P·N praeses provinciae Numidiae; — **M·C** Mauretaniae Caesariensis
PPO praefectus praetorio
P·P·P proconsul, pater patriae; propria pecunia posuerunt; pecunia publica posuit
P·P·P·C primipilaris, patronus coloniae
P·P·R praeses provinciae Raetiae
P·P·S provincia Pannonia superior
PP·VV perfectissimi viri, p. 193 f; piae vindices (legiones)
P·Q pedes quadrati; populusque
P·Q·Q·V pedes quoquo versus
P·Q·R populusque Romanus
P·R populus Romanus; post reditum *vel* pro reditu (Wilmanns, 2445)
PR praedium; praefectus (pp. 223, 225); praetor (*App.* v 33), praetores; praetorius, -oria; pridie; (legio) primigenia; primus; pro; probante; procurator; promotus; provincia
P·R provincia Raetia
PRAE(F) praefectus, pp. 223, 225, 227; *App.* v 39; **PRAEF·AEG** — Aegypti, **AER** — aerarii, — **ANN** — annonae, — **CAP·CVM** — Capuam Cumas, — **CL** — classis, p. 228, — **F·D** frumenti dandi, p. 225, — **I·D** — iure dicundo; — **PRAET** — praetorio, p. 227, — **TIR** — tironum, — **V(RB)** — urbi, — **VIG** — vigilum; **PRAEFF** praefecti
PR·BR·LON (publicani) provinciae Britanniae Londinienses, p. 154
PRAEP praepositus; **PRAEP·P·FRVM** — publici frumenti *vel* pecuniae frumentariae
PR·AER praefectus aerarii; praetor aerarii (p. 223)
PRAES praeses; praesentes
PRAET praetor,-orius(a); **PRAETT** praetoriae
PRAT pratum
PR·CER·I(VR)·D(IC)·QQ praetor cerialis iure dicundo quinquennalis (at Beneventum)
P·R·C·A post Romam conditam anno (Dessau, ii 5025)
PR·CAND praetor candidatus
PR·COS proconsul

PR·C·R praetoria civium Romanorum (ala)
PR·DES praetor designatus
PRI pridie; primus, -a; princeps
PR·I·D praefectus (praetor) iure dicundo
PRI(MIG) (legio) primigenia (p. 154)
PRINC princeps; principalis; **PRINC·PRAET** princeps praetorii; **PRINC·PEREG** — peregrinorum
PR·IVV praetor iuventutis; **PR·IV(EN)** princeps iuventutis
PR·K praetor candidatus; **PR·K·TVT** — tutelaris; **PR·PER** — peregrinus; **PR·VRB** — urbanus (p. 223)
PRO proconsul; procurator; pronepos; provincia; proficiscetur, Wilm. 1482
PROB probavit, -erunt; probante
PROC *vel* **PROCO** *vel* **PROCOS** (*App.* v 33) *vel* **PROCOSS** proconsul
PROC procurator; **PROC·AD B** — ad bona; — **P·V** — portus utriusque; — **IIII P·A** — quattuor publicorum Africae
PRO·M processum meritus; **PROM** promotus
PRON pronepos (pp. 72, 214)
PRO·PR propraetor (*App.* v 54)
PRO PR·EX·S·C pro praetore ex senatus consulto
PROQ proquaestor
PRO S pro salute, p. 88
PROT protector
PROV provincia; provocator, **PROV·SP** provocator spectavit (*vel* spectator), Dessau, ii 5084
PROX·CIPP proximus cippus
PR·PER praetor peregrinus
PR·P·R praetor populi Romani
PR·POS(T) princeps posterior
PR·P·F (legio) primigenia pia fidelis
PR·PR praefectus praetorio; pro praetore (p. 224; *App.* v 37)
PR·P·V (cohors) praetoria pia vindex
P·R·Q populus Romanus Quiritium, p. 223
PR·V praefectus vigilum
PR·VRB praetor urbanus
PR·XX·LIB procurator vicesimae libertatis
P·S Pannonia superior; pater sacrorum (*App.* v 29); pecunia sua (*ib.* 47); provincia Sicilia; **P·S·F**

(*ib.* 24) pecunia sua fecit: **P·S·F·C**
— faciundum curavit, **P·S·P** posuit, **P·S·P·D** — posuit dedicavit
P·S pro salute, p. 88, — **D·D**
— domus divinae; — **D·N** — domini nostri; **P·S·S·P** — sua posuit; — **S·S** — sua (et) suorum
P·V perfectissimus vir, p. 193 f; (legio, cohors, classis) pia vindex; praefectus urbi (pp. 185, 193); praetor urbanus; portus uterque
P·V·A pius vixit annis
PVB(L) publicus, -ca, -ce
PVB Publilia (tribu, p. 215)
PVB·P·R·Q (augur) publicus populi Romani Quiritium (Dessau, ii 4153)
PVP Pupinia (tribu, p. 215); Pupus

Q

Q quaestor (p. 223, *App.* v 33), quaestoricius; quando; que; qui; quinquennalis; Quintus; Quirina (tribu); quondam
Q·A quot annis
Q·A(ER) quaestor aerarii; **Q·ALIM** — alimentorum; **Q·C·V** — coloniae Viennae
Q·B·F·F quod bonum felix faustum (sit)
Q·D quondam, p. 292
Q·D·A qua *vel* quibus de agitur
Q·(D·E·R·)F·P·D·E·R·I·C quid (de ea re) fieri placeret, de ea re ita censuerunt (p. 161, *App.* v 45)
Q·D·R qua de re; — **A** agitur
Q·E qui (quae) est
Q·E·R·E·T·P (*App.* v 60) quanti ea res erit, tantam pecuniam
Q·F qui fuit; quo facto
Q·F·P·D·E·R·I·C quid fieri placeret, de ea re ita censuere
Q·I(NF)·S·S quae infra scripta sunt
Q·K quaestor candidatus
Q·M quo minus
Q·M(IL) qui militavit; **Q·M·C** qui militare coeperunt
Q·P·P quaestor pecuniae publicae
Q·PR quaestor provinciae—(p. 223); **Q·PR·PR** quaestor pro praetore (*ib.*)
Q·Q (*App.* v 27) Quinti; **QQ(Q·Q)** quinquennalis (-es) (*ib.* 39), p. 197; quinquennalitas (*App.* v 38); — **C·M** — corporis mensorum; — **C·P** censoria potestate (*ib.* 41);

P (*ib.* 19) praefectus; — **P·P(PER)** — perpetuus(-i), p. 229
QQ(Q·Q·)V·P quoquo versus pedes; — **L·P** locus pedum; (*App.* v 6, 7)
Q·R·C·F quando rex comitiavit, fas (p. 173)
Q·R·T·P·D·S·T·T·L qui rogat te, praeteriens dicas: sit tibi terra levis
Q·S qui (quae) supra
Q·S·P·P·S qui sacris publicis praesto sunt
Q·S·S·S qui subscripti (*vel* supra scripti) sunt
Q·V· (*vel* **VIX**) **A** qui (quae) vixit annis(os) — (p. 63)
QVADR quadrigae
QVAE(S) *vel* **QVAEST** quaestor; **QVAEST·SAC·P·ALIM** quaestor sacrae pecuniae alimentariae
QVAESIT·IVD quaesitor iudex
QVANTI·E·R·E·T·P quanti ea res erit, tantam pecuniam
Q·V·F·S quod verba facta sunt
QVI(R) Quirina (tribu, *App.* v 39, pp. 215, 218); **QVIR** Quirites
QVIN quinquennium, -nalis, -nalitas
QVINQ quinquies; quinquennalis
Q·VRB quaestor urbanus (p. 223)
QVM cum (*App.* v 25)

R

R ratio; restituit; retiarius; retro; revocatus; Romanus; rubrica; rubrum; rufus; russata (factio)
R(A) *vel* **RAP** (legio) rapax
RAT ratio (rationalis); **R·D·A** ratio dominica Augusta
R·C reficiendum curaverunt
REBELLES·H·H·P·P rebelles hostes publicos (Haverfield in Dessau, iii p. clxxiv, 1140)
REC·PROV rector provinciae
REF refecit; **REFIC·D·C·S·C** reficiendas de conscriptorum sententia curaverunt
REG regio
RES(T) restituit (*App.* v 47)
RES·P res publica; **RES·P·C·L·F** res publica coloniae Lambaesitanae fecit
RET retiarius
REVOC revocatus
RHOD Rhodanici
ROG rogat, rogant
ROM Romanus; Romilia (tribu, p. 215)

ROS ιυsalia (Dessau, ii 6719)
R·P ratio privata; retro pedes
R·P res publicae (p. 224; *App.* v 38);
R·P·C (*ib.* 34) rei publicae constituendae; **R·P·C·L** res publica coloniae Lambaesitanae; **R·P·M·D** — municipii Dianensium; **R·P·N** — nostra; **R·P·P·D·D** — Phuensium decreto decurionum; **R·P·P·R·Q** populi Romani Quiritium; **R·P·R** — Ricinensis
R·R (p. 141; *App.* v 55) recto rigore (Dessau, ii 5922–4; cp. rect. rigore, *ib.* 5932 : recta regione *semper perscr. ib.* 5936, 5946[8-9])
R·T ripa Thraciae

S

S sacerdos; sacrum, p. 83; salus; scripsit; secundae; semis; sententia; Servius; servus (p. 219); sestertium -a; (legio) Severiana; Severus; sextarius; Sextus; sibi; singuli; spectabilis (p. 117); Spurius; suus, sui cet
S·A Salutis Augustae (*App.* v 30); legio (*vel* cohors) Severiana Alexandriana
SA(L) Salvius
SAB Sabatina (tribu, p. 215)
SAC sacerdos (**SAC·P** sacerdos publicus; **SAC·VRB** sacerdos urbis); sacer, sacrum; sacravit
SACER(D) sacerdos
SACR sacrum; **SACR·FAC** sacris faciundis
S·A(S)·D sub ascia dedicavit (pp. 78—82; *App.* v 13)
SAG sagittarius
SAL salius (p. 224); Salonitani; Salvius; salus; salaria; salinae
SAM Samnis
SAR(M) *vel* **SARMIZ** Sarmizegetusa (in Dacia)
SAR(M) *vel* **SARMAT** Sarmaticus
S·ARK servus arcarius
S·A·S Saturno (*vel* Silvano) Augusto sacrum
S·C sacra cognoscens; senatum consuluerunt; senatus consultum (p. 135; *App.* v 41); singularis consularis; sub cura; summus curator
SCA(P) Scaptia (tribu, p. 215)
S·C·C senatus consulto consuluerunt; **S·C·F·C** — faciundum curaverunt; **S·C·L·D** — locus datus; **S·C·R·C** — restituendum curaverunt; **S·C·P·R** senatus consultum populi Romani
SCRI(B) scriba; scripsit
SC(RIB)·ADF (*App.* v 45) or **ARF** (*App.* iv 1) scribundo ad(r)fuerunt
SCRIB·LIBR·Q scriba librarius quaestorius; **SCRIB·Q·VI·PR** — quaestorius sex primus (Dessau, i 1893); **SCRIB·R·P** — rei publicae
S·CRI·VLL sine crimine ullo
SCY(TH) Scythica (legio)
S·D·L·S·D sacerdos dei Liberi, sacerdos deae
S·D·M (*App.* v 60) sine dolo malo; **SC·D·M** scientem dolo malo (*ib.*)
SEC secundae; secutor; **SEC·H** secundus heres; **SEC·TR** secutor tribuni
SEI·V·E sei videatur eis
SEM semel; semestris
SEN senatus; senior; **SEN·SEN(T)** senatus sententia
SEP Septimius; Septembris
SER (*App.* v 45) Sergius
SER(G) Sergia (tribu, p. 215); **SER** Servius; servus; **SER·4SC** servus contrascriptor; **SER·VIL** servus vilicus
SESQ sesquiplicarius
SE·TR secutor tribuni
S·ET·S sibi et suis, p. 65; **S·ET·S·L(IB)·L(IB)·P(OST)Q·E(OR)** sibi et suis libertis libertabus posterisque eorum
SEV·AVG sevir Augustalis
S(EX) Sextus
SEXM sexmestris
S·F sacris faciundis, p. 223
S·F·S sine fraude sua; — **C·L** capere liceto; — **F·L·I·PQVE·E** facere liceto, ius potestasque esto
S·I stlitibus iudicandis
SIG(N) signifer, p. 228
SIL·SILV Silvano silvestri
SING singuli; singularis, p. 228; **SING·COS** singularis consularis
S·L·L·M solvit laetus libens merito
SL·IVDIK stlitibus iudicandis
S·L·R·I·C·Q·O·O·R·E siremps lex res ius caussaque omnibus omnium rerum esto (*lex Rubria*)
S·M·D sacrum matri deum
S·M·V·S·D·D Soli Mithrae votum solvit, donum dedit (Dessau, ii 4199)
SOD sodalis (p. 224)

SOL·L·M solvit libens merito (*App.* v 22)
SP(E), *vel* **SPECT** spectavit, spectator, spectatus (p. 146 f)
SP Spurius (pp. 60, 208); **SP·F** Spurii filius (pp. 209, 216)
S·P subpraefectus; sua pecunia, **S·P·D·D** sua pecunia dono dedit, **S·P·F** — fecit (*App.* v 56), **S·P·F·C** — faciundum curavit, **S·P·P** — posuit (p. 112); — **D·D** — dedicavit
SPEC speculator (p. 228)
S·P·L senatus populusque Lanuvinus
SPL splendidus (-dissimus); **SPL· EQ·R** splendidus eques Romanus
S·P·P·Q·R senatus populus plebesque Romanus
S·P·P·S sacris publicis praesto sunt
S·P·P·S·F solo privato pecunia sua fecit (Dessau, ii 5612)
S·P·Q senatus populusque, p. 108, — **A** Anagninus, **C** Carsiolitanus, **F** Ferentinus, **R** Romanus (*App.* v 35), **T** Tiburs (*ib.* 39)
S·PR sine pretio
S·P·R sua pecunia restituit
SPR subpraefectus
S·Q·H·A·P·E·S·S·A·V·D·F si quis hanc arcam post excessum supra scriptorum aperire voluerit, dabit fisco — Cp. Bruns, *Fontes,* 172 § 17
SS sestertius
S·S senatus sententia; subscriptus; supra scriptus; sumptu suo
SS·DD·NN salvis dominis nostris (duobus)
S·S·S sicut supra scripsi; summa supra scripta; supra scripta sunt
S·T *vel* **S·TR** secutor tribuni (p. 228)
ST(A) Statius; **ST** stipendia
STAT statio (*App.* v 20); statua
STE(L) *vel* **STELL** Stellatina (tribu, p. 215)
STIP stipendia (*App.* v 10)
STL(IT)·IVD(IC) stlitibus iudicandis
S·T·T·L sit tibi terra levis (pp. 15, 63, 293; *App.* v 5, 6)
S·V spectatus (?) victor (Dessau, ii 5092)
SVB subheres
S(VB)·A(SC)·D(ED) sub ascia dedicavit (pp. 78–82; *App.* v 13)
SVB·PR subpraefectus
SVBSEQ subsequens
SVC Suburana (tribu, p. 215)
S·VE·C senatusve consulto (*App.* iv 4 § 9)
SVM summa (*App.* v 38); **SVM· SVM** summa summarum
SVMP sumptuarius
SVPR·S supra scriptum
S·V·Q sine ulla querella (cp. Wilmanns, 196 n)
S·V·T·L sit vobis (*vel* volo) terra levis

T

T tabula, p. 183; (ala) Tampiana; te; testamentum; tiro; titulus; Titus; tribunus; tumulus; turma
T·A taurus auratus
TAB tabula; tabulatio; **TAB(VL)** tabularius
TAVR taurobolium
TER Teretina (tribu, p. 215); Terminalia; terminus; Tertia; tertiae
TES(S) tesserarius (p. 228)
TEST·IVSS testamento iussit (*App.* v 58)
T·F·I·H·F·C testamento fieri iussit, heres faciundum curavit; — **H·P** heres posuit (*App.* v 10)
THAMV Thamugadina (advocatio)
THIB Thibursicum
THR Threx
T·I·A (de nostris ann. augeat) tibi Iuppiter annos (Dessau, i 451)
TI(B) Tiberius; **TIB** Tibur
TIG(N) tignarius
TIR tiro
TIT titulus
T·M Threx murmillo
T·M·Q·F·E·REV tene me quia fugi, et revoca (cp. Dessau, ii 8726-33; Bruns, *Fontes,* 159 § 2; Gradenwitz, *Simulacra,* xxxiv)
T·P tanta pecunia; termini positi; titulum posuit; tribunicia potestate (*App.* v 37)
T·P·I testamento poni iussit; **T·P· IVSSIT H·F** — heres fecit
T·Q·D totiusque domus
TR Threx; Trebius; tribunus; (— **L·C** laticlavius); trierarcha (p. 228); Tromentina (tribu, p. 215); Traianopolis; Traianus
TR·M(IL), tribunus militum (p. 223), — **PL** plebis; **TR·POT** tribunicia, -ae, potestate, -is
TR(A)·FOR (legio) Traiana fortis
TRAM tramare (= trans mare, Dessau, i 2354)

TRI trierarchus -a (p. 228)
TRIB tribus; tribunus, — **P(L)** plebis (p. 223)
TRI(B)·LAT(IC) *vel* **LATICL** tribunus laticlavius; **TR(IB)·MIL·A·P(OP)** tribunus militum a populo
TRIB·P(OT) *vel* **PT**, *vel* **TR·POT**, tribunicia potestate
TRIB·SVC tribu Succusana, p. 215 n. 4
TRIP Tripontium
TRIVMF *vel* **TRIVMP** triumphator
TRO Tromentina (tribu, p. 215)
T·R·P·D·S·T·T·L te rogo praeteriens dicas, sit tibi terra levis
T·T·L·S terra tibi levis sit (*App.* v 8); *perscr.* Dessau, ii 7286
T·V titulo usus; ture vino
TVB·SAC·P·R tubicen sacrorum populi Romani (p. 227)
TVDER Tudertini
TVL Tullus
TVM tumulus
TVR turma; **TVRR** turres

V

V Valerius; verna; Vibius; vicit; victrix (legio); Vienna; vir; vivus -a; vivit; vixit; votum; vovit; utere; valeat (Diehl, *Pomp. Wand-inschr.* 559)
VA compendio scriptum pro 'vale'; 'va(le) va(le) usque va(le)' (Diehl, *l.c.* 541 f, 554–8; cp. *C.I.L.* vii 1273). Ligature for VA ('vale') in Pompeian *graffiti*, Wilmanns, 1964, 1987, **VAL** *ib.* 1976, 1988
V·A vices agens (**V·A·L** — legati); vixit annis (p. 73; cp. Wilmanns, 168 n)
VAL Valens; Valerius; Valerianus; valetudinarius -um
V·A·S(ACR)·P·P(ROC) viis aedibus sacris publicis procurandis (Dessau, ii 6357 n)
V·B vir bonus (p. 161); **V·B·D·R·P** — dignus re publica; **V·B·O·V·F** virum bonum, oro vos faciatis, p. 161, *App.* v 44
V·B·M·P voto(?) bene merenti posuit (Dessau, i 1594)
V·C vir clarissimus, pp. 108, 185, 193, 205; *App.* v 29; — **D·D** — dedit dedicavit; — **CONS·P·N** — consularis provinciae Numidiae; — **P·P** — pater patrum; — **Q·K** — quaestor candidatus; — **ET INL** — et inlustris, p. 194
V(T)·D·P·R·L·P ut de plano recte legi possit (*App.* v 45, Dessau, ii 6089 li, lxiii)
V·E vir egregius (p. 194); **V·E·A·V·P** — agens vicem praesidis; **V·E·EQ·R** — eques Romanus; **V·E·PP** — primipilaris
VEC vectura; **VEC(T)** *vel* **VECTIG** vectigal
VEL velarius; Velina (tribu, p. 215); velites
V·EM vir eminentissimus, p. 193 f
VER(N) verna
VERB verbeces
VERC Vercellenses
VET veteranus (*App.* v 10); Veturia (tribu, p. 215)
VEX(I) *vel* **(IL)** *vel* **(ILL)** vexillarius; vexillatio, p. 58
V·F verba fecit (*App.* v 45); vivus (-a, -o) fecit, p. 61, *vel* vivi fecerunt; — **S·E·S** — sibi et suis
V·I vir industris, p. 194
VIAT viator, viatorium, viaticum
VI(C)·AVG Victoria Augusta
VIB Vibius
VIC Vicetia, Wilm. 2151, *Vicenza*; vicit; victimarius; victoria (p. 148); vicus, vicani
VICE·S·C vice sacra cognoscens
VICIM vicimagistri (Wilmanns, 2112, =Dessau, ii 7364)
VIC·N victoriatus nummus
VIC·POR vicani Portuenses, Ostia
VICT(R) (legio) victrix
VIG vigiles
VIL vilicus
VIND(EL) Vindelici (cohors)
V·INL vir industris, p. 194; **V·INL·COM** — comes
VIN·VRB·ET OST vinarii urbani et Ostienses
V·I·S verba infra scripta
VIS visu
VIV vivit; **VIX** vixit
V·L veteranus legionis; vir laudabilis
V·L·A·S votum libens animo solvit
V·L·M votum libens merito; **V·L·S** — solvit; **V·L·P** — posuit
VNC(T) unctor
VO Volusus?; Vopiscus?, Wilmanns, p. 402; p. 209 *supra*
VOC Vocontii

VOL(T) Voltinia (tribu, p. 215)
VOL voluntarii (cohors); **VOL·C·R** — cives Romani
VOT Voturia (tribu, p. 215, *App.* v 49)
VOT·X(XX) votis decennalibus (vicennalibus), p. 127
VOTI C·D voti compos dat
V·P vir perfectissimus, p. 193; **V·P·A·V·P** — agens vices praesidis; **V·P·D** — dux; **V·P·P·P· MAVR·SITIF** — praeses provinciae Mauretaniae Sitifensis; — **N·M** — — Norici mediterranei (Dessau, ii 4197); — **N** — — Numidiae; — **R** — Raetiae
V·P (*a*) votum posuit (vota posuerunt); — **L·M** libens merito; — **M** merito; (*b*) vivus posuit
V·Q viator quaestorius (*App.* v 23)
V·Q·R·F·E·V (*App.* v 60) uti quod recte factum esse volet
V·R urbs Roma
VRB urbanus; **VRBB** urbanae (cohortes)
V̄S̄ vir spectabilis, p. 194

V·S (*App.* v 18) votum solvit (*vel* voto soluto); **V·S·L** — libens; **V·S·A·L** (Dessau, ii 3881, 3883); — animo libens; **V·S·L·A** (*ib.* 3874) — libens animo (*perscr.* 3513, 4455 — lib. animo, *ib.* 3390 f); **V·S·L·L·M** — laetus libens merito (p. 83); **V·S·L·M** (*App.* v 16, 25, 27) — libens merito
V·S·P·S·S votum susceptum pecunia sua solvit
V·V (legio) Valeria victrix, Vlpia victrix; Venus Victrix; virgo Vestalis (p. 224); ut voverat (Dessau, ii 3674, 4202)
VV·CC viri clarissimi; — **EE** — egregii; — **PP** — perfectissimi
V·V·V vale, vale, vale (sepulcro inscriptum, p. 197), sed ne **VA** quidem (multo minus **V**) pro 'vale' sepulcris inscribi solitum (vide supra **VA**); ergo placet potius litteras has dubias interpretari, 'vixi, vixi, vixi,' propterea praesertim quod in sepulcris **V** pro 'vixit' passim inventum est

NUMERALS (cp. pp. 54 f, 132, 134, 136; Roby's *Latin Grammar*, i 441, 447–9; and Mommsen, *Ges. Schriften*, vii 765—791).

↓, ⊥, 50. C 100. Ɔ 500, half of ⊕, ∞, 1000. ⊢, I⊃⊃, III 5000, half of ⊕, CCI⊃⊃, IIIII 10,000. Ⓓ, 50,000, half of ⊕, 100,000 (p. 96). |X| 1,000,000. |XI| 1,100,000. |XVI| 1,600,000.

NUMERICAL ABBREVIATIONS

IIS (duo asses et semis, 2½ asses = semis-tertius) sestertius (*App.* v 41). To show that these three signs were used not as letters but as numerals, a short horizontal line was drawn across the middle of all three, making **IIS** resemble **HS**, the equivalent used for convenience in modern print. Similarly, from **X** for 'decem' is derived the crossed X (✶), for 'denarius' (p. 285).

(In inscr. relating to officials) **II** bis, iterum (p. 137); **II·V(IR)** duumvir (*App.* v 19, 51, 59), in Pompeian election placards **II** sometimes stands for 'duumvir'; **III** tertium; **III·V(IR)** triumvir (*ib.* 54); **IIII·VIR** quattuorvir (*ib.* 41, 48, 50); **V·VIR** quinquevir, **VI·**(*vel* IIIIII·)**VIR** sevir (*ib.* 13); **VII·VIR** septemvir; **X·V(IR)** decemvir; **XV·VIR** quindecimvir; **XX·VIRI** viginti viri; **C·V** centumviri.

LX sexagenarius; **C̄** centenarius; **C̄C̄** ducenarius; **C̄C̄C̄** trecen. (p. 226 f).
(Galleys) **III** trieris; **IIII** quadrieris; **V** penteris; **VI** hexeris.
(Taxes) **XX** vicesima (*sc.* pars), — **HER** — hereditatium; — **LIB** — libertatis; — **P·R** — populi Romani (*App.* v 40); **XXXX·G** quadragesima Galliarum; **C** *vel* **O** centesima.

INDEX

A, 47, 200; Aulus, 60, 208
Abbreviated phrases in inscr., 286–90
Abbreviations, 291–311; in dedicatory inscr., 83; epitaphs, 62–5; *Fasti*, 173–6; honorary inscr., 108 ff; municipal decrees, 161; in inscr. on portable objects, 143, 147 f, 154; on public works, 119 f, 138 f; *nomina*, 211; names of freedmen or slaves, 219 f; of Roman tribes, 215; *praenomina*, 60, 209; titles of emperors, 231–56; officials, 222–9; persons of senatorial or equestrian rank, 193 f; sources of error, 196–8
Accius, 36, 71
Accusative, without verb, in honorary inscr., 95
Acta (or *Instrumenta*), 156–188; — *fratrum Arvalium*, 25, 29, 90, 165 f; — *sacrorum saecularium*, 32, 176 f; — *triumphorum*, 176 f
Actium, 171, 172, 271
Adiabenicus, cognomen of Septimius Severus, 247; 'Caracalla', 248; Constantine, 255; Constantinus II, 255
Adlectus inter consulares, 116
Adoption, change of name on, 216 f
Advertisements, 14 f, 57, 150, 161; election placards, 44, 65, 161, 311
Aedes, 'a temple' 118 f, 191, 268 f; list in Dessau iii (2) p. 641
Aedificium, decree of Puteoli on, 160 (*e*); *S.C. de aedificiis* in Rome, 158 (*d*)
Aediles, 223, 228
Aegyptus, 272
Aemilianus, Q. Fabius Maximus (consul 145 B.C.), 97
Aemilianus, (Imp.) M. Aemilius, 250
Aemilius Lepidus, M., (1) censor, 179 B.C.; (2) consul, 78 B.C.; *Basilica* (*Fulvia et*) *Aemilia*, built by M. Fulvius Nobilior, the colleague of (1), and restored by the latter's descendant (2), 10, 95
Aemilius Paullus, L. (1) defeated by Hannibal at Cannae (216 B.C.); his forged epitaph, 204; (2) his son, praetor in Spain (189 B.C.), 161 f; conqueror of Macedonia (168 B.C.), 97, 122; his *elogium*, 101
Aemilius Regillus, L., his naval victory over Antiochus in 190 B.C., 5, 6
Aerarium, 267
Aethiopia, 271
Agnomen, 212 n. 3
Agrippa, 119, 159, 177, 270
Agrippina, the elder, urn of, 72
Alamannicus, cognomen of Constantinus II; *Germanicus Al.*, Constantius II, 255; *Al.*, Valentinian, 256
Alcántara on the Tagus, inscr. on bridge, 120
Aldus (son of Paulus) Manutius, 25 f
Aletrium, inscr. of, 119
Alimentariae tabulae, 180
Allectus, emp. in Britain, 254
Alpes, 271; *tropaeum Alpium*, 10, 19, 122
Alphabet, Latin, 34–53; Greek, 34; archaic, 37; ancient, 48; of Augustan age, 44; Claudian age, 44 f
Altar, funerary, 73; of Augustus, 86, 164; *Fortunae Reducis*, 265, *Neptuni etc.*, 83, *Pacis Augustae*, 265; of nine gods, 87; of an unknown god, 89
Amphitheatrum Flavianum, 142, 166
Amphorae, 154
Araunorum, civitas, 180
Ancona, Arch of Trajan at, 125 f, 242
Ancyra, milestone at, 136; *monumentum Ancyranum*, 119, 131, 176, 178, 258–276
Anio novus, 12; *nova*, 130
Antioch in Pisidia, Sir W. M. Ramsay's discovery at, 260
Antoninus Pius, 243; Column of, 128; Vallum of, 138 f
Antonius, M., triumvir, 170; 270 n. 5
Apex, 53; Dessau, iii (2) p. 805 f
Apianus, Petrus, 25
Apollini Mapono, 190
Apollo, 84, 90, 268
Aponus, fons, 165

INDEX 313

Apparitores, 227 f
Aquae Apollinares, 149
Aqueducts, 129-131 ; *Aqua Marcia*, 129 f, 131 ; *Tepula*, 129, 131 ; *Iulia*, 129, 131 ; *Claudia*, 130 ; *Anio novus*, 12 ; *nova*, 130 ; *Virgo*, 91 ; at Venafrum, 180
Arabia, 271 f
Arabicus, cognomen of Septimius Severus, 247 ; 'Caracalla', 248; Constantine, 255
Arcadius and Honorius, *doctissimi et felicissimi*, 108; *invictissimi*, 256
Arcarius, 228
Arches, inscr. on, 21, 95, 121-5, 242
Archimedes, his tomb, 6 f
Ariminum, bridge and arch of Augustus at, 121, cp. 269
Ariobarzanes I, King of Media, 274, 285; II, his grandson, 272, 274, 285
Aritium in Lusitania, 156
Armenia, 272
Armeniacus, cognomen of M. Aurelius, 244 ; L. Verus, 244 ; Diocletian and Maximian, 253 ; Constantius I, and Galerius, 254 ; Constantine, 255
Armour, inscribed, 148
Arretium (*Arezzo*), *elogia* at, 98-101
Artabazus, 272 l. 12, alternative name for Artavasdes II, *infra*
Artavasdes, 285 *addendum* ; I, King of Armenia, 273 (in Gk version of § 27, 4, ΑΡΤΑΟΤΑΣΔΟΤ). II, King of Media, 273 f (§§ 32 f, ΑΡΤΑ-ΟΤΑΣΔΗΣ in § 32, *Artabazi*, ΑΡΤΑΒΑΖΟΤ in § 27, 9, *Artavazdis*, ΑΡΤΑΒΑΖΟΤ in § 33). IV, grandson of II, 273 (§ 27, 10)
Artaxes, 272
Arvalis, frater, 223 ; *Arvalium*, *Acta fratrum*, 26, 29, 90, 165 f
Ascia, figured with D. M., 70, 79 ; *sub ascia dedicavit*, 78-82
Asconius, 8
Asculum, sling-bolts of, 148 ; many forged, 206
Assisi, temple at, 57
Atilius Calatinus, A., 5 f, 93
Atticus, T. Pomponius, 103, 217
Augsburg, inscriptions, 24
Augur, 223
Augur, Cn. (Cornelius) Lentulus, consul 14 B.C., 266
Augustalis, flamen, 223 ; *sevir*, 78; *sodalis*, 224
Augustinus, Antonius (of Saragossa), 24

Augustus, his father, 103 ; his early career, 260 ; his benefactions, 266 ; his buildings, 268 f, aqueduct at Venafrum, 180, arch and bridge at Ariminum, 121, at Segusio, 122, and in Rome, 123, *Forum Augustum* (with its *elogia*), 12, 16, 97-103, his milestones, 133, his repair of *Via Flaminia*, 121, 269, his statues, 270, his *tropaeum Alpium*, 10, 19, 122 ; honours received, 261, 265, the title *Augustus*, 230, 233, 275, *pater patriae*, 275 ; offices held 263 f (*pontifex maximus*, 171) ; *spectacula et ludi*, 270, *ludi saeculares*, 158, 176 ; *res gestae divi Augusti* (*monumentum Ancyranum*) 178 (13, 119, 131, 176), text and notes, 258-276 ; copies at Apollonia and Antioch in Pisidia, 260 ; *Mausoleum* of Augustus, 178, 259 ; *ara numinis Augusti* at Narbo, 86, 164
Augustus, as imperial title, 230, 233, 275
Aurelian, 190, 251 f
Aurelius, Marcus, 159, 193, 208, 244; Column of, 128
Aurum coronarium, 269, n. 7
Ausonius, 18
Ave, 63 ; *have*, 64

B, 47 : B and V interchanged, 198 n. 6
Baebiani Ligures in Samnium, 180 (Gradenwitz, *Simulacra*, xxi)
Bacchanalibus, Sctum de, 161 f, 257 f
Baiae, souvenirs of, 151 f.
Balbinus, emp., 249
Baltimore, inscr. in Johns Hopkins Univ., 33
Bantina, tabula, 156, Gradenwitz, *Simulacra*, v
Basilica Aem., 10, 95, *Iulia*, 268, 276
Bassaeus Rufus, M , inscr. on, 109, 115
Beguensis, saltus, N. Africa, 159
Bellini, Jacopo, 23
Bellona, temple of, 10, 95 ; *apud aedem Duelonai*, 257
Beneventum, Arch of Trajan at, 124 f
Bibulus, L. Poplicius, his tomb, 105
bisellium, 78 ; *bisellarius*, 78, 229
Boissard, J. J., 29
Boissieu, A. de, 70, 79 f
Borghesi, Bartolommeo, 29, 103, 112, 170 f
Boundary-disputes, 163, 179, 180 ; boundary-stones, 140
Bridges, inscr. on, 119-121

INDEX

Britain, Roman inscriptions in, 89, 90, 138, 149, 187; milestone in Leicester, 136; distance-slab in Edinburgh, 140; local museums, 33 n. 1
Britanni, 123; 273 f
Britannicus, cognomen of Commodus, 246; Septimius Severus, 247; 'Caracalla', Geta, 247 f; Aurelian, 251; Diocletian, Maximian, Constantius I, Galerius, 253 f; Constantine, 255. On Claudius, see Dio Cassius, lx 22, and cp. inscr. on his Arch, 123. For exx. of form in *Britt.* see Dessau iii (2) p. 804
British Museum, Latin inscr. in, 70, 71, 73, 76, 83, 85, 144, 148, 151, 159
Bronze, inscr. on, 3 f, 57, 149; bronze letters, 57, 122, 125
Brunelleschi, Battista, 24
Bullae(?), 147
Buoncompagno, 20
Burbuleius, L., inscr. on, 112 f
Busts, 70 f, 104
Byron, 109, 205

C, 47; *Gaius*, 35, 60, 208; Ↄ *Gaia*, 60, 209 f, 219; C and G, 35, 49
Caecilia Metella, tomb and epitaph of, 42, 69
Caesar, C. Iulius, 12, 141; his legislation, 157; forged inscr. relating to Caesar and Cicero, 204
Caesar, imperial title, 230
Caesares, Gaius and Lucius, adopted sons of Augustus, 159, 265
Calendars, 25, 172–176
'Caligula', 13, 236; oath on accession of, 156
Cambridge, Latin inscr. in; St John's College, 90 n. 7; Fitzwilliam Museum, 80 n. 6; cast of archaic inscr. in Roman Forum, Museum of Classical Archaeology, 38 n
Camulodunum, 90
Camulus, Mars, 90 f
Candelabrum, 74
Capua, colony of, 141
'Caracalla', 248
'Caractacus' (Carataeus), 123
Carausius, 'emp.', 254
Carinus, A., emp., 253
Carmen Arvale, 165; *Saeculare*, 177; *Saliare*, 36, 264
Carpi (Dacian tribe on the Danube); *Carpicus*; *cognomen* of Philippi, 249 f; Aurelian, 251; Diocletian, Maximian, Constantius I, Galerius, 253 f
Carus, emp., M. Aurelius, 253
Cassiodorus, 42 n. 1, 194
Catullus, 15, 83, 86, 164
Censitor, 224
Censor, Ap. Claudius Caecus (312 B.C.), 10, 98 f; Q. Fabius Maximus (230 B.C.), 100; L. Aemilius Paullus (164 B.C.), 101; imperial title, 231, *c. perpetuus*, 241
Censorinus, 119 n. 9; the author, 6; the 'tyrant', 18
Census, 211; *censum egi* (Augustus), 263
Centenarii, 226
Centurio, 226, 228; tombs of *centuriones*, 77 f, 117
Ceres, 85
Cestius, C., 69; *Cestius, pons*, 121
Cicero, inscr. in, 5–8 (cp. 14); inscr. on his bust, 104, his orthography, 50; uses *clarissimus vir* oftener than *vir clarissimus*, 193 n. 3; the forged epitaphs on his daughter Tullia, 205; quotations from *ad Atticum* (85), *de Or.* (6, 90), *pro Balbo* (4, 181), *in Vatinium* (122).
Cimbri, 271
Cippus, (1) 'tombstone', used once in Horace, 64, (2) 'boundary stone,' 131, 140 f
Circus Maximus, inscr. on obelisk formerly in, 43
Ciriaco of Ancona, vi, 22
Cistae, 'jewel-boxes', 149
Citizenship, grants of, 181
Clarissimus vir, 117, 193 f
Classification of inscriptions, 59 f, 259 (cp. Mommsen, *Ges. Schr.* iv 249 f)
Classis (*navalis*) 96; *praefectus* etc. 227, 228 (*b*)
Claudian, inscr. in honour of, 108
Claudius Caecus, Ap., consul 307, 296 B.C., 10, 95; *elogium* of 98 f
Claudius Pulcher, Ap., consul 54 B.C., 85
Claudius Sabinus (I), Ap., consul 495 B.C., 10
Claudius, emperor (41–54 A.D.), 236 f; his new letters, 36, 45; his edict on the civitas Anaunorum (46 A.D.), 180, cp. Gradenwitz, *Simulacra*, xv; his speech (of 48 A.D.) preserved at Lyons, 179, 276–280; his former Arch, 123; his milestones, 133, 137; the *aqua Claudia*, 130, 237

INDEX 315

Claudius II (emp. 268-270 A.D.), 251
Clipei, 'portrait-medallions', 10, 95
Cogidubnus, Ti. Claudius, British king, 218
Cognomen, 211 f; transmission of, 216; *cognomina virtutis ergo*, 232
Collars of slaves, and of dogs, inscriptions on, 150
Collegia, gilds, 229; *cursus honorum* in, 117; decrees of, 166; admission to, 150. Cp. Bruns-Gradenwitz, *Fontes*, II xiii 174 (ed. 1909) pp. 388-401[7]; J. S. Reid, *Municipalities of the Roman Empire*, 1913, pp. 511-520
Coloniae, magistrates of, 228, 272
Columbarium, 74 f
Column of Trajan, 127; Antoninus Pius, 128, and Marcus Aurelius, 128
Columna rostrata, 95 f
Comes Augusti, 224
Commodus, emp., 120, 246
Consonants, double, 36; unaspirated, *p, c, t*, 202
Constans, 255
Constantinus I ('Constantine the Great'), 254 f, dedicatory inscriptions etc. from his defeat of Maxentius (312 A.D.), to 327 A.D., 91 f; inscr. on Arch of, 92, 127; inscr. in honour of, 190; his reforms in official titles, 194
Constantinus II, 255
Constantius (I) 'Chlorus', 254; inscr. on, 190; II, 255
Constitutiones, imperial, 180
Consul, 223, 231
Consul ter, 14 n. 1; *tertium*, 119; *tert.* Dessau, 154, 6543; *procos. tertio, ib.* 158, *tr. mil. tertio, ib.*, 57
Consulares, Fasti, 25, 167-172
Consularia, Diptycha, 185
Contrascriptor, 228
Conubium and *civitas*, granted to veteran soldiers of foreign birth, 180 f
Corbridge lanx, 149
Cornelio, old nom. for *-us*, 67; cp. *Fourio(s)*, 41
Cornelius Balbus, L., 170
Corona civica, 8, 78
Corpus Inscriptionum Latinarum, 30 f and Bibliography, xviii-xx
Corrector, 224
Cossus and cos., 4 n. 6
Criticism of inscr., 196-206
Curatores, 224

Curia Iulia, 275
Cursive hand, 45 f, 186-8
Cursus honorum, 2; 110-117; 193 f; 222-9
Cyzicus, S.C. on, 159

D, 49; 60, 208; abl. in *d*, 87 *ult.*, 162; final *d*, 10, 163, 202, 257
Daci, 273
Dacian waxed tablets, 187
Dacicus, cognomen of Trajan, 242; Maximinus, 249; Gallienus, 250; Aurelian, 251
Dalmatia, inscr. on bridge in, 120 f
Damnatio memoriae, 126 n. 5, 232
Dasumius, will of, 185
Dates determined by lettering, 200 f, spelling, 202 f, internal evidence, 203; dates in imperial reigns, 117, 232-56
Dative of gift or dedication in 'dedicatory' inscr., 83, 86 f; also used in 'honorary' inscr., 104-6, 111, 139
Dea Dia, grove of, 165 f
Decemvir stlitibus iudicandis, 222; 110
Decimus, praenomen, 60, 208
Decius, emp., 250
Decrees of *Collegia*, 160, 166; magistrates, 161 f; municipal senates, 159; honorary, 160 (*d*) (*e*); imperial, 180
Dedicatory inscr., 83-92
Demonstrative pronouns rare in dedications, 88, 164, 204; cp. 109
Diana, dedications to, 89; temple of, 3, 164
Dictator, 83, 98, 100; cp. 262 (5)
Didius Julianus, emp., 246
Digamma, inverted, 36
Diocletian, 253 f; Iovius, 91; his edict *de pretiis rerum venalium*, 180, 254, 283-5
Dionysius of Halicarnassus, 3
Diplomata militaria, 180-185
Diptycha Consularia, 185
Dis Manibus, in the Augustan age, 62; 70, 76, 79, 81
'Distance-slabs', 138-140
Divinities, Roman and foreign, 90 f; cp. Toutain, *les cultes païens dans l'empire romain*
Divus, 232; 230
Documents, 156-188; imperial, 158-161; 179 f; private, 185-8; public and sacred, 163 f, 176 f; of the army, 180-185; of *collegia*, 166 f; of municipalities, 159-161

316 INDEX

Doliare, opus, 153
Dolichenus, Iuppiter, 90; cp. Cumont, *Études Syriennes*, 1917
Dominus, imperial title, 253, 292
Dominus noster, 253 ult.
Domitian, 11, 86, 240 f
Domitius Calvinus, Cn., 168, 172
Donati, Sebastiano, 28
Donatus equo publico, 225; *hasta pura, corona vallari*, 87
Dondi, Giovanni, 21
Doni, Giovanni Battista, 27
Double consonants, 36, 202; vowels, 36, 72 f, 86, 119, 202; Dessau, iii (2) 803 f
Drusus, M. Livius, *elogium* of, 103
Ducenarii, 226
'Duenos' inscr., 37, 40, 51
Duilius, C., *elogium* of, 10, 95 f
Dumnobellaunus, 274
Duoviri iure dicundo, quinquennales, 228 f

E, 49
Edicts of emperors, 180
Edictum Diocletiani, 180, 254, 283–5
Egregius, vir, 126, 194
Einsiedeln, *Anonymus Einsiedlensis*, 20; *Codex Eins.*, 69
'Elagabalus', 'Heliogabalus', 248
Election placards, 44, 65, 161, 311
Elogia, 93–104; *elogium*, 15 n. 3, 61, 67, 69
Eminentissimus, vir, 193 f
Emperors, names and titles of, 230–256
Emporium on the Tiber, 152
Ennius, 7, 36, 67
Epigraphy defined, 1
Epitaphs, 60–82; in classical authors, 4–19; two on the same tomb, 63, 73
Equestrian order, *cursus honorum* for, 111 f, 114; military functions of, 116; three ranks of equestrian officials under M. Aurelius, 193 f
Equites Romani equo publico, 225; *equites singulares Augusti*, 75 f, 87
Equo publico donatus or *exornatus*, 191 n. 13, 225
Et, use of, in inscriptions, 195
Evans, (Sir) John, 274 n. 2
Exactum, 143
Exsecrationes (or *defixiones*), 5, 41, 187

F, 49
Faber duplarius, ship's carpenter on double pay, 228

Fabianus, Arcus, 95, 97, 122
Fabius Maximus, Q., (*a*) 'Cunctator', dictator 221 and 217 B.C., *elogium* of, 100 f; (*b*) Aemilianus, consul 145 B.C., 97; (*c*) 'Allobrogicus', consul 121 B.C., 122; (*d*) curule aedile *c*. 56 B.C., 122
Fabius Titianus (350 A.D.), 108
Fabretti, Rafaello, 27
Fabricius, pons; inscr., 119 f
Fasti, 167; *Consulares*, 25, 29, 167–172; *anni Iuliani* (*Maffeiani*), 25, 172; drawn up by priestly colleges, 172; *Praenestini*, 173; *Menologia Rustica*, 174.
Feci, refeci, of public works, 119, 268 f
Fecit, inscr. on tombs, 16
Felicianus of Verona, 23
Fetialis, 223; *ius fetiale*, 104
Fibula Praenestina, 38, 149
Ficoroniana, cista, 149
Figlina, 153 f
Fistulae aquariae (*plumbeae*), 131, 150
Flamines, 223
Flaminia, via, 121, 269 n. 2
Flavius, praenomen of Vespasian, 238; Titus, 240; Domitian, 240
Flavius Severus, 254
Florence, *elogium* of Q. Fabius Maximus now in, 100 f
Florianus, emp., 252
Foreigners, naturalised, 217 f; foreign towns assigned to Roman tribes, 218
Forged inscriptions, 28 f, 204–6; alleged forgeries found to be genuine, 206; precautions against forged documents, 184
Formello vase, alphabet on, 34
Formulae, and Formularies, 293
Fortuna, 87, 265
Forum, archaic inscr. in the, 37–39
Fractions, 56
Francicus, cogn. of Valentinian, 256
Fratres Arvales, 165 f
Freedmen, names of, 220
Frontinus, 12, 130 n. 3
Frumentatio, 74; cp. 144
Fulvius Nobilior, M., 87
Furfo, inscr. from Sabine town of, 163 f
Furius, M., 87; Fourios, 41

G and C, 35, 49; G. for Gaius, rare, 89 n. 1
Gaius, C. for, 35, 60, 208
Galba, emp., 238
Galerius, emp., 254
Galliae, 271

INDEX

Gallienus, emp., 17, 250; Arch of, 126
Gallus, emp., C. Vibius Trebonianus, 250
Gellius, inscr. in, 13 f
Gelt, inscr. from the river, 58
Genetiva Iulia, colonia, 158
Genio populi Romani, 83, 92; *sing. Aug.*, 87
Genitive of person honoured, placed at head or foot of honorary inscr., 108, 213 f
Gentile vel gentilicium, nomen, 210 f
Germania, 271
Germanicus, inscr. on, 11; Germanicus and the younger Drusus, their posthumous honours, 158
Germanicus, cognomen of 'Caligula', Claudius, Nero, 236; Domitian, 240; Nerva, 241; Trajan, 87, 242; M. Aurelius, 244; Commodus, 245; 'Caracalla', 248; Maximinus, 249; Philippi, 249 f; Valerian, Gallienus, 250; Claudius II, 251; Aurelian, 251; Probus, 252; Carus, 253; Diocletian etc., 253 f; Constantinus I, Constantinus II (*Germ. Alamannicus*), Constantius II, 255; Julian, Valentinian, 256
Geta, emp., 248
Giocondo, Frà Giovanni del, 23, 25
Gladiatoriae, tesserae, 146 f
Gladiatorial games, 159, 161
Glandes plumbeae, 148, 206
Glasgow, the Hunterian Museum, 140
Glass, inscriptions on, 151 f
Gnaeus, Cn. for, 60, 208
Gold, inscr. on, 149
Gordianus, 17, 249
Gori, A. F., 27, 206
Gothicus, cognomen of Claudius II, Aurelian, 251; Tacitus, Probus, 252; Constantinus I, II, Constantius II, 255; Valentinian, 256
Gracchus, C., his roads, 135; his boundary-stones, 140; his agrarian laws annulled, 157
Graffiti, Pompeian, 46, 57, 188
Gruter, Janus, 27 f
Gulielmus, Paulus, forger, 205
Gutenstein, L., forger, 29

H, forms of; origin of modern h, 50
Hadrian, 243; 69, 87; his *adlocutio ad exercitum Africanum*, 282; his *Vallum*, 140, his Wall, 149, 152
Hadrianum mare, 271 f
Hagenbuch, epigraphical critic, 30

Hawkwood, Sir John (*Ioannes Acutus*), source of *elogium* on, 101
'Heliogabalus', 248
Hederae distinguentes, 54
Henzen, W. (1816–87), 165, 201
Heraclea in Lucania, inscr. from, 157
Hercules, 83–5, 87 f
Herculius, title of Maximianus, 91, 253
Heredem non sequetur, monumentum, 81
Higuera, H. R. de la, forger, 29
Hirtius and Pansa, 43 B.C., 106, 261
Hispaniae, 271, cp. inscr. of Spain, 158, 162
Honesta missione, missi, 87
Honorary inscriptions, 93–117, suggested, or amplified, by recipient of honour, 116
Honori, at head of inscr., 109
Honorius, emp., 256
Honorum, cursus, 2; 110–117; 193 f; 222–9
Horace, his *carmen saeculare* mentioned in *acta sacrorum saecularium*, 177; his own references to inscriptions, 15 f, 64; his *votiva tabula* dedicated to Neptune, 86; *vinum 'natum' aut 'diffusum'*, 155; *aures liberti 'gaudent praenomine'*, 219
Hospitalis, tessera, 145 f
Hospitii, tabulae patronatus et, 146; *facsimile* in Gradenwitz, xiv; on *ius hospitii*, cp. Bruns, *Fontes, Pars II*, c. xii § 173
Hostilianus, emp., 250
Hübner, Emil, 32, 62 n. 2

I, 50; tall form of, 179; origin and rare use of J; late appearance of the dotted I, 50
(*Ianum*) *Quirinum...clausum*, 265 § 13
Illegitimate children, names of, 209, 216
Illyricum, 273
Imagines maiorum, 71, 93 f, 97
Imperator, 230 f
India, 273
Indicium (advt) of runaway slave, 150; *Facs.* in Gradenwitz, xxxiv
Inlustris, vir, 194
Inscriptions, their value, 2; survey of those mentioned or quoted in classical authors, 3–19; modern collections of, 20–33; the earliest extant examples, 37 f; process of making inscr., 56 ff; inscr. left un-

finished, 57 f. Classification of, 59 f, 159 (cp. Mommsen, *Ges. Schr.* iv 249 f); (I) inscriptions proper, sepulchral, 60–82, dedicatory, 83–92, honorary, 93–117; on public works, 118–142; on portable objects, 143–55. (II) *acta* (laws, legal agreements, etc.), 156–88. Language and style, 189–195; mechanical copies, 196; sources of error, 196–8; restoration of inscriptions, 198–200; their date determined by lettering, 200 f, spelling, 202 f, or internal evidence, 203; forgeries, 204–6

Instrumentum, 'articles used in public or private life', 143; *pl.* 'documents', 59

Invictus, epithet in inscr. of Commodus, 246, and Constantinus I, 255, and on coins of Sept. Severus; *invictissimi*, of Arcadius and Honorius, 256

Iovi optimo maximo, 83, 87 f
(*Iovi*) *Poenino sacrum*, 85
Iovius Diocletianus, and *Herculius Maximianus*, 91, 253
Itineraries on cups, 149
Itur, precario, 142; cp. inscr. on *iter privatum*, in Bruns, *Fontes*, II, 141, 4, and Gradenwitz, *Simulacra*, xxxi *b*
Iulianus, (Imp.) Flavius Claudius, 256
Iulius Iunianus Martialianus, *cursus honorum* of, 114
Iunoni Reginae, 83
Iuno Sospita, temple dedicated to, 201
Iuppiter Capitolinus, temple of, 5, 9, archives in, 4; restoration begun by Sulla (83 B.C.), continued and completed by Q. Lutatius Catulus (78–60 B.C.), 118
Iuppiter Dolichenus, 90
Iuridici, 224

Jars, inscribed, 155
Jerusalem, inscr. on capture of, 123
Josephus, 12
Julian 'the apostate', 256
Justinian, 256
Juvenal, 16, 84

K, 51; K(aeso), 60, 208
Kellermann, O., 30

L, 51; 60, 208
Lacunae, restoration of, 198
Lambaesis, 282

Lamps, inscribed, 150
Language and style of inscriptions, 189–195
Lanifica, 64 f
Lanuvium, decree of, 160
Latin, alphabet, 34–53; language in inscriptions, 189–195; archaic, 37–41, 60, 84 f, 87, 95, 119, 162 f, 200; changes in spelling under Roman republic, 202 f
Laudatio funebris, 65
Laws, 157 f; see *lex*
Lead, inscr. on, 5, 130, 147, 152, 187
Legati, 224
Legiones, 154, 184, 194
Letters, forms of, 34–53; reversed for *praenomina* of women, 60, 219 f; cut on stone or bronze, 56 f; made of bronze or lead, 57, 125; painted, 56; punctured, 57; stamped in relief, 58
Letronne, J. A. (1787–1848), 30
Leugae ('*leagues*'), Gallic, 136
Lex (the Roman numerals refer to the facsimiles in Gradenwitz, *Simulacra*, 1912), *Acilia*, 157 (vii f); *Agraria*, 157 (vii f); *Antonia de Termessibus*, 157 (x); *latina tabulae Bantinae*, 156 (v); *Cornelia de xx quaestoribus*, 157; *coloniae Genetivae*, 158 (xii); '*Iulia municipalis*', 157, 211, 215 (xi); *Malacitana*, 158 (xix); *parieti faciundo*, 159 (ix); *Rubria*, 157; *Salpensana*, 158; *de imp. Vespasiani*, 21, 280 f (xvi); *metalli Vipascensis*, 158; *Villia annalis*, 110; *leges arae Augusti*, 86, 164 (xiii); *leges templorum*, 163
Liberti, 219 f
Licinius, emp., 254
Ligatures, 53
Ligorio, Pirro, forger, 25, 28 f, 204
Lipsius, 26, 205
Litterae quadratae, lapidariae, 42
Livia, *columbarium* of, 74
Livy, inscriptions in, 4 f; (i 26), 18 n. 6; (ii 30, 4 f, Manius Valerius), 100 n. 1, 2; epitaph regarded as his by Petrarch, 27; by Dessau, 61
London, inscriptions in British Museum, 70, 71, 73, 76, 85, 144, 148, 151, 159; Roman flange-tile, 154
Lucan, 16
Lucius, praenomen, 60, 208
Lucius Verus, emp., 244 f; inscr. 233, 246
Lucretius, 164, 188

INDEX 319

Lucullus, L. Licinius, *elogium* of, 102
Ludi Martiales, 270; *saeculares*, 158, 176 f, 270
Lug(u)dunum (*Lyon*), speech of Claudius preserved at, 276-280
Lusitania, inscr. in, *Alcántara*, 120, (*lex metalli Vipascensis*) 158
Lutatianum, S.C., 158
Lyon(s) Museum, inscriptions in, 70, 79, 179, 276-280

M, forms of, 51, 127 n. 3; M, 60, 131, 208 (cp. Ritschl, *Opusc.* iv 718, 726)
ʍ, Manius, 51, 60, 171, 208
Macrinus, emp., 248
Maffaeus, Bp Hieronymus, 25; *Fasti Maffeiani*, 25; *Kalendarium Maffeianum*, 172
Maffei of Verona, Scipione, 28, 101, 201, 204, 206
Magistratus Romani, 222-27; *municipales*, 228
Mainz, inscriptions, 24
Malacitana, lex, 158
Manius, abbreviation for, 51, 60, 100 n. 1, 171, 208
Mantegna, 23
Manutius (Aldi filius), Paulus (†1574), 25; his son, the younger Aldus (†1597), 25 f
Marble-blocks, inscr. on, 152
Marcanova, 23
Marcellus (conqueror of Syracuse, 212 B.C.), 6, 87
Marcelli, tres, 8
Marcomani, 274
Marcus, praenomen, 60, 208
Marcus Aurelius, 244 f
Marini, Gaëtano, 29, 165
Marius, C., *elogium* of, 102; cp. 107; forgery relating to his daughter, 204
Marliani, 25
Mars, 87, 166
Martial, epitaphs in, 16 f
Matres or *Matronae*, 91
Maxentius, 254
Maximian, 253
Maximinus, 249
Maximinus Daia, 254
Mazochi, Roman printer (*fl.* 1521), 24, 25
Mazzochi, A. S., Neapolitan archeologist (†1771), 28
Medi, 272-4
Medicus, cognomen of M. Aurelius, 244 f; L. Verus, 245; Diocletian, etc., 253 f; Constantine, 255

Memoriae, 81; *memoriae causa, in memoriam*, 162
Menologia Rustica, 174 f
Michigan, inscr. in University of, 33
Milestones, 133-8
Miliaria, 133-8
Miliarium Popilianum, 132
Military diplomas, 180-85
Minicius, C., *cursus honorum* of, 114
Minium, 'vermilion', 56 f, 61
Minuciorum sententia, 163; Gradenwitz, *Simulacra*, vi
Missiles, inscribed, 148
Mithras, 91
Mommsen, Theodor (†1903), 30, 147, 179, 189, 197 f, 201 f, 206, 259 f, 279 n. 1
Monumentum Ancyranum, 178 f; 13, 119; text and notes, 258-276
Morcelli, Antonio, 29, 190 n. 1
Mother, eulogy of an exemplary, 65
Mummius, conqueror of Corinth, 84, 88
Munatius Plancus, L., founder of Lyons 42 B.C., his tomb at Gaëta, 69, 97
Municipal decrees, 159 ff
Municipia, 117, 228
Muratori, 28, 196
Murdiao, laudatio, 65
Murgantia, forgery relating to, 204
Muses, temple of the, 87
Museums, 33.

N, 51
Naevius, 14
Names, Roman, 207-221; *praenomen*, 208 f; *nomen*, 210 f; *cognomen*, 211 f; *signum* (or nickname), 213; names of women, 209; name of father, 214; of tribe, 215; transmission of *praenomen* and *cognomen*, 215 f; names of natural sons, 209, 216; change of name on adoption, 216 f; names of naturalised foreigners, 217 f, slaves, 219, freedmen, 220
Naples Museum, 108 n. 5, 174
Narbo, 80, 164
Natural children, names of, 209, 216
Naturalised foreigners, 217 f
Nefas, nefastus, 173
Nennig, near Trier, forged inscriptions of, 206
Neptuni, ara, 83
Neptuno ex voto, 86
Nero, 237; precautions against for-

geries under, 184; *ara incendii Neroniani*, 164
Nerva, 241
Nicknames (or familiar names), 213; of slaves, 219
Nomen, 210 f
Numerals, 54, 311
Numerianus, 18, 253
Nundinales, litterae, 173

O, 51
Octavius, C., father of Augustus, 103
Oculist's stamps, 150 f
Officials, titles of Roman, 222–9
Officina or *figlina*, 154
Olivieri, Annibale Camillo, 29, 204
Optimus, cognomen of Trajan, 242
Optio, 'adjutant', 77
Orange, triumphal arch at, 57
Ordo decurionum; *ordo Augustalis*, in *municipia*, 228
Orelli, J. C. († 1849), 30
Orsato, Sertorio, 27
Orthography, 2, 26; cp. 50, 202 f
Otho, emp., 238
Ovid, epitaphs in, 15; *Fasti*, 173; in Pompeian *graffiti*, 46, 188; on *Regia*, 168
Oxford, Ashmolean Museum, cast of archaic inscr. in Roman Forum, 38 n.

P, 52; 60, 208
Pacuvius, 14, 273 n. 3
Padua, 27, 61, 101 n. 1
Pallas, freedman of Claudius, his epitaph, 11
Palmyrenicus, irregular *cognomen* of Aurelian, 251
Pantheon, inscr. on, 119
Panvinius, Onophrius, 24, 25, 26
Passus, and *pedes*, 138 f
Parthi, 274
Parthicus, *cognomen* of Trajan, 242; M. Aurelius, L. Verus, 244 f; Sept. Severus, 'Caracalla', 247; Gallienus, 250; Claudius II, 251; Aurelian, 251
Patavium, contract for bridge at, 121; *Padua*, 27, 61, 101 n. 1
Pater patriae, imperial title, 231; 197
Perfectissimus, vir, 193 f
Perpetuus, in imperial titles, 190, 256 ult.
Persicus, cognomen of Philippus I, 249 f; Gallienus, 250; Carus, Valerian, Diocletian, etc., 253; Constantine, 254 f

Persius, (*Sat.* i 112 f) 16; (iv 13) 61; (v 78 f) 219
Pertinax, emp., 246
Petrarch, 20 f
Petronius, inscr. in, 9
Peutinger, Conrad, 25
Phalerae, 78
Philippus I, II, (Imp.) M. Iulius, 249
Phrates, name of Armenian kings, 273 f
Pilotimus, 203
Pisana, decreta, 159; suspected by Scaliger, 206
Pisaurum, archaic inscr. in sacred grove of, 41, 83
Pius and *Felix, cognomina* of, Commodus, 246; 'Caracalla', 247; 'Heliogabalus', 248
Plautius (near Tivoli), tomb of, 61
Plautus, epitaph of, advt in, 14; *tessera hospitalis*, 145
Plebeian officials, 227 f
Plebiscita, 157
Plebs, in *municipia*, 228, and *collegia*, 229
Pliny the elder, on inscriptions, 9 f; on ancient statues in the Forum, 94; on use of *minium* to pick out lettering of inscr., 37; on use of impf. in inscr. of Greek artists, see *N.H., Praef.*, § 26 f
Pliny the younger, his name on adoption by the elder Pliny, 217; his benefactions to his native town, 199; quotes the epitaph of Pallas, and of Verginius Rufus, 11; epitaph on a proconsul's daughter lamented by Pliny, 72; dedication to Vulcan by Pliny's friend Titinius Capito, 87
Pocolom, 83, 202
Poets quoted in *graffiti*, 46, 188; cp. Dessau, iii (2) p. 751, *Carmina*
Poggio, collected inscriptions, 20 ff; saw the Arch of Claudius, 123
Pollia, tribus, sons of Roman legionaries assigned to, 218
Polybius records Roman treaties in obsolete Latin, 3
Pomerium enlarged by Claudius (281 n. 2), Vespasian, Titus, 141
Pompeii, election placard, 44; banker's receipt, 186; other inscr. from, 45, 161; *graffiti*, 46, 51, 57, 188
Pompeius (Magnus), Cn., 9, 13, 16
Pompeius Priscus, Q., his thirty names, 212
Pomponius Laetus, 24 f

INDEX

Pontifex maximus, 167, 223, 231
Popilius Laenas, M., censor 158 B.C., 94
Popillius Laenas, P., consul 132 B.C., 133, 137
Poplice, obsolete form of *publice*, 106
Poplicius Bibulus, C., 105
Poplilius Flaccus, L., 106
Portraits on tombs, 69–71
Postumus, emperor in Gaul, 251
Potestas, tribunicia, 231, 233–255 *passim*
Praefecti, 225–8; *Praefectus praetorio*, 108, 115, 227; *urbi*, 115, 225
Praefectura, 225 f
Praeneste, early epitaphs, 41, 60; *fibula* of, 38, 50, 149; *sortes* of, and sundial at, 5; temple at, 206; *Fasti Praenestini*, 173
Praenomen, 207–209; abbreviations for, 60, 208; transmission of, 215
Praeses provinciae, 111, 225; cp. Dessau, iii (1) pp. 293–5, and W. T. Arnold, *Roman Provincial Administration*, 187, ed. 1914
Praetores, 223
Priesthoods open to the Senatorial (223), or the Equestrian (227) Order
Princeps (Augustus), 265 § 13, 273 § 30; *princeps senatus*, 263 § 7
Princeps iuventutis, 266 l. 1
Probavit, 2 n, 118–120
Probus, M. Valerius, grammarian, 291
Probus, (Imp.) M. Aurelius, 18, 252
Proconsul, 231
Procurator, 111, 195, 226 f; *p. columnae Divi Marci*, 128
Profession of deceased denoted on tomb, 78
Propertius, quoted in *graffiti*, 46, 188; literary inscriptions in, 15
Public works, inscr. on, 117–142
Publice, 105, 108; *poplice*, 106
Publius, praenomen, 60, 208
Punctuation, 54
Punic War, First; consuls of, 171; naval victory of Duilius in, 95 f; Second, recovery of Saguntum, 107
Pupienus, 249
Pupus, praenomen of infant, 208
Puteoli, 10, 159 f; *lex parieti faciendo*, 160, 203 (Gradenwitz, ix); *decretum de aedificio*, 160 f (*ib.* xxvii)

Q, 52, 60, 208

Quadratae, litterae; quadratorii, quadratores, 42
Quaestores, 223, 228
Quarries, inscriptions in, 58, 152
Quattuorvir viarum curandarum, 222
Qui et vocatur, phrase preceding a nickname, 213
Quindecimviri sacris faciundis, 176 f, 223; Bruns, *Fontes, Pars I*, c. vi §§ 74 f (Gradenwitz, *Simulacra*, xxx)
Quinquennalis, 117
Quintilian, on final *d*, 10; on milestones, 137
Quintillus, emperor, 251
Quintus, praenomen, 60, 208, 219 n. 2

R, 52, 200 f
Ravenna, inscriptions, 24
R(ecto) r(igore), abbreviated, and *recta regione*, inscribed in full, 141
Refeci, of public works, 119, 268 f
Regia, 25, 167 f
Regium, Latin form of Greek *Rhegium*, 132 f, 135
Reinesius, Thomas; his posthumous *Syntagma*, 27
Resende, L. A. de, forger, 29
Restitutae ab imp. Nerva, libertati, 203
Restitutori aedium sacrarum (Vespasian), 191; *orbis* (Aurelian), 190; *humani generis* (Constantine), 190; *libertatis et Romanae religionis* (Julian), 256
Restoration of inscriptions, 198
Rienzi (*Cola di Rienzo*), discoverer of Roman inscriptions, 20 f
Ritschl, Friedrich, 31, 48, 201, 202 f
Roads, 131–8; *via Aemilia*, 134; *Appia*, 134 f; *Caecilia*, 135; *Claudia Augusta*, 133; *Domitia*, 137; *Egnatia*, 134; *Flaminia*, 121, 135, 269; *Latina*, 135; *Ostiensis*, 134; *Popillia*, 134; *Postumia*, 134; *Salaria*, 135; *Traiana*, 133. Cp. Konrad Miller's *Itineraria Romana*, 1916
Robortelli, ed. *Fasti Capitolini*, 25
Rome, collections of inscriptions in published works, 20–22; 24–27; in public Museums, 32 f: inscr. on Aqueducts, 129 f; on Altar to unknown god, 89: archaic inscr. in Forum, 39 (cp. *Year's Work in Cl. Studies*, xii (1918) 65); *elogia* from Forum of Augustus, 97–103: Arch of Claudius, 123; Constantine, 127;

INDEX

Gallienus, 126; Sept. Severus, 126; Titus, 123, 125; Trajan, 124 f: *Columna Rostrata*, 95 f; Column of Antoninus Pius, 128; Trajan, 127; Forum of Trajan, 128, (Stilicho) 108: Obelisk in Piazza del Popolo, 43: Columbarium of Livia, 74; Pantheon, 119; Pons Cestius, 121; Pons Fabricius, 119 f; Regia, 167–172: Statue of Phocas, 109; Tomb of Bibulus, 105; Caecilia Metella, 42; C. Cestius, 69; *eques singularis Augusti*, 76; Scipios, 66–68; Tomb of Scipio Barbatus, *Frontispiece*, 66 f; inscr. in Vatican Museum, 33; Roman tile, 153; votive tablet of Mummius, 84. Praefects, *praef. praetorio*, 108, 115, 227; *urbi*, 115, 225; regulations for rebuilding houses, 158

Rossi, G. B. de, 31

S, 52; 60, 208
Sacerdotia, senatorial, 223; equestrian, 227; 113
Sacred inscriptions, 82 ff, 163, 165
Sacrom, 83
Saeculares, ludi, 158; *ludos saeclares*, 270; *Acta sacrorum saecularium*, 176 f
Saguntum, recovery of, 107
Saliare carmen, 264; *c. Saliorum*, 36
Salius, 224; Alban *Salii*, 70
Salpensana, lex, 158
Salve, viator, 63; *salve, vale*, Wilmanns, no. 181
San Cesareo on *Via Appia*, archaic epitaphs from, 6
Sanctio, 282 n. 1
Sarcophagus, Frontispiece; 66, 69 f
Sarmaticus, cognomen of M. Aurelius, 244 f; Commodus, 245; Maximinus, 249; Aurelian, 251; Diocletian etc., 253; Constantine, 255
Saturnian lines, 6, 61, 67 ff, 85, 93 f
Scaliger, Joseph Justus, 4 n. 3, 26, 206
Scipio family, tombs and epitaphs of, 26, 65 ff, 206; inscr. on Africanus maior, 7, 107, 122, minor, 7, 10, 97, 122; Barbatus, *Frontispiece*, 66, 69; filius Barbati, 67, 94; flamen Dialis, 68; Hispalli, 68; Hispanus, 61; Asiagenus, 94; see also title of *Frontispiece*
Scriptores Historiae Augustae, epitaphs in, 17 f
Scriptura monumentalis, 42 f (*litterae quadratae* or *lapidaria*, 42); *actuaria*, 43 f; *cursiva*, 45 f, 186–8; *uncialis*, 46 f; *vulgaris*, 58
Segusio (*Susa*), Arch of Augustus at, 122
Senatorial order, *cursus honorum* for, 110 f, 222–5; titles and ranks of Senators, 193 f; three highest classes under Constantine, 116 f
Senatus Consulta, 12, 158 f; letter embodying *Senatus Consultum de Bacchanalibus*, 161; text, 257 f
Senatus sententia, de, 118
Seneca, inscr. in, 8 f
Septemvir epulonum, 224
Septimius Severus, 247; Arch of, 126; his *ludi saeculares* (204 A.D.), 177
Sepulcrorum, iura, 64; cp. Bruns, *Fontes*, II xi § 172, and Dessau, ii 8156 (Gradenwitz, *Simulacra*, xxxii)
Servius, praenomen, 60, 208
Sestertius, 55, 311
Severus Alexander, 249
Severus, Flavius, 254; Šeptimius, 126, 247.
Sevir Augustalis, 78; *s. equitum Romanorum*, 199
Sexagenarii, 226
Sextus, *praenomen*, 60, 208
Sicilicus, mark denoting double letter, 53
Sigla, littera singula, 291
Signa militaria, 272
Signum, sobriquet or nickname, 213
Sigonius, *Fasti consulares*, 25
Silvanus, dedication to, 89
Silver, inscr. on, 149
Slaves, names of, 219
Smetius, Martin, of Bruges, 26
Sodalis Augustalis etc., 224
Sol invictus, 92 f
Sōlarium, 'ground-rent' (distinguished from *sŏlarium*, a 'solar', or 'sunny room'), 129 n., 160
Sortes, 5, 165
Spectabilis, vir, 194
Spectavit, on gladiatorial *tesserae*, 146 f
Spelling, 2, 26, 50; archaic, 202
Spoletium, inscr. from sacred grove at, 163
Spurius, praenomen, 60, 208, 209; *Spurii f.* for *spurius f.*, 209, 216
Stamps, 58, and seals, 150 f; oculist's stamp, 151; date-stamps on bricks and tiles, 27, 152 f
Statues, honorary, 94, 106 f, 108 ff, 115 f, 159, 160

INDEX

Steelyards, 143 f
Stertinius, L. (Arch of 196 B.C.), 122
Stilicho, inscr. on, 108, 117
Strabo, C. Julius Caesar, *elogium* on 103
Suetonius, inscriptions in, 12 f
Sugambri, 274
Surnames (*cognomina*), 211 f
Symmachus, *praefectus urbi*, 115

T, 52
Tablets, waxed, 1, 186 f
Tabula votiva, 16, 86
Tabulae alimentariae of Trajan, 180; *t. ceratae*, 186 f; *t. civitate donatorum*, 181–5; *t. patronatus et hospitii*, 146 (Gradenwitz, *Sim.* xiv); *t. plumbeae*, 5 n. 8, 187
Tacitus, 152 n. 2; inscr. in, 5, 11 f; *oratio Claudii*, 179; *Iulius Alpinus*, 205
Tacitus, (Imp.) M. Claudius, 252
Temples, 268; inscr. on, 118 f, 178
Templorum, leges, 163
Tennyson, 58
Tergeste, decree of, 160
Termessus in Pisidia, autonomy of, 157 (*lex* in Gradenwitz, *Sim.* x)
Termini, 140–2
Testamenta, 65, 185 f
Tesserae, 144–8; '*consulares*', 146; *conviviales*, 147; *frumentariae*, 144 (*et nummariae*, 267 n. 10); *gladiatoriae*, 146 f; *hospitales*, 145; *lusoriae*, 144 f; *plumbeae*, 147; '*theatrales*', 144
Tetricus, emp. in Gaul, 251
Theatrales ?, tesserae, 144
Theatres, 119; and Amphitheatres, seats assigned in, 142, 166
Theodosius the Great, 256
'Third class' (or *plebs*), careers in the, 117
Tiberius (Claudius Nero), stepson of Augustus, 272 f; emperor, 235 f; former Arch of, 123; milestones of, 137
Tiberius, praenomen, 60, 208
Tibullus, epitaphs in, 15; on Messala's repair of *via Latina*, 135 n. 10
Tiburtes, *S. C.* on the, 163
Tigranes, I, II, III, kings of Armenia, 272
Tiles, inscribed, 188 n. 3; stamped, 152–4
Timesitheus, 17
Timgad, inscr. from, 47, 114
Tin(commius), 274 n. 2

Titinius Capito (friend of younger Pliny), 11, 87
Titles of Roman officials, 222–9; and Roman emperors, 230–256
Tituli, 59; *honorarii*, 93–117; *sacri*, 83–92; *operum publicorum*, 118–142; *sepulcrales*, 60–82; *instrumentum*, 143–155
Titus, emperor, 240; Arches of, 123 f
Titus, praenomen, 60, 208
Tombs decorated with emblems of the occupation of the deceased, 78
Trade-marks, 154
Trajan, 242; his Arches at Beneventum and Ancona, 124-6, and (formerly) in Rome, 126; his Bridge, 120; his Forum, 108; his Column, 127, 190; his roads, 133; his *tabulae alimentariae*, 180; prayer for his safe return from Dacia, 166; style of his inscriptions, 189 f; Pliny's *Panegyricus* on Trajan, 242, 253; Constantine calls him *Parietaria*, 230
Treaties, 3 f, 156
Trecenarii, 226
Tribes; Roman; their names, with the abbreviations for each, 215; foreign towns assigned to specified tribes, 218; natural sons often assigned to *tribus Collina, Suburana*, or *Esquilina*, 216
Tribunicia potestas; its annual renewal determines the year of the emperor's rule, and the date of the corresponding inscriptions, 231, 232, 233–55 *passim*
Tribunus, (1) *legionis*, 225; (2) *militum laticlavius*, 223; (3) *plebis*, 223
Triumphorum, acta, 25, 167–172
Triumvir capitalis,—monetalis, 222
(Tudme)rus (?), 274 n. 4
Turiae, laudatio, 65 n. 3
Tusculum, archaic epitaphs from, 41, 60

U and V, 52; 273 n. 3; in *scriptura uncialis*, 46 f
Uncial letters, 46
Urn, funerary, 72
Ursinus (*Orsini*), F., librarian of Cardinal Alessandro Farnese, 174

V and U, 52; 46, 273 n. 3; V before a name in epitaphs, 62; Claudius' letter for Latin V and Greek Υ, 36
Vaarus, old form of *Varus*, 119
Vale, 63 f, 197, 213 (cp. 311)

324 INDEX

Valentinian, 194, 256
Valerian, 17, 250
Valerius Maximus, Manius, dictator of 494 B.C., *elogium* of, 100
Valerius Messala, M., his repair of *Via Latina*, 135
Vallum of Hadrian, 140; of Antoninus Pius, 138 f
Varianum, bellum, 77 f, 123
Varro, on inscriptions, 5; on *praenomina*, 207, 209 f; his chronology, 170; his *Imagines*, 13 f, 97, 103; *L.L.* 36
Veleia near Parma, *tabula alimentaria* from, 180 (Bruns, *Fontes, Pars* II, c. vi § 145 *a*)
Velleius Paterculus, 8
Venafrum, edict of Augustus on aqueduct at, 180 (Bruns, *Fontes, Pars* I, c. vii § 77)
Verginius Rufus, epitaph of, 11
Verrius Flaccus, 173
Verus, Lucius, emperor, 244 f; inscr., 233, 246
Vespasian, 238 f; his restoration of the tablets of the laws, 11, 13; *lex de imperio Vespasiani*, 21, 158, 206; text and notes, 280–2; his decrees, 180; inscriptions, 233, 239, *divus*, 123, 125; military diploma of, 182 f
Veteran soldiers, privileges granted to, 180 f
Viae, 131–8; see *Roads*
Victor, in imperial titles, of Probus, 18; *victor ac triumfator semper Aug.*, of Constans, Dessau, i 727 f
Victor, Aurelius, 103
Victorinus, emperor in Gaul, 251
Vienna (*Vienne* on the Rhone), 278 n. 4, n. 8
Vigintiviri, 110, 116, 222; *vigintisex viri*, 110

Vipascensis, lex metalli, 158
Vir clarissimus, egregius, eminentissimus, inlustris, perfectissimus, spectabilis, titular significance of these epithets, 117, 193–4
Virgil, often quoted in Pompeian *graffiti*, 188; dedicatory inscr. in, 15; 'Aminean' vines (*Georg.* ii, 97) mentioned in a will, 186
Virgo Vestalis, 177, 224
Vitellius, 238; inscr. on his father, 13
Vitis, 78
Vivŏs, 202
Vivus fecit, 61
Volcanus, an imperial secretary's dedication to, 87
Vopiscus, praenomen, 208; Flavius Vopiscus, 18
Votive inscr., 83–5, 150
Vowels, double, 36, 72 f, 86, 119, 202

Water-pipes, 131, 150
Waxed tablets, 1, 186 f
Weights and Measures, 142 f
Wife, eulogy of an exemplary, 65
Wills, 65, 69, 185 f
Women, names of, 209 f
Wood, tablets of, 187 n. 3
Words in inscr., order of, 190–193

X, 52; symbol for *decem*, 54

Y, 35 f, 53

Z, 35 f, 53
ZEPHYRVS, Greek Υ and Ζ added to Latin alphabet for spelling of words such as, 35 f (cp. Cicero's *Orator*, 160), and ZMYRNA, special form of 'Smyrna', Catullus 95, 1 (cp. Dessau, i 74, 'divo Iulio civit(as) Zmyrnaeorum')